BUSINESS RESEARCH SOURCES

THE IRWIN/McGRAW-HILL SERIES
Operations and Decision Sciences

BUSINESS RESEARCH SOURCES
A Reference Navigator

F. Patrick Butler

Irwin McGraw-Hill

Boston   Burr Ridge, IL   Dubuque, IA   Madison, WI   New York   San Francisco   St. Louis
Bangkok   Bogotá   Caracas   Lisbon   London   Madrid
Mexico City   Milan   New Delhi   Seoul   Singapore   Sydney   Taipei   Toronto

Irwin/McGraw-Hill

*A Division of The **McGraw·Hill** Companies*

Irwin/McGraw-Hill
A Division of The McGraw-Hill Companies

Business Research Sources: A Reference Navigator

This book is printed on acid-free paper.

1 2 3 4 5 6 7 8 9 0 DOC/DOC 9 3 2 1 0 9 8

ISBN 0-256-23003-X

Vice president and editorial director: *Michael W. Junior*
Publisher: *Jeffrey J. Shelstad*
Executive editor: *Richard T. Hercher, Jr.*
Senior sponsoring editor: *Scot Isenberg*
Senior developmental editor: *Gail Korosa*
Senior marketing manager: *Zina Craft*
Project manager: *Christine A. Vaughan*
Senior production supervisor: *Melonie Salvati*
Freelance design coordinator: *Gino Cieslik*
Compositor: *Electronic Publishing Services, Inc.*
Typeface: *10/12 Times Roman*
Printer: *R. R. Donnelley & Sons Company*

Library of Congress Cataloging-in-Publication Data

Butler, F. Patrick.
    Business research sources : a reference navigator / F. Patrick
Butler.
        p.   cm.
    ISBN   0-256-23003-X
    Includes bibliographical references and index.
        1. Business information services — United States.   2. Business —
Bibliography.   3. Reference books — Business — Bibliography.
    4. Business — Computer network resources — Directories.   I. Title.
    HF54.52.U5B88   1999
016.33 dc—21   98-21172

http://www.mhhe.com

DEDICATION

For some reason, one of which I am not aware, dedications often seem harshly simple and direct, just a few words on a blank page. I would like my appreciation voiced a little more (anyone fifty-seven or older can understand the necessity of covering as many bases as possible). This book is dedicated to my family and to those members of the campus community who, over so many years of my academic life, have enriched not only my experience, but thousands of students intent on bettering themselves and their society as well. I can't name them all of course, so here are just a few:

To my former dean, Dr. Jim Miller, who had to suffer my moments at times with abiding patience and kindness, and whose friendship supported me, thank you.

To my good friends on faculties in the United States, Sweden, Mexico, Austria, Germany, and Romania who fit so much more easily in my heart than names on this page. As colleagues, your humor, energy, commitment, and encouragement makes me proud to be associated with you. To Ellen Bruno, my former student and gracious colleague whose assistance helped begin this book, and Dr. Ralph Norcio whose review and corrections helped to improve it; and to my faithful mentor Sol Bloomenkranz, thank you.

To Judy Durnbaugh, our secretary whose job it was to serve in a maelstrom of students, copiers, coffee, phones, and faculty, but still found time to write poetry and philosophize; to Kathleen Clunan and her staff, whose library resources greatly assisted my efforts; to Mary Ann and Rita in the bookstore who selected gifts, wrapped them, and sent them off across the Atlantic or across the street to help smooth my way at a distant university or a birthday at home; and to Hugo Hervitz and Tina Klingberg, my friends . . . thank you all.

Finally, to those whose encouragement and expectations made it possible for me to write this book: my lovely and intelligent companion Ines Gassner who had to live with all my frustrations but made colorful my aspirations; to my loving sisters MaryLane Butler and Taffy Farese; my dear daughters Erin Butler, Shannon Butler, Robyn and husband Scott Crennan; plus, brothers in spirit, Kim Martiny and Roland Hansson—when that long day is done a call or letter from you takes me home no matter where I rest.

fpb

F. Patrick Butler is presently a professor of international business at the Monterrey Institute of Technology, Monterrey, Mexico. Previously he served as a faculty member for the Georgetown University School of Business and as visiting professor on the faculties of the University of Innsbruck, Austria, University of Stockholm, Sweden, University of Paderborn, Germany, and Georgetown University in Washington, D.C. Dr. Butler, who has taught for 22 years, was twice selected as a Fulbright Scholar for the Academy of Economic Studies in Bucharest, Romania. He has guest lectured at a number of international universities including the former Leningrad International Management Institute. He received his Ph.D. and M.A. in International Relations from The American University and B.S. at St. Bonaventure University.

Dr. Butler founded a consulting company, The Spirit of '76, Inc., in Washington, D.C. He was a member of the Domestic and International Business Administration of the U.S. Department of Commerce, and served as Field Director for the Ford Administration's White House Public Forums on Domestic Policy. Dr. Butler was a Marketing Engineer for the Lockheed Aircraft Corporation. Commissioned as a Naval Flight Officer in the U.S. Navy, Dr. Butler served in an active-duty status for seven years.

Dr. Butler has three daughters, Erin, Robyn, and Shannon.

"Knowledge is of two kinds. We know a subject ourselves, or we know where we can find information upon it."

Samuel Johnson

"A person's judgment is only as good as his or her information."

Unknown

This book is a guide for over 100 selected reference works described in 50 chapters. It has been designed and written to help you quickly identify and efficiently use business and economic reference information.

Business Research Sources is intended primarily as an introduction to secondary reference works for university students. My most important goal is to make this book readable, practical, and interesting to help those dedicated souls who are committed to learning to better understand and positively affect their environment. The text describes selected reference works and databases that can provide information that is essential for sound analytical judgments and business decisions.

Despite the excellent ability and efforts of librarians everywhere, students (and sometimes faculty) are ill-prepared to use library resources. Business schools generally do not require courses in training students in information retrieval, analysis, and application. Since there is now a deluge of data creating an ocean of information, the challenge is a formidable one. (LEXIS-NEXIS for example, offers 6,900 databases and adds 9.5 million documents each *week*.) *Business Research Sources* meets this challenge by identifying and reviewing both the classic and contemporary reference works required to serve the analytical needs of young professionals in a rapidly changing business world.

In the past, research has often been a confusing exercise in hunting for esoteric and unique reference books buried on the shelves or in databases, only to find that it was not right for the researcher's needs and a waste of time. *Until now there has not been a textbook that simply and directly takes the reader between the covers of over 100 selected reference publications to explore the nature and utility of their service.* This book gives you guidance for quick and easy access to particularly useful reference works in business.

Considerations in Structuring the Book

Time

A recent survey in the *International Herald Tribune* pointed out that 73 percent of Americans felt they were stressed and didn't have enough time. This textbook aims to reduce the time needed to evaluate which reference works best suit the needs of the researcher by portraying the salient parts of each reference publication and providing the information necessary (ISBN/ISSN number, publisher's telephone/fax number, Web site, e-mail address, etc.) to read or obtain it.

Learning Technique

If you try to devour this book quickly you will not grow stronger, regardless of the considerable fiber involved. If you try to read this book in small bites (or bytes), however, it may digest quite well. Fifty chapters of reference material is a lot. One way to approach this book is to learn it by sections. Each section focuses on a different area of reference material (biographies, statistics, financial ratios, indexes, directories, etc.). Once you have learned the format of the different types of references and their application to business questions, the easier it will become to think of them as specific tools to do specific analytical jobs.

Format

The reference works are categorized into eight sections. Each chapter has a *primary* and a *secondary* research source. However, to provide as many opportunities as possible for the researcher, other reference publications are mentioned, usually with their telephone numbers and Web site addresses. While some references are easily classified, others overlap, creating a problem of whether, for example, one should look under a section dealing with international sources, governmental sources, functional sources, databases, and the like. The indexes and directories are listed in various chapters under private publishers, yet they are also found in the CD-ROM databases and on-line services of the government. Therefore, the question of where to look is often a subjective one. (An easy definition of *reference publication* is the material you *cannot* check out of the library.)

Each Chapter Is Divided into Four Parts

Part I: Description of Publication

Part I of each chapter gives a brief portrayal of the reference book and where to find it. A box at the beginning of each chapter, called the "Reference Navigator," accompanies the ISBN or ISSN numbers and telephone and fax numbers. *This important box (see sample on page xxii) includes Web site addresses, e-mail, databases, CD-ROM availability, and library reference numbers* (see Chapter 21 for more information on Web sites).

Web Sites.   The researcher's primary access point for almost all reference works is the publisher's Web site. However, the simple click that opens the door also turns into an often bewildering array of information alternatives that may appear to have little or nothing to do with the research goal. Some reference sources covered in this text have their own Web sites and the research task is easy. But some are arduous. For example if one wishes to find *Tax Guide for Business Publications 314,* one has to enter the U.S. government on-line service and then go to—Treasury Department—IRS—tax information—publications. The effort is often a challenge. Remember, persistence and practice make very good (there is no "perfection").

E-mail.   E-mail addresses can be used for contacting personnel within the organization (publisher, government, etc.) one is seeking information from. They are a function of each researcher's particular interest (back copies, permissions, editorial, etc.), and no one simple e-mail address will answer all questions. Sometimes the organization has an e-mail address, and this is included in the text if available; personnel e-mail addresses are usually not included.

Databases.   There are thousands of databases that may, or may not, cover the reference source in question and may do so in a variety of forms: bibliographic, abstract, or full text. In some cases the publishers or government have their own databases that may be accessed through their Web site (e.g., Gale Research), a common server (e.g., AOL), or another database (e.g., Lexis-Nexis). In short, the environment is very dynamic, and the researcher is cautioned to be flexible. *Also refer to* Directory of Business Information *(Chapter 15) for database availability and format.*

CD-ROM.   On average, most references are not available on CD-ROM unless they cover substantial fields of data, such as census tracks, which serve as the basis for the *Statistical Abstracts of the United States.* Some companies, like SIRS (Social Issues Resources Series), sell their databases on CD-ROM and on-line. The CD-ROM category in the "Reference Navigator" indicates the publisher CD-ROM only. See Chapter 15 for information on CD-ROM reference availability on the market.

Library Reference Number.   It should be noted that all libraries vary somewhat in their reference system, so if you want a record of the book's reference number from your library, *you must insert the number yourself.* Some of the reference works cited in this book may not be at your local library. Nevertheless, there is a comprehensive interlibrary loan system in the United States, and many reference works are available on-line. Also, e-mail and Web site addresses, database and CD-ROM products may not be available as this book is being published; you should add this information to your book when you find it becomes available. There is a section for notes at the back of the book. Since this is one book you should hold on to, use the space provided to write down information in the future.

Reference Navigator

Web site:	CD-ROM:
E-mail:	Library Reference Number:
Database:	(student fills in blanks when necessary)

Incidentally, advertising information appearing in these references can be informative and useful with regard to research services. Take the opportunity to read it.

Part II: Sample Table of Contents

The table of contents of any book gives an immediate impression as to its . . . its . . . contents, as we say in academia. This page, besides showing the conceptual framework of the text, may also include a short description of some of the interesting attributes included in various chapters. In some chapters the tables of contents have been deleted because the table of contents is simply too brief to be of consequence or too large to reproduce (examples are then given).

Part III: Sample Page

Although some critics may believe this part is superfluous, I feel that even a small exposure to the publication's number of pages, writing style, and general format are good introductions to the researcher's familiarity with the work. In some instances, highlighted parts may be used to explain the information portrayed. For example, the *U.S. Industry & Trade Outlook* (Chapter 45) has the name of the industrial specialist at the Department of Commerce who wrote the piece, plus his or her telephone number, and the date the piece was written at the end of each section.

Part IV: Recommended Supplement

After 20 years of teaching with textbooks, I would guess that while the "Summary" is the most-read page in any chapter, "Suggested Readings" is probably the least. Many students can barely find time to read the chapter and, despite the advantages, usually have no interest in looking up more material to read. Since there are 50 (short!) chapters in this textbook, additional suggested readings are not included. Instead, the concept of a "Recommended Supplement" has been put in its place. A "recommended supplement" is another quality reference work that may not have the specific focus or versatility of the first resource in the chapter, but offers some excellent supporting information or otherwise unique attributes.

For example, in Chapter 50 (*World Development Report,* published by the World Bank) the recommended supplement is *World Resources: A Guide to the Global Environment.* Here the focus of world economic development is enhanced by a comprehensive report on environmental development. The "Recommended Supplement" section at the end of each chapter summarizes each work into one or two pages. You will also find small boxes at the end of different sections in the chapter offering "Something to do" or "Something to think about," which will challenge you to give some thought to what you have just read.

Principles Underlying the Philosophy of This Text

Ignorance

The great majority of people have almost no idea what business reference books or databases exist or how to use them, yet many of these same people are employed in the exercise of, for the want of a better phrase, commercial judgments. The mission of this text is to help dispel this ignorance.

Competence

Those individuals with management experience know that in the soul of competent decisions, the substance of good information is always found. Those who can define, identify, retrieve, apply, and evaluate information from an ocean of data will, in our rapidly changing economy, be responsible for the progress and survival of organizations.

Selectivity

Depending on who is counting, there are at least 4,000 references of specific use in the business environment. *Harvard Business School Core Collection,* for example, contains 3,500 selected works "reflecting the research teaching and general business reading interests of the Harvard Business School." And that doesn't include periodicals. The point is not how many sources exist or which seem the most important, but rather, which specific sources best meet the research goal. This text could not contain even 300 much less 3,000 sources that might have a bearing on a certain commercial issue. Therefore, to accommodate the needs of the average researcher, the reference works selected were limited to the number of works that would roughly meet the needs of all (including the publisher who insisted that this book be limited to 400 pages). Management professors may wonder why the *Administrative Science Quarterly* was not included; the finance and exchange analyst will wonder about the exclusion of *Institutional Investor;* and the varsity football team the absence of *Sports Illustrated.* They all are right; some relevant publications are left out.

Presentation

Only a decade or two ago, a good student's research ability might have been determined by the stack of his or her 3-by-5 cards. Today it is a given that information retrieval must utilize computer databases. *Computer literacy is, therefore, essential to the research philosophy and the substance of this text. Almost every research source now has an Internet home page, and each student should be familiar with its use.*

A Short Note about Textbooks and Research Papers

Textbooks

Everyone who has graduated from a university has used a textbook. Conversely, very few use textbooks after they leave school. Most managers, for example, obtain their information from business periodicals and industry or government reference works, relatively few of which they have seen or been required to use in school. Education should be modified to incorporate more emphasis on the use of reference works and databases in accomplishing the course requirements. On average, in my opinion, the balance between textbook and reference use should be equal.

Research Paper

If it is true that none have graduated without the use of a textbook, it might similarly be said that few have graduated without doing a research paper. All reference works need to be cited in term papers, yet many students are not trained in any specific method to make the citations. There are a number of style guides, including the Modern Language Association's *The Handbook for Writers of Research Papers* and the American Psychological Association's *Publication Manual of the APA*. Also, since many business references are (or will soon be) available on-line, the challenge is how to cite such material from the Internet, particularly when these citations are based on evolving standards. Instructors and students should look for new publications as they come out. Aside from the MLA and APA, other sources to keep in mind are *Elements of E-Text Style* and *A Guide to Citing Electronic Information*. If you want some help on-line, contact Janice R. Walker, Department of English, University of South Florida (jwalker@chuma. cas.usf.edu), who also has a forthcoming book (with Todd Taylor) titled *The Columbia Guide to Online Style*.

Understanding the Role of Research References to Business Applications

A systems theory axiom has it that "a person's judgment is only as good as his or her information." The competitive environment is changing from stable to dynamic in almost every industry (the buggy whip industry, however, has managed to remain stable). Like the sine curve, the *frequency* and *amplitude* of change are now both rapid and global, from placing ads to building factories. Judgment in this environment carries a great deal of weight when it comes to the survivability of an organization. Business applications of information technology must be viewed from their functional perspective (i.e., marketing, finance, human resource, production/service) and their process requirements (i.e., location, people, equipment, resources, relationships, and policies). Your professional judgments will help decide the fate of your company.

A Description of the ISSN and ISBN

The ISSN and ISBN are the codes by which serials and books can be identified. ISSN stands for International Standard Serial Number. It is an internationally accepted, concise, unique, and unambiguous code for the identification of serial publications. The ISSN is employed as a component of bar codes and as a tool for the communication of basic information about a serial title and for such processes as ordering, billing, inventory control, abstracting, and indexing. In library processes, the ISSN is used in operations such as acquisitions, claiming, binding, accessioning, shelving, cooperative cataloging, circulation, interlibrary loans, and retrieval of requests. ISBN is an abbreviation for International Standard Book Number, which is assigned to each volume or edition by the publisher. The ISSN, which is assigned by the International Center (Paris) or national ISSN centers, remains the same for each issue. For full information contact: National Serials Data Program (NSDP) at the Library of Congress, Washington, DC 20540-4160. Telephone: (202) 707-6452.

Keep this book handy

This is a book you should plan on keeping. It is the source book to help you quickly research many business information problems; therefore, interact with the information as you are using it by keeping notes on references.

And one final note. Research guides are by their nature incomplete so, if you know of a particularly good business reference that is not included, please feel free to write and describe why you like it. We will be grateful for the information and appreciate the time you took to do it.

Author e-mail: profpatbut@aol.com

Publisher's Web site: http://www.mhhe.com

A C K N O W L E D G M E N T S

I would like to recognize, with special thanks, the kind and efficient support of the faculty and staff at the schools of business from the following universities: University of Stockholm (Sweden)—Deans Sikander Kahn, Sten Kopniwsky, Jan-Erik Gröjer, Olle Högberg, and Professor Roland Hansson (former Director of the International Business Academy), and administrators Kiki Winnersten and Linnea Shore; University of Paderborn (Germany)—Professors Peter Weinberg, Andrea Groppel, and Wolfgang Weber; University of Innsbruck (Austria)—Professor Hans Hinterhuber; and Monterrey Institute of Technology (Mexico)—Dean Gerardo Lujan, Associate Dean Juan Bruno Garcia-Sordo, professors Felipe Saravia, Luis Garcia and Mohammed Ayub Khan. Thanks also to the following associates who helped guide this book: Dr. Jennifer Braaten, Mr. Arthur Snyder, Mr. Michael Petrowski, Ms. Donna Sullivan, Mr. E.K. Morris, Ms. Lisa Prue, Dr. Eldon Bernstein, Dr. John Pickering, and Dr. Carolyn Spencer. Also, without the support of Wendy Hegel and the expertise of the McGraw-Hill Companies staff, Gail Korosa, Christine Vaughan, Scott Isenberg, and Dick Hercher, this book could not have been written.

Finally, I would like to thank the following reviewers, of the first and second stages of manuscript for their suggestions: David Adams, Marywood College; John P. Flemming IV, Troy State University; Bruce Stern, Portland State University; Abu T. Shaharier, University of Phoenix: John Hanke, Eastern Washington University; Craig Swenson, University of Phoenix; David Ketcham, Bryant College; Mary Meredith, University of Southwestern Louisiana; and Marie Flatley, San Diego State University.

F O R E W O R D

How I wish that Patrick Butler's book had been available years ago! The grief it would have spared me.

During my years reporting on the economy, I could have used his *Business Research Sources* on countless occasions. The hours I could have saved in researching sources of information. But I'll get to that in a moment.

First, though, I should mention that beyond being an invaluable guide to specific sources of information, Patrick Butler's book serves a broader purpose in helping readers to develop invaluable research skills. Let me tell you how, many years ago, I learned the hard way the importance of developing such skills.

I had it drummed into me by some tough city editors.

My earliest newspaper job was writing obituaries for the *Providence* (Rhode Island) *Journal*. The very first day at the paper I wrote that a deceased person was interned in the Woodlawn Cemetery.

"Dummy," exclaimed the city editor, a man not noted for his diplomacy, "interned is what happens to prisoners of war. Interred is for corpses."

Quick research into a basic research tome (not tomb) known as the dictionary would have spared me the sneers I could sense from others in the newsroom.

I also learned about the importance of speed in getting at research information in my first real job as a journalist on the midnight shift of the foreign-news desk at International News Service in New York. INS was, to put it bluntly, cheap. The company pinched pennies, liras, rubles, centimes, and every other currency in the countries where it had correspondents covering the news.

This was in the days before satellites and other high-tech forms of communication. Correspondents sent their dispatches by cable, an international telegram transmitted by radio or under-the-ocean cables. The cost per word of the dispatches depended on the speed of service desired; the faster the service, the higher the rate. To save money INS correspondents were instructed to send only the first few words of a news story "urgent," the most expensive rate, and to follow up with details by the cheapest rate, even though it might take an hour or more for the details to reach New York. In the meantime, the writer (me, for one) on the foreign desk was to take the few words (such as "STALIN DEAD") in the urgent-rate cable and spin it into a story to move quickly on the news wire in the usually futile hope of beating the Associated Press and United Press in servicing clients with the news.

That meant drawing on whatever knowledge the writer might have on the particular subject to expand immediately on the cryptic cable ("JOSEF STALIN, WHO RULED THE SOVIET UNION WITH AN IRON HAND, DIED TODAY . . . ETC.") and then to flesh out the report in short takes with material gleaned from reference sources. That was the challenge: to quickly go to sources available in the INS office for background material—the date of Stalin's birth, his career in the Communist Party, his meetings with American presidents, and so on.

Those sources were limited, including little more than the bureau news clippings "morgue," the encyclopedia, and the *World Almanac*.

Happily, the average researcher today—whether a student, a journalist, a businessman or woman—has a virtually unlimited reservoir of sources (an overabundance, might be a more accurate description) where answers are to be found. The big problem is to identify the sources and to know how to use them effectively.

Enter Patrick Butler.

Dr. Butler has skillfully undertaken the role of Sherpa on the treacherous slopes of the mountains of available business data, and he guides the reader with precision and even a generous ration of wit.

The problem for anyone doing research in the information age is not a lack of information, but rather how to target the information required for a particular project and how to get to it quickly.

That's what this book accomplishes.

Which brings me back to my regrets that it was not available earlier. As an economics correspondent, I would have used it to seek out people and companies to illustrate television stories. For example, when the monthly government report on the U.S. trade deficit was released, the inevitable problem was how to translate statistics into a visual television piece. That time-consuming task would have been simplified by turning to Dr. Butler's *Business Research Sources: A Reference Navigator* to locate reference sources that would identify firms engaged in foreign trade and cite the names of officers of those corporations.

The next step would be to arrange to shoot videotape of a corporation's production facilities and do an interview with an officer . . . and presto! sterile statistics would have been converted into the ingredients of a TV report.

Finally, a word about our able and self-effacing guide Patrick Butler, who brings to his project the experience not only of a widely respected college professor, but also of wide-ranging careers as a naval flight officer, a marketing engineer for the Lockheed Aircraft Corporation and in U.S. government.

By Irving R. Levine
former NBC News chief economics correspondent

C O N T E N T S

BUSINESS RESEARCH SOURCES

I GENERAL CONCEPTS ABOUT BUSINESS REFERENCE BOOKS

Description of Section Pages

This book is segmented into *eight* distinct sections. Each section (except this one) begins with a page that lists 10 optional reference works, assisting the reader in further exploring research sources other than those described in the subsequent chapters. For example, the Section II page will provide industry references. Although I have tried to correlate the list of suggested reference sources shown on the section page with the chapters from that topic area, the fit is not always close and some research sources could easily overlap. (Reference works cited in the chapters are not included in the section page list.)

Section I: Description of section pages
Section II: Industry references
Section III: Economic references
Section IV: Business database references
Section V: Statistics and demographic references
Section VI: Government affairs references
Section VII: Company references
Section VIII: International references

1   BUSINESS INFORMATION

Description of Publication

For information on this publication (ISBN 0-89774-643-0) call Oryx Press at: (602) 265-2651 or (800) 279-6799 or fax: (800) 279-4663.

 Reference Navigator

Web site: http://www.oryxpress.com

E-mail: info@oryxpress.com

Database: not available

CD-ROM: not available

Library Reference Number:

Michael Lavin's *Business Information: How to Find It, How to Use It* is perhaps one of the preeminent books on business reference information. It will show you a great number of business resources and how to find them and use them. Unfortunately, it is a thick book, covering over 500 pages with small print and a great deal of information you may not always need. Nevertheless, it is reader-friendly and essential for those who wish an in-depth coverage of business information. Although it is not a book about specific companies, statistics, functional areas (marketing, human resources, etc.), or regulations, it has such a comprehensive listing and description of business references that it is useful for anyone interested in business research, and it is particularly recommended for senior-level and graduate students and business faculty. The book Web site is: http://www. oryxpress.com/books/bi2.htm

    If *Business Information* is so good, why should you purchase *Business Research Sources: A Reference Navigator*? The answer lies in the depth and complexity of understanding reference works. *Business Information* is written for professional information analysts and students dedicated to a deeper understanding of the subject. *Business Research Sources* is written for those who simply need a road map to their goals of research versus those who relish the sophistication of an atlas.

The second edition is an improvement on the first and is comprised of 20 chapters, which can be seen in the following table of contents. My hypothesis, and no doubt that of a great host of educators, about the research techniques of students is succinctly stated in Lavin's book.

> When confronted with a research project, or even a request for a few simple facts, businesspeople seldom know how to launch their campaign. Once started, they proceed in a lurching, haphazard manner, trusting to luck and a small network of familiar contacts.

Business Information combines knowledgeable descriptions of major business publications and databases with explanations of concepts for using them effectively. The book explains how to begin a research project, where to look for information, and how to analyze what is found. According to Lavin, a business and management subject specialist at Lockwood Memorial Library, State University of New York at Buffalo, *Business Information* requires no prior knowledge of economics or business. Every chapter discussion begins with an explanation of the basic concepts required to understand the resources described. *Two overriding themes are found in the book: the importance of planning a search strategy, and the need to develop a critical eye when using business information.* Equally important, he says, is what the book is not intended to do. First, it should not be viewed as a comprehensive guide to the literature of business, and second, the book is not a guide to the "core" resources in business since, despite their respectability, the selections represent his personal preferences and biases. He offers, "Perhaps the most notable change in business information has been the increasing importance of electronic databases, especially CD-ROMs." In the past many databases were expensive and access was limited; however, most reservations regarding this matter now have long since disappeared. Many publications are produced in several formats: a single product may be available in print, on CD-ROM from several publishers, and offered on-line through many vendors, with each variation differing in some respects.

> Lavin has organized the book into five sections.
>
> Part I introduces ideas and methods important to all business research activities. These include how business information is used, its characteristics, the sources of published and unpublished data, and the forms in which publications and databases appear.
>
> Part II is devoted to the tools that determine where to look for information—the directories, indexes, bibliographies, and catalogs that describe other business sources.
>
> Part III surveys the challenging task of investigating companies, both private and publicly held. Research needs in this area cover directory data, financial profiles, investment information, and specialized news.

Part IV deals with statistical data of various types: demographic, economic, and industrial. A separate chapter introduces general statistical concepts and research problems.

Part V explores four special topics—information about local areas, business and labor law, marketing, and taxation and accounting.

In every chapter, key concepts and terminology are introduced before the related information products are described. The number of major resources varies per chapter, from about a dozen to 25 or more. Chapters conclude with discussions of strategic issues, the research problems encountered, how to initiate a project, choosing the best tools, and how to cope with information overload, which may be the only major criticism of the book itself.

One of the most significant aspects of using information is understanding the numbers offered within—the statistics. Chapter 13, "Introduction to Statistical Reasoning," is particularly useful for the novice information gatherer, who avoids statistics like the proverbial plague. In "Topics Covered," for example, special note is made of "Statistical Abuses and Mistakes: Averages, Percents, Index Numbers, Rankings, Charts and Graphs, and Tables."

If you thought trying to find some information about business in the United States was hard, wait until you try Saudi Arabia or some other such exotic place. Well, there is hope...with *International Business Information: How to Find It, How to Use It,* second edition (ISBN 1-57356-050-2) also published by Oryx Press (http://www.oryxpress.com/books/ibi2.htm). It describes key international business publications and databases and provides the subject background needed to understand them.

From any national perspective, much international business information is, as the authors Ruth Pagell and Michael Halperin point out, truly foreign. The sources are different, the language is different, the coding is different, and the definitions are different. This book is designed to help its users overcome the obstacles to finding and understanding international business information. An important goal for the authors has been to provide the reader with the information and techniques needed to evaluate and select information products for international business research. They believe that identifying and explaining the problems in relation to existing international business sources will help the reader evaluate new sources that will appear after their book is published.

The material the authors looked for was authoritative, available, and affordable; things near and dear to all our hearts. Most of the sources they describe are in English or have at least partial English translations. Their book is not a bibliography. Rather, their emphasis is on what they consider the core of business research: companies, industries, markets, and finance. Most of the sources described are serial publications.

Each chapter of their book consists of a subject background followed by a description of the subject's information sources. In the preface they advise that they occasionally strayed from this plan when it seemed appropriate to describe a source while discussing a business subject. Most of the chapters, they say, can stand alone and can be consulted as needed. They also warn that the inclusion of a source in their book should not necessarily be seen as a recommendation for its use or purchase. In fact, they occasionally describe a source with the recommendation that it *not* be purchased. In their description of sources, they have presented hundreds of extracts of entries, tables, and records, believing that seeing an actual record, or even partial record, will often give a better sense of the contents of a source than the most elaborate description. As a practical matter, they have focused their presentation on English-language directories, yearbooks, reports, databases, and electronic files.

Throughout the book, the authors emphasize that care should be taken in the use and interpretation of international business data. Business vocabulary often changes meaning when it crosses a border. Terms and concepts familiar in the United States, such as CPI, may not be used or have different definitions abroad. Something as simple as comparing the GDP of two countries has pitfalls.

Something to Think About

According to *Business Information,* what are the benefits of an on-line system? Can you name the three broad database categories cited in the book and give a short discussion of each?

CHAPTER 3
Finding Reference Materials

Topics Covered

1. General Guides to the Literature
2. Guides to Directories
3. Guides to Periodicals and Other Serials
   a. General Serials Directories
   b. Trade Journal Directories
   c. Newsletter Directories
   d. Newspaper Directories
   e. Guides to Special Issues
4. Guides to Specialized Business Publications
5. Guides to Computerized Information Sources
   a. Directories of On-line Databases
   b. Specialized On-line Directories
   c. CD-ROM Directories
   d. Directories of Magnetic Tape Files and Diskettes
6. Honing Research Skills
7. For Further Reading

Major Sources Discussed

- *Encyclopedia of Business Information Sources*
- *Directories in Print*
- *Ulrich's International Periodicals Directory*
- *Business Publications Rates & Data*
- *Oxbridge Directory of Newsletters*
- *Editor & Publisher International Year Book*
- *Business Rankings Annual*
- *Findex: The Directory of Market Research Reports, Studies and Surveys*
- *Information Industry Directory*
- *Directory of Online Databases*
- *Fulltext Sources Online*
- *CD-ROMs in Print: An International Guide*
- *Directory of Computerized Data Files: A Guide to U.S. Government Information in Machine Readable Format*

Samuel Johnson wrote: "Knowledge is of two kinds. We know a subject ourselves, or we know where we can find information upon it." To know the answers ourselves certainly seems preferable; at the very least, it saves us the trouble of looking it up. Realistically, there will probably be more instances in our lives when we don't know the answer than when we do. The accelerating rate at which knowledge is created makes it impossible to learn and retain everything that is relevant to us. And even if we could, it is unlikely we would be able to anticipate all our future information needs. That is where research skills come into play. Knowing where to look is the researcher's stock-in-trade, but numerous finding tools are published to assist novice and expert alike. The focus of this chapter is on these guides—the directo-

ries, handbooks, and bibliographies that can lead the user to the proper source of information.

Learning what reference materials are available is a vital part of the research process, but a bewildering array of published materials exists for every business topic imaginable. Finding exactly the right source to address a specific question often seems like an overwhelming task. Common sense might suggest that a particular type of publication must exist, but identifying it when needed can be challenging. Library catalogs are frequently too general for specific inquiries, and popular guides such as *Books in Print* typically do not cover specialized reference works. One of the best ways to learn about potentially useful information sources is to consult guides to . . .

Recommended Supplement: American Library Association's *Guide to Reference Books*

Reference Navigator

Web site: http://www.ala.org

E-mail: ala@ala.org

Database: See Web site

CD-ROM: not available

Library Reference Number:

_____

One of the primary sources for reference research is the *Guide to Reference Books* (ISBN 0-8389-0669-9). The present version of the *Guide to Reference Books (GRB)* is the 11th full edition of a continuing publication by the American Library Association that reaches back to the first edition of 1970. Like other full editions, this one, according to the editors, represents an attempt to reassess the body of reference sources and select those that have been found most useful. As one might expect, the *GRB*, in keeping with growth in the number and variety of reference sources, has itself increased in size with each edition. The number of titles listed in the 11th edition is roughly 15,500. The 11th edition also includes a higher proportion of titles that support the study of non-Western cultures and of diverse viewpoints than its predecessors.

The present edition has been compiled by 50 librarians from institutions ranging geographically from Harvard and Columbia in the East to the University of California and the Graduate Theological Union in the West. The Economics and Business Section, researched by Bessie Carrington, Duke University, and Rita Moss from the University of North Carolina at Chapel Hill, covers:

General works	Economic conditions and world trade
Finance and investment	Company information and industry analysis
Commerce	Marketing and advertising
Organizational behavior	

No discussion of business information would be complete without acknowledging the huge input of business and economics textbooks and teaching materials. Without any bias in this text, the McGraw-Hill Publishing Cos. is one of the top suppliers in the country if not the world. Those interested in business information should avail themselves of the McGraw-Hill catalogs, which are published annually. Most books are annotated, with tables of contents, plus videos and study guides described. Call the customer relations representative at: (708) 789-4000; or fax: (708) 789-6937.

A second source of reference information is the *Walford's Guide* (ISBN 0-85365-539-1), published in annual intervals by the Library Association Publishing Company in London. It has been an essential component of the standard reference collection for over 35 years. With its international coverage and ordering information and its evaluation of works, the *Guide* has become an important tool in building up and in revising reference collections worldwide. The *Guide* is also for use in general and special inquiry work, particularly for the research student in the initial stages of research. Each edition, usually published in three volumes, covers reference works published in English, although significant material in other languages is not overlooked. The three volumes are identified as:

   I. Science and technology
  II. Social and historical sciences, philosophy and religion
 III. Generalia, language and literature, the arts

Critical annotations and reviewers' comments accompany the citations. The entries are selective and evaluative in order to guide the inquirer to the best source of reference in each subject area, whether that source be a journal article, a textbook, a database, a bibliography, a progress report, or a monograph. The subject arrangement is based on the Universal Decimal Classification. A comprehensive subject index reflects the importance of the subject arrangement. The economic section of the book (II) is listed below:

Social Sciences
    Economics
        Labour & Employment
        Land & Property
        Business Organizations
        Finance & Banking
        Economic Surveys, etc.
        Trade & Commerce
    Business & Management
    Law and Public Administration

SECTION

II GENERAL BUSINESS REFERENCE SOURCES

Optional industry references:

- *Manufacturing USA*
- *Commodity Yearbook*
- *Aluminum Statistical Review*
- *International Petroleum Encyclopedia*
- *Standard Industrial Classification Manual*
- *Moody's Public Utility Manual*
- *Life Insurance Factbook*
- *Aviation Week and Space Technology*
- *Industrial Statistics*
- *Industry Review*

2   HOOVER'S HANDBOOKS

There are four books in this collection: (1) *Hoover's Handbook of American Business 1998;* (2) *Hoover's Handbook of World Business 1998;* (3) *Hoover's Handbook of Private Companies 1998;* and (4) *Hoover's Handbook of Emerging Companies 1998.* Only the first two will be covered.

Descriptions of Publications

For information on these annual business publications, contact Hoover's, Inc. at: (800) 486-8666; or fax: (512) 374-4501.

 Reference Navigator

Web site: http://www.hoovers.com
E-mail: info@hoovers.com
Database: see Web site

CD-ROM: available
Library Reference Number:

The *Hoover's Handbooks* cited above provide profiles on specific companies, both domestic and international, in terms of size, growth, visibility, and so on. The good news is the detailed profiles of 1,500 companies (all large); the bad news is that there are approximately 20 million of them (almost all small), not including farms. The top 500 companies represent about 55 percent of the U.S. gross national product.

One primary reason the *Hoover's Handbooks* are offered at the beginning of this book is the service that its publisher, Hoover's Inc., provides. Hoover's, Inc. is a leading provider of business information to the mass market. Its *Hoover's Company Database,* for example, is the only "reasonably priced source" (according to its editors) for information on the operations, strategies, histories, financial performance, and products of major U.S. and global public and private companies.

The format is simple, well organized, and easy to read. A list of the databases produced by Hoover's includes:

Hoover's Company Profiles

> Detailed profiles on 2,700 companies. Each profile contains an overview, history, officers, geographic presence, products, key competitors, and up to 10 years of financial and stock data.

Hoover's Company Capsules

> A database of 11,000 companies, including all the public companies traded on the three major U.S. stock exchanges and the largest and fastest-growing private companies; plus 1,000 non-U.S. companies (added in 1996). This database contains key company information, including company name, address, phone, fax, CEO, CFO, human resources officer, annual sales, change in sales, fiscal year-end, employment, ticker symbol and exchange (for public companies), and a brief description of the company's business.

Business Rankings

> A list-lover's compendium, containing lists of the largest companies in various industries. The lists range from the "50 Top U.S. Defense Contractors" to the "25 Largest Law Firms in the U.S. by Revenue."

Hoover's has a point about low price. The set of four *Hoover's Handbooks* sells for $294.95. But *Hoover's* strength is also its weakness. It has excellent thumbnail sketches of domestic and international companies; however, these sketches are very basic, which could be exactly what's needed or analytically not sophisticated enough to be appropriate.

Nevertheless, *Hoover's* has a lot of reference products in print, on-line, CD-ROM, and diskette formats. *Hoover's Company Profiles,* for example, is ideal for executives, investors, career changers, salespeople, consumers, and scholars—anyone who needs to know about companies. Do yourself a favor and get the catalog (call [800] 486-8666). The company makes its database available on Hoover's Online (http://www.hoovers.com) and through America Online, Bloomberg, CompuServe, Dow Jones News Retrieval, LEXIS-NEXIS, and other services.

Hoover's Handbook of American Business is, according to James F. Ryan, president of Zacks & Perrier, "exactly the kind of business reference book I've been looking for most of my life." It's a useful book for the developing analyst as one can see from the table of contents.

"Using the Profiles" addresses the question, "What companies will our readers be most interested in?" In answering that question, four general criteria were used: size, growth, visibility, and breadth of coverage. The 750 profiles are presented in alphabetical order. The overview section covers such important questions as: where, who, what, when, rankings, and key competitors.

A particularly interesting section of the handbook is "A List-Lover's Compendium," which has such lists as: "30 Years of Change in the Fortune 500," "20 Most Advertised Brands," "Largest Beer Companies in the U.S."

The largest and probably most important section of the book is dedicated to "The Company Profiles," an example of which can be seen in the sample pages from *Hoover's Handbook of American Business* and *Hoover's Handbook of World Business*.

Finally, the book finishes with three Indexes: "Index of Profiles by Industry"; "Index of Profiles by Headquarters Location"; and "Index of Brands, Companies, and People Named in the Profiles."

Hoover's Handbook of World Business is very similar in format to *Hoover's Handbook of American Business*. Some aspects of the book that are almost identical to the previous volume include: A List-Lovers Compendium, The Company Profiles, and three indexes. This volume has some excellent, but very basic information.

ABOUT *HOOVER'S HANDBOOK* OF AMERICAN BUSINESS 1998

American business is changing every day. From the first snake-oil salesmen hawking patent medicines to the online entrepreneur selling Internet access, American business has gone through many changes over the years. *Hoover's Handbooks of American Business* have followed these stories since 1990, when we first published *Hoover's Handbook 1991: Profiles of Over 500 Major Corporations*. We've changed, too, to keep pace with the times, but we think you will find the *Hoover's Handbook of American Business 1998* to be the same reliable source of quality, reasonably priced company information that you have come to depend on. We've expanded our coverage of the top public companies to make this version, at 750 profiles, our largest *Hoover's Handbook of American Business* to date.

This two-volume 1998 version of *Hoover's Handbook of American Business* is the first of a four-title series that will be made available as an indexed set. The three other titles are *Hoover's Handbook of Emerging Companies*, *Hoover's Handbook of Private Companies*, and *Hoover's Handbook of World Companies*.

In addition to the 1,500 companies covered in our books, more than 1,200 other profiles are available in electronic format as part of our World Wide Web site, Hoover's Online (www.hoovers.com), and on CD-ROM (Hoover's Company Profiles on CD-ROM). This year we redesigned our Web site to make it more accessible and informative, adding feature stories; links to news articles, CEO biographies, and related sites; and more financial information.

As the online medium has grown, so have our offerings. In addition to Hoover's Online, we also offer three sites of specific interest to business information consumers: Cyberstocks (www.cyberstocks.com), the companion Web site to the book *Cyberstocks: An Investor's Guide to Internet Companies*; Stockscreener (www.stockscreener.com), which enables potential investors to search for stocks based on up to 20 different performance criteria; and IPO Central (www.ipocentral.com), which offers free information on companies filing to go public. Additionally, Hoover's Company Information is available on over 25 other sites on the Internet, including *The Wall Street Journal*, *The New York Times*, and online services Infoseek and Pathfinder.

We welcome the recognition we have received as the premier provider of high-quality company information — electronically, online, and in print — and continue to look for ways to make our products more available and more useful to you.

We believe that anyone who buys from, sells to, invests in, lends to, competes with, interviews with, or works for a company should know about that enterprise. Taken together, this book and the other Hoover's products and resources represent the most complete source of basic corporate information readily available to the general public.

This latest version of *Hoover's Handbook of American Business* contains, as always, profiles of the largest and most influential companies in the United States. Each of the 750 companies profiled here was chosen because of its important role in American business. For more details on how these companies were selected, see the section of this book titled "Using the Profiles."

This book consists of four sections:

1. Using the Profiles describes the contents of our profiles and explains the ways in which we gather and compile our data.

2. A List-Lover's Compendium contains lists of the largest, smallest, best, most, and other superlatives related to companies involved in American business.

3. The profiles make up the largest and most important part of the book — 750 profiles of major U.S. enterprises, arranged alphabetically, with A-K in Volume 1 and L-Z in Volume 2.

4. Three indexes complete the book: In addition to the main index, the companies are indexed by industry group and headquarters location. The main index contains the names of brands, companies, and people mentioned in the profiles in the book. The indexes are at the end of Volume 2.

To help you find a particular company, a complete list of all profiled companies is found near the front of each volume.

As always, we hope you find our books useful. We invite your comments via phone (512-374-4500), fax (512-374-4501), mail (1033 La Posada Drive, Suite 250, Austin, TX 78752), or e-mail (comments@hoovers.com).

The Editors
Austin, Texas
December 1997

The 100 Fastest-Growing Companies by Sales in
Hoover's Handbook of American Business 1998

Rank	Company	Annual % Change	Rank	Company	Annual % Change
1	Republic Industries, Inc.	808.8%	51	Enron Corp.	44.6%
2	MedPartners, Inc.	563.3%	52	Ticketmaster Group, Inc.	43.2%
3	Netscape Communications		53	National City Corporation	42.9%
	Corporation	329.0%	54	The Gillette Company	42.7%
4	U.S. Office Products Company	304.0%	55	NIKE, Inc.	42.0%
5	AmeriServe Food Distribution, Inc.	220.1%	56	Praxair, Inc.	41.4%
6	Ultramar Diamond Shamrock		57	InaCom Corp.	41.0%
	Corporation	202.4%	58	MacAndrews & Forbes Holdings Inc.	40.4%
7	Morrison Knudsen Corporation	188.4%	59	Massachusetts Mutual Life	
8	LG&E Energy Corp.	161.1%		Insurance Company	40.1%
9	Allegheny Teledyne Incorporated	155.3%	60	Ingram Micro Inc.	39.5%
10	Hilton Hotels Corporation	138.9%	61	AirTouch Communications, Inc.	39.1%
11	Budget Group Inc.	138.7%	62	Service Corporation International	38.9%
12	H&R Block, Inc.	136.2%	63	CompuCom Systems, Inc.	38.4%
13	Berkshire Hathaway Inc.	134.0%	64	Central and South West Corporation	38.0%
14	Canandaigua Brands, Inc.	112.1%	65	Gateway 2000, Inc.	37.0%
15	Washington Mutual, Inc.	109.7%	66	Solectron Corporation	36.4%
16	Cisco Systems, Inc.	107.0%	67	Tosco Corporation	36.2%
17	Corporate Express, Inc.	101.0%	68	JP Foodservice, Inc.	36.1%
18	NGC Corporation	98.0%	69	Safeguard Scientifics, Inc.	35.9%
19	The Quaker Oats Company	90.2%	70	Lennar Corporation	35.7%
20	The Chase Manhattan Corporation	84.2%	71	Applied Materials, Inc.	35.4%
21	Travelers Property Casualty Corp.	79.4%	72	3Com Corporation	35.2%
22	United HealthCare Corporation	77.6%	73	Oracle Corporation	34.6%
23	Micron Electronics, Inc.	76.5%	74	WellPoint Health Networks Inc.	34.2%
24	Oxford Health Plans, Inc.	74.2%	75	Westinghouse Electric Corporation	34.2%
25	Packard Bell NEC, Inc.	73.9%	76	Olsten Corporation	34.1%
26	Sonat Inc.	70.6%	77	Domino's Pizza, Inc.	33.3%
27	CUC International Inc.	65.9%	78	Harnischfeger Industries, Inc.	33.1%
28	Valero Energy Corporation	65.3%	79	Thermo Electron Corporation	32.9%
29	Crown Cork & Seal Company, Inc.	64.9%	80	Metro-Goldwyn-Mayer Inc.	32.6%
30	Smithfield Foods, Inc.	62.4%	81	Lear Corporation	32.6%
31	Wells Fargo & Company	61.3%	82	Burlington Northern Santa Fe	
32	Furniture Brands International, Inc.	58.0%		Corporation	32.4%
33	HSN, Inc.	57.0%	83	Computer Sciences Corporation	32.4%
34	HEALTHSOUTH Corporation	56.5%	84	Foster Wheeler Corporation	31.7%
35	Tenet Healthcare Corporation	56.3%	85	Cabletron Systems, Inc.	31.5%
36	UtiliCorp United Inc.	54.8%	86	K-III Communications Corporation	31.4%
37	The Walt Disney Company	54.7%	87	Travelers Group Inc.	31.3%
38	America Online, Inc.	54.1%	88	Microsoft Corporation	31.0%
39	Penske Corporation	53.8%	89	The Charles Schwab Corporation	30.4%
40	First Union Corporation	53.2%	90	Tyco International Ltd.	29.6%
41	Host Marriott Corporation	51.2%	91	Halliburton Company	29.6%
42	The TJX Companies, Inc.	50.4%	92	Staples, Inc.	29.3%
43	Tech Data Corporation	49.0%	93	Intel Corporation	28.7%
44	EOTT Energy Partners, L.P.	46.8%	94	Kaufman and Broad Home Corp.	28.3%
45	Dell Computer Corporation	46.5%	95	Rite Aid Corporation	28.0%
46	Micro Warehouse, Inc.	46.5%	96	MBNA Corporation	27.8%
47	CoreStates Financial Corp	46.3%	97	The First American Financial Corp.	27.8%
48	Western Digital Corporation	45.8%	98	Freddie Mac	27.3%
49	PETsMART, Inc.	45.6%	99	The Columbia Gas System, Inc.	27.3%
50	Humana Inc.	45.0%	100	E. & J. Gallo Winery	27.3%

Note: These rates are for the most recent fiscal year and may have resulted from acquisitions.
Source: Hoover's, Inc., Database, June 1997.

THE GAP, INC.

OVERVIEW

From infancy to affluence, the Gap has got you (or your body) covered. Based in San Francisco, the vertically integrated clothing company operates about 1,900 retail outlets under the names babyGap, Banana Republic, Gap, GapKids, and Old Navy. Almost all of the Gap's merchandise is private label.

Though the company has experienced record sales and earnings, its newest chain, Old Navy, is the Gap's main source of growth. Old Navy has quickly expanded to almost 200 locations. The units resemble upscale warehouses, with concrete floors and exposed pipes, and offer casual apparel at low prices. The Banana Republic division, which offers upscale

clothing and accessories for the over-30 crowd, has introduced a shoe line as well as personal care products with success.

The company's Gap stores are lagging behind its other chains, in part because they strayed from the tried-and-true classics male customers had come to expect (jeans, T-shirts, and khakis) in favor of trendier styles. The chain is trying to recapture this market and update its image through a new advertising campaign pitching Gap's "Easy Fit Jeans." Gap stores have also introduced high-end items such as perfume and skin products.

Founders Donald and Doris Fisher own 24% of the company.

WHEN

In 1969 Donald Fisher and his wife, Doris, opened a small store near what is now San Francisco State University. The couple named their store the Gap (after "the generation gap") and concentrated on selling Levi's jeans. The couple opened a second store in San Jose eight months later, and by the end of 1970 there were six Gap stores. In the beginning the Fishers catered almost exclusively to teenagers, but in the 1970s they expanded into active wear that would appeal to a larger spectrum of customers. Nevertheless, by the early 1980s the Gap was still dependent upon its largely teenage customer base.

In a 1983 effort to revamp the company's image, Fisher hired Mickey Drexler, a former president of Ann Taylor who had a spotless track record in the apparel industry, as the Gap's new president. Drexler immediately overhauled the motley clothing lines to concentrate on sturdy, brightly colored cotton clothing. He also consolidated the stores' many private clothing labels into the Gap brand. As a final touch Drexler ripped out the stores' circular clothing racks and installed white shelving where the clothes could be neatly stacked and displayed.

Also in 1983 the company bought Banana Republic, a unique chain of stores that sold safari clothing in a jungle decor. The company expanded the chain, which enjoyed tremendous success in the mid-1980s; however, after the novelty of the stores wore off in the late 1980s, sales went into a slump. Drexler responded by introducing a broader range of clothes (including higher-priced leather items) and playing down the jungle image. By 1990 Banana Republic was again profitable.

The retailer opened its first GapKids in 1985 after Drexler couldn't find clothing that he liked for his son. During the late 1980s and early 1990s, the Gap continued to grow rapidly, opening its first stores in Canada and the UK. In 1990 it introduced babyGap in 25 GapKids stores, featuring miniature versions of its GapKids line. The company announced in 1991 it would no longer sell Levi's (which had fallen to less than 2% of total sales) and would go completely private label.

The Gap's earnings fell in fiscal 1993 because of Gap division losses brought on by low margins and high rents. It shuffled management positions and titles as part of a streamlining effort. The company rebounded in 1994, concentrating more on improving profit margins than increasing sales. That year the Gap launched Old Navy Clothing Co., which by 1996 accounted for 16% of sales.

In 1995 the company launched a line of body and bath products at Banana Republic, which that year opened its first two stores outside the US, in Canada's Edmonton and Toronto.

During 1996 the company opened 203 new stores. The Gap also teamed up with the NBA to offer kid's clothes featuring the New York Knick's, Los Angeles Laker's, and Chicago Bull's logos, making it the first major retailer allowed to use team logos on its own clothes.

In 1997 Robert Fisher (the founders' son) became the new president of the Gap division (including babyGap and GapKids), and was charged with turning around the segment's sales decline.

WHO

Chairman: Donald G. Fisher, age 68, $1,845,360 pay
President and CEO: Millard S. "Mickey" Drexler, age 52, $3,130,385 pay
EVP; President, The Gap, GapKids: Robert J. Fisher, age 42, $1,478,440 pay
EVP and Chief Administrative Officer: John B. Wilson, age 37, $1,194,848 pay
Division EVP Stores, GapKids: Ronald G. Franks
Division EVP Stores: Dennis R. Parodi
Division EVP Stores and Operations, Old Navy: Kevin M. Lonergan
SVP Finance and CFO: Warren R. Hashagen Jr., age 46, $486,660 pay
SVP and Chief Information Officer: Dennis M. Connors
SVP Strategic Planning and Business Development: Charles K. Crovitz
SVP Offshore Sourcing; Managing Director, Gap International Sourcing: James P. Cunningham
SVP and General Counsel: Anne B. Gust, age 39
SVP Distribution: George A. Joseph
SVP Real Estate: Steven B. Kaplan
SVP Personal Care: Gary L. McNatton
SVP Sourcing and Logistics: Stanley P. Raggio
SVP Human Resources: Adrienne M. Johns
VP Human Resources: Susan L. Cooper
CEO, Banana Republic: Jeanne Jackson
President, International: William S. Fisher
Auditors: Deloitte & Touche LLP

WHERE

HQ: One Harrison St., San Francisco, CA 94105
Phone: 650-952-4400   **Fax:** 650-427-2795
Web site: http://www.gap.com

Stores

	No.
US	1,666
Canada	109
UK	71
France	18
Japan	11
Germany	8
Total	**1,883**

WHAT

Stores

	No.
The Gap	947
GapKids	491
Banana Republic	229
Old Navy Clothing	199
babyGap	17
Total	**1,883**

KEY COMPETITORS

Benetton	J. C. Penney	NIKE
Bugle Boy	L.A. Gear	Nordstrom
Calvin Klein	Lands' End	OshKosh B'Gosh
Dayton Hudson	Levi Strauss	Polo
Dillard's	The Limited	Reebok
Edison Brothers	L.L. Bean	Sears
Esprit de Corp.	Luxottica	Spiegel
Federated	May	TJX
Guess?	Mercantile Stores	Toys "R" Us
Gymboree	Nautica	VF
J. Crew	Enterprises	

HOW MUCH

NYSE symbol: GPS FYE: January 31	Annual Growth	1988	1989	1990	1991	1992	1993	1994	1995	1996	1997
Sales ($ mil.)	19.5%	1,062	1,252	1,587	1,934	2,519	2,960	3,296	3,723	4,395	5,284
Net income ($ mil.)	23.1%	70	74	98	145	230	211	258	320	354	453
Income as % of sales	—	6.6%	5.9%	6.2%	7.5%	9.1%	7.1%	7.8%	8.6%	8.1%	8.6%
Earnings per share ($)	22.9%	0.25	0.26	0.35	0.51	0.81	0.74	0.89	1.10	1.23	1.60
Stock price - FY high ($)	—	9.73	5.42	7.69	10.69	29.69	28.13	21.44	24.69	25.50	36.50
Stock price - FY low ($)	—	2.00	2.33	4.41	4.88	10.00	14.06	12.75	14.44	14.88	23.19
Stock price - FY close ($)	31.5%	2.44	4.63	5.84	10.63	26.63	17.25	21.13	16.25	23.56	28.75
P/E - high	—	39	21	22	21	37	38	24	22	21	23
P/E - low	—	8	9	13	10	12	19	14	13	12	14
Dividends per share ($)	17.6%	0.07	0.07	0.09	0.11	0.15	0.16	0.19	0.23	0.24	0.30
Book value per share ($)	22.8%	0.95	0.93	1.20	1.65	2.38	3.08	3.88	4.75	5.70	6.03
Employees	17.3%	15,700	19,800	23,000	26,000	32,000	39,000	44,000	55,000	60,000	66,000

STOCK PRICE HISTORY

HIGH/LOW/CLOSE

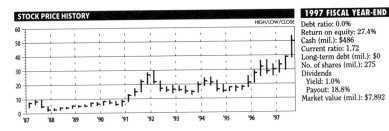

1997 FISCAL YEAR-END

Debt ratio: 0.0%
Return on equity: 27.4%
Cash (mil.): $486
Current ratio: 1.72
Long-term debt (mil.): $0
No. of shares (mil.): 275
Dividends
 Yield: 1.0%
 Payout: 18.8%
Market value (mil.): $7,892

ABOUT *HOOVER'S HANDBOOK*
OF WORLD BUSINESS 1998

World business is a relative term — and is as varied as the different cultures of the world. Big changes in foreign stock markets, wild fluctuations in currencies, and dramatic shifts in the telecommunications and banking industries have made international business in the 1990s extremely volatile. Many of the companies directly involved in and affected by these changes are profiled in this fifth edition of *Hoover's Handbook of World Business*, which features 250 of the most influential companies based outside the United States.

This book is one of the most complete sources of in-depth information on large, non-US–based business enterprises available anywhere. In addition to this volume, we have other international reference products that you may find useful. *Hoover's MasterList of Major European Companies* provides basic information on more than 2,500 leading public and private enterprises in Europe. *Hoover's MasterList of Major Latin American Companies* covers 1,400 enterprises. And we still make available through our catalog many of the best business reference works from other countries, such as the *Brazil Company Handbook*, *Germany's Top 500*, *The Thornton Guide to Hong Kong Companies*, and many others. To see our complete selection, call us at 1-800-486-8666 and request a catalog of our products, or see our catalog online. Hoover's Online (www.hoovers.com) features company profiles and related information. In addition to our main site, we also offer three sites of specific interest to business information consumers: Cyberstocks (www.cyberstocks.com), the companion Web site to the book *Cyberstocks: An Investor's Guide to Internet Companies*; Stockscreener (www.stockscreener.com), which enables potential investors to search for stocks based on up to 20 different performance criteria; and IPO Central (www.ipocentral.com), which offers free information on companies filing to go public. Additionally, Hoover's Company Information is available on over 25 other sites on the Internet including *The Wall Street Journal*, *The New York Times*, and online services Infoseek and Pathfinder. Most of our information is also available in electronic format (Hoover's Company Profiles on CD-ROM), as well as on our Internet sites.

We believe that anyone who buys from, sells to, invests in, lends to, competes with, interviews with, or works for a company should know about that enterprise. If you are an investor, here's a chance to look at a few of the more than 1,300 foreign companies listed on the US stock exchanges. If you are in sales or marketing, check out the purchasing power of multinational companies such as Toyota or Nestlé. If you are looking for a job, consider the US opportunities available from major manufacturers such as BMW and Samsung, and financial service companies, from Nomura Securities to Credit Suisse Group. With the power of today's computer and telecommunications services, anyone with the right knowledge can move money, products, and even services on the other side of the globe. More than ever, good information is the key to successful business.

Hoover's Handbook of World Business 1998 is one of a four-title series that will be made available as an indexed set. The others are *Hoover's Handbook of American Business* (two volumes), *Hoover's Handbook of Emerging Companies*, and *Hoover's Handbook of Private Companies*. These books, together with our many other Hoover's products, represent the most complete source of basic corporate information readily available to the general public.

This book consists of four sections:

1. Using the Profiles describes the contents of our profiles and explains the ways in which we gather and compile our data.

2. A List-Lover's Compendium contains lists of the largest, most profitable, and most valuable companies in this book, and selected lists from other sources of superlatives related to these companies involved in world business.

3. The profiles — 250 business enterprises of global importance, arranged alphabetically, make up the largest and most important part of the book.

4. Three indexes complete the book: the companies are indexed by industry groups and headquarters location, and there is a main index of all the brand names, companies, and people mentioned in the profiles.

To help you find a particular company, a complete list of all profiled companies can be found at the front of the book.

As always, we hope you find our books useful. We invite your comments via telephone (512-374-4500), fax (512-374-4501), mail (1033 La Posada Drive, Suite 250, Austin, TX 78752), or e-mail (info@hoovers.com).

The Editors
Austin, Texas
February 1998

ABB ASEA BROWN BOVERI LTD.

OVERVIEW

ABB Asea Brown Boveri Ltd. doesn't fight the power: it produces it. The Zurich-based engineering firm, made up of 1,000 companies in more than 100 countries around the world, is a leader in power generation, transmission, and distribution, as well as industrial and building systems. It is also involved in rail transportation through a 50% joint venture with Daimler-Benz and operates a financial services unit to support its many construction and engineering projects. The company is jointly owned by ABB AB (formerly ASEA AB) of Sweden and ABB AG (formerly BBC Brown Boveri) of Switzerland. The Wallenberg family's Investor AB controls 50% of the firm.

Swedish chairman and former CEO Percy Barnevik has been a driving force in the continuing globalization of the company. He describes ABB as a "multidomestic" corporation with a decentralized structure, where national subsidiaries remain closely linked to their local customers and labor force.

ABB is investing heavily in emerging areas such as China, Eastern Europe, and Latin America, where infrastructure and energy plant construction, as well as modernization, is booming. ABB is stepping up its investment in China to more than $1 billion and hopes to double its sales in that area by 2002.

WHEN

Asea Brown Boveri (ABB) was formed in 1988 when two lackluster giants, ASEA AB of Sweden and BBC Brown Boveri of Switzerland, combined their electrical engineering and equipment businesses. Percy Barnevik, head of ASEA, became CEO of the new company.

Ludwig Fredholm founded ASEA in Stockholm in 1883 as Electriska Aktiebolaget to make engineer Jonas Wenstrom's electric dynamo. In 1890 he merged his company with Wenstrom's brother's to form Allmanna Svenska Electriska Aktiebolaget (ASEA), a pioneer in industrial electrification. Early in the 1900s ASEA participated in its first railway electrification project; by the 1920s and 1930s it provided locomotives and other equipment for Sweden's national railway. ASEA became one of Sweden's largest electric equipment makers by buying its rival, Elektromekano, in 1933. It entered the US market in 1947, and in 1962 it bought 20% of electric appliance maker Electrolux and formed Scandinavian Glasfiber with Owens-Corning Fiberglas (US). ASEA created the nuclear power venture ASEA-ATOM with the Swedish government in 1968, buying full control in 1982.

BBC Brown Boveri had been formed as a partnership, Brown, Boveri, and Company, by Charles Brown and Walter Boveri in Baden, Switzerland, in 1891 to make electrical generation equipment. It produced the first steam turbines in Europe in 1900. BBC established companies in Germany (1893), France (1894), and Italy (1903) to produce and distribute its steam and gas turbine equipment. After WWII it diversified into nuclear power generating equipment. Electrical machinery production expanded with the purchase of Maschinenfabrik Oerlikon (1967), a Swiss

company that manufactured electrical equipment in France and Spain. In 1979 BBC formed a joint venture with Gould (US) to produce electrical equipment.

In an unusual merger, both ASEA and BBC withheld certain assets from the combination, such as ASEA's holdings in Electrolux. Each company continues as a separate entity, sharing equal ownership of ABB. ABB formed two joint ventures with Westinghouse in 1988: one to produce turbines and generators and the other to make electrical transmission equipment. In 1989 it bought Westinghouse's half of the transmission joint venture as well as Combustion Engineering for a total exceeding $2 billion. The purchase of Cincinnati Milacron in 1990 enhanced ABB's industry automation and environmental control systems segments.

An ABB-led consortium was awarded a $1.25 billion contract in 1992 to build one of the world's largest hydroelectric plants, in Iran. The company merged its transportation segment into ADtranz — a joint venture with Daimler-Benz that is the world's #1 maker of trains — in 1995. That year it added contracts in Colombia, Italy, Norway, Russia, Saudi Arabia, South Korea, Sweden, and the US.

ABB continued to confirm its global presence in 1996, winning contracts to expand Manila's light rail system and to build power plants in Thailand and Turkey, and an oil refinery in India. In 1997 ABB's involvement in a $5.7 billion hydroelectric dam in Malaysia was threatened when it failed to settle contractual disputes with its partner in the project, Ekran Bhd.

WHO

Chairman: Percy Barnevik
President and CEO: Göran Lindahl, age 52
EVP and CFO: Renato Fassbind, age 42
EVP Industrial and Building Systems: Sune Carlsson, age 56
EVP Power Transmission and Distribution: Sune Karlsson, age 51
EVP Power Generation: Armin Meyer, age 48
President and CEO, Asea Brown Boveri: Peter S. Janson
President and CEO, ABB Switzerland: Alois Sonnenmoser, age 57
EVP, Asia Pacific and South Asia: Alexis Fries, age 42
EVP, Americas: Howard Pierce, age 56
EVP, Europe, Middle East, and Africa: Eberhard von Koerber, age 59
SVP Human Resources Operations, Asea Brown Boveri: Richard Walsh
CFO, Asea Brown Boveri: Phillip Widman
Senior Corporate Officer, Corporate Projects, Finance, and Administration: Tomas Ericsson, age 62
Senior Corporate Officer, Research and Development, Technology Evaluation, and Process Technology: Craig Tedmon, age 58
Manager Financial Services: Jan Roxendal, age 44
Management Resources (HR): Arne Olsson
Auditors: KPMG Klynveld Peat Marwick Goerdeler SA; Ernst & Young AG

WHERE

HQ: PO Box 8131, CH-8050 Zurich, Switzerland
Phone: +41-1-317-7334   **Fax:** +41-1-311-7958
US HQ: Asea Brown Boveri Inc., 501 Merritt Seven, Norwalk, CT 06851
US Phone: 203-750-2200   **US Fax:** 203-750-2263
Web site: http://www.abb.com

1996 Sales

	$ mil.	% of total
Europe	19,679	57
Asia/Pacific & South Asia	6,465	18
The Americas	6,136	18
Middle East & Africa	2,294	7
Total	**34,574**	**100**

WHAT

1996 Sales

	$ mil.	% of total
Industrial & building systems	16,067	40
Power generation	9,697	24
Power transmission & distribution	9,025	22
Transportation	2,008	5
Financial services	479	1
Other	3,321	8
Adjustments	(6,023)	—
Total	**34,574**	**100**

Selected Segments, Products, and Services

Industrial and Building Systems
Air handling equipment
Automation and drives
Installation material
Instrumentation
Low-voltage apparatus and systems
Motors

Power Generation
Environmental systems
Fossil combustion systems and services
Power plant control
Power plant production
Power plants (including gas turbine and combined-cycle, hydro, nuclear, and utility steam)

Power Transmission and Distribution
Cables
Distribution transformers
Medium-voltage equipment
Network control and protection
Power lines, systems, and transformers

KEY COMPETITORS

AIG	General Signal	McDermott
Alcatel Alsthom	Halliburton	Mitsubishi
Bechtel	Hitachi	Nippon Steel
Broken Hill	Honeywell	Peter Kiewit
CBS	Ingersoll-Rand	Sons'
Fluor	Johnson Controls	Rolls-Royce
GE	Mannesmann AG	Siemens
GEC	Mark IV	Toshiba

HOW MUCH

Joint venture FYE: December 31	Annual Growth	1987	1988	1989	1990	1991	1992	1993	1994	1995	1996
Sales ($ mil.)	8.6%	—	17,832	20,560	26,688	21,864	26,688	28,883	29,718	33,738	34,574
Net income ($ mil.)	15.6%	—	386	589	590	353	590	609	760	1,315	1,233
Income as % of sales	—	—	2.2%	2.9%	2.2%	1.6%	2.2%	2.1%	2.6%	3.9%	3.6%
Employees	3.0%	—	169,459	189,493	215,154	214,399	213,407	206,490	207,557	209,637	214,894

NET INCOME HISTORY

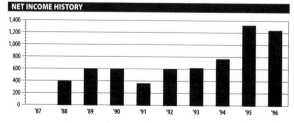

1996 FISCAL YEAR-END

Debt ratio: 23.7%
Return on equity: 21.0%
Cash (mil.): $5,553
Current ratio: 1.23
Long-term debt (mil.): $1,823

Recommended Supplement: *Gale Research Information Solutions 1997*

For information on Gale Research services call: (800) 877-GALE; or fax: (800) 414-5043.

Reference Navigator

Web site: http://www.gale.com   CD-ROM: available

E-mail: galeord@gale.com   Library Reference Number:

Databases: Gale Research, DIALOG   _____

These people do great work; unfortunately many students can't afford the material, only libraries can. So here is a project for your business school club. Review the material (the author is not employed by Gale Research Inc. to say this) and check it against what your library has. If the library doesn't have what you're looking for, perhaps it will buy it or the club could donate money for the publication or database. Gale has been growing for more than 40 years in the information market. Known in the past for its reliable contact data, now you (or the library) can look to Gale (or other providers) to supply you with complete information solutions. The editors, programmers, writers, and researchers act as information filters, personally evaluating and interpreting data. Then it's further customized by incorporating and blending indexes, charts, photographs, glossaries, sound bites, video chips, and hypertext links that offer extra insight into the subjects you are investigating. Eventually, you may be responsible for putting together an information center for your business. Gale is a name to remember.

Gale puts out material in all sorts of formats: GaleNet, commercial on-line, CD-ROM, diskette, magnetic tape, and custom edition. GaleNet is a new subscription on-line service that links you directly to Gale resources. Several of Gale's most-frequently consulted information sources are: *Encyclopedia of Associations* (see Chapter 19), *Gale Directory of Databases* (see Chapter 20), *Gale Guide to Internet Databases, Research Centers and Services Directory,* to name a few. As of January 1996, all electronic databases with one or more annual updates (within a calendar year) were available to the public on an annual or multiyear subscription basis.

Gale Business Resource provides a single-source access to an extensive, integrated database of industry, product, and brand name information, as well as statistics and company profiles and histories. For direct access to vital information on more than 210,000 U.S. businesses, Gale Business Resource's CD offers menu-driven options to search by company, product and brand, or industry. Users can also construct extended searches by combining any of 28 items of information, including Standard Industrial Classification code, number of employees, annual sales/revenues, and location, using Boolean logic operators. Information for each industry will cover:

- An industry overview and analysis.
- Industry statistics.
- Leading companies' addresses, officers, employment and financial data.
- Full-text Securities and Exchange Commission reports for the Fortune 1,000.
- Article-length company histories.
- 12,000 market share reports.
- 16,000 rankings and industry associations.

This type of information is valuable, but you have to know how to put it together to get good business research results for, among other things, analyzing market share and market share participants, determining parent/subsidiary relationships, finding specific industry trends, and the like.

Something to Do

Go to the Gale Research Web site and review the catalog of materials to familiarize yourself with the types of information available.

---

3   STANDARD & POOR'S

Description of Publication

For information on this set of publications (ISSN 0196 4666), call Standard & Poor's Corporation, a division of McGraw-Hill Inc., at: (800) 525-8640, fax: (212) 412-0395.

Reference Navigator

Web site: http://www.standardpoor.com
E-mail: webmaster@mcgraw-hill.com
On-line database: M.A.I.D.

CD-ROM: Available
Library Reference Number:
_____

The most encyclopedic source of narrative and financial industry analysis is Standard and Poor's Corp. (S&P). It offers such a wide variety of publications (approximately 25) that could be useful to anyone engaged in business research that it is impossible to profile all of them in one chapter. So we won't. Nevertheless, it is important to cover a few of the S&P publications to get a feel for their topics and format and to note names of various other works (see below) to give readers an idea of what is available. *Business Research Sources* focuses on publications with a broad scope; therefore, some S&P references are *not* included due to their complexity and specific nature. Once again you are advised to take advantage of Michael Lavin's *Business Information* to get a more detailed explanation of how to utilize S&P publications.

This chapter covers *Standard & Poor's Industry Surveys* and *Standard & Poor's Corporation Records.* The following publications are available in many libraries in either hard cover, on-line, or CD-ROM versions.

OTC Profiles	*Trends & Projections*
Daily News	*Bond Guide*
Statistical Service	*Stock Reports*
Earnings Guide	*Industry Report Service*
Insurance Rate Service	*Stock Market Encyclopedia*
Lipper/S&P Special Situations	*Outlook*
Security Owner's Stock Guide	*Market Scope*
Emerging & Special Situations	*Credit Week*

Standard & Poor's Industry Surveys (annual with updates) is a comprehensive two-volume reference work offering a wealth of valuable data covering all major domestic industries. The information includes recent developments, industry basics, and company data. The analysis begins with an examination of the prospects for that particular industry. This is followed by an analysis of trends and problems presented in historical perspective. Major segments of the industry are spotlighted. Textual matter is accompanied by statistical tables and charts providing valuable background material. One unique section is titled "Comparative Company Analysis." Here one can compare the growth in sales and earnings of the leading companies in the industry and also track the profit margins, dividends, price–earnings ratios, and data for each firm over a five-year span.

The analysis provides the latest developments and available industry, market, and company statistics, along with appraisals by S&P's analysts of the investment outlook for the area covered. In using these surveys for investment research, readers must recognize that business and stock market conditions can change extremely rapidly.

More than 1,000 companies are covered in the "Comparative Company Analysis" section of *Industry Surveys*. Company ratio comparisons and balance sheet statistics are provided in the analytical survey. Interim revenue and income data for these same companies can be found in the earnings supplement. The earnings supplement lists the latest (at press time) revenues and earnings. This supplement is located in the front of the volume, immediately following the indexes. In addition to reporting the revenues and earnings for the latest quarter, the supplement also shows revenues and earnings for the most recent four quarters and indicates corporate return on revenues and return on equity. One especially valuable feature of the supplement is the rankings, which assist investors and other users in quickly identifying the most rapidly growing and most profitable companies within the various industry subgroups.

Standard & Poor's cautions that while a ranking system could imply that the companies included in the tables are specially selected, such isn't the case. The rankings are provided only to identify the fastest-growing and most profitable companies.

S&P Corporation Records (annual with updates) is a six-volume loose-leaf directory with detailed descriptions of 12,000 domestic and international public companies, with fullest coverage of the 9,000 firms that have most investor interest. Information includes history, finances, officers, directors, subsidiaries, and securities. It includes an index of firms by SIC number and a cross-reference index to subsidiaries. It's on-line with *Standard & Poor's Corporate Descriptions* (full text), and is available on Dialog and LEXIS-NEXIS (see Chapter 21). Its CD-ROM version is called *Corporations CD-ROM* and includes full text of coverage for approximately 9,200 companies in *Corporation Records.*

This publication and others from S&P are similar to Moody's publications in many important respects, so Moody's will not be covered in this textbook. The differences between *S&P Corporation Records* and *Moody's Manuals* is most obviously the size and format. *Corporation Records* is published in loose-leaf format and arranged alphabetically. *Moody's Manuals* is more comprehensive than its competitor, both in the number of companies and the amount of information. In short, what *Moody's* takes 20 volumes to cover, *Standard & Poor's* does in 7. An advantage of the S&P service is its faster updating. The main volumes of the *Corporation Records* are revised quarterly instead of annually, and the corresponding news service provides subscribers with late-breaking corporate information every business day. The updates appear in the seventh volume, called *Standard & Poor's Daily News.* Aside from these and other modest differences, the information in both publications is similar. Capitalization, description of securities, and lists of subsidiaries, properties, and officers can all be found in both publications.

Perhaps one of the quickest ways to get good solid investment information is to simply call one's broker. Reason enough to start your investment portfolio early so your broker can help supply information for your research paper. Morgan Stanley Dean Witter, for example, has an outstanding research department. However, its annual investment publication, called *The Competitive Edge,* is available only to its client base. If you really want the inside skinny on an industry, then you could try to contact an analyst in your area of interest. The analysts may be willing to help students, but clients obviously come first, and it may be a while before you get an answer.

Something to Think About

Where can one compare the growth in sales and earnings of the leading companies in the industry and also track the profit margins, dividends, price–earnings ratios, and other data for each company over a five-year period? Could you do it?

I N D E X   T O   S U R V E Y S

In July 1996, the format of *Industry Surveys* was revamped in two ways. First, the subjects were expanded from 20 broad topics to 52 more specialized ones. Each of these 52 topics will be the exclusive subject of an issue of *Industry Surveys*. By July 1997, each topic will have been covered at least once. Second, there are no longer "Basic" or "Current" issues. All future issues will have the same format, including recent developments, industry basics, and company data.

This index indicates whether the most recent coverage of each particular subject is in an issue of *Industry Surveys* in the new format or old format. If a subject is covered in a new-format issue, the relevant page number will be in bold san serif text **(like this),** and the issue's name will be abbreviated with *two* to *four* letters. If a subject is covered in an old-format issue, the relevant page number will be in regular serif text (like this), and the issue's name will be abbreviated with *one* letter.

The specific abbreviations for issue titles in the new format are listed below; the old-format abbreviations are on the next page. For example, if a subject is covered on page 6 of the Foods & Nonalcoholic Beverages issue in the new format, it would be referenced as **FNB-6.** If a subject is referenced on page 28 of the Oil & Gas Basic in the old format, it would be referenced as O-28. By July 1997, each subject will be covered in the new format.

New Format: Volume 1 (A–L)

Topic	Abbreviation	Published
Aerospace & Defense	AD	*
Agribusiness	AG	*
Airlines	AIR	*
Alcoholic Beverages & Tobacco	ABT	*
Apparel & Footwear	AF	*
Auto & Auto Parts	AAP	*
Banking	BA	8/22/96
Biotechnology	BT	*
Broadcasting & Cable	BC	8/1/96
Capital Goods	CG	*
Chemicals: Basic	CB	*
Chemicals: Specialty & Plastics	CSP	*
Communications Equipment	CE	*
Computers: Commercial Services	CCS	*
Computers: Consumer Services & the Internet	CCSI	*
Computers: Hardware	CH	9/19/96
Computers: Networking	CN	*
Computers: Software	CS	*
Electric Utilities	EU	9/26/96
Electrical Equipment	EE	*
Financial Services: Diversified	FSD	*
Foods & Nonalcoholic Beverages	FNB	8/8/96
Healthcare: Facilities	HF	*
Healthcare: Managed Care	HMC	*
Healthcare: Pharmaceuticals	HP	8/29/96
Healthcare: Products & Supplies	HPS	*
Homebuilding	HB	*

New Format: Volume 2 (M–T)

Topic	Abbreviation	Published
Metals: Industrial	MI	*
Metals: Precious	MP	*
Movies & Home Entertainment	MHE	*
Natural Gas Distribution	NGD	*
Oil & Gas: Equipment & Services	OGES	*
Oil & Gas: Production & Marketing	OGPM	*
Paper & Forest Products	PFP	*
Pollution Control	PC	*
Publishing	PUB	*
Restaurants	RES	*
Retailing: General	RG	*
Retailing: Specialty	RS	*
Savings & Loans	SL	*
Semiconductor Equipment	SCE	*
Semiconductors	SC	*
Supermarkets & Drugstores	SD	*
Telecommunications: Wireless	TWLS	*
Telecommunications: Wireline	TWLN	9/12/96
Transportation: Commercial	TC	9/5/96

* = not yet published

Old-format abbreviations and publication dates are listed on the following page.

Commercial Space Products

HEADY GROWTH FOR COMMERCIAL SPACE APPLICATIONS

Although military and civil space agencies are established customers of the space-related aerospace industry, they are not the only ones. The market for commercial space products is large, and it has been growing at double-digit annual rates for several years. Some analysts estimate that by 2000, commercial spending in this sector will eclipse both military and space agency purchases.

The mention of "commercial aerospace products" usually brings to mind large aircraft and other general aviation vehicles. However, the actual menu of products is far broader. Satellites, satellite launchers, and earthbound items like control tower communications equipment are increasingly important commercial aerospace products.

Although estimates vary widely, Teal Group, a Fairfax, Va.-based consulting firm, estimates the annual worldwide commercial space services market was worth more than $7 billion as of mid-1995. It divides the market as follows: satellite equipment, $2.3 billion; launch vehicles, $1.7 billion; and ground equipment, $3.3 billion. Another assessment of the size of this industry comes from Don Fuqua, president of the Aerospace Industries Association (AIA): he estimates the U.S. commercial space sector at about $6.5 billion in 1995. Regardless of the organization making the estimate, all analysts agree that this sector has been growing by at least 20% annually for several years.

Space Electronics & Telecommunications

Satellite Communications: the Biggest Commercial Use. Ground equipment, such as receivers and transmitters, comprise the space sector's largest component. However, because a space system is made up of both ground equipment and satellites, we will discuss the two groups together.

Satellites and their earthbound support equipment work together to observe the earth, conduct scientific research, and perform industrial services. But by far the most mature space-related commercial service is satellite communications. Owners and operators of communications satellites continually need space access; they account for virtually all of the current private sector market for commercial launch services.

According to Teal Group, seven of the 10 largest satellite manufacturers are based in the United States. Hughes Electronics (a subsidiary of General Motors), Lockheed Martin Corp., Space Systems/Loral (a subsidiary of Loral Corp.), TRW Inc., and others still set the pace technologically and commercially in satellite production. Foreign competitors, however, have an edge in launching satellites, as discussed later. Currently U.S. aerospace contractors are moving beyond satellite production and are becoming service providers. For example, Hughes not only makes direct broadcast satellites but also operates the DirecTV unit, which sells direct broadcast services to consumers. Major projects underway in these satellite-related areas include:

Global Satellite-Based Mobile Telephone Services. In January 1995, the Federal Communications Commission (FCC) issued three companies licenses to operate satellite-based communications services in the United States. Big LEO (low earth orbit) satellite systems, as they are known in the industry, will let customers receive telephone services via handheld receivers anywhere in the world. Competing in this arena will be Motorola Inc.'s Iridium, Loral Corp.'s Globalstar, and TRW Inc.'s Odyssey systems.

Global Wireless Systems in the Works

System	Leading Organization(s) Involved	Date Scheduled to Begin	Number of Satellites	Expected Service Cost ($/minute)	Estimated Telephone Cost	Estimated System Cost (bil.$)	Comments
Iridium	Motorola, Inc.	1998	66	$3.00	$2,500	$3.4	High-quality service; few ground stations needed
Globalstar	Loral Corp., Qualcomm Inc.	1998	48	$0.70	$750	$2.0	Least expensive system; will require costly earth stations; direct ownership interest available through Globalstar Telecommunications Ltd.
Odyssey	TRW Inc.	2000	12	$1.00	$500-$700	$2.3	Will operate in connection with local service providers
ICO Global Communications	Owned by the International Mobile Satellite Organization	2000	10	$2.00	$1,500	$2.6	Has not yet been granted an FCC license

Source: Company reports.

I N D E X   T O   C O R P O R A T I O N   R E C O R D S

This Volume Should Contain The Following Sections, in the order Listed:
Yellow Index dated January 1997
Blue Pages dated January 9, 1997
White Pages 9037–9998 & 1523–2878

This section is an index to all basic descriptions in this volume, and to all subsequent news items through November 22, 1996.
Reference to previous A-B Index Section and to White Pages 2879 to 3322 is no longer necessary.

This index refers to all companies carried in Corporation Records. The page numbers of descriptions and subsequent news, as well as items of interest on companies not fully described, are shown. The blue cross-reference section, which should be filed below these yellow pages, contains the names of subsidiaries, affiliates, etc., of companies on which a description is published, as well as names of predecessor and merged companies, changes in names, etc. Users of Corporation Records not finding a company name in the yellow index should consult the blue cross-reference section.

Standard & Poor's Corporation may from time to time release the names of subscribers/customers to our services to other reputable mailers whose offers we feel may be of interest to them. If you are unwilling to allow us to do this, kindly remove the mailing label from this publication and return it to us with your instructions to make your name unavailable for such use. We will then make every effort to have your name deleted from any list rental or exchange.

STANDARD & POOR'S BOND RATINGS

Standard Corporation Records includes the Standard & Poor's Bond Rating for publicly-held issues described in the publication. Although the rating published was current at the date indicated, subscribers should check the currentness of such rating by referencing the Cumulative News Section and the Daily News Section of the service or by calling the CORPORATE RATINGS DESK at (212) 208-1527.

-NOTE-

This service contains descriptions of various publicly held corporations, including those listed on the New York and American Stock Exchanges and the larger unlisted and regional exchange companies. Full or standard coverage treatment is accorded to corporations included herein for a fee. Other corporations will receive less than such coverage. Full coverage companies listed on the New York Stock Exchange are charged $2,040 per year, while American Stock Exchange, regional exchange and unlisted companies are charged $925. In some circumstances, a one-time premium of $1,525 may be charged for initial company descriptions. An additional fee is charged to companies for either (a) reprinting from annual reports, the full unedited text of the President's annual message to stockholders ($410); or (b) the President's message plus the management's review of operations contained in the annual report, the message or review contained in quarterly reports to stockholders, and the President's remarks at the annual meeting of stockholders ($1,395).

The star (*) appearing after a company's name in this index identifies those companies that are presented in tabular form in Standard Corporation Records. The bullet (•) and the diamond (♦) appearing after a name are for Standard & Poor's internal purposes only.

ALPHABETICAL INDEX

ADVANCED DIGITAL INFORMATION CORP.

Capitalization

(July 31, '96, after spin-off of Co. by Interpoint Corp. and forgiveness of intercompany debt Oct. 16 '96)

LONG TERM DEBT—None.

STOCK—	Auth. Shs.	Outstg.Shs.
Preferred no par	2,000,000	None
Common no par	†40,000,000	7,932,200

*Incl. 475,000 for options, with shs. for future grants.

Corporate Background

Company designs, makes, markets and supports specialized data storage peripherals used to back up and archive electronic data for PC/LAN and Unix client/server network environments.

Company's products consist of stand-alone tape drives and automated tape libraries ranging from 4 gigabytes to over three terabytes of data storage capacity. Co.'s principal products are automated tape libraries which combine proprietary electro-mechanical robotics, electronic hardware and firmware developed by Co. with industry standard, technologically advanced tape drives made by third parties.

SUBSIDIARY—wholly owned—ADIC Europe SARL.

PROPERTY—A manufacturing and research and development facility is leased in Redmond, Wash.

CAPITAL EXPENDITURES, Yrs. End. Oct. 31: Thou. $
1995....................................757   1994.................................451

RESEARCH & DEVELOPMENT EXPENDITURES, Yrs. End. Oct. 31: Thou. $
1995................................1,097   1994.............................1,037

EMPLOYEES—July 23, 1996, 132 (full-time).

INCORPORATED in Wash. in Aug. 1984. Feb. 11, 1994, acquired by Interpoint Corp.

Oct. 16, 1996, Interpoint Corp. distributed all 7,932,200 Com. shs. of Co. held by it to Interpoint shareholders of record Oct. 15, 1996, on the basis of one Com. share of Co. for every Com. share of Interpoint held.

CHAIRMAN, PRES & CHIEF EXEC OFFICER, P. H. van Oppen; SR V-P & CHIEF OPER OFFICER, C. H. Stonecipher, V-Ps, W. C. Britts, B. W. Brugman, N. H. Searle.

DIRECTORS—C. T. Bayley, W. P. Kistler, R. F. McNeill, P. H. van Oppen, J. W. Stanton, W. F. Walker.

OFFICE—10201 Willows Rd., Redmond, WA 98052 (Tel.:206-881-8004)

ANNUAL MEETING—In Feb.

Stock Data

PREFERRED STOCK PURCHASE RIGHTS—Oct. 15, 1996, Com. stockholders received one Pfd. Stock Purchase right, expiring Oct. 16, 2006, for each Com. share. Privilege to entitlement trades with Co.'s Com. At the time the rights became exercisable, separate certificates will be distributed and the Rights could begin to trade separately from Co.'s Com. Rights become exercisable 10 days after an announcement that a person or group (Acquiring Person) had acquired, or obtained the right to acquire, 15% or more of Co.'s Com. shares, or following the commencement of an offer that would result in ownership of 15% or more of Co.'s Com. shares. Upon occurrence of such events, each Right would entitle the holder to buy from Co. one one-hundredth of a share of Ser.A Pfd. of Co. for $50. If Co. is involved in a merger or other business combination or more than 50% of its assets or earning power are sold or transferred, the Rights will be modified so as to entitle the holder to buy a number of the acquiring company's Com. shares having a market value of twice the exercise price of each Right. In the event a person becomes an Acquiring Person, each Right not owned by the Acquiring Person would become exercisable for the number of Co.'s Com. shares having a market value of two times the exercise price of each Right. After the Rights become exercisable, Co. may exchange each Right not owned by an Acquiring Person for consideration of one-half the securities issuable upon the exercise of each Right. Rights are redeemable in whole, but not in part, at $0.01 per Right by Co. prior to the tenth day after a public announcement that 15% or more of Co.'s Com. shares have been acquired.

PRINCIPAL STOCKHOLDERS—Oct., 16, 1996, officers and directors owned or controlled 15.2% of the Com, incl. 5.9% by J.W. Stanton.

TRANSFER AGENT & REGISTRAR—ChaseMellon Shareholder Services, L.L.C., Ridgefield Park, N.J.

LISTED—Nasdaq (Symbol ADIC) Oct. 17, 1996.

DIVIDENDS—Com. no par: none.

Earnings and Finances

AUDITORS—Price Waterhouse LLP, Seattle, Wash.

CONSOL. EARNS., Y-E Oct. 31 (Sept. 30 prior to 1994): Thou. $

	Net Sales	Inc. Taxes	Net Inc.
1995	31,716	cr78	292
1994	20,083	cr99	d42
1993	17,109	308	1,285
1992	12,837	22	964
1991	11,735	cr68	d1,365

dDeficit.

Note: On Feb. 11 '94, Advanced Digital Information Corp. ("ADIC" or "Co.") was acqd. by Interpoint Corp. ("Interpoint") pursuant to an Agreement and Plan of Merger dated Oct. 29 '93, in which Co. was merged into a wholly owned subsidiary of

Interpoint. Consolidated financial statements for all periods subsequent to Sept. 30 '93 reflect the results of operations, financial position, and cash flows of ADIC as a component of Interpoint.

Annual Report—Consol. Inc. Acct.,Yrs. End.: Thou. $

	Oct. 31 '95	Oct. 31 '94	Sept. 30 '93
Net sales	31,716	20,083	17,108
Cost & exps.	30,721	19,202	15,286
Oper. income....................	995	881	1,822
Other income	—	—	1
Fgn. currency transl.	dr19	32	
Total income	976	913	1,823
Depr. & amort..................	484	331	164
Acquisition costs	—	590	—
Interest exp., net	278	134	66
Income tax	176	cr184	445
Defr. inc. tax	cr254	84	cr137
Net income..................	292	d42	1,285
dDeficit.			

Note A: Co. reported pro forma share earns. of $0.04 in 1995 (based on 8,010,000 avge. com. & com. equiv. shs., adjtd. for June '96 Interpoint 2-for-1 stk. split), assuming the spin-off of ADIC from Interpoint had occurred on Nov. 1 '95.

Note B: On Feb. 11 '94, Advanced Digital Information Corp. ("ADIC" or "Co.") was acqd. by Interpoint Corp. ("Interpoint") pursuant to an Agreement and Plan of Merger dated Oct. 29 '93, in which Co. was merged into a wholly owned subsidiary of Interpoint. Consolidated financial statements for all periods subsequent to Sept. 30 '93 reflect the results of operations, financial position, and cash flows of ADIC as a component of Interpoint.

Consol. Bal. Sheet, Oct. 31: Thou. $

Assets—	1995	1994
Cash...	624	184
Accts. rec., net..........................	5,816	4,133
Inventories...............................	5,384	2,770
Income tax...............................	—	161
Defr. inc. tax............................	320	50
Other curr. assets	227	182
Tot. curr. assets....................	12,371	7,480
*Net property	1,177	859
Defr. inc. tax............................	46	59
Other assets	349	312
Total assets	13,943	8,710
Liabilities—		
Accts. pay.................................	3,937	2,493
Accruals	981	832
Income tax...............................	204	—
Tot. curr. liabs.....................	5,122	3,325
Intercompany debt....................	5,434	2,358
†Com. stk. p.$0.01	a	a
Paid-in cap...............................	702	702

Fgn. currency transl.................	133	66
Retained earns.	2,552	2,259
Total liabs............................	13,943	8,710
Net wkg. cap.	7,249	4,155
dDeficit.		
•Depr. & amort. res.	1,234	928
†Com. shs. (Thou.):	1	1
aRepresents $10.		

Interim Report July 31 '96—†9 Mos. Consol. Inc.

Acct.:	Thou. $
Net sales	39,571
Cost & exps.	35,853
Oper. income	3,718
Fgn. currency transl....................	38
Total income	3,756
Depr. & amort.	417
Interest exp., net	407
Income tax.................................	991
Net income	1,941
†Unaudited.	

Note: Co. reported pro forma share earns. of $0.24 (based on 8,158,000 avge. com. & com. equiv. shs., adjtd. for June '96 Interpoint 2-for-1 stk. split), assuming the spin-off of ADIC from Interpoint had occurred on Nov. 1 '95.

bConsol. Bal. Sheet, July 31 '96: Thou. $

Assets—	
Cash...	444
Accts. rec., net..........................	10,867
Inventories...............................	7,499
Defr. inc. tax............................	318
Other curr. assets	207
Tot. curr. assets....................	19,335
•Net property	1,437
Defr. inc. tax............................	45
Other assets	452
Total assets	21,269
Liabilities—	
Accts. pay.................................	5,078
Accruals	1,610
Income tax.................................	835
Tot. curr. liabs.....................	7,523
Intercompany debt....................	8,442
†Com. stk. p.$0.01	a
Paid-in cap...............................	702
Fgn. currency tranl.	109
Retained earns.	4,493
Total liabs............................	21,269
Net wkg. cap.	11,812
dDeficit.	
•Depr. & amort. res.	1,623
†Com. shs. (Thous):	1
aRepresents $10.	
bUnaudited.	

Recommended Supplement:
Value Line Investment Survey

Reference Navigator

Web site: http://www.valueline.com

E-mail: vlsoft@valueline.com

Databases: See Web site

CD-ROM: Available

Library Reference Number:

_____

One could guess that if a college library has only one investment service, it is most likely to be the *Value Line Investment Survey.* The service was founded in the 1930s, and has appeared in its present format since the mid-60s. The service provides in-depth coverage of 1,700 stocks, grouped into approximately 90 industries. For sheer volume of information, few sources can compare with the magnitude of this publication.

Value Line is issued weekly in three parts. Part I, the "Summary and Index," serves as a cumulative index to the entire set. The index leads the reader to the page on which each company report appears, as well as summarizing key data for all 1,700 stocks. This section lists the Value Line ratings, recent price, EPS, dividends, and other measures for each stock. The second section of Part I consists of about 20 screening lists that rank stocks by various characteristics such as "best performers," "lowest P/E," "highest dividend yield," and "widest discount from book value."

Part II, "Selection and Opinion," is a weekly newsletter of approximately 10 pages that contains articles on the economic outlook, the state of the market, current investing trends, and statistical indicators, including data on the Value Line Stock Index. Part II also offers a "stock highlight," which recommends an especially good investment buy, with an article discussing the company's virtues. A table listing all stocks that received a rating change in the previous week rounds out this section. Part III, "Ratings and Reports," carries full-page coverage for every one of the 1,700 companies, plus an industry overview for the 90 industry groups. Each company analyses is updated four times per year on a rotating schedule.

Something to Do:

Many companies now file reports electronically with the SEC under a system called EDGAR (Electronic Data Gathering Analysis and Retrieval). At this writing, approximately 11,000 companies are using it. Check with the SEC for information (see Chapter 28).

---

4 ROBERT MORRIS ASSOCIATES'
ANNUAL STATEMENT STUDIES

Description of Publication

To obtain information on this annual publication (ISBN 1-57070-019-2) call Robert Morris Associates Customer Service Department at: (800) 677-7621; Fax: (888) 762-8500

 Reference Navigator

Web site: http://www.rmahq.org	CD-ROM: available
E-mail: RMA@Smartmail	Library Reference Number:
Database: See Web site	

This book is filled with financial statistics. If you don't like a lot of numbers, find someone who does and get that person to explain them to you because it's important and because it isn't that hard. The numbers are given in percentages of assets and sales. This book is about small business financial statements: balance sheets, income statements, and financial ratios. *It is an excellent business resource.*

Robert Morris Associates (RMA) is the national association of bank loan and credit officers. Founded in 1914, RMA has grown (as of publication date) to nearly 3,000 commercial banks and thrift institutions, which account for almost 80 percent of the consumer and industrial lending done by these types of U.S. financial institutions. RMA members are represented in the association by nearly 15,000 commercial loan and credit officers and related personnel in all 50 states, Puerto Rico, Canada, and offshore cities.

The RMA *Annual Statement Studies* is made possible through the voluntary cooperation of RMA member banks; therefore, it is designed primarily for commercial bankers. However, the material is very useful for those contemplating going into business or facing financial questions in an ongoing business. The mass of financial information on the page can be intimidating, but is actually quite easy to apply. Two perspectives can be taken: (1) microeconomic, which shows how one can compare his or her business with an industry average, and (2) macroeconomic, which shows statistical averages (national) for company activities in different asset ($500 million in total assets or less, depending on the industry studied) and sales sizes.

The *Statement Studies* contain composite financial data on manufacturing, wholesaling, retailing, service, and contracting lines of business. Financial statements on each industry are shown in common size form (those whose numerical amounts are expressed as percentages of an important summary figure) and are accompanied by widely used ratios. In Parts I through III, data for a particular industry appear on both the right- and left-hand pages of the spread (see the sample statement pages provided). The heading "Current Data Sorted By Assets" is on the far left. The center section of the double page presentation contains the "Comparative Historical Data," with the "All Sizes" column for the current year shown under the heading "4/1/96–3/31/97." Comparable data from past editions of the *Annual Statement Studies* also appear in this section. To the far right is the display "Current Data Sorted by Sales."

The information shown at the top of each page includes the identity of the industry group; its Standard Industrial Classification (SIC) number; a breakdown by size categories of the types of financial statements reported; the number of statements in each category; the dates of the statements used; and the size categories. For instance, 225(4/1–9/30/96) means that 225 statements with fiscal dates between April 1 and September 30, 1996 make up part of the sample. When there are fewer than 10 financial statements in a particular size category, the composite data are not shown because such a small sample is not considered representative and could be misleading. However, all the data for that industry are shown in the "All Sizes" column. The total number of statements for each size category is shown in bold print at the top of each page.

At the bottom of each page, the sum of the net sales (or revenues) and total assets for all the financial statements in each size category are shown. These data are provided to allow recasting the common size statements into dollar amounts. To do this, divide the number at the bottom of the page (either net sales or total assets, depending on which one you are analyzing) by the number of statements in that size category. Then multiply the result by the percentages in the common size statement.

Below the common size balance sheet and income statement presented on each data page is a list of ratios that have been computed from the financial statement data. Each ratio has three values: the upper quartile, median, and lower quartile. For any given ratio, these figures are calculated by first computing the value of the ratio for each financial statement in the sample. Theses values are then arrayed in an order from the strongest to the weakest. The values are then divided into four groups of equal size. The three points that divide the array are called quartiles—upper, median, and lower quartile.

From the service of skating rinks to the manufacture of ophthalmic goods, the *Annual Statement Studies* can give the budding analyst a look at how the company he or she is studying compares to the industrial average in all the important items: trade receivables, inventory, fixed assets, trade payables, long-term debt, net worth, net sales, gross profit, profit before taxes, current ratios, debt/worth ratios, and the like. These averages can be used to compare a specific company or simply used to determine the dynamics of a particular industry. The averages also show very specific trends over a period of five years ("Comparative Historical Data"). When you study the common size sheets in particular industries, the numbers begin to reveal certain characteristics of the industry. For example, do inventories in retail trade among department stores have any parallels to those of the hardware industry? Can you read into these figures the economic, political, technological, or international implications for the industry in question?

The information offered by the *Annual Statement Studies* is really the beginning of financial analysis in that if the company being studied is different from the national average, the immediate question is why? Knowing what questions to ask is always at the heart of each good company strategy.

A very important part of this publication can be found at the back of the book: "Sources of Composite Financial Data—A Bibliography." Although the *Annual Statement Studies* edition covers move than 400 industries, some industries are not covered. Information on industries not covered or supplemental data on some of the ones that are can be found in this section. The information contained in this section is divided into two parts:

1. A subject index that enables you to determine which entries cover a particular line of business. For example, if you need data on drugstores, the index indicates entry numbers (not page numbers) of the listed sources that provide it.
2. The actual list of sources of information, citing title, publisher, price, and a brief explanation of the data available.

The *Annual Statement Studies* data are taken directly from the financial statements of close to 138,000 customers of RMA member institutions. Data on 483 specific industries is organized by SIC (4-digit level) and sorted by both sales and assets. Robert Morris Associates cautions that the *Studies* be regarded only as a general guideline and not as an absolute industry norm. This is due to limited samples within categories, the categorization of companies by their primary SIC number only, and different methods of operations by companies within the same industry. For these reasons, RMA recommends that the figures be used only as general guidelines in addition to other methods of financial analysis.

Retailers—Gasoline Service Stations. SIC# 5541

	Current Data Sorted By Assets							Comparative Historical Data	
							# Postretirement Benefits	5	21
							Type of Statement		
1	8	27	40	7	6		Unqualified	55	69
12	24	57	23	1			Reviewed	84	79
92	84	46	7	1			Compiled	175	161
57	16	3		1	1		Tax Returns	28	30
64	59	50	29	3	5		Other	125	121
	225 (4/1-9/30/96)			499 (10/1/96-3/31/97)		100-250		4/1/92- 3/31/93 All	4/1/93- 3/31/94 All
0-500M	500M-2MM	2-10MM	10-50MM	50-100MM	MM				
226	191	183	99	13	12		Number of Statements	467	460
%	%	%	%	%	%		Assets	%	%
13.5	10.2	9.6	7.6	5.3	10.4		Cash & Equivalents	10.5	11.3
10.6	10.7	10.2	8.9	9.1	5.8		Trade Receivables - (net)	11.1	10.7
23.2	14.8	13.0	10.5	12.1	11.6		Inventory	17.9	17.0
1.7	1.0	2.5	1.5	4.4	.7		All Other Current	1.8	1.9
49.0	36.7	35.2	28.5	30.9	28.4		Total Current	41.3	41.0
37.5	51.5	53.4	61.3	58.8	64.3		Fixed Assets (net)	48.1	48.5
5.8	4.3	3.1	2.7	3.8	2.8		Intangibles (net)	2.9	2.4
7.6	7.5	8.3	7.5	6.5	4.5		All Other Non-Current	7.6	8.1
100.0	100.0	100.0	100.0	100.0	100.0		Total	100.0	100.0
							Liabilities		
5.1	4.6	4.2	4.1	6.4	4.6		Notes Payable-Short Term	5.5	5.7
4.7	3.8	3.7	4.3	3.0	2.5		Cur. Mat.-L/T/D	4.7	4.5
16.3	14.9	18.3	15.9	12.5	10.6		Trade Payables	16.6	15.0
.3	.2	.3	.2	.3	.6		Income Taxes Payable	.3	1.5
10.0	8.1	9.1	7.5	11.9	5.0		All Other Current	9.0	9.5
36.4	31.6	35.6	32.1	34.0	23.3		Total Current	36.2	36.2
26.6	36.4	27.2	29.1	28.3	29.4		Long Term Debt	27.9	26.8
.0	.2	.5	1.2	1.9	3.0		Deferred Taxes	.5	.5
5.8	3.7	4.3	2.9	4.2	2.3		All Other Non-Current	3.4	2.9
31.2	28.1	32.4	34.7	31.6	42.0		Net Worth	32.0	33.7
100.0	100.0	100.0	100.0	100.0	100.0		Total Liabilities & Net Worth	100.0	100.0
							Income Data		
100.0	100.0	100.0	100.0	100.0	100.0		Net Sales	100.0	100.0
20.5	19.0	17.6	17.1	17.0	22.2		Gross Profit	19.7	19.9
18.5	17.6	16.2	15.1	15.1	18.2		Operating Expenses	18.2	17.9
2.0	1.5	1.4	2.0	2.0	4.0		Operating Profit	1.5	2.0
.3	.5	.1	.5	.4	1.3		All Other Expenses (net)	.4	.2
1.7	1.0	1.4	1.6	1.6	2.6		Profit Before Taxes	1.2	1.8
							Ratios		
2.7	1.9	1.3	1.1	1.2	1.4			1.8	1.7
1.6	1.2	1.0	.8	.9	1.2	Current		1.1	1.1
.9	.8	.7	.6	.7	.5			.8	.8
1.4	1.3	.8	.7	.5	.9			.9	1.0
.6	(188) .6	.6	(98) .5	.5	.4	.6	Quick	(466) .6	.6
.3	.3	.3	.3	.3	.1			.3	.3
0 887.8	1 246.2	2 157.7	3 117.7	3 126.2	1 387.0			1 269.0	2 213.0
2 162.1	4 101.0	6 61.8	6 61.9	7 51.1	7 56.0	Sales/Receivables		4 88.6	5 76.1
7 55.6	9 39.0	11 34.7	12 31.6	21 17.3	19 19.2			10 35.5	11 32.9

Retailers—Gasoline Service Stations. SIC# 5541 (concluded)

Current Data Sorted By Assets							Comparative Historical Data	
6 66.0	7 51.2	7 49.7	9 42.6	9 39.8	9 41.4	Cost of Sales/Inventory	7 49.3	7 49.3
9 38.5	10 35.0	11 33.2	11 33.6	12 29.3	12 30.5		11 32.9	11 33.8
15 25.0	15 24.4	14 25.8	15 24.8	18 20.2	35 10.5		17 21.8	17 20.9
2 171.3	4 88.0	11 32.6	13 27.2	12 29.4	14 26.4	Cost of Sales/Payables	6 60.7	5 78.7
6 65.2	10 36.7	16 23.0	17 20.9	17 21.0	20 18.2		12 30.7	12 31.3
12 30.5	16 22.9	22 16.9	24 15.4	21 17.7	24 14.9		18 20.8	18 20.1
25.6	26.0	56.5	222.1	76.0	30.5	Sales/Working Capital	33.7	32.3
73.9	119.0	571.0	−85.6	−80.3	47.1		219.9	190.8
−176.8	−75.6	−48.0	−32.0	−29.3	−32.4		−64.0	−65.0
5.6	3.6	4.6	5.4	7.8	4.1	EBIT/Interest	5.1	7.2
(172) 2.4	(172) 1.9	(168) 2.1	(95) 2.5	2.6	(10) 2.9		(420) 2.4	(414) 3.3
.8	.9	1.2	1.5	2.2	2.2		1.1	1.9
4.0	4.4	5.6	7.3			Net Profit + Depr., Dep., Amort./Cur. Mat. L/T/D	2.9	4.2
(16) 2.3	(40) 2.0	(75) 2.2	(46) 2.4				(171) 1.7	(148) 1.9
.7	1.0	1.5	1.4				.9	1.1
.5	.8	1.1	1.3	1.4	1.1	Fixed/Worth	.8	.8
1.6	2.1	2.0	2.1	1.9	1.8		1.7	1.5
UND	9.3	3.8	3.7	5.2	3.1		3.7	3.3
.9	1.3	1.3	1.2	1.7	1.0	Debt/Worth	1.0	1.0
2.4	3.3	2.7	2.3	2.3	1.6		2.4	2.2
NM	16.8	5.8	4.2	7.3	2.6		6.1	5.3
73.4	32.5	26.0	27.6	36.4	25.1	% Profit Before Taxes/Tangible Net Worth	34.0	49.7
(170) 25.7	(155) 14.4	(172) 12.9	(96) 17.7	(12) 22.3	(11) 19.5		(403) 15.2	(422) 23.5
.0	1.1	4.1	4.4	17.0	11.1		2.8	10.9
21.5	8.8	6.5	8.5	8.4	8.4	% Profit Before Taxes/Total Assets	11.1	14.5
6.5	3.8	3.5	4.4	5.6	6.7		4.8	7.0
−1.0	−.3	1.0	1.8	3.4	4.5		.4	2.8
96.6	24.6	15.7	8.9	7.8	4.7	Sales/Net Fixed Assets	28.9	25.7
30.7	10.4	8.4	6.2	6.0	4.0		11.4	10.1
9.8	5.0	5.1	4.3	4.7	2.6		6.5	6.0
14.7	7.9	6.7	5.2	4.4	3.4	Sales/Total Assets	8.4	8.0
9.0	4.9	4.6	3.7	3.6	3.0		5.4	5.2
4.6	3.0	3.0	3.0	3.0	1.8		3.9	3.6
.4	.8	1.0	1.4	.5		% Depr., Dep., Amort./Sales	.8	.8
(184) 1.0	(173) 1.3	(171) 1.5	(95) 1.8	1.6			(443) 1.3	(417) 1.3
1.8	2.1	2.1	2.3	2.3			1.8	2.0
1.3	1.2	.4	.5			% Officers', Directors', Owners' Comp/Sales	.9	.9
(121) 2.2	(83) 1.8	(74) .9	(19) .8				(204) 1.8	(204) 1.6
4.1	2.7	2.0	1.2				3.4	3.1
517396M	1242876M	4103657M	8831751M	3431236M	8599561M	Net Sales ($)	11722701M	14033029M
56376M	205515M	827187M	2203426M	956272M	1818378M	Total Assets ($)	2890057M	3082042M

©RMA 1997, M = $ thousand, MM = $ million, See Pages 1 through 20 for Explanation of Ratios and Data

Source: Reprinted with permission, copyright Robert Morris Associates, 1997.

Retailers—Gasoline Service Stations. SIC# 5541

Comparative Historical Data				*Current Data Sorted By Sales*					
36	41		**# Postretirement Benefits**						
			Type of Statement						
88	100	89	Unqualified	2	6	3	5	8	65
85	102	117	Reviewed	4	6	10	21	31	45
200	194	230	Compiled	19	83	37	32	40	19
44	63	78	Tax Returns	7	43	14	7	5	2
172	175	210	Other	13	53	24	26	40	54
4/1/94-	**4/1/95-**	**4/1/96-**			**225 (4/1-9/30/96)**		**499 (10/1/96-3/31/97)**		**25MM**
3/31/95	**3/31/96**	**3/31/97**		**0-1MM**	**1-3MM**	**3-5MM**	**5-10MM**	**10-25MM**	**& Over**
All	**All**	**All**							
589	634	724	**Number of Statements**	45	191	88	91	124	185
%	%	%	*Assets*	%	%	%	%	%	%
11.4	11.7	10.6	Cash & Equivalents	9.7	10.4	14.0	11.8	10.5	9.0
10.1	9.7	10.2	Trade Receivables - (net)	10.4	9.1	10.3	8.9	13.1	10.0
16.5	15.9	16.3	Inventory	22.3	17.5	18.1	16.9	16.8	12.0
2.2	2.2	1.7	All Other Current	.4	1.6	1.4	2.2	1.8	2.1
40.2	39.4	38.8	Total Current	42.7	38.6	43.8	39.7	42.1	33.0
49.4	49.9	49.3	Fixed Assets (net)	48.3	48.0	41.9	49.9	46.3	56.1
3.2	3.2	4.2	Intangibles (net)	6.2	5.5	6.1	2.4	3.4	3.0
7.3	7.5	7.7	All Other Non-Current	2.8	7.9	8.2	7.9	8.3	7.8
100.0	100.0	100.0	Total	100.0	100.0	100.0	100.0	100.0	100.0
			Liabilities						
5.0	5.5	4.6	Notes Payable-Short Term	7.4	4.1	5.7	4.5	4.2	4.4
4.2	4.3	4.1	Cur. Mat.-L/T/D	3.3	5.2	4.1	3.3	3.6	3.9
16.0	15.4	16.2	Trade Payables	9.3	12.8	15.9	16.4	20.6	18.5
.4	.3	.2	Income Taxes Payable	.1	.2	.3	.2	.3	.3
9.3	9.5	8.9	All Other Current	7.9	7.4	10.2	7.8	11.0	9.2
34.9	34.9	34.1	Total Current	27.9	29.7	36.3	32.2	39.7	36.2
28.7	28.5	29.8	Long Term Debt	37.6	36.6	26.6	29.8	24.2	26.0
.4	.5	.5	Deferred Taxes	.0	.1	.1	.5	.2	1.3
4.0	3.8	4.4	All Other Non-Current	3.0	5.1	3.8	7.0	4.0	3.2
32.1	32.3	31.3	Net Worth	31.5	28.5	33.3	30.5	31.8	33.4
100.0	100.0	100.0	Total Liabilities & Net Worth	100.0	100.0	100.0	100.0	100.0	100.0
			Income Data						
100.0	100.0	100.0	Net Sales	100.0	100.0	100.0	100.0	100.0	100.0
20.3	19.8	18.9	Gross Profit	30.8	21.0	17.7	16.8	16.9	16.7
18.1	17.8	17.1	Operating Expenses	25.3	18.9	15.7	16.0	16.4	15.1
2.2	2.0	1.8	Operating Profit	5.4	2.1	2.0	.8	.6	1.6
.2	.4	.3	All Other Expenses (net)	1.2	.7	.5	.0	−.3	.3
2.0	1.6	1.4	Profit Before Taxes	4.2	1.5	1.5	.8	.8	1.3
			Ratios						
1.7	1.8	1.8		4.5	2.6	2.3	1.9	1.5	1.1
1.1	1.1	1.1	Current	1.6	1.5	1.4	1.1	1.1	.9
.8	.7	.8		.9	.8	.8	.8	.8	.7
1.0	1.0	1.0		1.6	1.4	1.5	1.1	.9	.7
(587) .6	(631) .6	(720) .6	Quick	.6	(190) .6	.7	(90) .6	(123) .6	(184) .5
.3	.3	.3		.3	.3	.4	.3	.3	.3

Retailers—Gasoline Service Stations. SIC# 5541 (conclude)

Comparative Historical Data — *Current Data Sorted By Sales*

1 255.5	1 260.9	1 283.9	Sales/Receivables	1 541.5	1 622.5	1 612.2	1 291.2	2 169.9	3 131.1
4 85.1	4 92.0	4 88.0		7 54.7	2 151.4	3 127.6	3 109.4	6 62.5	6 61.9
10 38.0	9 38.9	10 37.8		17 22.1	7 55.7	7 51.7	7 49.8	12 30.2	11 32.1
8 48.4	7 48.8	7 51.7	Cost of Sales/Inventory	13 27.1	7 53.3	5 73.2	7 54.8	7 50.3	7 49.7
11 32.3	11 32.8	11 34.4		21 17.0	11 34.3	9 42.5	9 39.2	11 34.2	10 35.2
17 21.4	16 23.4	15 24.7		37 9.9	15 24.5	13 27.5	14 25.7	13 27.8	14 25.6
6 63.5	6 62.5	5 72.3	Cost of Sales/Payables	3 138.9	2 170.2	2 153.9	5 72.8	9 38.8	13 28.8
13 28.2	13 29.0	12 30.2		12 30.0	6 61.8	8 45.2	12 31.4	14 25.7	17 21.5
20 18.6	19 19.1	19 19.6		25 14.6	12 30.3	15 25.1	18 20.4	19 19.3	22 16.8
36.6	29.8	33.9	Sales/Working Capital	14.8	22.4	26.2	33.3	37.0	169.4
153.3	202.4	270.7		32.6	79.8	75.4	140.4	148.6	−87.5
−70.2	−51.0	−56.6		−82.8	−88.0	−139.6	−77.8	−86.2	−36.8
7.9	5.4	4.7	EBIT/Interest	5.1	3.9	5.9	5.3	4.6	4.8
(532) 3.3	(560) 2.5	(630) 2.2		(34) 1.8	(159) 1.8	(74) 2.3	(80) 1.8	(109) 2.2	(174) 2.6
1.7	1.4	1.1		.5	.9	1.0	.7	1.0	1.6
4.1	4.2	5.6	Net Profit + Depr., Dep., Amort./Cur. Mat. L/T/D		2.6	12.8	2.3	5.6	6.3
(195) 2.3	(178) 2.2	(189) 2.1			(18) 1.9	(10) 4.2	(28) 1.6	(43) 2.0	(89) 2.5
1.3	1.5	1.4			.7	2.4	1.1	1.2	1.6
.8	.9	.9	Fixed/Worth	.5	.7	.7	.7	.9	1.2
1.9	1.9	2.0		2.3	2.0	1.9	2.0	1.7	2.0
4.0	5.2	5.3		52.5	67.8	UND	6.3	3.7	3.5
1.1	1.1	1.1	Debt/Worth	.8	1.0	.9	1.2	1.2	1.4
2.4	2.4	2.6		3.3	2.8	2.2	3.1	2.2	2.6
5.7	7.8	8.4		64.7	−562.0	UND	6.9	6.6	4.2
47.1	38.3	35.0	% Profit Before Taxes/Tangible Net Worth	87.5	42.3	53.2	40.3	25.0	29.0
(523) 24.2	(551) 19.2	(616) 16.2		(35) 26.4	(143) 16.3	(67) 22.2	(82) 14.6	(111) 12.9	(178) 17.2
10.3	7.4	2.9		.0	.0	6.6	−1.7	2.9	7.3
15.2	12.2	10.5	% Profit Before Taxes/Total Assets	19.4	14.8	20.8	9.9	7.7	8.3
7.8	5.5	4.4		5.2	4.9	6.7	4.1	3.7	4.4
2.7	1.9	.4		−2.7	−1.0	.7	−1.0	.3	2.2
22.0	21.9	29.7	Sales/Net Fixed Assets	41.7	42.2	50.5	31.4	29.7	13.0
9.8	9.6	10.1		7.1	11.0	24.3	11.4	12.7	7.7
5.5	5.2	5.1		2.7	5.1	7.2	5.3	7.0	4.7
7.7	7.4	8.6	Sales/Total Assets	4.8	10.0	13.6	9.0	9.5	6.3
5.0	4.9	5.1		3.5	5.0	7.7	4.9	5.8	4.5
3.4	3.2	3.3		2.1	3.1	3.8	3.1	3.8	3.3
.9	.8	.8	% Depr., Dep., Amort./Sales	1.0	.6	.5	.6	.8	1.1
(542) 1.4	(583) 1.5	(642) 1.4		(34) 1.8	(160) 1.6	(76) 1.0	(86) 1.4	(114) 1.3	(172) 1.5
2.0	2.2	2.1		3.4	2.6	1.7	2.2	1.8	2.1
.9	1.0	.8	$ Officers', Directors', Owners' Comp/Sales	1.7	1.3	.8	1.1	.6	.3
(244) 1.8	(247) 1.8	(298) 1.6		(15) 6.0	(99) 2.5	(44) 1.5	(40) 1.4	(54) 1.4	(46) .6
3.4	3.4	3.0		8.5	3.8	2.0	2.3	2.1	1.0
21657271M	24996429M	26726477M	Net Sales ($)	30573M	365749M	335685M	671790M	2022777M	23299903M
5325035M	5669565M	6067154M	Total Assets ($)	11705M	103964M	67786M	152247M	398203M	5333249M

© RMA 1997, M = $ thousand, MM = $ million, See Pages 1 through 20 for Explanation of Ratios and Data

Recommended Supplement:
Industry Norms and Key Business Ratios

For information on this annual publication, call Dun & Bradstreet Information Services at: (908) 665-5000.

Reference Navigator

Web site: http://www.dnb.com

E-mail: dnbmdd@mail.dnb.com

Database: See Web site

CD-ROM: available

Library Reference Number:

_____

This publication is very similar to the RMA publication except it costs a lot more and has 800 industry groups, approximately twice that of the *Annual Statement Studies*. It is the product of D&B's unique database of credit reports and draws on the financial statements of more than a million companies. It is used to evaluate the financial performance of companies against averages in their own industries, such as profit to sales, and for comparing one industry to another on many items, such as return on investment. D&B calculates 14 ratios, while RMA provides 16. An important difference is that, although median and quartile figures are presented, data are not grouped by size of company, and no historical information is provided. In addition to common size analysis, D&B calculates a "typical balance sheet and summary income statement" for each industry by multiplying the common size percentages by the median total assets and sales for that industry group. The common size presentation of income statement data is much briefer than for balance sheet items.

In addition to the desktop edition described above, D&B also sells more detailed ratio data to commercial customers. Various formats offer breakdowns by asset size, geographic region, and time period. Each can be purchased in printed format or on floppy disk. Industry norms from D&B also appear in several other products. Selected company and industry ratios are presented in several of D&B's more specialized credit reports. The on-line reports typically cite eight industry norms and four key ratios for every company.

5 FASB ACCOUNTING STANDARDS

Description of Publication

For information on this annual publication, call the American Institute of CPAs at (800) 862-4272 or fax: (800) 362-5066.

 Reference Navigator

Web site: http://www.aicpa.org
E-mail: personal only
Database: See Web site

CD-ROM: available
Library Reference Number:

According to most accounting experts (e.g., Robert May, et al. *Accounting*), financial statements that a U.S. business publishes and distributes to outsiders must conform to professional standards called Generally Accepted Accounting Principles (GAAP). Before the mid-1930s, GAAP consisted of a relatively few foundation elements that had evolved over several centuries. Considerable judgment was required to apply GAAP to individual businesses and circumstances. In fact, managers of U.S. firms made most judgments regarding what constituted GAAP and how financial statements were to conform. After the stock market crash of 1929 and the ensuing Great Depression, however, many abuses of the system were discovered. Although the crash and depression were not caused by accounting abuses, such abuses apparently were considered contributing factors. In the mid-1930s, the U.S. government passed the Securities Act of 1933 and the Securities and Exchange Act of 1934. Both acts gave the newly formed Securities and Exchange Commission (SEC) the authority to set accounting standards for financial statements filed with the SEC, affecting virtually all publicly owned U.S. corporations. The SEC turned to the accounting profession, represented by the American Institute of Certified Public Accountants (AICPA). The AICPA's Committee on Accounting Procedure (CAP) and later its Accounting Principles Board (APB) set standards for financial statements until 1973. In 1973, the Financial Accounting Standards Board (FASB), a new body independent of the AICPA, was formed to bring representatives of businesses and users of financial statements, as well as CPAs, directly into the standard-setting process.

According to the FASB director of research and technical activities, it is the job of the FASB to publish its *FASB Accounting Standards—Original Pronouncements* (in two volumes) with the intent of communicating consensus and pronouncements on issues relating to accounting. This has been done from FASB's inception in 1973 to the present. The first volume depicts the FASB statements. A status page at the beginning of each pronouncement identifies *(a)* the source of changes to the pronouncement, *(b)* other pronouncements affected by that pronouncement, and *(c)* the effective date. The status page also identifies, where applicable, other interpretive pronouncements and releases that further clarify that pronouncement. In addition, the status pages of applicable pronouncements reflect either the impact of a given pronouncement on an Emerging Issues Task Force (EITF) issue or the relationship of an EITF issue to a given pronouncement.

The *Comprehensive GAAP Guide* (ISBN 0-15-601815-2), published by Harcourt Brace Jovanovich in Orlando, Florida, contains all the promulgated and many of the nonpromulgated accounting principles in use today. Each promulgated pronouncement is thoroughly reviewed in a comprehensive format that is easy to assimilate and understand. Many chapters contain in-depth illustrations on the application of the specific accounting principle. Important nonpromulgated accounting principles have been integrated throughout the text in an effort to provide a more complete picture of the material.

The second volume contains the following materials issued by the American Institute of Certified Public Accountants or its committees through June 1973 and by the FASB to the present.

- Accounting Research Bulletins.
- Accounting Principles Board Opinions.
- Interpretations of Accounting Research Bulletins and Accounting Principles Board Opinions.
- FASB Interpretations and FASB Technical Bulletins.
- FASB Statements of Financial Accounting Concepts.

The books use a shading technique to alert the reader when paragraphs containing accounting standards have been amended or superseded. All terms and sentences that have been amended or superseded are shaded. Paragraphs and subparagraphs that have been amended simply by the addition of terms, sentences, or new footnotes are marked with a vertical solid bar in the left margin. A status page at the beginning of each pronouncement identifies *(a)* the source of changes to the pronouncement, *(b)* other pronouncements affected by that pronouncement, and *(c)* the principal effective date (still want to be a CPA?). The CAP issued 51 Accounting Research Bulletins, the APB issued 31 Opinions, and the FASB has issued over 100 Statements of Financial Accounting Standards by the early 1990s. As a consequence, GAAP now includes the original foundation elements, those that have evolved over centuries, plus an ever-expanding set of authoritative pronouncements on the ways to apply them to specific situations.

Perhaps the most important feature of this guide is its readability. Considerable care has been exercised to avoid incomprehensible language. Sentence structure has been simplified as much as possible to foster the maximum comprehension in a minimum period. Finally, an innovative "Disclosure Index" contains both required and recommended disclosures currently in use. This index has been designed to assist the preparer or reviewer of financial statements in determining whether necessary disclosures have been made.

Something to Think About

Can you cite some of the functions of the FASB Emerging Issues Task Force?

The *Comprehensive GAAP Guide* will be used as the representative materials in the sample table of contents and sample pages sections.

SPECIALIZED INDUSTRY ACCOUNTING PRINCIPLES

Pension Plans—Employers

OVERVIEW

Promulgated GAAP for employers' accounting for pension plans center on the determination of annual pension expense (identified as net periodic pension cost) and the presentation of an appropriate amount of pension liability in the statement of financial position. Net periodic pension cost has often been viewed as a single homogeneous amount, but it is actually made up of several components that reflect different aspects of the employer's financial arrangements, as well as the cost of benefits earned by employees.

In applying principles of accrual accounting for pension plans, the FASB has emphasized three fundamental features:

1. *Delayed recognition*—This feature means that changes in the pension obligation and changes in the value of pension assets are not recognized as they occur, but are recognized systematically and gradually over subsequent periods.
2. *Net cost*—This feature means that the recognized consequences of events and transactions affecting a pension plan are reported as a single net amount in the employer's financial statements. This approach results in the aggregation of items that would be separately presented for any other part of the employer's operations: the compensation cost of benefits, interest cost resulting from deferred payment of those benefits, and the results of investing pension assets.
3. *Offsetting*—This feature means that pension assets and liabilities are shown net in the employer's statement of financial position, even though the liability has not been settled. The assets may still be controlled and substantial risks and rewards associated with both are clearly borne by the employer.

Promulgated GAAP for accounting for pensions by employers are located in the following pronouncement:

FASB-87, Employer's Accounting for Pensions

Recommended Supplement: *The CPA Journal*

For information on this monthly publication (ISSN 0732-8435) call the New York State Society of Certified Public Accounts at (212) 719-8336.

Reference Navigator

Web site: http://www.cpajournal.com

E-mail: cpaj@luca.com

Database: See Web site

CD-ROM: not available

Library Reference Number:

_____

The *CPA Journal,* as one might suspect, has a certain tax information bias to the contents, ads, and articles. This magazine is not heavy into format presentation. It's relatively short—80 pages—and somewhat, dare I say it, colorless. Look for about six articles of six to eight pages each that are analytical and relatively easy to read if one is somewhat familiar with accounting-speak. Departmental segments cover such items as:

News and views	The CPA and the computer
Accounting	The CPA consultant
Auditing	State and local taxation
Federal taxation	The CPA in industry

Two other valuable sources are the *Journal of Accountancy* and *Accounting Horizons.* The *Journal of Accountancy* is from the American Institute of Certified Public Accountants ([212] 575-3857). The AICPA also has an on-line database called *National Automated Accounting Research System* (NAARS), which offers financial statements, proxy statements, accounting literature, and the like, the most current of which goes back five years. Information on cost and availability can be obtained by calling (212) 575-6200. *Accounting Horizons* is published quarterly by the American Accounting Association ([941] 921-7747). According to the editors, *Horizons* publishes carefully edited, articulately written, practice-based papers. Practitioners are widely used in the review process because their views concerning what is relevant are invaluable. *Horizons* represents a partnership between the accounting profession and academia. The common thread among all articles published in *Accounting Horizons* is that they are applied. The journal is approximately 200 pages, covering seven or eight articles, a commentary section, reviews, and placement section.

Something to Do:

The AICPA offers *Professional Standards, U.S. Auditing Standards, Accounting Review Services, Bylaws, International Accounting, Ethics, International Auditing, Management Advisory Services, Quality Control,* and *Tax Practice* (two volumes). Give the AICPA a call at (312) 583-8500 and ask for promotional material on any of the sources that seem to be of interest for your business career.

6   THE WALL STREET JOURNAL

Description of Publication

For information on this newspaper, published on the days the New York Stock Exchange is open (Eastern Edition ISSN 0099-9660) call Dow Jones Directory Assistance at (800) 832-1234. The table of contents and sample pages of *The Wall Street Journal* are not included.

 Reference Navigator

Web site: http://wsj.com

E-mail: Info@interactive.wsj.com

Database: Dow Jones Interactive

CD-ROM: UMI

Library Reference Number:

_____

The Wall Street Journal (WSJ) may be the most renowned business newspaper in the world; it certainly is in the United States, the largest economy in the world. Regional editions are also published. *The Wall Street Journal Europe* is edited and published in Brussels and printed in Germany, Great Britain, Switzerland, and Belgium.

The WSJ is one of the most frequently consulted financial dailies in the United States. Any casual reader will enjoy going to the center column on the first page for some trivia or plain old fun, such as, "Quizz: How do U Spel Milenium? Not That Way, Actually" (June 25, 1997). *The WSJ* provides much more than just securities quotations; nevertheless, the detailed financial tables are one main reason for its popularity. The data are provided by a variety of sources. Stock quotes appear daily for the New York Stock Exchange, the American Stock Exchange, and other domestic and foreign exchanges. *The WSJ* has a large "Directory of Services," which will help the reader find information provided by Dow Jones & Co. For example:

The Wall Street Journal Interactive Edition:	http://wsj.com
Personal Journal	1 (800) 291-9382
DJIA Centennial Products	1 (800) 975-DJIA
Dow Jones Customclips	1 (800) 445-9454
Plan Ahead For Your Financial Future	1 (800) 522-3567
Subscription Services:	1 (800) JOURNAL
Dow Jones Directory Assistance:	1 (800) 832-1234

The Wall Street Journal is divided into three sections: the first covers general business, political, and economic news, the second reports on marketing, media, technology, law, and Who's News (called "Marketplace"), and the third section (called "Money & Investing") covers the financial markets. Regular updates of the monthly and quarterly statistical indicators usually appear in summary form in the second column on the first page of the first section. The news stories to which these summaries refer are almost always published on the second page of the first section. On Mondays the *WSJ* publishes on this page a tabular summary (called "Tracking the Economy") of all the statistics that appeared in the previous week as well as a calendar of those you can expect in the present week. In short, *The Wall Street Journal* is replete with statistics that come out at various times: daily, weekly, monthly, and quarterly. *The Wall Street Journal* publication schedule is available on-line and includes statistics such as these:

Day of the month: 1st—leading indicators; 25th—GDP, 5th, 15th, 25th—Auto sales.
Day of the week: Monday—Bond yields (chart); Friday—Federal Reserve Data.
Daily: Foreign exchange rates; Treasury bill rates.

Mutual funds, bonds, stock options, commodity futures, futures contracts for indexes and interest rates, cash prices for selected commodities, and a separate table for daily oil prices are some of the quotations provided by the paper. Also, detailed foreign exchange data are reported daily. Exchange rates are given both in U.S. dollars and the national currency for 50 countries. Every Monday, the Bank of America publishes an extensive list of exchange rates for nearly every country in the world. General market barometers also appear daily (e.g., the Stock Market Data Bank), along with Markets Diary, which describes the activities of the New York and American exchanges and the over-the-counter market. A special edition on learning, *The Wall Street Journal Educational Edition,* is provided for students by Dow Jones, as are student subscription rates.

One great little book that serves the needs of students, academicians, and investors alike is Michael Lehmann's *Real World Economic Applications: The Wall Street Journal Workbook* (ISBN 0-256-13153), published by Richard D. Irwin (now McGraw-Hill Higher Education) at (800) 338-3987. According to the editors, *Real World Economic Applications: The Wall Street Journal Workbook* is not a typical study guide or workbook. It incorporates a proven, successful method for teaching fundamental principles of the macroeconomy by focusing on a number of key statistical reports that appear regularly and predictably in the *WSJ*. Their belief is that a student using this workbook and *The Wall Street Journal* acquires a surprisingly quick and firm comprehension of the ups and downs of the American business economy "in a systematic, pleasing, and non-technical manner." The true-to-life aspect of the data and applications goes a long way in supporting theoretical arguments and a student's motivation to learn them. The table of contents for the *Real World Economic Applications: The Wall Street Journal Workbook* is as follows:

Recommended Supplement: *Barron's*

Reference Navigator

Web site: www.barrons.com

E-mail: editors@news.barrons.com

Database: Dow Jones Interactive

CD-ROM: Not available

Library Reference Number:

_____

Barron's ([800] 628-9320), a sister publication to *The Wall Street Journal,* published by Dow Jones & Company in 1921. Written exclusively for investors, it is one of the best-known business periodicals in the United States. It is known for its detailed financial tables. For example, the "Market Week" Section contains 55 pages of securities quotations. It is also known for investment articles that often take a contrarian stand.

The tables in *Barron's* also list prices for every security, whether traded the previous week or not. At first glance one can see that the tables are easier to read than those in the *WSJ;* larger print and more spacing create listings that are much less cramped. Also, the stock tables give slightly more data than standard listings, showing more complete information on dividends and corporate earnings.

The "Market Laboratory" section provides summary measures of security performance similar to the *WSJ's* "Data Bank," but in more complete fashion. It is considered, according to Michael Lavin, to be the most convenient form of comprehensive market information available on a weekly basis and offers the most diverse compilation of market indicators of any investment publication.

No other information company in the world can match Dow Jones at business news and coverage of financial markets—whether by newspaper or news wire, in magazines or on television, on the Internet or real-time networks. Just as innovation is crucial to the business community, it's also central to Dow Jones. Dow Jones keeps coming up with new ways to deliver its product; it has more than 1,000 reporters and editors around the globe focusing on the most authoritative business news and information, in new forms, times, and places. Every business day, for example, the global *Wall Street Journal* reaches over 7 million executives in more than 125 countries. For more information on what Dow Jones is up to, visit the Dow Jones home page at http://www.dowjones.com or e-mail to jan.abernathy@cor.dowjones.com.

Having said all that, one should also be aware of another useful source called *Investor's Business Daily* (ISSN 1061-2890) published by Investor's Business Daily, Inc. ([800] 831-2525). It was created "For People Who Choose To Succeed," just in case you were ambivalent about whether to purchase the newspaper. The daily newspaper (except Saturdays, Sundays, and holidays) was launched as an alternative to the *WSJ.* According to Lavin, *Investor's Business*

Daily eschews the lengthy, wide-ranging articles that are the hallmark of the *WSJ* and concentrates on investment information. The articles are brief, emphasizing news of public companies, economic conditions, and market behavior. The great strength of *Investor's Business Daily* is the quality of its financial tables; its strength, however, may also be its weakness since most of the pages are devoted to financial tables and should not be considered as a replacement to the *WSJ* as the primary source of business news. *Investor's Business Daily* is an excellent source of additional information, and presents numerous articles analyzing companies, industries, and political issues. For example, "Is the U.S. Importing Poverty?" by Anna J. Bray is replete with useful statistical information about the economic impact of this issue and does not get involved in debating the human interest and political dilemmas.

To assist readers in locating articles of interest, a weekly "Index of Investor's Business Daily Features" appears on Fridays. This column provides an alphabetical index to the companies and industries covered in special articles during the prior three months. The complete text of *Investor's Business Daily* is also available electronically through LEXIS-NEXIS. The table of contents includes:

Amex Tables	Classifieds	Companies/News
Computers & Tech.	Credit Markets	Dividends
Earnings	Futures	Industry Groups
Market Charts	Mutual Funds	Nasdaq Short Interest
Nasdaq Small Caps	Nasdaq Tables	New America
New Highs & Lows	New Issues	NYSE Tables
Options	World Markets	

Something to Do

According to Michael Lehmann (*Real World Economic Applications: The Wall Street Journal Workbook*), economists have never agreed on a single economic indicator to predict the future. Some indicators are better than others, he says, but none is consistently accurate. To deal with this, economists have devised a *composite* of statistical series drawn from a broad spectrum of economic activity, each of which tends to move up or down ahead of the general trend of the business cycle. These series are referred to as leading indicators because of their predictive quality. Eleven have been combined into the *composite index of leading economic indicators*. The series usually appears around the first of the month. Try locating it and reviewing it.

7   OCCUPATIONAL OUTLOOK HANDBOOK

Description of Publication

If you wish information on this annual publication (ISBN 0-16-043044-5) call the Government Printing Office at (301) 457-4100 or the Bureau of Labor Statistics regional office nearest you.

 Reference Navigator

Web site: http://stats.bls.gov/ocohome.htm   CD-ROM: available

E-mail: M@bls.gov   Library Reference Number:

Database: Stat-USA   _____

The *Occupational Outlook Handbook,* the government's premier publication on career guidance, provides essential information about prospective changes in the world of work and the qualifications that will be needed in the future work environment. The *Handbook* describes about 250 occupations in detail, covering about 104 million jobs, or 85 percent of all jobs in the nation.

     The *Handbook* is best used as a reference; it is not meant to be read from cover to cover, which you probably hadn't considered anyway since it is 496 fairly large pages with very small print, no color, and only a few photos. Start by exploring the table of contents, where related occupations are grouped in clusters, or look in the alphabetical index at the end of the book for specific occupations that interest you. The introductory chapter explains how the occupational descriptions, or statements, are organized. The next two chapters, "Sources of Information on Career Preparation and Training" and "Tomorrow's Jobs," tell you where to obtain additional information and discuss the forces that are likely to determine employment opportunities in industries and occupations through the year 2005.

For any occupation that sounds interesting to you, use the *Handbook* to find out what the work entails; what education and training you need; what the advancement possibilities, earnings, and job outlook are; and what related occupations you might consider. Each occupational statement in the *Handbook* follows a standard format, making it easier for you to compare occupations:

- Nature of the work
- Working conditions
- Employment
- Job outlook
- Earnings
- Related occupations
- Training, other qualifications, and advancement

Two particularly useful special features are (1) sources of state and local job outlook information; and (2) reprints. State and local job market and career information is available from state employment security agencies and State Occupational Information Coordinating Committees (SOICCs). State employment security agencies develop occupational employment projections and other job market information. SOICCs provide or help locate labor market and career information. The *Handbook* provides a complete list giving the title, address, and telephone number of state employment security agency directors of research and SOICC directors. For example:

Florida

Chief, Bureau of Labor Market Information, Florida Department of Labor and Employment Security, 2012 Capitol Circle SE, Room 200 Tallahassee, FL 32399-2151. Phone: (904) 488-1048

Manager, Florida Department of Labor and Employment Security, Bureau of Labor Market Information, 2012 Capitol Circle SE, Hartman Building, Suite 200, Tallahassee, FL 32399-0673. Phone: (904) 488-1048

All the occupational statements in the *Occupational Outlook Handbook* are available in reprint form. Reprints are especially useful for job seekers who want to know about a single field and for counselors who need to stretch the contents of a single *Handbook* among many students. An example of the bulletin numbers, prices, and titles of the reprints is shown below:

Bulletin No.	*Price*	*Title*
2450-5	$2.00	*Social Scientists and Legal Occupations*

Something to Do

If your supervisor asked you to find the telephone number of the Director, Division of Research and Statistics, New York State Department of Labor, could you do it?

Registered Nurses

(D.O.T. 075.124-010 and -014, .127-014, -026, -030 and -034, .137-010 and -014, .167-010 and -014, .264-010 and -014, .364-010, .371—010, .374-014, -018, and -022)

NATURE OF THE WORK

Registered nurses (R.N.s) care for the sick and injured and help people stay well. They are typically concerned with the "whole person," providing for the physical, mental, and emotional needs of their patients. They observe, assess, and record symptoms, reactions, and progress; assist physicians during treatments and examinations; administer medications; and assist in convalescence and rehabilitation. R.N.s also develop and manage nursing care plans; instruct patients and their families in proper care; and help individuals and groups take steps to improve or maintain their health. While state laws govern the tasks R.N.s may perform, it is usually the work setting which determines their day-to-day job duties.

Hospital nurses form the largest group of nurses. Most are staff nurses, who provide bedside nursing care and carry out the medical regimen prescribed by physicians. They may also supervise licensed practical nurses and aides. Hospital nurses usually are assigned to one area such as surgery, maternity, pediatrics, emergency room, intensive care, or treatment of cancer patients or may rotate among departments.

Office nurses assist physicians in private practice, clinics, surgicenters, emergency medical centers, and health maintenance organizations (HMOs). They prepare patients for and assist with examinations, administer injections and medications, dress wounds and incisions, assist with minor surgery, and maintain records. Some also perform routine laboratory and office work.

Home health nurses provide periodic services, prescribed by a physician, to patients at home. They care for and instruct patients and their families. Home health nurses care for a broad range of patients, such as those recovering from illnesses and accidents, cancer, and childbirth. They must be able to work independently.

Nursing home nurses manage nursing care for residents with conditions ranging from a fracture to Alzheimer's disease. Although they generally spend most of their time on administrative and supervisory tasks, R.N.s also assess residents' medical condition, develop treatment plans, supervise licensed practical nurses and nursing aides, and perform difficult procedures such as starting intravenous fluids. They also work in specialty-care departments, such as long-term rehabilitation units for strokes and head injuries.

Public health nurses work in government and private agencies and clinics, schools, retirement communities and other community settings. They instruct individuals, families, and other groups in health education, disease prevention, nutrition, and child care. They arrange for immunizations, blood pressure testing, and other health screening. These nurses also work with community leaders, teachers, parents, and physicians in community health education.

Occupational health or *industrial nurses* provide nursing care at worksites to employees, customers, and others with minor injuries and illnesses. They provide emergency care, prepare accident reports, and arrange for further care if necessary. They also offer health counseling, assist with health examinations and inoculations, and work on accident prevention programs.

Head nurses or *nurse supervisors* direct nursing activities. They plan work schedules and assign duties to nurses and aides, provide or arrange for training, and visit patients to observe nurses and to insure that care is proper. They may also insure that records are maintained and that equipment and supplies are ordered.

At the advanced level, *nurse practitioners* provide basic health care. They diagnose and treat common acute illnesses and injuries. Nurse practitioners can prescribe medications in some states. Other advanced practice nurses include *clinical nurse specialists, nurse anesthetists,* and *certified nurse-midwives.*

WORKING CONDITIONS

Most nurses work in well-lighted, comfortable medical facilities. Home health and public health nurses travel to patients' homes and to schools, community centers, and other sites. Nurses may spend considerable time walking and standing. They need emotional stability to cope with human suffering, emergencies, and other stresses. Because patients in hospitals and nursing homes require 24-hour care, nurses in these institutions may work nights, weekends, and holidays. They may also be on-call. Office, occupational health, and public health nurses are more likely to work regular business hours.

Nursing has its hazards, especially in hospitals, nursing homes, and clinics where nurses may care for individuals with infectious diseases such as hepatitis and AIDS. Nurses must observe rigid guidelines to guard against these and other dangers such as radiation, chemicals used for sterilization of instruments, and anesthetics. In addition, they face back injury when moving patients, shocks from electrical equipment, and hazards posed by compressed gases.

EMPLOYMENT

Registered nurses held about 1,906,000 jobs in 1994. About 2 out of 3 jobs were in hospitals. Others were in offices and clinics of physicians, home health care agencies, nursing homes, temporary help agencies, schools, and government agencies. More than one-fourth of all R.N.s worked part time.

Recommended Supplement: *Monthly Labor Review*

If you need information on this publication (ISSN 0098-1818) call the Bureau of Labor Statistics at (202) 606-7828 or fax: (202) 512-2250; communication to the editor-in-chief: (202) 606-5900.

Reference Navigator

Web site: http://www.bls.gov/emphome.htm   CD-ROM: Available

E-mail: M@bls.com   Library Reference Number:

Database: Stat-USA

According to the *Monthly Labor Review,* its job is to "provide the pieces." In other words, bringing you the raw data is its mission. Then, the publication helps you put the pieces together, since each issue also brings you insights on employment, wages and benefits, prices and productivity, and the rest of the economic puzzle. In the end, of course, you get the picture!

The *Monthly Labor Review* is published by the Bureau of Labor Statistics, which is represented in 10 federal districts by the Bureau of Labor Statistics regional offices. They are prepared to...

- Help you find the information you need about prices, the labor force, wages, employee benefits, safety and health, productivity, and other current statistical series.
- Explain what the data mean to your region, your industry, and your labor market.
- Deliver the information promptly and help you use the data correctly.

If you are in the academic world and looking for a job, an additional source of occupational information that no self-respecting faculty member or future faculty member should be without is *The Chronicle of Higher Education* (ISSN 0009-5982) published weekly by the Chronicle of Higher Education, Inc. The *Chronicle* is divided into two parts, A and B. Despite the fact that there are excellent articles in the publication, Section B is probably the most often read. Section B has a comprehensive listing of jobs (e.g., 87 pages in the November 1, 1996, issue) available in the academic community, which covers faculty, administrators, and associations in the domestic and international field. Call (202) 466-1000 or e-mail: member-today@chronicle.com or visit http://www.chronicle.com.

Something to Do

If you would like to get information from the International Labor Organization (ILO) go on-line at http://www.ilo.org.

---

8   HARVARD BUSINESS REVIEW

Description of Publication

For information on this bimonthly publication (ISSN 0017-8012) call *Harvard Business Review* at (800) 274-3214 or fax: (617) 496-1029.

  Reference Navigator

Web site: http://www.hbsp.harvard.edu   CD-ROM: available

E-mail: custserv@cchbspub.harvard.edu   Library Reference Number:

Database: See Web site

Despite its academic roots, *Harvard Business Review (HBR)* has matured into an excellent market magazine (i.e., it has colorful articles in both senses of the word, editorials, advertisements, book reviews, etc.). It is very useful for perusing erudite topics and issues of recent interest in the business environment. Its layout, language, and format are done in a user-friendly and pleasing manner.

If the $13.50 per copy (as of this date) at the newsstand puts you off, you should know that it costs just about double overseas, where you obviously get some very serious readers. The bottom line, of course, is whether you should spend the money in any case (you get two months' worth...since it comes out once every two months). You can find *HBR* in practically every library in the developed world—the rest is up to you.

Today *HBR* has a very nice layout compared to the old stodgy times. One particularly useful attribute is the comprehensive table of contents. Each article, department, and special piece in the magazine is annotated to brief the reader on what may be interesting and what is not. Besides the articles, there are four "departments": (1) "HBR Case Study," which creates a fictitious company and its problems, and then solicits some reactions by experts offering solutions; (2) "Thinking About..." identifies a business issue and analyzes it; (3) "Ideas at Work," discusses the practical applications of concepts (e.g., getting the most out of your product development process); and (4) "Books in Review," which reviews a couple of recent books relating to business or economics. One unique section, not listed as one of the departments, is called "Executive Summaries" and provides a brief overview of each article in that particular issue of *HBR,* as well as information on ordering reprints and what to expect in the next issue. There are also special topics, for example, information on the McKinsey awards or something called, "Strategic Humor." Throw in the letters to the editor and you have it!

If you really like what you read and wish to get a reprint, call: (617) 496-1449 or (800) 988-0886, which gets you HBR's Customer Service Team.

*HBR'*s relatively new format still has the soul of an academic publication and as such may be courted by writers who seek fame and fortune in one of the world's most prestigious journals. If you are one of those, the *HBR*'s editors strongly suggest that you obtain a copy of *HBR*'s "Guidelines for Authors" before submitting manuscripts. To obtain a copy, write: The Editor, *Harvard Business Review,* 60 Harvard Way, Boston, MA 02163 or fax (617) 495-9933 or e-mail hbr_editorial@cchbspub.harvard.edu.

This is good material. If you want to be a professional manager, you better get used to reading professional literature that will help train and educate you to your job. While we are on the topic of Harvard, I would be remiss in not pointing out that there are two other sources of excellent information: (1) the *Harvard Business School Core Collection* and (2) the *Harvard Business School Teaching Materials Catalog.*

The *Harvard Business School Core Collection* is part of the Baker Library Reference Series. The *Core Collection* contains a variety of books (no periodicals are included) reflecting the research and teaching interests of the Harvard Business School; included are a selection of graduate textbooks, certain business classics, handbooks, most of the more recent Harvard Business School faculty publications, as well as current business books of general interest. According to the editors, the collection was begun about 20 years ago to enable Baker's patrons to browse easily through a compact, choice selection. Books are added throughout the year, and titles no longer in demand are weeded regularly. It now contains over 3,500 titles. Each entry contains full bibliographic information along with the price. There are four indexes: Geographic, Detailed Subject, Name, and Title. There is also a list of publishers' addresses.

The *Harvard Business School Teaching Materials Catalog* is for business educators and provides information on such items as case studies (including 200 Stanford case studies and 30 Design Management Institute case studies), videos, *Harvard Business Review* articles (including 50 *California Management Review* articles), and Harvard Business School Press books. The catalog contains annotated listings and comprehensive indexes of teaching materials available for purchase from Harvard Business School Press. One other unique service that the Harvard Business School provides is its new *Custom Coursebook Series.* The

Series publishes customizable coursebooks that have been developed to incorporate case studies, background and industry notes, and *HBR* articles, as well as selected reading from outside sources. At the professor's request, HBS will provide a sample coursebook containing an entire semester of readings. The class can use the entire coursebook, or the professor can select only those readings he or she wishes to use.

Want to Go to Harvard?

If you're interested in going to Harvard, there are a couple of things you may want to know. Costs for 1997–98 tuition and fees were listed as $22,800 and room and board, $7,278; personal expenses, books, supplies, and similar costs averaged $2,624; travel expenses vary. All financial aid awards at Harvard/Radcliffe are based on need. Approximately two-thirds of the undergraduates receive some form of financial assistance.

Undergraduates come from every state and nearly 100 countries. More than 16,000 applicants from both public and private schools compete for 1,600 spots in the freshman class. Application deadlines are November 1 and January 1. Call (617) 495-9707 for transfer admissions.

Harvard and Radcliffe's faculty is an outstanding group of scholars, teachers, and researchers. The Faculty of Arts and Sciences consists of 700 full-time members, all of whom hold a doctorate; they may be assisted by teaching fellows who are doctoral candidates. In a typical course, a faculty member teaches a group of approximately 25 students.

Will She Fit In?

"And then, well, he just lunged at me."

"He did *what?*" Nancy asked incredulously.

"He lunged at me," Susan replied. "One minute we're sitting on the couch in his hotel room, rehearsing his board presentation, and the next minute he lurches toward me, knocking me over. I just couldn't believe it."

"Wow." There was silence on the phone line.

"Yeah, wow," Susan repeated. "Now what do I do?"

Susan Carter was a partner at the Crowne Group, a strategy consulting firm based in New York. Her good friend Nancy Richfield was an investment banker. In the 12 years since they had graduated from business school, the two women had kept in touch, often seeking advice and support from each other at difficult moments in their careers. Susan and Nancy were among a handful of women who had "joined the club"—attaining the rank of partner at elite, privately held firms in which 95 percent of the partners still were men. Crowne's New York office had the kind of partner mix typical of most consulting and investment-banking firms: there were 98 partners in all, 4 of them women.

Promotion to partner four years earlier was a goal Susan had worked hard to achieve. And her successes on the Pellmore account had given her a lot of visibility in the firm. In particular, her work with Brian Hanson, a group senior vice president at Pellmore Industries, was responsible for the dramatic turnaround of a troubled business. The turnaround had made Brian look like a hero, and he was so pleased that he had begun to champion Crown to other executives at Pellmore. Almost overnight, Pellmore became Crowne's largest and most profitable client. Billings mushroomed to $28 million—more than 20 percent of the New York office's revenue. And Crowne's senior partners were hoping to expand the Pellmore budget even further during the annual account review the following month.

Susan could feel the tension in the back of her neck.

"So then what happened, after he lunged at you?" Nancy asked.

"I pushed him aside, jumped up off the couch, and said, 'This is not a good idea,'" Susan replied. "And—can you believe this?—*I'm* the one who picked up the slides, which by now were scattered all over the floor. Then I just got the hell out of there. I still can't believe Brian Hanson would pull a stunt like this. I've worked so hard. How am I going to get past this with him? Talk about the things they never teach you in business school!"

****

Joan Magretta is an editor-at-large at HBR. She was formerly a partner at Bain & Company, an international strategy consulting firm based in Boston, Massachusetts.

Recommended Supplement:
California Management Review

For information on this publication (ISSN 0008-1256) published quarterly by the University of California, Walter A. Haas School of Business, Berkeley, call (800) 777-4726, or (310) 825-4321.

Reference Navigator

Web site: http://haas.berkeley.edu

E-mail: personal only

Database: See Web site

CD-ROM: not available

Library Reference Number:

_____

Since the eastern establishment has always been a political entity with schools like Harvard at its center, no self-respecting unbiased publication can do without the western point of view, ergo the University of California and the *California Management Review (CMR)*. According to the editors, *CMR* serves as a bridge of communication between those who study management and those who practice it. The *CMR* is an excellent journal (for east or west) focusing on contemporary issues written by competent authors, such as Tom Peters, who wrote "Get Innovative or Get Dead."

The periodical is usually broken down into four or five sections, with a book advertisement or two thrown in at the end. For example:

- Strategy and Organization
- High Technology
- Public Policy
- Executive Forum

It's fairly difficult to mention big-name business schools, however, without referencing Massachusetts Institute of Technology's Sloan School of Management. No aspiring manager should ever write a management paper without consulting MIT's *Sloan Management Review* (ISSN 0019-848X) to make sure he or she covered all the bases. *SMR* is an academic journal written by management and academics, consultants and practitioners, and edited for professional managers. It strives to "present what's most useful in current management theory and practice." While it emphasizes general management issues, the choice of material does reflect MIT Sloan School's focus on organizational change, management techniques, and international management. If you are contemplating writing an article, the publication is particularly interested in cross-functional perspectives on management issues. E-mail SMR@MIT.Edu or go to http://web.edu/sloan/www. An example of an article in the fall 1996, issue is "Three Cultures of Management: The Key to Organizational Learning," by Edgar H. Schein.

One excellent source that needs to be mentioned is *Business Horizons* (ISSN 0007-6813), a bimonthly journal published for the Indiana University Graduate School of Business by JAI Press, Inc. (Editorial office: [812] 855-6342; fax: [812] 855-8679). The articles are relatively brief, running from five to seven pages, but very reader-friendly and informative covering any number of relevant topics in the business area with an across-the-board functional approach (marketing, finance, personnel, etc.) plus a strong international perspective. One good example of interest to faculty members is "The Faculty-in-Residence Program," by B. Beatty, R. Lamy, P. Peacock, and B. Saladin; annotation: offering faculty members residencies in host firms may be one answer to strengthening the relevancy of teaching and research in today's business schools. (January–February 1996, vol. 39, no. 1).

There are far too many academic journals to include in this book that try to fill a particular niche in the market. For example, the University of Chicago's business school publishes the *Journal of Business,* (312) 753-2247, and also boasts of the Center for Research in Security Prices, (312) 702-7275; therefore, it would behoove the research student to identify those universities that have reputations for journals and research centers in unique business areas.

Something to Think About

Considering all the student research papers that are being written, few students ever try to get their papers published. Review a copy of *Writer's Market* in the economics and business area for the name of a publishing company that would be interested in publishing your work.

9   Who's Who in America

Description of Publication

For information on this annual publication (ISBN 0-8379-0159-6) call Marquis Who's Who (Reed Reference Publishing Co.) at: (908) 464-6800; or fax: (908) 771-8645.

 Reference Navigator

Web site: http://www.reedref.com

E-mail: jdanzig@reedref.com

Database: See Web site

CD-ROM: available

Library Reference Number:

Only a few reference sources specifically cover prominent business leaders. Three national directories specialize in executive profiles: (1) the *Reference Book of Corporate Managements* will be covered briefly below; (2) *Who's Who in Finance and Industry* is presented in this chapter as a recommended supplement; and (3) Volume 2 of the S&P Register (see Chapter 3 for more information on *Standard & Poor's* publications).

Nevertheless, *Who's Who in America* does a good job of covering everybody, including executives, which is perhaps best for the researcher's needs and so will be the primary focus here.

According to its editors, Marquis *Who's Who in America* was first published in 1899 and has become the standard of contemporary biography throughout the nation. The "Big Red Book" is known for its readily available store of life and career data on noteworthy individuals. The book has grown from 8,602 names in the first edition to more than 90,000 biographees at this publication date. From its inception, *Who's Who in America* has endeavored to profile the leaders of American society: those men and women who are influencing their nation's development. In 1898, when A. N. Marquis, the original publisher, recognized the need for an American biographical directory, he declared that the guiding principle behind such a venture would be to chronicle the lives of individuals whose achievements and contributions to society made them subjects of widespread reference interest and inquiry.

Who's Who in America primarily focuses on U.S. citizens and prominent individuals from other countries, particularly Canada and Mexico, as well. (There is also an international edition.) The biographical data comes from the biographees, which usually results in accurate and current biographical information. Selection is based on reference value. Individuals become eligible for listing by virtue of their positions and/or noteworthy achievements that have proven to be of significant value to society. Wealth or social position are not criteria. The preface lists 12 standards of admission.

Users can identify and locate individuals in any of 38 categories, as well as by country, state, or city. To produce the most efficient reference source available, *Who's Who in America* provides several useful features. First, the latest edition contains a cumulative "Retiree Index" of persons whose names were deleted from the last three years because they have retired from active work. Second, there is a "Necrology of Biographees" whose sketches appeared in the most recent edition and whose deaths were reported before the closing of that edition. The third feature is an expanded listing of individuals whose sketches appear in one of the Marquis regional or topical directories.

Many of the women and men profiled in *Who's Who in America* have included in their biographies a listing of their avocations, thus providing additional insights into their personal lives and interests. Some of the sketches also end with an italicized feature, "Thoughts on My Life." The statement is written by the biographees and reflects those principles, goals, ideals, and values that have been guidelines for success and high standards.

The *Reference Book of Corporate Managements* is published by Dun & Bradstreet and boasts a list of 12,000 companies and their executives in the United States. It lists corporate officers by their companies and not alphabetically, like most other directories. Personal information includes: year of birth, marital status, colleges attended, military service, employment history, and principal outside affiliations. The information is contained in a four-volume set arranged alphabetically by company, with a description of each company and the biographical profiles. The last volume is the index. The *Reference Book of Corporate Managements* is available in CD-ROM.

Periodicals that can be referenced for biographical information are: *Biography,* University Press of Hawaii, a quarterly publication, (808) 948-8694, and *Current Biography,* H. W. Wilson Co., monthly, (800) 367-6770.

Something to Think About

The reference value for biographees in *Who's Who in America* is based on either or both of what two factors? Are you in a position to nominate a candidate for *Who's Who in America?* How would you undertake to do such a project?

LEVINE, HAROLD, lawyer; b. Newark, Apr. 30, 1931; s. Rubin and Gussie (Lifshitz) L.; children: Brenda Sue, Linda Ellen Levin Gersen, Louise Abby, Jill Anne Levine Zuvanich, Charles A., Cristina Gussie, Harold Rubin II; m. Cristina Cervera, Aug. 29, 1980. B.S. in Engring., Purdue U., 1954; J.D. with distinction, George Washington U., 1958. Bar: D.C. 1958, Va., 1958, Mass. 1960, Tex. 1972, U.S. Patent Office, 1958. Naval architect, marine engr. U.S. Navy Dept., 1954–55; patent examiner U.S. Patent Office, 1955–58; with Tex. Instruments Inc., Attleboro, Mass., 1959–77, asst. sec., Dallas, 1969–72, asst. v.p. and gen. patent counsel, 1972–77; ptnr. Sigalos & Levine, Dallas, 1977–93; prin. Levine & Majorie LLP, 1994—; chmn. bd. Vanguard Security, Inc., Houston, 1977—; chmn. Tex. Am. Realty, Dallas, 1977—; lectr. assns., socs.; del. Geneva and Lausanne (Switzerland) Intergovtl. Conf. on Revision, Paris Pat. Conv., 1975–76. Mem. U.S. State Dept. Adv. Panel on Internat. Tech. Transfer, 1977. Mem. ABA (chmn. com. 407 taxation pats. and trdmks. 1971–72), Am. Patent Law Assn., Dallas Bar Assn., Assn. Corp. Pat. Csl. (sec-treas. 1971–73), Dallas-Fort Worth Patent Law Assn., Pacific Indsl. Property Assn. (pres. 1975–77), Electronic Industries Assn. (pres. pat. com. 1972), NAM, Southwestern Legal Inst. on Patent Law (planning com. 1971–74), U.S. C. of C., Dallas C. of C., Alpha Epsilon Pi, Phi Alpha Delta. Republican. Jewish. Club: Kiwanis. Contbr. chpt. to book, articles to profl. jours. Editor: Geroge Washington U. Law Rev., 1956–57; mem. adv. bd. editors Bur. Nat. Affairs, Pat., Trdmk. and Copyright Jour., 1979–87. Office: Levine and Majorie LLP 12750 Merit Dr Ste 1000 Dallas TX 75251-1243

LEVINE, HENRY DAVID, lawyer; b. N.Y.C., June 7, 1951; s. Harold Abraham and Joan Sarah (Price) L.; m. Barbara Wolgel, Aug. 28, 1976; children: David, Rachel, Daniel. AB, Yale U., 1972; JD, M in Pub. Policy, Harvard U., 1976. Bar: N.Y. 1977, D.C. 1978, U.S. Supreme Ct. 1980. Assoc. Wilmer, Cutler & Pickering, Washington, 1976-80; assoc. Morrison & Foerster, Washington, 1981-83, ptnr., 1983-92; ptnr. Levine, Blaszak, Block & Boothby, Washington, 1993—; cons. to GSA on FTS2000 Successor System, 1994—. Editor Telematics, 1984-89. Mem. Nat. Rsch. Coun. Com on High Tech. Bldgs., 1985-88. Named one of the twenty-five most powerful people in networking Network World, 1996. Mem ABA, Fed, Communication Bar Assn., Forum Com. on Comm. Law. Home: 5208 Edgemoor Ln Bethesda MD 20814-2342 Office: Levine Blaszak Block & Boothby 1300 Connecticut Ave NW Ste 500 Washington DC 20036-1708

LEVINE, HOWARD ARNOLD, state supreme court justice; b. Mar. 4, 1932; m. Barbara Joan Segall, July 25, 1954; children: Neil Louis, Ruth Ellen, James Robert. B.A., Yale U., 1953, LL.B., 1956. Bar: N.Y. 1956. Asst. in instrn., research asso. in criminal law Yale Law Sch., 1956-57; asso. firm Hughes, Hubbard, Blair, Reed, N.Y.C., 1957-59; practiced in Schenectady, 1959-70; asst. dist. atty. Schenectady County, N.Y., 1961-66, dist. atty., 1967-70; judge Schenectady County Family Ct., 1971-80; acting judge Schenectady County Ct., 1971-80; adminstrv. judge family cts. N.Y. State 4th Jud. Dist., 1974-80; asso. justice appellate div. 3d dept. N.Y. State Supreme Ct., 1982-93; asso. judge N.Y. Ct. of Appeals, 1993—; vis. lectr. Albany Law Sch., 1972-81; mem. N.Y. Gov.'s Panel on Juvenile Violence, N.Y. State Temp. Commn. on Child Welfare, N.Y.

State Temp. Commn. on Recodification of Family Ct. Act, N.Y. State Juvenile Justice Adv. Bd., 1974-80; mem. ind. rev. bd. N.Y. State Div. for Youth, 1974-80; mem. rules and adv. com. on family ct. N.Y. State Jud. Conf., 1974-80. Contrbr. articles to law revs. Bd. dirs. Schnecatady County Child Guidance Ctr., Carver Community Ctr., Freedom Forum of Schnectady. Mem. Am. Law Inst., N.Y. State Bar Assn. (chmn. spl. com. juvenile justice), Assn. Family Ct. Judges State N.Y. (pres. 1979-90). Home: 2701 Rosendale Rd Niskayuna NY 12309-1300 Office: Country Bldg 620 State St Schenectady NY 12305-2112

LEVINE, HOWARD HARRIS, health facility executive; b. Bklyn., Sept. 30, 1949; s. Roy and Lucille Levin. MPH in Hosp. Administrn., UCLA, 1974; BBA in Mktg., Baruch Coll., 1972. Adminstrv. resident Inter-Community Hosp., Covina, Calif., 1973-74; adminstrv. asst. to exec. dir. John F. Kennedy Med. Ctr., Edison, N.J., 1974-75; assoc. exec. dir. John F. Kennedy Med. Ctr., Edison, 1975-78; adminstr. Robert Wood Johnson Jr. Rehab. Inst., Edison, 1975-78; asst. dir. Beth Israel Med. Ctr., N.Y.C., 1978-81, assoc. dir., 1981-84, sr. assoc. dir. for ops., 1984-87; v.p. Staten Island Univ. Hosp., 1988, sr. v.p. chief oper. officer, 1988-91; CEO Chapman Med Ctr., Orange, Calif., 1992-96; v.p. OrNda Health Corp., 1994-95; pres., CEO Columbia West Hills (Calif.) Med. Ctr., 1996—; adj. lectr. dept. health care adminstrn. Bernard M. Baruch Coll./Mt. Sinai Sch. Medicine, N.Y.C., 1982-93; Health Profl. adv. com. March of Dimes, 1992—; joint com. patient svcs. Calif. Hosp. Assn., 1992—; guest lectr. svcs. Calif. Hosp. Assn., 1992—; guest lectr. NYU Grad. Sch. Pub. Adminstrn., 1984-86; mem. mental health and substance abuse com. Greater N.Y. Health Adminstrn., 1988-91; profl. affairs and hosp. ops. com., 1989-91, chmn. com. on utilization rev., 1988-91; exec. and planning com. Hosp. Coun. So. Calif., 1992—, coun. on profl. practices N.J. Hosp. Assn., Princeton, 1977-78, dist. bd. Health Svcs. Adminstrn., N.Y.C., 1979-80. Mem. editorial adv. bd. The Malpractice Reporter, N.Y.C., 1980-88. Mem. ins. profl. adv. com. Fedn. Jewish Philanthropies Ins., 1981-87; mem. tech. adv. panel N.J. State Health Coordinating Coun., Princeton, 1976-78; bd. dirs. Meals-on-Wheels Program, Metuchen, Edison and Woodbridge, N.J., 1974-76; mem. budget com. United Crusade L.A., 1973-74. Fellow Am. Coll. Healthcare Execs. mem. Coun. Hosp. Adminstrs. (pres. 1986-87), Met. Health Adminstrs. Assn. (pres. 1980-82), Am. Coll. Healthcare Mktg., Hosp. Adminstrs. Discussion Group. Home: 865 Comstock Ave # 14 B Los Angeles CA 90024 Office: Columbia West Hills Med Ctr 7300 Med Ctr Dr West Hills CA 91307

LEVINE, IRVING RASKIN, news commentator, university dean, author, lecturer; b. Pawtucket, R.I.; s. Joseph and Emma (Raskin) L.; m. Nancy Cartmell Jones, July 12, 1957; children—Jeffrey Claybourne Bond, Daniel Rome, Jennifer Jones. BS, Brown U., 1944, LHD (hon.), 1969; MS, Columbia, 1947; LHd (hon.), Bryant Coll., 1974; D.Journalism (hon.), Roger Williams Coll., 1985, LLD (hon.), U. R.I., 1988; LHD (hon.), Lynn U., 1992; LLD (hon.), Northeastern U., 1993; D in Journalism (hon.), R.I. Coll., 1996. Writer obits. Providence Jour., 1940-43; fgn. news editor Internat. News Service, 1947-48; chief Vienna (Austria) bur., 1948-50; with NBC, 1950-95; war corr. NBC, Korea, 1950-52; radio anchor

World News Roundup, Moscow, 1953-54; chief corr. NBC, Moscow, 1955-69, Rome, 1968-71, London, 1967-68; chief econs. corr. NBC, Washington, 1971-95; dean Sch. Internat. Studies, Lynn U., Boca Raton, Fla., 1995—; commentator Consumer News and Bus. Channel Cable TV affiliate svc. NCB TV News, 1990-96; commentator Pub. Broadcasting Sys., WPBT, Miami, 1997—; spl. writer London Times, 1955-59; covered assignments in Can., China, Czechoslovakia, Bulgaria, Poland, Japan, Vietnam, Formosa, Thailand, Eng., France, Germany, Switzerland, Algeria, Congo, Israel, Turkey, Tunisia, Greece, Yugoslavia, Union of South Africa, Denmark, Sweden, Ireland; press group with pres. Ford, Carter, Reagan, Bush, Clinton; attended G-7 Econ. Summits, 1975-95; lectr. univs., bus. groups, cruise ships. Author: Main Street, USSR, 1959, Travel Guide to Russia, 1960, Main Street, Italy, 1963, The New Worker in Soviet Russia, 1973; contbr. articles to nat. mags.; guest on numerous TV shows including Murphy Brown, 1989, David Letterman Show, 1990, Jay Leno Show, 1990. With Signal Corps. U.S. Army, 1944-47, Philippines, Japan. Recipient award for best radio-TV reporting from abroad Overseas Press Club, 1956, award for outstanding radio network broadcasting Nat. Headliners Club, 1957, 50th Anniversary award Columbia Sch. Journalism, 1963, Emmy citation 1966, Martin R. Gainsbrugh award for best econ. reporting, 1978, William Rogers award Brown U., 1988, Silver Circle award Nat. Acad. TV Arts and Scis., 1990, 93; named one of 10 Outstanding Young Men, U.S. Jaycees, 1956; named to R.I. Hall of Fame, 1972, Pawtucket Hall of Fame, 1986, Nat. Broadcasters Hall of Fame Lifetime Achievement award, 1995; honoree Loyola Coll.'s Beta Gamma Sigma, 1994,. Mem. Coun. on Fgn. Rels. (fellowship 1952-53), Cosmos, Phi Beta Kappa, Beta Gamma Sigma. Office: Lynn U 3601 N Military Trl Boca Raton FL 33431-5507

LEVINE, ISRAEL E., writer; b. N.Y.C., Aug. 30, 1923; s. Albert Ely and Sonia (Silver) L.; m. Joy Elaine Michael, June 23, 1946; children: David, Carol. BS, CCNY, 1946. Asst. dir. pub. rels. CCNY, 1946-54, dir., 1954-77, editor Alumnus Mag., 1952-74, 87-89; editor Health Care Week, 1977-79, William H. White Publs., 1979-81; dir. communcations Am. Jewish Congress, 1981-87; COO Richard Cohen Assocs., N.Y.C., 1987—. Author: (with A. Lateiner) The Techniques of Supervision, 1954; The Discoverer of Insulin: Dr. Frederick G. Banting, 1959, Conqueror of Smallpox: Dr. Edward Jenner, 1960, Behind the Silken Curtain: The Story of Townsend Harris, 1961, Inventive Wizard: George Westinghouse, 1962, Champion of World Peace: Dag Hammarskjold, 1962, Miracle Man of Printing: Ottmar Mergenthaler, 1963, Electronics Pioneer: Lee DeForest, 1964, Young Man in the White House: John Fitzgerald Kennedy, 1964, 91, Oliver Cromwell, 1966, Spokesman for the Free World: Adlai Stevenson, 1967, Lenin: The Man Who Made a Revolution, 1969, The Many Faces of Slavery, 1975; contbr. over 200 articles to mags. Mem. exec. com. Com. for Pub. Higher Edn., N.Y.C., 1987—. 2d lt., navigator USAAF, 1943-45, ETO. Decorated Air medal with 3 oak leaf clusters, 3 battle stars USAAF; recipient 125th Anniversary medal; CCNY, 1972, Svc. medal CCNY Alumni Assn., 1974. Mem. The Authors Guild, Authors' League Am., Soc. of Silurians, 2d Air Divsn. Assn. Jewish. Avocation: gardening. Address: Richard Cohen Assocs 40 W 55th St Ste 503 New York NY 10019-5316

LEVINE, JACK, artist; b. Boston, Jan. 3, 1915; s. Samuel Mayer and Mary (Grinker) L.; widowed; 1 child, Susanna Levine Fisher. AFD, Colby Coll., Waterville, Maine, 1956. One-man shows include Downtown Gallery, N.Y.C., 1938, Artists, 1942, Mus. Modern Art, N.Y.C., 1943; exhibited in group shows at Jeu de Paume, Paris, 1938, Carnegie Internat. exhbns., 1938-40, Artists for Victory, Met. Mus., N.Y.C., 1942, retrospective at Jewish Mus., N.Y.C., 1978-79; represented in permanent collections Mus. Modern Art, Met. Mus. Art, N.Y.C., William Hayes Foggs Mus., Harvard U., Addison Gallery, Andover, Mass., Mus. Vatican, D.C. Moore Gallery, N.Y. With AUS, 1942-45. Mem. Am. Acad. Arts and Letters (pres., chancellor), Inst. Arts and Letters (pres. 1993), Nat. Acad. Design, Century Club.

LEVINE, JACK ANTON, lawyer; b. Monticello, N.Y., Dec. 23, 1946; s. Milton and Sara (Sacks) L.; m. Eileen A. Garsh, Sept. 7, 1974; children: Matthew Aaron, Dara Esther. BS with honors, SUNY, Binghamton, 1968; JD with honors, U. Fla., 1975, LLM in Taxation, 1976. Bar: Fla. 1975, U.S. Ct. Appeals (11th cir.) 1981, U.S. Tax Ct., 1982. Tax atty. legis. and regulations divsn. Office chief counsel IRS, Washington, 1977-81; assoc. Holland & Knight, Tampa, Fla., 1981-83, ptnr., 1984—; lectr. in field. Contbr. articles to profl. jours. Mem. ABA, Fla. Bar Assn. (sect. taxation exec. coun. 1984—, chmn. ptnrship. com. 1985-88, chmn. taxation regulated public utilities com. 1988-92, co-chmn. corps. and tax-exempt orgns. com. 1992—, bd. cert. in tax law 1984—). Democrat. Jewish. Avocations: golf, reading, traveling. Home: 10905 Carrollwood Dr Tampa FL 33618-3903 Office: Holland & Knight 400 N Ashley Dr Ste 2300 Tampa FL 33602-4327

LEVINE, JAMES, conductor, pianist, artistic director; b. Cin., June 23, 1943; s. Lawrence M. and Helen (Goldstein) L. Studied piano with Rosina Lhevinne and Rudolf Serkin, studied conducting with Jean Morel, Fausto Cleva and Max Rudolf, studied theory and interpretation with Walter Levin; student, Juilliard Sch. Music; hon. degree, U. Cin., New Eng. Cons., Northwestern U., SUNY, Potsdam. Music dir. Ravinia Festival, 1973-93; artistic dir. Met Opera, 1986—; guest lectr. Sarah Lawrence Coll., Harvard U., Yale U. Piano debut with Cin. Symphony, 1953; conducting debut at Aspen Music Festival, 1961; Met. Opera debut, 1971; Chgo. Symphony debut at Ravinia Festival, 1971; regularly appears throughout U.S. and Europe as condr. and pianist, including Vienna Philharm., Berlin Philharm., Chgo. Symphony, Phila. Orch., Boston Symphony, N.Y. Philharm., Dresden Staatskapelle, Philharmonia Orch., Israel Philharm., Wagner Festival at Bayreuth; made Bayreuth debut in new prodn. Parsifal, 1982; condr. Salzburg Festival, 1975-93; Salzburg premiers include Shcönberg's Moses und Aron, 1987, Offenbach's Tales of Hoffmann, 1980, Mahler's Seventh Symphony, Mendelssohn's Elijah; condr. Met. premiere prodns. of Verdi's I Vespri Siciliani, Stiffelio, I Lombardi, Weill's The Rise and Fall of the City of Mahagonny, Stravinsky's Oedipus Rex, Berg's Lulu, Mozart's Idomeneo and La Clemenza di Tito, Gershwin's Porgy and Bess, Schönberg's Erwartung, world premiere Corigliano/Hoffman The Ghosts of Versailles, 1991; subject of documentary for PBS; artistic dir. Met. Opera. Recipient Smetana medal, 1987, 8 Grammy awards. Office: Met Opera Assn Inc Met Opera House Lincoln Ctr New York NY 10023

74

Recommended Supplement: *Who's Who in Finance and Industry*

Reference Navigator

Web site: http://www.reedref.com   CD-ROM: available

E-mail: jdanzig@reedref.com   Library Reference Number:

Database: See Web site

This annual publication (ISBN 0-8379-0325-4) is also published by Reed Reference Publishing and contact can be made by calling the numbers listed above. According to the editors, in compiling names for inclusion in *Who's Who in Finance and Industry,* the aim has been to select qualified men and women in all lines of useful and reputable financial endeavor. The standards of admission provide for the selection of those individuals who, because of prominence in particular branches of business, have become subjects of interest, inquiry, or discussion in the business world. Others are chosen because of positions held in financial and industrial concerns defined by size based on assets or sales, or by other specialized rating criteria. The editors present comprehensive coverage of approximately 25,000 North American and international professionals who are of current business reference interest.

The listings in *Who's Who in Finance* are the most detailed of the three major directories mentioned above. Using volume of business as the criteria for selection, numerous officers from the largest American companies and the key officers from companies doing business of smaller designated volume are included, as well as management-level professionals. In addition, the directory covers professionals in business-related fields, such as selected government officials, heads of stock exchanges, business educators and researchers, directors of professional and trade associations in business, and labor union officers. Listings are arranged alphabetically by personal name, with no additional indexes. CD-ROM data are also available.

Each candidate for inclusion in *Who's Who in Finance and Industry* is invited to submit biographical data about his or her life and business career. This information is reviewed by the Marquis editorial staff before being written into sketch form. In the event that a reference-worthy individual fails to submit biographical data, the Marquis staff compiles the information through independent research.

10 MIT's Technology Review

Description of Publication

For information on this publication (ISSN 00401692) published eight times a year, call the Association of Alumni and Alumnae of the Massachusetts Institute of Technology at (617) 253-8250; or fax: (617) 258-7264.

  Reference Navigator

Web site: http://web.mit.edu/techreview/

E-mail: trcomments@mit.edu

Database: See Web site

CD-ROM: not available

Library Reference Number:

_____

OK, OK, so *Technology Review* is from MIT, a prestigious engineering school, and it is a magazine about technology, but that's no reason to run scared . . . right? Right! This is an eminently reader-friendly publication (80 pages). It is not a periodical about engineering, math, or the so-called hard sciences, and it certainly is easier to read than your average organic chemistry book. Yet it is about technology, in all its forms. For example, from "Mindful Healing: A Talk with Herbert Benson" (October 1996):

> The author of *The Relaxation Response* describes his quest to understand the mind/body link—activated by meditation, belief in a particular medical procedure, or even religious faith—in reducing stress and promoting a patient's recovery. But he decries those who would take his ideas to an unwarranted extreme by proselytizing or blaming patients for their disease.

Its reputation is supported by some interesting facts: (1) the average number of years as a subscriber are 11; (2) 73 percent of the readers are professionals/managers; and (3) 91 percent have at least one college degree. The format is long on essay and short on advertising, an attribute of no little consequence to those bent on learning instead of buying. Four or five feature articles are offered at approximately 10 pages each, so the prospects for useful reference works are good. The departments have the usual letters, careers, and trends section, but economic perspectives are also included, which is useful for targeting business interests. For example, the April 1997 issue included "The Economic Perspective," by Bennett Harrison:

> New technologies do boost productivity as long as they are complemented by policies that, for example, enhance infrastructure or reorganize workplaces.

Despite *Technology Review* being a technology magazine, it frequently overlaps the interests of business. Businesspeople, after all, cannot avoid being involved with technology by either using it, funding it, or producing it.

By the way, those interested in getting information about the MIT Sloan School of Management MBA programs or the Executive Short Courses should visit the Web site at: http://www/web.mit.edu/sloan/ or call: (617) 253-7166; or fax: (617) 252-1200.

Another technology source, somewhat friendly to the noninitiated, is the *Scientific American* (ISSN 0036-8733), published monthly by Scientific American, Inc. ([800] 333-1199). Computer sources are: e-mail at info@sciam-com or visit their Web site at http://www.sciam-com/. This is not a business reference publication, but it has left the rather rigid and esoteric formats of the past scientific articles for the more reader-friendly style that accomplishes the same goal while including a far greater number of readers. The magazine does include business articles (e.g., sections on "Technology and Business" and "Working Knowledge"). A recent feature article, for example, focused on "Semiconductor Subsidies," by Lucien P. Randazzese.

> The federally funded research consortium SEMATECH is often credited with restoring vigor to the U.S. semiconductor industry. The ability of such cooperative efforts to foster competitive technology can be severely limited, however, as illustrated by the noteworthy failure of GCA Corporation. A once successful manufacturer of microlithography tools, SEMATECH tried to resuscitate GCA's business but could not. That experience holds lessons for other public and private policy makers.

DEPARTMENTS

Phenomena

By David Brittan

Waiting for Uncle Bill

The lives of the self-made often follow a symmetrical curve, wherein a mounting acquisitiveness peaks in middle age and mellows into philanthropy as the person grows in wisdom, leisure time, and (perhaps) abhorrence at the thought of his or her heirs driving around in fancy cars. True to form, Andrew Carnegie devoted his youth to building an empire. By his mid-fifties, when he consolidated his holdings into Carnegie Steel, he was thinking seriously about "the improvement of mankind" and declaring that a "man who dies rich dies disgraced." After his retirement in 1901, at age 65, Carnegie went on a giving spree that lasted 18 years and dispatched $350 million. Electronics pioneer David Packard traced a similar curve, setting up a modest foundation in his early fifties and, later, in 1988, when he was 75, enriching it with his $2 billion stake in the Hewlett-Packard Co. There is beauty and logic in this progression: first you inhale, then you exhale. But there is also danger in taking it for granted.

Bill Gates, the president of Microsoft, has adopted this curve as a template for his own financial career, perhaps not realizing what a slippery slope he is on. At 41, he has amassed the largest private fortune in the world—currently $23.9 billion, and probably somewhat larger by the time you finish this paragraph. So far, he has barely stopped to exhale. Gates's charitable expenditures, according to *Time,* consisted of the following as of January: $34 million to the University of Washington, $15 million to Harvard University, $6 million to Stanford, $3 million in book royalties to inner-city libraries, and $200 million in the form of a foundation fund. By ordinary standards, $258 million is a generous sum. But seen as a mere 1 percent of his net worth, Gates's philanthropic record is on a par with the average person's lifetime contribution to wishing-wells.

Gates knows this. It's all part of a plan he articulates whenever he's pressed to rationalize his enourmous wealth. "Remember," he told a *Playboy* interviewer three years ago, "95 percent of it I'm just going to give away . . . I'm saving that for when I'm in my fifties. It's a lot to give away and it's going to take time." Until then, Gates is marshalling his excuses. As he frenquently reminds people, his billions are tied up in Microsoft stock. So, presumably, if he wanted to liquidate assets, there'd be phone calls to make, papers to sign. A 1991 *New York Times* profile quoted him as complaining, "I don't have time to figure out what charities make sense," to which he added a postscript that set a new standard for procrastination: "And to the degree Microsoft can do well, it's just that much more to give later."

It is understandable that somebody in the midst of one of the biggest inhalations in the history of capital might regard the future as his to control. The time and resources at his command appear to be infinite, inexhaustible. He will "give later," when he reaches a suitable point on the curve. If only the curve of empire building were so predictable.

At Gates's age, Howard Hughes was a bright young man, too—breaking speed records with his flying and hard at work designing the largest airplane ever built. In his late forties, right on schedule, he turned to philanthropy, using the profits from the Hughes Aircraft Co. to found the Howard Hughes Medical Institute. It seems unlikely that Hughes could have forseen the years of seclusion and madness that would close out his life. In his waning days he spoke of his interest in supporting medical research, according to James Phelan's *Howard Hughes: The Hidden Years.* "Eventually that is where the bulk of my estate will go," Hughes claimed in an interview. But "eventually" never came: he died intestate, and most of his wealth was divided among his cousins.

The decline of Howard Hughes may be an extreme case, but it is only one of many cautionary tales from which a self-made billionaire might profit. Two of the richest nineteenth-century Americans, John Jacob Astor and Cornelius Vanderbilt, never really got around to major philanthropic works, despite physical and financial longevity. Donald Trump—formerly *the* Donald, now just *a* Donald—found that his chance to make a contribution in proportion to his fortune was cut short by the vicissitudes of the market. The list could go on and on. The point is that anyone who counts on a policy of deferred giving is ignoring the role played by Fortune with a capital "F"—kismet, Lady Luck, destiny.

In an uncertain world, the best insurance policy may be to give it while you've got it. A living testament to this philosophy is Charles Feeney, cofounder of Duty Free Shoppers, Ltd. In 1984, still in his early fifties, he relinquished the chance to become a Billionaire for Life when he signed over most of his wealth—some $500 million—to the charitable fund he founded, Atlantic Foundation and Atlantic Trust. The fund has since mushroomed to $3.5 billion, according to *Newsweek.* Another adherent, Percy Ross, a Minneapolis millionaire, looks for unusual ways to brighten people's lives. He once threw a Christmas Eve dinner for 1,050 disadvantaged children and gave them each a bicycle, for example, and he writes a newspaper column in which he grants readers' requests for money. "I don't need any hospital wings or libraries named after me," Ross told *People* magazine. "I want to enjoy giving my money away while I'm alive."

It's hard to picture Bill Gates handing out bicycles (which, by the way, he could do for every American man, woman, and child). Then again, it's difficult to imagine how *anyone* might spend $24 billion. Gates appears confident that the answer will come to him in due season. As his friend and fellow billionaire Warren Buffett has put it, "He will spend time, at some point, thinking about the impact his philantrhopy can have. He is too imaginative to just do conventional gifts." Let us hope Gates makes up his mind in this lifetime. For when a road is paved only with good intentions, who knows where it might lead?

Recommended Supplement:
Research-Technology Management

For information on this bimonthly publication (ISSN 0895-6308) call the Industrial Research Institute at (202) 296-8811; or fax: (202) 776-0756.

Reference Navigator

Web site: http://www.iriinc.org

E-mail: personal only

Database: ABI/INFORM

CD-ROM: not available

Library Reference Number:

The publisher of this publication, Industrial Research, Inc., is a nonprofit organization whose members are approximately 300 industrial companies with technical research departments. These member companies are responsible for the conduct and management of a large portion of all industrial research and development activity being carried on in the United States.

This publication, formerly called *Research Management,* has a very readable format and definitely qualifies as excellent reference material. It has an impressive board of editors who help to maintain the quality of the material (e.g. vice president of corporate R&D, The Gillette Company; director, product engineering, Snap-on-Tools; director of research, Olin Corporation; etc.). Two examples of feature articles are "Strategic Alliances in the Global Market Place," by Bruce Merrifield (describes the exponential growth of international alliances and predicts it will progressively undermine nationalistic economic and security policies) and "Critical Success Factors in R&D Projects," by Jeffrey Pinto and Dennis Slevin (authors found that the relative importance of 10 factors critical to and predictive of success varies with the particular stage in a project's life cycle).

The departments include Profiles (e.g., "Managers at Work"), Perspectives (e.g.. "MIT dean wants radical redesign of engineering education"), and Information Resources (e.g., "The Business of Science, Mastering Technology," etc.).

Contents of *Research-Technology Management* are indexed and abstracted in the ABI/INFORM database. A case could be made by some business school pundits that American business education is too dedicated to the marketing and finance areas. The Industrial Research Institute can be a helpful resource for trying to balance this bias by helping to develop areas of educational interest for students.

The purposes of the Industrial Research Institute are listed as follows: (1) to promote, through the cooperative efforts of its members, improved, economical, and effective techniques of organization, administration, and operations of industrial research; (2) to foster interaction between research and other corporate functions; (3) to generate understanding and cooperation between the academic and industrial research communities; (4) to afford a means for industry to cooperate effectively with government in matters related to research; (5) to stimulate and develop an understanding of research as a force in economic, industrial, and social activities; and (6) to encourage high standards in the field of industrial research.

Something to Do

Here are some other valuable sources of reference service you may wish to consider contacting for either research or job (internships, fellowships, etc.) opportunities:

American Institute for Economic Research, (413) 528-1216.

Brookings Institution, (202) 797-6000.

Research and Development (monthly), Cahners Publishing Co., Inc., (212) 645-0067.

Review of Business and Economic Research (semiannual), University of New Orleans, (504) 283-6248.

Competitor Intelligence: How to Get It—How to Use It, by Leonard Fuld, John Wiley and Sons, Inc., (800) 526-5368; reveals how to gather business and industrial information and includes sources and critical annotations.

How To Find Information About Companies (annual), Washington Researchers, (202) 333-3533.

AUBER Bibliography, Association for University and Business Economic Research, (304) 293-5837.

11 SMALL BUSINESS SOURCEBOOK

Description of Publication

If you would like information on this publication (ISBN 0-8103-6850-1) call Gale Research Inc. at (800) 877-4253.

 Reference Navigator

Web site: http://www.gale.com/gale.html
E-mail: galeord@gale.com
Database: Dialog

CD-ROM: available
Library Reference Number:

Small Business Sourcebook (*SBS*) provides expanded and updated coverage of a wide variety of sources of information and assistance for all entrepreneurs. Volume 1 includes profiles of 225 generic small businesses (e.g., antique shop, apparel shop, appliance store, art gallery, etc.). Volume 2 covers general small business topics; programs and assistance in U.S. states and territories and many Canadian provinces; and U.S. federal government agencies and offices. This book—1,550 pages in Volume 1 alone—is comprehensive and informative. The two together deserve to be perhaps the best source book for small business.

The *Small Business Sourcebook* groups information in four sections:

1. *Specific small business profiles*. This section includes the following types of resources: start-up information, primary associations, other organizations of interest, educational programs, directories of education programs, reference works, sources of supply, statistical sources, trade periodicals, trade shows and conventions, consultants, franchises and business opportunities, computerized databases, computer systems/software, information services, libraries, research centers, and other resources of interest—all arranged by business type.

2. *General small business topics.* This section offers such resources as associations, books, periodicals, articles, pamphlets, videos, databases, educational programs, trade shows and conventions, consultants, and libraries, arranged alphabetically by business topic.

3. *State listings.* Entries include government, academic, and commercial agencies and organizations, as well as selected coverage of relevant state-specific publications; listings are arranged by state, territory, and Canadian province.

4. *Federal government assistance.* Listings are arranged alphabetically by U.S. government agency or office; regional or branch offices are listed alphabetically by state.

A "Master List of Small Business Profiles" provides the beginning page number of each profile. Also included in a separate section are the four-digit SIC codes and corresponding classification descriptions for the 225 small businesses profiled in the fifth edition. The SIC system, which organizes businesses by type, is a product of the Statistical Policy Division of the U.S. Office of Management and Budget. Statistical data produced by government, public, and private organizations usually are categorized according to SIC codes, thereby facilitating the collection, comparison, and analysis of data as well as providing a uniform method for presenting statistical information. Hence, knowing the SIC code for a particular small business increases access to and the use of a variety of statistical data from many sources. For example:

Athletic Shoe Store
5661   Shoe Stores

Auto Supply Store
5531   Auto and home supply stores

There are other good resources for small businesses. *Nation's Business* runs a column called "Direct Line," which is a popular advice column for small business owners and managers, plus gives you answers from the experts about starting and running your business. Now you can have even more answers at your fingertips with *Mancuso's Small Business Resource Guide* ([800] 230-7700 or fax [202] 463-5641). This updated guide contains a complete list of names, addresses, and telephone numbers of the best sources of small business information about various topics, including:

- Computer purchasing directories and warehouses.
- Incorporating and forming partnerships.
- Franchising directories, associations, and advisers.
- Government assistance, including loans and grants.
- Obtaining venture capital.
- Import/export government contacts.

Small business information also can be acquired from the following Web sites:

Small Business Administration: gopher://www.sbaonline.sba.gov.

Franchise Handbook: http://www.franchise1.com.

For information dealing with European small and medium-size enterprises see *Enterprises in Europe* (ISBN 9-28267-692-7), a strong supplement to *Eurostate Yearbook*. This publication is available through UNIPUB at (800) 274-4888 or fax (301) 459-0056.

Something to Do

Select a generic small business example from one of those listed in the *Small Business Sourcebook* and review the profile with an actual small business owner in your community for comparison.

Recommended Supplement: *The Source Book of Franchise Opportunities*

Reference Navigator

WebSite: http://www.franchise-update.com   CD-ROM: not available

E-mail: 103042.3305@compuserve.com   Library Reference Number:

Database: See Web site

The *Source Book,* (ISBN 1-55623-331-0) according to Robert E. Bond, president of the publisher, Bond & Associates, a business research and development firm, offers the sophisticated potential franchisee the most up-to-date and definitive information on more than 2,700 franchising options. This comprehensive reference book is based on a 41-point questionnaire seeking information about:

- Company history, size, and geographic distribution.
- Investment requirements of franchisees.
- Start-up assistance/training provided by franchisors.
- Ongoing royalty and advertising fees.
- A detailed listing of ongoing franchisor support services.
- Franchisor expansion plans.

In case you're wondering if it's a good book, a testimony from U.S. Congressman Bill Archer (R, Texas) should help:

> Unquestionably the most up-to-date, comprehensive, and definitive handbook for data on the ever-changing franchising industry. Bond's research, clarity and presentation are unequaled. Truly *required reading* for anyone seriously considering an investment in franchising.

Bond writes that for an industry that has such a dramatic impact on the national economy ($1 in every $10 in the retail trade) and that presents a vast and ready market for true value-added publications, the paucity of sophisticated current literature on franchising is disconcerting. But Bond & Associates does recommend four books to any serious potential franchisee.

1. *The Continental Franchise Review,* Trend Communications, (303) 740-7031. This is an eight-page analytical newsletter that discusses current topics of interest to both franchisees and franchisors alike.

2. *The Franchise Option, Expanding Your Business Through Franchising,* DeBanks M. Henward, III, and William Ginalski, Franchise Group Publishers, 3644 E. McDowell, Suite 214, Phoenix, AZ 85008. An excellent overview of the inner workings of the industry from the franchisee's point of view.

3. *Franchise Law Bibliography,* American Bar Association, (312) 988-6064. According to the authors, perhaps the most complete (if dated) bibliography of books, periodicals, and articles about the subject of franchising. Although the thrust is toward a legal orientation, the bibliography covers all areas of franchising.

4. *Franchising Opportunities,* International Franchise Association (IFA), 1350 New York Avenue, NW, Suite 90, Washington, DC 20005. Gives the most current news on what's happening in franchising (at least with regard to its membership) in a newsmagazine format.

There is at least one other journal you should be familiar with—*Entrepreneur: The Small Business Authority* (e-mail: www.EntMag.com or fax: [714] 755-4211). This is a substantial monthly journal (see Chapter 17) of approximately 230 pages, usually found on newsstands, that boasts of a monthly circulation of around 4.5 million. Examples of articles include:

"Best Sellers," by Robert McGarvey. (Five of the nation's top sales professionals share their best secrets to sales success.)

"Danger Zone," by Brian Steinberg. (Scam artists are targeting capital-hungry entrepreneurs. Could you be next?)

Departments cover such items as "The Business Beat" (small enterprise at a glance); "Travel Smarts"; "Entrepreneurial Woman"; "Global Vision" (trademark registration, export regulations, etc.); and "Book Reviews" fill out the rest.

Something to Do

Compare starting a Jiffy Lube versus Grease Monkey franchise. There are a number of considerations for comparison; for example, company-owned units; cash investment; area development agreement; passive ownership; expansion plans, etc. Which would you prefer starting out as a franchisee? Why?

---

12 PETERSON'S GUIDE TO FOUR-YEAR COLLEGES

Description of Publication

For information on this annual publication (ISSN 0894-9336), call Peterson's Guides, Inc., at (609) 243-9111.

 Reference Navigator

Web site: http://www.petersons.com
E-mail: info@petersons.com
Database: See Web site

CD-ROM: available
Library Reference Number:

For over 30 years, according to its editors, Peterson's has given students and parents the most comprehensive, up-to-date information on undergraduate institutions in the United States and Canada. The data published in *Peterson's Guide to Four-Year Colleges* are obtained directly from the colleges and updated every year. However, if you are ambivalent or your parents are not too enthusiastic about the four years of expense and turmoil in sending you to college, the Marine Corps recruiting number is: (1–800–MAR–INES).

The book contains

- Comparative data on more than 2,000 accredited U.S. and Canadian colleges (*Peterson's* makes no effort to distinguish between colleges and universities). It lists majors and degrees, costs, admission requirements and procedures, financial aid, ROTC, campus life, and other interesting facts.
- Over 800 detailed two-page descriptions written by admissions directors that paint a complete picture of what the colleges have to offer.
- Detailed maps to help you locate each college and plan how to get there.

- Advice on evaluating the quality of your choice (either just starting out or as a transfer student) from Dr. Ernest Boyer, former U.S. Commissioner of Education.

Two important sections of the book deal with the "College Profiles and Special Announcements" and the "In-Depth Descriptions of the Colleges."

The college profiles section contains detailed factual profiles of colleges, covering such items as background facts, enrollment figures, faculty size, admission and graduation requirements, expenses, financing, special programs, career services, housing, campus life and student services, sports, majors and degrees, and whom to contact for more information. In addition, there are special announcements from college administrators about new programs or special events.

The in-depth descriptions section shifts the focus to a variety of other factors, some of them intangible, that should also be considered. Two-page descriptions are offered to provide a greater overview of nearly 900 of the 2,026 colleges and universities profiled. Prepared exclusively by college officials, they are designed to help give you a better sense of the individuality of each institution, in terms that include campus environment, student activities, and lifestyle. The absence from this section of any college or university does not constitute an editorial decision on the part of Peterson's Guides. In essence, this section is an open forum for colleges and universities, on a voluntary basis, to communicate their particular message to prospective college students.

Finding a school that meets your needs is, of course, only one step—applying is another. If there's a high school senior in your household, then you know that filling out applications may seem to be the hardest thing about getting into college. The old paper and pencil-age relics, which one expects to be perfect, are complex, confusing, and unforgiving. Completing one by hand or typewriter—if you can find a typewriter—is an ordeal. In September 1997, Peterson's announced the opening of www.ApplyToCollege.com, home of POLARIS (Peterson's Online Application, Registration, and Information Service)—a revolutionary and free admissions service that gives college-bound students the resources to organize and manage the application process by using The Universal Application^{sm} program. The Universal Application is a set of proprietary online forms that includes an application officially accepted by nearly 900 colleges (and the number grows daily). Another alternative is APPLY! '98, a Windows CD-ROM with digitized applications to over 500 popular colleges, including top-rated schools like Princeton, Harvard, and Duke; smaller private colleges like Middlebury, Bard, and Kenyon; and a handful of state colleges. All you have to do is pick a school, fill in the blanks onscreen, and hit the print button. Out comes a completed application, with all the proper fonts and graphics, ready for mailing. The software produced by Apply Technology of Burlington, Massachusetts, works like a dream if you've got a PC with lots of horsepower. Best of all, the program is free. APPLY! '98 is not available in stores. You can get your free copy by calling (203-740-3504); or try your luck by visiting APPLY's Web site at: www.weapply.com

OK, now let's assume you're ready for graduate school and *Peterson's Guide to Graduate & Professional Programs* (ISBN 1-56079-291-4). Peterson's full *Graduate Database* is also available on-line through Dialog and on CD-ROM through SilverPlatter. According to the editors, since 1966 the six-volume *Guides to Graduate Study* have been the only complete, up-to-date resource for students, academic advisers, researchers, and librarians. The overview provides details on more than 1,500 universities offering graduate and professional degree programs. Special features include:

- Expert advice: Applying to graduate school and professional schools; plus financial aid for graduate and professional education.
- In-depth profiles: Degrees offered, enrollments, admission and degree requirements, tuition, financial aid, housing, faculty research projects and facilities, and contacts at each institution.
- Specialized directories: Graduate and professional programs by field, programs by institution, and combined-degree programs.
- Full descriptions: Two-page essays written by grad school officials— offering important information to all prospective graduate students.

Of the six volumes, Book 6 provides information on graduate programs in business, education, health, and law. Book 1 presents several directories to help you identify programs of study that might interest you; you can then research those further in Books 2 through 6. The "Graduate Adviser" in Book 6 helps in describing: applying to graduate and professional schools; financial aid, for graduate and professional education; tests required of applicants; and accreditation and accrediting agencies. The academic and professional programs in business include, but are not limited to: business administration, accounting, finance/banking, hospitality administration, nonprofit management, international business, marketing, and real estate.

Something to Do

Assume you are a career development counselor at The American University in the District of Columbia and that a senior student from your school wanted to attend a relatively small liberal arts university in Florida and pursue an MBA degree with a specialization in international business. The student is 26 years old, a Swedish citizen, and has never held a full-time job. The student has not taken the GMAT, needs financial assistance, and has a grade point average of 3.1. What would be your recommendations to her?

She has mentioned how much she would like to do an advertising internship in the United States. Review *Peterson's Guides: Internships* 1997 (ISBN 1-56079-149-7) and help her research possibilities with Abramson Ehrlich Manes; Adams Sandler, Inc.; and Ads Unlimited.

Make ample use of the written materials available, plus computer resources.

BOSTON COLLEGE
Chestnut Hill, Massachusetts

Enrollment: 14,830
UG: 8,958
Entrance: Very Difficult
SAT I≥500: 96% V, 98% M* (R)
Tuition & Fees: $19,298
Room & Board: $7,530
Application Deadline: 1/10
ACT≥21: N/R

The Jesuit philosophy of education emphasizes a rigorous intellectual grounding in the liberal arts, the formation of critical leadership skills, and the opportunity for reflection upon personal paths of development. A new computing and communication network provides Internet, telephone, and cable television services to all classrooms, offices, and dorm rooms, and is the latest evidence that Boston College intends to offer cutting-edge learning technologies, while always fostering respect and concern for each student.

GENERAL

Independent Roman Catholic (Jesuit), coed. Awards bachelor's, master's, doctoral, first professional degrees (also offers continuing education program with significant enrollment not reflected in profile). Founded 1863. *Setting:* 240-acre suburban campus with easy access to Boston. *Endowment:* $449.7 million. *Research spending 1995–96:* $7.8 million. Education spending 1995–96: $9982 per undergrad. *Total enrollment:* 14,830. *Faculty:* 982 (591 full-time, 95% with terminal degrees, 391 part-time); student-undergrad faculty ratio is 15:1. *Graduate and professional fields:* area and ethnic studies, biological and life sciences, business management and administrative services, education, English language literature/letters, foreign language and literature, health professions and related sciences, law and legal studies, mathematics, philosophy, physical sciences, psychology, social sciences, theology/religion.

UNDERGRADUATES

8,958 students from 53 states and territories, 91 other countries. 53% women, 47% men, 28% state residents, 72% live on campus, 3% international, 0% 25 or older, 5% Hispanic, 4% black, 8% Asian or Pacific Islander. *Retention:* 93% of 1995 full time freshman returned. *Areas of study chosen:* 24% business management and administrative services, 18% social sciences, 10% education, 10% English language/literature/letters, 9% biological and life sciences, 8% psychology, 5% communications and journalism, 3% health professions and related sciences, 2% foreign language and literature, 2% mathematics, 2% philosophy, 2% physical sciences, 1% fine arts, 1% performing arts, 1%

theology/religion. *Most popular recent majors:* finance/banking, English, political science/government.

FRESHMEN

2,474 total; 16,501 applied, 41% were accepted, 37% of whom enrolled. 7 National Merit Scholars.

ACADEMIC PROGRAM

Core, honor code. *Calendar:* semesters. ESL program offered during academic year, services for LD students, advanced placement, accelerated degree program, self-designed majors, freshman honors college, tutorials, honors program, Phi Beta Kappa, summer session for credit, part-time degree program (daytime, evenings), adult/continuing education programs, internships. More than half of graduate courses open to undergrads. Off-campus study at Boston University, Brandeis University, Hebrew College, Pine Manor College, Regis College (MA), Tufts University. Study abroad in Belgium, China, England, Ireland, Japan, Netherlands (3% of students participate). ROTC: Army (c), Naval (c), Air Force (c). Unusual degree programs: 3-2 engineering with Boston University, nursing, social work, education, BA/MA, BA/MSW in arts and sciences; BS/MS with School of Nursing; BA/MA, BA/MSW with School of Education.

GRADUATION REQUIREMENTS

114 credits; 2 semesters of math/science; computer course for business, math majors.

MAJORS

Accounting, American studies, art history, biochemistry, biology/biological sciences, business administration/commerce/management, chemistry, classics, communication, computer information systems, computer science, (pre)dentistry sequence, early childhood education, economics, education, elementary education, English, environmental sciences, finance/banking, French, geology, geophysics, German, Germanic languages and literature, Greek, Hispanic studies, history, human development, human resources, interdisciplinary studies, Italian, Latin, (pre)law sequence, linguistics, management information systems, marketing/retailing/merchandising, mathematics, (pre)medicine sequence, music, nursing, operations research, philosophy, physics, political science/government, psychology, Romance languages, Russian, Russian and Slavic studies, science, secondary education, Slavic languages, sociology, Spanish, special education, studio art, theater arts/drama, theology.

LIBRARY

Thomas P. O'Neill Library with 1.4 million books, 15,075 periodicals.

COMPUTERS ON CAMPUS

200 computers available on campus for general student use. Computer purchase/lease plans available. A computer is recommended for all students. A campus-wide network can be

accessed from student residence rooms and from off-campus. Students can contact faculty members and/or advisers through e-mail. Computers for student use in computer center, computer labs, learning resource center, classrooms, library provide access to the Internet/World Wide Web. Staffed computer lab on campus provides training in use of computers, software. *Academic computing expenditure 1995–96:* $5 million.

COLLEGE LIFE

Orientation program (3 days, $91, parents included). Drama-theater group, choral group, marching band, student-run newspaper, radio station. *Social organizations:* 140 open to all. *Most popular organizations:* Ski Club, The Bostonians, Boston College Bop. *Major annual events:* Homecoming, Middlemarch Ball, Student Leadership Awards Banquet. *Student services:* health clinic, personal-psychological counseling, women's center. *Campus security:* 24-hour emergency response devices and patrols, late-night transport-escort service, controlled dormitory access.

HOUSING

6,580 college housing spaces available; 6,550 were occupied 1996–97. Freshmen given priority for college housing. Off-campus living permitted. *Options:* freshmen-only, coed, single-sex, international student housing available. Resident assistants live in dorms.

ATHLETICS

Member NCAA. All Division I except men's football (Division I-A). *Intercollegiate:* baseball M, basketball M(s)/W(s), crew M(c)/W(c), cross-country running M/W(s), fencing M/W, field hockey W(s), football M(s), golf M/W, ice hockey M(s)/W, lacrosse M/W(s), rugby M(c)/W(c), sailing M/W, skiing (downhill) M/W, soccer M(s)/W(s), softball W(s), squash M(c)/W(c), swimming and diving M/W(s), tennis M/W(s), track and field M(s)/W(s), volleyball W(s), water polo M, wrestling M. *Intramural:* basketball, crew, cross-country running, football, ice hockey, lacrosse, racquetball, sailing, skiing (downhill), softball, squash, swimming and diving, table tennis (Ping-Pong), tennis, track and field, volleyball, water polo. *Contact:* Mr. Chester S. Gladchuk Jr., Director, Athletic Association, 617-552-4681.

CAREER PLANNING

Placement office: 10 full-time, 5 part-time staff; $506,000 operating expenditure 1995–96. *Director:* Mr. Frank Fessendon, Director of the Career Center, 617-552-3430. *Services:* job fairs, resume preparation, resume referral, career counseling, careers library, job bank, job interviews.

AFTER GRADUATION

27% of class of 1996 went directly to graduate, professional school: 10% graduate arts and sciences, 9% law, 6% business, 4% medicine. 4 Fulbright scholars.

EXPENSES FOR 1996–97

Application fee: $45. Comprehensive fee of $26,828 includes full-time tuition ($18,820), mandatory fees ($478), and college room and board ($7530 minimum). College room only: $4200 (minimum).

FINANCIAL AID

65% applied for aid, 84% of those who applied for aid were judged to have need, 100% of those were aided. Average percent of need met: 92%. Average amount received per student (from all sources): $12,350. Non-need awards available. *Required forms:* CSS Financial Air PROFILE, institutional, FAFSA; required for some: state *Financial aid (priority) deadline:* 2/1. *Payment plans:* tuition prepayment, installment. *Waivers:* full or partial for employees or children of employees.

APPLYING/FRESHMEN

Options: electronic application, early entrance, early action, deferred entrance, midyear entrance. *Required:* essay, school transcript, 2 recommendations, SAT I or ACT, 3 SAT II Subject Tests, SAT II: Writing Test, TOEFL for international students. *Recommended:* 4 years of high school math, 3 years of high school science, 4 years of high school foreign language, interview. Test scores used for admission and counseling/placement. *Application deadlines:* 1/10, 11/1 for early action. *Notification:* 4/15, 12/15 for early action.

APPLYING/TRANSFER

Required: essay, standardized test scores, high school transcript, 1 recommendation, college transcript, minimum 2.5 GPA (3.0 preferred), good standing at previous institution. *Recommended:* 3 years of high school math and science, 4 years of high school foreign language, interview. *Entrance:* very difficult. *Application deadline:* 5/1. *Notification:* 6/15. *Contact:* Ms. Lesa Loritts, Associate Director of Transfer Admission, 617-552-3295.

CONTACT

Mr. John L. Mahoney Jr., Director of Undergraduate Admission, Boston College, Chestnut Hill, MA 02167-9991, 617-552-3100 or toll-free 800-360-2522. *E-mail:* admissions@bcvms.bc.edu. *Web site:* http://www.bc.edu/. College video and electronic viewbook available.

Recommended Supplement: *International Handbook of Universities*

If you wish to get information on this publication (ISBN 3-11-013907-3), which is published every two years by the International Association of Universities (IAU), call France: (33-1) 45 68 25 45; fax: (33-1) 47 34 76 05.

Reference Navigator

Web site: http://www.macmillan-press.co.uk   CD-ROM: not available

E-mail: IUTRA@FRUNES21   Library Reference Number:

Database: see Web site

This very handy book, over 1,300 pages long, is a quick guide to all the degree-granting institutions of university level in 169 countries and territories and comprises over 4,000 individual entries. A second source of information may be obtained on "Other Institutions of Higher Education" (the *World List of Universities,* published by IAU) containing more than 9,000 entries. The difference between the two categories of institutions is based solely on the distinction made for each country by the competent national higher education body that provided the authoritative information for the *World List* entries.

The institutional entries within each country are generally listed in geographical order, by town or province, with postal address and telecommunication information. The name of each institution is systematically given first in English, followed by the name in the national language(s) in italics, where appropriate.

The lists of faculties, colleges, departments, schools, institutes, and so on are intended primarily as a guide to the academic structure of the institutions of which they are a part.

These are followed by brief descriptions of the history and structure of the institutions and by notes on cooperation with university institutions in other countries.

Admission requirements are usually listed for courses leading to a first degree or similar qualification; special requirements for admission to studies leading to higher degrees and specialized diplomas are indicated where appropriate.

The names of degrees, diplomas, and professional qualifications are generally given in the language of the country concerned. The duration of studies, indicated in years or semesters, is normally the minimum period required. Translations into English of fields of study are included where they are likely to be helpful.

The tables on the composition of academic staff follow a descending order of rank, and the respective titles are given in the language of the country concerned.

Information on fees, language of instruction, size of staff, and student enrollment, plus volumes in the library are also included.

Some Information on the GMAT and TOEFL Examinations

Graduate Management Admissions Test

The *GMAT Bulletin* is prepared for people who will take the Graduate Management Admissions Test to apply for admission to graduate schools of management. The policies, fees, and procedures described in this edition of *Business Research Sources* apply to all aspects of the GMAT program for the 1997–98 academic year. Their fees are subject to change without notice.

Reference Navigator

Web site: http://www.gmat.org

E-mail: gmat@ets.org

Database: See Web site

CD-ROM: available

Fax: (609) 883-4349

The GMAT is sponsored and directed by the Graduate Management Admissions Council, consisting of representatives of 121 graduate schools of management. The council provides information to schools and prospective students to help both make reasoned choices in the admission process. Educational Testing Service (ETS) consults with the council about general policy, develops test material, administers the test, and conducts research projects to improve the test. For information contact ETS at (609) 771-7330. The GMAT is designed to help graduate schools of business assess the qualifications of applicants for advanced study in business and management. GMAT scores are used by nearly 1,300 graduate management programs throughout the world, and about 850 schools require GMAT scores from each applicant. But GMAT scores are only *one* predictor of academic performance in the first year of graduate management school.

The GMAT test consists of nine separately timed sections: two 30-minute writing tasks and seven 25-minute multiple-choice sections. The GMAT measures general verbal, mathematical, and analytical writing skills that are developed over a long period and are associated with success in the first year of study at graduate schools of management. It does not presuppose any specific knowledge of business or of other specific content areas. It does not measure achievement in any particular subject area.

Test of English as a Foreign Language

Reference Navigator

Web site: http://www.ets.org

E-mail: toefl@ets.org

Database: see Web site

CD-ROM: available

Fax: (609) 771-7500

The TOEFL evaluates the English proficiency of people whose native language is not English. The test uses a multiple-choice format to measure the ability to understand North American English. The test consists of three sections:

- Listening comprehension—measures ability to understand English as it is spoken in North America.
- Structure and written expression—measures ability to recognize language that is appropriate for standard written English.
- Reading comprehension—measures ability to understand nontechnical reading matter.

For more information about TOEFL, call (609) 771-7100.

Getting Ready for the Big Day

It might be best if you considered using a test-preparation company to help you get ready for your exams. There are a number around, and one good one is The Princeton Review (1-800-2-Review) or try on the Web at http://www.review.com. The Princeton Review's Web site includes information on GRE, GMAT, TOEFL test dates, topics, and scores. One of the publications you should look at is *Cracking the GMAT 1997,* which gives information on strategic shortcuts for the math and verbal sections. Another useful source is: Student Advantage Guide to The Best Business Schools 1997 (ISBN 0-679-77125-5).

13   AMERICAN HERITAGE

Description of Publication

For information on this monthly (and bimonthly) publication (ISSN 0002-8738) call Forbes and American Heritage at (800) 888-9896, or (212) 620-2200.

 Reference Navigator

Web site: http://www.americanheritage.com

E-mail: mail@americanheritage.com

Database: not available

CD-ROM: not available

Library Reference Number:

As Ralph Waldo Emerson put it, "The years teach much which the days never know." Feeling the need for a business historical perspective in this textbook, I wanted to include a magazine called *Audacity,* but it has, unfortunately, been discontinued. The mission of *Audacity* was to make connections between yesterday and today, and thereby help business and government leaders move more confidently and knowledgeably into tomorrow.

Its parent, the venerable *American Heritage,* is still with us (since 1954) and a source of considerable value and interest for business historians. It is approximately 115 pages, replete with interesting stories and anecdotes from America's past, with great black-and-white pictures and only a few ads. There are usually four or five substantial articles averaging 25 or so pages each, which makes the journal quite useful for reference research. One special section in each edition, called "The Business of America," gives small vignettes (two to three pages) into the chronicles of America's business past; for example, "The Atlantic Stakes," by John Steele Gordon (The most glamorous business of the industrial era almost always lost money. But nobody paid a steeper price than Edward Knight Collins).

American Heritage is formatted well, a pleasure to read, and informative. For those who put stock in a liberal arts education and employ the tools of business,

American Heritage is an excellent choice. Another product from the same publisher is *American Heritage of Invention & Technology* (ISSN 8756-7296) and has as its founding sponsor General Motors. The history of technological innovation offers valuable lessons about the nature of progress and the roots of problems facing America.

One more source that should not be overlooked is *Great Events from History II: Business and Commerce Series* (ISBN 0-89356-813-9) from the Magill family of reference books. The current five volumes of *Great Events* address the major developments in the worldwide evolution of business and commerce in the 20th century. The history of business and commerce provides a unique perspective on history as a whole, showing how economic life progressed and describing the forces that shaped it. The articles in *Great Events from History II: Business and Commerce* are arranged chronologically by date of event, beginning in 1897 with the first publication of the Dow Jones Industrial Average and ending in 1994 with the effective date of the North American Free Trade Agreement. A broad range of topics is addressed. Business is defined broadly to include any activity concerned with the production of goods or with the rendering of financial or other services. Commerce involves the exchange of commodities or services.

Significant 20th century events in the evolution of all these aspects of business and commerce are described in 374 articles, arranged chronologically in five volumes. The articles run a little long, to approximately 2,500 words. Each article begins with ready-reference matter listing the category of the event discussed, from advertising to transportation; a brief summary of the event's significance in the history of business and commerce; and descriptions of principal personages who were key players in the event. The text of each article follows and is divided into two subsections: "Summary of Event" describes the event itself and the circumstances leading up to it, and "Impact of Event" analyzes the influence of the event on the evolution of business practice and/or a major industry in both the short and long terms. There follows a select bibliography, which lists publications to consult for further information, accompanied by annotations indicating the focus and usefulness of each source, chosen for relevance to the topic in question and accessibility through most libraries.

The Business of America

By John Steele Gordon

The Atlantic Stakes

The most glamorous business of the industrial era almost lost money. But nobody paid a steeper price than Edward Knight Collins.

When I was a child, the most magical day of the year for me was the one—usually a week or two after New Year's—when my grandparents would leave on their annual trip to someplace warm. My brother and I got a day off from school, and a hired car took everyone to the piers that then lined the West Side of Manhattan for several miles. There we would board a passenger ship bound for the Mediterranean, South Africa, Hong Kong, or some other place as distant from New York as it was exotic to my young mind.

There would be a small party in my grandparents' cabin; my grandfather would take us around to inspect the ship, and I would wave to the people on the pier far below, pretending that I was going too. Then, inevitably, the loudspeakers would begin announcing departure, and visitors were asked to disembark. I obediently went along and stood on the pier watching fascinated while tugs pushed the great ship out of her dock and she set off down the Hudson River, headed for the ends of the earth.

I was perhaps too obedient a child, for I have often wondered what would have happened had I simply turned left when everyone else turned right, vanished in the crowd, and hidden out until the ship was past Sandy Hook and had dropped the pilot. To be sure, there would have been hell to pay when I finally got back to New York. But I seriously doubt that whatever the inevitable punishment, it could possibly have been too high a price to pay for such an adventure. But I never got to sail on a passenger ship out of New York Harbor, and by the time I was grown up, almost all were gone, unable to compete with the Boeing 707s that began flying in 1958. One of the most storied and romantic businesses in history simply vanished in less than a decade.

Curiously, the passenger-ship business had a precise beginning. Until 1818 passenger carrying had been nothing more than a supplement to cargo hauling, and ships left when they had full holds. But then a New York merchant named Isaac Wright decided to change things. Engaged in trans-Atlantic trade that required frequent crossings, Wright hated having to wait, so he put up twenty-five thousand dollars—as did each of his four partners—to found the Black Ball Line. According to an early advertisement, it would operate a fleet of vessels "between New York and Liverpool, to sail from each place on a certain day in every month throughout the year." The first ship, the *James Monroe,* left New York on January 5, 1918, right on schedule.

Equally curious, although the United States was present at both the creation and, as we shall see, the end of the passenger-ship business, it was perhaps the only major business of the industrial era that the United States not only did not dominate but, for most of the era, had virtually no role in at all. There was a brief exception to this, in the 1850s, and it involved a now nearly forgotten man, Edward Knight Collins. He would fail utterly in the business and pay a staggering personal price as well, but he would also profoundly affect it.

Though the first regularly scheduled passenger service was in sailing ships, steam quickly replaced sail. But, under steam, the passenger-ship business was seldom really profitable. For most of its existence it depended on the kindness of governments to stay viable. The names of British passenger liners, for instance, were usually preceded by the initials RMS, standing for Royal Mail Steamship (translation: big government subsidies hidden in mail contracts).

Recommended Supplement: *Business History Review*

For information on this quarterly publication (ISSN 0007-6805) call Harvard Business School Publishing Corporation at (617) 495-6154; or fax: (617) 496-5985.

Reference Navigator

Web site: http://www.hbsp.harvard.edu

E-mail: kdonahue@hbsp.harvard.edu

Database: not available

CD-ROM: not available

Library Reference Number:

_____

There is a certain irony to this reference work dealing with history when one realizes how little history about itself is contained within its covers: no mission statement, no vignettes about its founders, and no information about the subject of business history, even in the annual association publication! Surely the editorial board will reconsider the oversight.

Perhaps the most unique aspect of this little green academic publication (the format is very basic with only a few pictures to enliven the imagination) is the large number of book reviews. Each review is done by a different reviewer and includes all the necessary information to call and purchase the book. One would like to believe such scholarly works get reviewed in other venues, but that is not often the case. If one wishes to develop an acquaintance with or build a collection of books on business history, these reviews are an efficient way to do it. Also, the "Editor's Corner" is interesting because it provides information on awards for fellowships, prizes, grants, announcements on pertinent publications dealing with scholarships, and the like. There are approximately four feature articles each amounting to 30 or 40 pages. They are briefly abstracted, heavily footnoted, but user-friendly, nevertheless, and provide for comfortable and informative reading. The spring 1996 issue included "Chain Building: The Consolidation of the American Newspaper Industry, 1953–1980," by Elizabeth MacIver Neiva.

A second publication to consider is the *Journal of The History of Economic Thought* (ISSN 1042-7716) published each spring and fall by the History of Economics Society (HES) since 1974. The Web page address for the HES is http://cs.muohio.edu/HisEcSoc/. The Spring 1997 edition included "Adam Smith on the Virtues: A Partial Resolution of the Adam Smith Problem," by Spencer J. Pack. The publication is approximately 175 pages, with approximately eight reader-friendly articles covering some 15 to 20 pages, including six or seven book reviews. If you would like to offer an article, you can get information at http://www.iup.edu/ec/.

14   THE WORLDLY PHILOSOPHERS

The Lives, Times, and Ideas of the Great Economic Thinkers

Description of Publication

For information on this publication (ISBN 0-671-63318-X) call Touchstone Books, Simon & Schuster, Inc., at (515) 284-6751.

 Reference Navigator

Web site: http://www.pocketbooks.com

E-mail: personal only

Database: see Web site

CD-ROM: not available

Library Reference Number:

_____

> My dog is worried about the economy because Alpo is up to 99 cents a can. That's about $7.00 in dog money.
>
> Joe Weinstein

Robert L. Heilbroner, the author of *The Worldly Philosophers,* is a wonderful writer, and he would enjoy Weinstein's comments about economics. This book is one of Heilbroner's classics, appearing now in its sixth edition. Adam Smith was no slouch in his day either when he wrote *The Wealth of Nations* (see "Recommended Supplement" below). Although the two books are fundamentally different—Heilbroner's being an overview of the lives of the economists whose ideas set in motion the development of the Western world, and Smith's the voluminous investigation of the nature of what was to become capitalism—they both help to explain the paradigms that created the intellectual foundation of our economy.

Unlike communism and socialism, American capitalism had no ideology specifically adopted by the political process, except that government should stay out of its way. Nevertheless, capitalism is the strongest political–economic force on the planet. The two books in this chapter offer a representative perspective on capitalism and the evolution of economic thinking.

If given the chance, I would insist that every business school student would have to read *The Worldly Philosophers* before being allowed to graduate. Two things make this book so enjoyable: (1) the subjects (i.e., the economists themselves) and (2) the storytelling (i.e., the writing should appeal to almost every student). Read how Heilbroner describes these "Great Economists."

> An odder group of men . . . could scarcely be imagined. There were among them a philosopher and a madman, a cleric and a stockbroker, a revolutionary and a nobleman, an aesthete, a skeptic, and a tramp. They were of every nationality, of every walk of life, of every turn of temperament. Some were brilliant, some were bores; some ingratiating, some impossible. At least three made their own fortunes, but as many could never master the elementary economics of their personal finances. Two were eminent businessmen, one was never much more than a traveling salesman, another frittered away his fortune.
>
> Their viewpoints toward the world were as varied as their fortunes—there was never such a quarrelsome group of thinkers. One was a lifelong advocate of women's rights; another insisted that women were demonstrably inferior to men. One held that "gentlemen" were only barbarians in disguise, whereas another maintained that non-gentlemen were savages. One of them—who was very rich—urged the abolition of riches; another—quite poor—disapproved of charity. Several of them claimed that with all its shortcomings, this was the best of all possible worlds; several others devoted their lives to proving that it wasn't.
>
> All of them wrote books, but a more varied library has never been seen. One or two wrote best sellers that reached to the mud huts of Asia; others had to pay to have their obscure works published and never touched an audience beyond the most restricted circles. A few wrote in language that stirred the pulse of millions; others—no less important to the world—wrote in prose that fogs the brain.
>
> Thus it was neither their personalities, their careers, their biases, nor even their ideas that bound them together. Their common denominator was . . .

I hope you will want to read on in this book and in others, such as John Kenneth Galbraith's *The New Industrial State* or Jude Waniski's *How the World Works*.

According to the editors, more than 2 million copies of Heilbroner's universally celebrated book have been sold in five editions and in two dozen languages. For over 35 years it has been the standard text in hundreds of economics courses, educating and entertaining millions of readers, teachers, and students alike.

> If ever a book answered a crying need, this one does. Here is all the economic lore most general readers conceivably could want to know, served up with a flourish by a man who writes with immense vigor and skill; who has a rare gift for simplifying complexities.
>
> The *New York Times*

VIII
The Savage Society of Thorstein Veblen

One hundred and twenty-five years had now passed since *The Wealth of Nations* appeared in 1776, and in that span of time it seemed as if the great economists had left no aspect of the world unexamined: its magnificence or its squalor, its naïveté or its sometimes sinister overtones, its grandiose achievements in technology or its often mean shortcomings in human values. But this many-sided world, with its dozens of differing interpretations, had nonetheless one common factor. It was European. For all its changing social complexion, this was still the Old World, and as such it insisted on a modicum of punctilio.

Thus it was not without significance that when Dick Arkwright, the barber's apprentice, made his fortune in the spinning jenny he metamorphosed into Sir Richard; the threat to England's traditional reign of gentlemanliness was nicely solved by inducting such parvenus wholesale into the fraternity of gentle blood and manners. The parvenus, it is true, brought with them a train of middle-class attitudes and even a strain of antiaristocratic sentiment, but they brought with them, as well, the sneaking knowledge that there was a higher social stratum than that attainable by wealth alone. As countless comedies of manners testified, there was a difference between the beer baron, with all his millions and his purchased crest, and the impoverished but. . .

Recommended Supplement: *An Inquiry Into the Nature and Causes of the Wealth of Nations*

Political economy had been studied long before Adam Smith, but the *Wealth of Nations* may be said to constitute it for the first time as a separate science. The work was based on considerable historical knowledge, and its principles were worked out with skill and ingenuity. Despite more than two centuries of criticism, new facts, and fresh experiences, the work still stands as the best all-around statement and defense of some of the fundamental principles of the science of economics.

Perhaps the most notable feature of the teaching of the *Wealth of Nations,* from the point of view of its divergence from previous economic thought as well as of its subsequent influence, is the statement of the doctrine of natural liberty. Smith believed that "man's self-interest is God's providence" and held that if government abstained from interfering with free competition, industrial problems would work themselves out and the practical maximum of efficiency would be reached. This same doctrine was applied to international relations, and Smith's development of it is the classical statement of the argument for free trade.

Smith wrote the *Wealth of Nations* in five books:

Book I: Of the Causes of Improvement in the Productive Power of Labour, and of the Order According to which its Produce Is Naturally Distributed Among the Different Ranks of the People.

Book II: Of the Nature, Accumulation, and Employment of (Capital) Stock.

Book III: Of the Different Progress of Opulence in Different Nations.

Book IV: Of Systems of Political Economy

Book V: Of the Revenue of the Sovereign or Commonwealth.

To explain in what has consisted the revenue of the great body of the people, or what has been the nature of those funds, which, in different ages and nations, have supplied their annual consumption, is the object of these Four first Books. The Fifth and last Book treats of the revenue of the sovereign, or commonwealth.

Adam Smith

III DIRECTORIES, ALMANACS, PERIODICALS, INDEXES, AND ENCYCLOPEDIAS

Optional Economic References

- *Economics, Bibliographic Guide to Reference Books and Information Sources*
- *Environmental Economics*
- *Encyclopedia of Economics*
- *Economic Handbook of the World*
- *Encyclopedia of American Economic History*
- *The Student Economist's Handbook*
- *Handbook of United States Economic and Financial Indicators*
- *Journal of Economic Literature*
- *American Economist*
- *Journal of Comparative Economics*

15　Directories

Description of Publication: *Directory of Business Information*

If you would like information on this publication (ISBN 0-471-59816-X) call John Wiley & Sons, Inc., at (800) 526-5368 or (212) 850-6000.

 Reference Navigator

Web site: http://www.wiley.com

E-mail: info@jwiley.com

Database: See Web site

CD-ROM: not available

Library Reference Number:

_____

This very useful text authored by Lawrence Rasie complements Michael Lavin's *Business Information.* It is not intended to describe sources, but instead lists business sources usually with address and telephone numbers plus other resources, including electronic formats (CD-ROM and on-line) and microfilm, which are not included in Lavin's book (see also Chapter 19).

According to Rasie, business sources now appear in a bewildering variety. You must choose among business newspapers, business journals, on-line indexes, on-line abstracts of articles, on-line full-text copies of articles, CD-ROM indexes, CD-ROM abstracts of articles, CD-ROM full-text copies of articles, plus microfilm copies of materials, and more.

Rasie's book helps to tie it all together. It presents direct links from conventional sources you know to thousands of printed indexes, on-line databases, and CD-ROM databases. It's a network of direct links to advanced research technology, source by source, topic by topic—across the entire business spectrum. Unfortunately, not all of the citations have telephone numbers and addresses. (See *Business Phone Book USA* mention in this chapter.)

A sample citation for *The Economist* (see Chapter 43) demonstrates this network of specific sources (abbreviations for the format of databases are: *ind* = indexing only; *abs* = abstracts of articles; and *ful-tx* = full text articles):

The Economist. Economist Newspaper NA Inc.

This weekly offers world business and economic coverage. Edited for management, it has a reportorial and analytical approach to business, economy, finance, and politics. Very helpful on the global economy. Regular section "Economic and Financial Indicators" focuses on selected countries.

It's indexed in BPI, F&S, EnvironAbs, MgmtMark-Abs(abs), PAIS, Promt(abs), SocSciInd, and TextilTechDigst (abs).

It's on-line with ABI(ful-tx), AcadInd, BPI(ind,abs), DatTim(ful-tx), Dowj (some ful-tx), F&S, LEXIS-NEXIS(ful-tx), MagInd(ful-tx), MgmtMarkAbs(abs), Ne4wsPerAbs (abs), PAIS(abs), SocSciInd(ind,abs), and TradInduInd (ful-tx).

It's on CD-ROM with ABI(abs), AcadInd, Acad-Abs(ful-tx), AcadSerch(abs), BPI, BusI(ful-tx), BusSorce (ful-tx), F&S, MagArtSums(abs), MgmtMarkAbs, MagInd, PAIS, and SocSciInd. It's on microfilm with UMI.

The book has four major parts, each with sources for various kinds of business information. Part I describes general sources covering many business topics. These sources are good for simple research and as a launching pad for complex research. Chapter 1 describes general databases and broad business databases, directories, yearbooks, business newspapers and periodicals, major business broadcasts and transcripts, business statistics, prepared market research, and general management sources. Chapter 2 describes specialized databases for business research, such as *Dow Jones News/Retrieval, PROMT*, and *Social Science Index*.

Part II covers three essential business and investment topics: the economy, industries, and leading companies. It provides business and investment sources for the national economy, 350 leading industries, and their top companies. Chapter 3 helps readers navigate these unfamiliar waters. It starts with a brief summary or abstract of the overall economy, including future projections for several years. It also includes broad sources for the economy, industries, companies, and investments. Chapter 4 describes specific industries in a separate section. It summarizes the status and outlook for each, lists the top companies in each, and describes specialized sources of information for each. Chapter 4 also includes some general business functions, such as advertising and marketing and general management services.

Part III covers specific business functions:

- Chapter 5 for new and small business.
- Chapter 6 for international business.
- Chapter 7 for sources in the federal government.
- Chapter 8 for selected topics from antiques to taxes.

Part IV covers business in the 50 states and libraries in the 50 states. Chapter 9 covers state and regional information. The chapter begins with broad sources that have information about all states or regions. Then, each state has its own separate section. Each begins with a brief abstract describing the state's economy and its outlook for several years. Next are key business sources in that state, including state government offices important to business, state data centers and local/regional publications, and the like. Each section concludes with a list of the 10 or so largest companies (by revenue) in that state. A second list names the leading employers within that state. Chapter 10 lists the largest public libraries and college libraries in every region of the country. The Appendix lists major publishers whose works are cited throughout the book.

A company that specializes in lists is American Business Information, Inc. located in Omaha, Nebraska, (402) 593-4600. In its 23 years of existence, it has been perhaps the leading provider of sales leads to businesses. A staff of approximately 300 people compile information from more than 5,000 *Yellow Pages, Business White Pages,* and other public sources. And, according to their representatives, they make over 14 million phone calls a year to verify the database and to collect additional information. Of particular interest is the American Business Directories division (Internet e-mail: directory@abii.com), which publishes over 2,000 different business directories. If you would like to see a sample page from a specific directory just call. The directories include:

- Business name, address, and phone number.
- Name of owner or manager and number of employees.
- Sales volume and credit rating codes.

PART III

SOURCES FOR SPECIFIC BUSINESS TOPICS

PART IV

STATES AND REGIONS; LARGER LIBRARIES

JOURNAL OF BUSINESS STRATEGY

Warren Gorham & Lamont Inc.

Practical, well written articles aimed at managers responsible for strategic business planning. Looks at decisions and activities from practical point of view. Core issues explored in depth.

It's indexed in Anbar (abs), BPI, HospLitInd, Mgmt-MarkAbs, PAIS, and WorkRelatAbs (abs).

It's online with ABI (abs), BPI (ind, abs), MgmtCntnts (abs), MgmtMarkAbs (abs) (on PIRA), and PAIS (abs).

It's on CD-ROM with ABI, AcadSerch (abs), BPI, BusI, BusSorce (abs), MagSerch (abs), MgmtMarkAbs (on PIRA), and PAIS.

It's on microfilm with BusColl and UMI.

MERGERS & ACQUISITIONS

MLR Enterprises Inc. 6/yr.

Covers techniques, news and trends in mergers, acquisitions and leveraged buyouts of U.S. companies.

It's indexed in Anbar (abs), BPI, and PAIS.

It's online with ABI (abs), BPI (ind, abs), LEXIS-NEXIS (ful-tx), PAIS (abs), and TradInduInd (ind, ful-tx).

It's on CD-ROM with ABI, AcadSerch (abs), Anbar (abs), BPI, BusI, BusSorce (abs), and MagSerch (abs).

It's on microfilm with BusColl and UMI.

MONEY

Time Inc. Magazine Co.

Written for the layman, this popular magazine covers personal finance, investment recommendations and current financial and business topics. Has yearly rankings of individual stock and bond mutual funds.

It's indexed in BPI and ReadGidePerLit.

It's online with ABI (ful-tx), AccountTax (ful-tx), Agelin (abs), BPI (ind, abs), DatTim (some ful-tx), Dowj (some ful-tx), MagInd (ind, ful-tx), LEXIS-NEXIS (ful-tx), NewPerAbs (abs), ReadGidePerLit (ind, abs), and TradInduind (ind, ful-tx).

It's on CD-ROM with ABI, AcadAbs (ful-tx), AcadSerch (abs), Agelin, BPI, BusI (ind, ful-tx), BusSorc (ful-tx), MaArtSums (ful-tx), MagInd, MagSerch (abs), PerAbs, and ReadGidePerLit.

It's on microfilm with BusColl and UMI.

MONTHLY LABOR REVIEW

U.S. Dept. of Labor, Bureau of Labor Statistics.

This is a basic publication of in-depth current statistics on employment, hours, wages, Consumer Price Index (retail prices), Producer Price Index (wholesale prices), and more. Each issue includes analysis and 50 pages of current statistics.

It's indexed in AmerStatInd, BPI, F&S, IndEconArts (abs), IndUSGovtPer, PAIS, PredFore (tables, U.S. only), ReadGuidPerLit, SocSciInd, and WorkRelated (abs).

Its online with ABI (ful-tx), AcadInd (ind, ful-tx), AgeLin (abs), BPI (ind, abs), DatTim (some ful-tx), Dowj (some ful-tx), EconLitInd (abs), F&S (ind), LEXIS-NEXIS (some ful-tx), MagInd (ind, ful-tx), NewsPerAbs (abs), PAIS (abs), PredFore (tabular), ReadGidePerLit (ind, abs), SocSciInd (ind, abs), and TradIndInd (ind, ful-tx).

It's on CD-ROM with ABI (abs), AcadInd (ind, ful-tx), AcadAbs (ful-tx), AcadSerch (abs), AgeLine, BPI, BusI (ful-tx), BusSorce (ful-tx), EconLit (abs), F&S, MagInd, MagArtSums (Ful-tx), MagSerch (abs), PAIS, PerAbs, ReadGidePerLit, and SocSciInd.

It's on microfilm with BusColl and UMI.

SALES AND MARKETING MANAGEMENT MAGAZINE

Bill Communications Inc. MO.

Practical articles and statistics of interest to sales, marketing specialists and general managers of large and small companies.

It produces a series of special issues packed with useful current information. They include:

Survey of Buying Power. Gives current U.S. and Canadian population, income, and retail business by metropolitan area, county, and city. Reports disposable income for four income groups and sales in six retail segements, for specific geographical areas.

Survey of Media Markets. Provides population, income, and retail sales data for specific media markets. This is helpful market data for many purposes, such as placing advertising in specific markets.

It's indexed in Anbar (abs), BPI, F&S, UrbanAffAbs (abs), TopMgmtAbs, MgmtBiblio, and MgmtMarkAbs.

It's online in ABI (ful-tx), BPI (ind or abs), DatTim (some ful-tx), Dowj (some ful-tx), F&S (ind), Inspec (abs), LEXIS-NEXIS (some ful-tx), MagInd (ful-tx), MARS, NewsPerAbs (abs), and TradInduInd (ful-tx).

It's on CD-ROM with ABI, AcadSerch (abs), Anbar (abs), BPI, BusInd (ful-tx), BusSorce (abs), MagSerch (abs), and PerAbs.

Recommended Supplement: *Ward's Business Directory of U.S. Private and Public Companies*

Reference Navigator

Web site: http://www.gale.com   CD-ROM: not available

E-mail: galeord@gale.com   Library Reference Number:

Database: See Web site   _____

According to its editors, *Ward's Business Directory of U.S. Private and Public Companies,* (800) 877-GALE, has been the leading source for hard-to-find information on private companies. It lists approximately 135,000 companies—90 percent of which are private. *Ward's* assists market researchers in identifying market participants and analyzing market share; plus, it helps sales managers identify potential clients, create targeted marketing, and determine parent/subsidiary relationships. For you young merger and acquisition specialists, *Ward's* is a valuable tool in analyzing market position and locating specific data on targeted companies.

Ward's Business Directory covers domestic private and public companies in seven volumes. Volumes 1, 2, and 3 provide current company information in a single A–Z arrangement and offer valuable data even on America's smallest companies. In addition to contact information, Volumes, 1, 2, and 3 include:

- Financial figures.
- Number of employees.
- Up to four four-digit SICs with descriptions of products and services offered.
- Up to five executive officers' names and titles.
- Year founded.
- Ticker symbol and stock exchange of publicly traded companies.
- Immediate parent name for corporate tree linkage.

Volume 4 is a geographic listing of the companies in Volumes 1, 2, and 3 (arranged by Zip code within state) and includes:

- Total number of companies, employees, and sales for each state.
- Special features, which offer at-a-glance evaluations of industry activity through rankings and analyses.

Volume 5 offers rankings by sales within SIC codes at the four-digit level. Volume 6 ranks companies by sales within 1987 SIC codes at the four-digit level, arranged by state, and provides an alphabetic company name index.

Another Gale Research Inc. product is *Ward's Private Company Profiles* (ISSN 1071-9555). Privately held companies account for much of the business activity in the United States and thus play a vital role in our economy. Moreover, many innovative products, services, marketing tactics, and management styles originate in these enterprises. It seems somehow ironic, then, that comprehensive information about private companies is difficult to locate.

As any good business student knows, public companies are required by law to reveal detailed information (see Chapter 28) about their business, finances, and operations. From these reports, which are widely available, a plethora of reference sources are published. Private companies are not obliged to release such information, so researchers must pore through a variety of sources to gain a true portrait of a private company.

The basic company data in *Ward's Private Company Profiles (WPCP)* was culled from *Ward's Business Directory of U.S. Private and Public Companies*, which lists more than 135,000 U.S. companies. The primary components of *WPCP* entries are articles and excerpts from a broad range of sources including *Cleveland Plain Dealer, Business Week,* and *Graphic Arts Monthly.*

Volume 1 of the annual series covers 150 privately held U.S. companies (see also: *Hoover's Handbooks* in Chapter 2). These companies represent the full spectrum of economic activity in the United States, from agriculture to construction to retailing to transportation.

A great deal of useful reference material is made available, including:

- Address and phone number, including fax, telex, and toll-free numbers.
- SIC numbers, parent company, number of employees, sales, revenues, etc.
- Excerpted and full-text articles arranged under topical headings, such as corporate overview, historical information, management; corporate operations, product/service news, employee news; corporate citizenship, environmental practices, and community relations, etc.

Anytime someone says *directory* most people will think *telephone*. That being the case, it seems natural that a phone directory is included in this section. According to its editors, *Business Phone Book USA,* formerly *The National Directory of Addresses and Telephone Numbers,* lists the largest and most important businesses, organizations, agencies, and institutions in the United States, as well as a selected number of high-profile individuals. The present edition (19th) contains more than 122,000 individual listings, presented both alphabetically by name and a classified subject arrangement.

Listings in *Business Phone Book USA* provide the company or organization name, address, and telephone number, and most include fax numbers. Toll-free telephone numbers are given where available; and electronic mail and World Wide Web addresses and Internet resources are also provided.

The *Business Phone Book USA's* best assets include:

- World Wide Web addresses for nearly 8,000 listings.
- E-mail addresses for more than 4,000 listings.
- Toll-free telephone numbers for some 33,000 listings.
- Top lists (e.g., *Forbes* 200 Best Small Companies in America).
- Time zone map; mileage chart; airport codes; federal information center.

While the principal emphasis of listings in *Business Phone Book USA* is on businesses, extensive listings also are provided for organizations that serve as important information resources for businesses, including:

Associations and organizations	Chambers of commerce
Colleges and universities	Consulates and embassies
Convention centers	Foundations
Government agencies	Libraries
Magazines, newsletters, newspapers	Military bases
Political organizations	Research centers
TV news and talk shows	UN agencies and missions

An example of a listing would be:

MacArthur John D & Catherine T Foundation
140 S Dearborn St. Chicago, Il. 60603 312 726-8000 fax 920-6235
Toll free: 800 662 8004 http://www.macfdn.org gopher.macfdn.org:3016/1

Something to Do

One very useful telephone number is that which lists all organizations listed on the 1- (800) directory: 1 (800) 555-1212. One number you may not think to call too often is the White House. Also, you can e-mail the president himself. Can you find the telephone number and e-mail address of the White House? Can you find the telephone number of *Business Phone Book USA*?

Description of Publication: *International Directory of Company Histories*

Information on this publication (ISBN 1-55862-342-6) may be obtained by calling St. James Press, Detroit, Michigan, at (313) 534-7730.

Reference Navigator

Web site: http://www.gale.com   CD-ROM: available

E-mail: galeord@gale.com   Library Reference Number:

Database: Dialog

International Directory of Company Histories provides detailed information on the development of the world's largest and most influential companies. *Company Histories* has covered more than 2,500 companies in 14 volumes. Most companies chosen for inclusion in *Company Histories* have achieved a minimum of $100 million in annual sales and are leading influences in their industries or geographical locations. State-owned companies that are important in their industries and that may operate much like public or private companies are also included. Wholly owned subsidiaries and divisions are presented if they meet the requirements for inclusion.

Each entry begins with a company's legal name, the address of its headquarters, its telephone number and fax number, and a statement of public, private, state, or parent ownership. A company with a legal name in both English and the language of its headquarters country is listed by the English name, with the native-language name in parentheses.

Also provided are the company's founding or earliest incorporation date, the number of employees, and the most recent sales figures available. Sales figures are given in local currencies with equivalents in U.S. dollars. For some private companies, sales figures are estimates. The entry lists the exchanges on which a company's stock is traded, as well as the company's principal Standard Industrial Classification codes.

Something to Do

An interesting aside could be had by reviewing Chapter 13's *Great Events from History II: Business and Commerce Series*. If you are looking at the *International Directory of Company Histories,* you may also need to peruse some substantial material about the history of the company you are studying.

Preface   page ix
List of Abbreviations   xi

Company Histories

122

Abercrombie & Fitch Co.
Abercrombie & Fitch Co.

Four Limited Parkway East
P.O. Box 182168
Columbus, Ohio 43218-2168
U.S.A.
(614) 577-6500
Fax: (614) 577-6565

Wholly Owned Subsidiary of The Limited, Inc.
Incorporated: 1904
Sales: $165 million (1994)
Employees: 1,000
SICs: 5611 Men and Boys Clothing & Accessory Stores;
5621 Women's Clothing Stores; 5632 Women's Accessory & Specialty Stores; 5947 Gift, Novelty & Souvenir Shops

During the first half of the 20th century Abercrombie & Fitch Co. was the definitive store for America's sporting elite, outfitting big-game hunters, fishermen, and other adventurers. After the chain went bankrupt in 1977, Oshman's Sporting Goods revived the Abercrombie & Fitch name but shifted its focus to more contemporary sporting goods and a wider array of apparel for men and women. The Limited, Inc., after acquiring the company in 1988, eliminated sporting goods entirely.

THE EARLY YEARS

Abercrombie & Fitch Co. was founded in 1892 in New York City by David T. Abercrombie and Ezra H. Fitch. Abercrombie, a former prospector, miner, trapper, and railroad surveyor or engineer, owned a small shop and factory producing camping equipment in lower Manhattan. Fitch, one of his customers, was a successful lawyer in Kingston, New York, but the outdoors was his chief interest.

The partners were ill matched. Fitch was the visionary of the two, anticipating a clientele far broader than merely those who camped out in the course of earning a living. Furthermore, both men were hot-tempered. Following the latest of many long and violent arguments, Abercrombie resigned in 1907 to return to manufacturing camping equipment. Fitch continued with

other partners. In 1909 he mailed out 50,000 copies of a 456-page catalogue. Since they cost a dollar each to produce, they almost bankrupted the company, but the subsequent flood of orders justified the expense. In 1917 Abercrombie & Fitch moved into a 12-story building on Madison Avenue at East 45th Street, a location the advertising department described as "Where the Blazed Trail Crosses the Boulevard." It included a luxuriously furnished log cabin that Fitch made his town house, with an adjoining casting pool.

By this time Abercrombie & Fitch's reputation as purveyor to the sporting elite already was well established. It had equipped Theodore Roosevelt for an African safari and also outfitted, or was soon going to outfit, polar expeditions led by Roald Amundsen and Admiral Richard Byrd and flights made by Charles Lindbergh and Amelia Earhart. Every president from Roosevelt to Gerald Ford eventually would buy something from the store.

ROARING TWENTIES AND DEPRESSION THIRTIES

Fitch retired in 1928, selling his interest in the company to his brother-in-law, James S. Cobb, who became vice president, and an employee Otis L. Guernsey, who became vice president. In his first year at the helm, Cobb acquired a similar New York business, Von Lengerke & Detmold, respected for its European-made sporting guns and fishing tackle, and Von Lengerke & Antoine, the Chicago branch, which became a subsidiary of Abercrombie & Fitch but continued until 1959 under its own name. In 1930 Cobb bought Griffin & Howe, a gunsmith shop. The merchandise that Von Lengerke & Detmold and Griffin & Howe had in stock was added to the Madison Avenue store.

By this time Abercrombie & Fitch was selling outdoor and sporting equipment not only for hunting, fishing, camping, and exploration, but also for skating, polo, golf, and tennis. It also carried a variety of outdoor clothing, boots, and shoes for both men and women and cameras, pocket cutlery, and indoor games. In the 1920s Abercrombie & Fitch became the epicenter of the burgeoning mah-jongg craze and *the* place in New York. . .

Recommended Supplement: *Ulrich's International Periodicals Directory*

If you would like information on this publication (ISBN 0-8352-3537-8) call in the United States 1-(800) 346-6049.

Reference Navigator

Web site: www.silverplatter.com/infoeq.htm   CD-ROM: available

E-mail: info@silverplatter.com   Library Reference Number:

Database: SilverPlatter   _____

For 62 years, *Ulrich's International Periodicals Directory* has been the premier serials reference source. The 33rd edition of *Ulrich's* contains information on more than 210,000 serials published throughout the world, arranged under 967 subject headings. This is a good research tool that you should be familiar with, so get a volume to look through.

The availability of serials in electronic formats, either on-line or on CD-ROM, continues to grow. This edition of *Ulrich's* includes 4,115 serials available exclusively on-line or in addition to hard copy and 1,119 serials available on CD-ROM.

Also included are more than 9,532 titles that are known to have ceased or suspended publication in the last three years.

This edition of *Ulrich's* is arranged within five volumes: the first three volumes comprise the "Classified List of Serials"; the fourth volume contains the "Refereed Serials," "Controlled Circulation Serials," "Serials Available on CD-ROM," "Producer Listing/Serials on CD-ROM," "Serials Available Online," "Cessations," "Index to International Organizations," ISSN, title change, and title indexes. The fifth volume comprises daily and weekly newspapers published in the United States. Ulrich's provides a toll-free number, (800) 346-6049, that subscribers can call to get help in solving particular serial research problems and questions.

The notation, ADONIS™, appearing in a serial entry indicates the availability of that serial for document delivery through ADONIS's service, by permission from the copyright owner. Contact ADONIS USA: (800) 944-6415, or fax: (617) 876-7022 for information.

Something to Think About

If you were searching for an article written in the *Miami Herald,* which of the five *Ulrich* volumes would you look in?

Description of Publication: *Law and Legal Information Directory*

Reference Navigator

Web site: http://www.gale.com/gale.html

E-mail: 72203.1552@compuserve.com

Database: DIALOG

CD-ROM: available

Library Reference Number:

A directory that could prove very useful researching legal information is the *Law and Legal Information Directory* (ISBN 0-8103-69524), which describes organizations, services, programs, and other sources of data about the legal field, bringing together in one work a considerable array of topics on an area of increasing significance to all walks of life. From the casual newspaper reader to the legal professional, everyone is aware of the impact of the law on everyday situations: malpractice for lawyers, dentists, doctors, and even clergy; compliance regulations to avoid gender, racial, or disabilities discrimination; waste disposal directives; and a myriad of other laws with ramifications for social, business, and political activities. *Law and Legal Information Directory* (Gale Research Inc.) profiles a wide range of organizations, services, and programs relating to law and the legal profession. Materials from the 6th edition are organized into 25 chapters, as outlined on the contents page. Of particular note to business students are Chapters 7, Law Schools; 8, Continuing Legal Education; 9, Paralegal Education; 10, Scholarships and Grants; 11, Awards and Prizes; 13, Information Systems and Services; 22, Small Claims Courts; and 23, Corporation Departments of States.

Something to Do

How about perusing a directory of directories? If you can't seem to find the directory you had your heart set on seeing, look up the *Directories in Print*. According to Lavin's book, *Business Information*, this indispensable guide lists over 10,000 directories published in the United States. It is divided into 16 broad categories; however, the majority of listings are for directories of companies and other business-related publications. Hundreds of business activities, for example, are represented by such titles as the *Tent Rental Directory*, the *Sandblasting Companies Directory*, and so on. The emphasis, according to Lavin, is on national and international directories, though some regional publications are described. Another tool for identifying directories is the *Guide to American Directories,* which concentrates on business topics and includes many directories not found in the Gale publications. Entries are arranged alphabetically by subject and accessed by a title index.

(15) Legal Periodicals

This section provides details on the primary journals, legal newspapers, regular law school publications, special subject journals, newsletters, and legal looseleaf services issued in the United States and Canada, as well as certain key international publications in the broad field of law. For further information on content, arrangement, format, and sources, please consult the Section Descriptions that begin on page ix.

A

A-E LEGAL NEWSLETTER. Monthly. Victor O. Schinnerer and Company Incorporated, Two Wisconsin Circle, Chevy Chase, Maryland 20815

A-G REPORT. Monthly. National Association of Attorneys General, 444 North Capitol Street, Northwest, #403, Washington, D.C. 20001

AALJ NEWSLETTER. Bimonthly. Association of Administrative Law Judges, 200 West Adams, #510, Chicago, Illinois 60606.

AAMA WASHINGTON REPORT. Biweekly. American Apparel Manufacturers Association, 2500 Wilson Boulevard, #301, Arlington, Virginia 22201-3816.

ABA/BNA LAWYER'S MANUAL ON PROFESSIONAL CONDUCT. Looseleaf service. Bureau of National Affairs, Incorporated, 1231 25th Street, Northwest, Washington, D.C. 20037.

ABA JUVENILE AND CHILD WELFARE REPORTER. Twelve times per year. American Bar Association, National Legal Resource Center for Child Advocacy and Protection, 1800 M Street, Northwest, Washington, D.C. 20036.

ABA LAWYER'S TITLE GUARANTY FUNDS NEWSLETTER. Irregular. John Atkinson Foundation, 750 North Lake Shore Drive, Chicago, Illinois 60611-4497.

ABA MONOGRAPH SERIES. Three to nine publications per year. University of Tulsa, College of Law, 3120 East Fourth Place, Tulsa, Oklahoma 74104.

ABA RETAIL BANKER. Twelve times per year. American Bankers Association, 1120 Connecticut Avenue, Northwest, Washington, D.C. 20036.

ABA STANDARDS FOR CRIMINAL JUSTICE, 2nd Edition. Looseleaf service. Little Brown and Company, Law Division, 34 Beacon Street, Boston, Massachusetts 02106.

ABA WASHINGTON LETTER. Monthly. American Bar Association, 1800 M Street, Northwest, Washington, D.C. 20036.

ABA'S COMPLIANCE SOURCEBOOK. Looseleaf service. American Bankers Association, 1120 Connecticut Avenue, Northwest, Washington, D.C. 20036.

ABDOMINAL INJURIES (COURTROOM MEDICINE SERIES). Looseleaf service. Matthew Bender and Company, Incorporated, 11 Penn Plaza, New York, New York 10001.

ABI BULLETIN. Fifteen to twenty-five times per year. American Bankruptcy Institute, 107 Second Street, Northeast, Washington, D.C. 20002.

ABI NEWSLETTER. Six times per year. American Bankruptcy Institute, 107 Second Street, Northeast, Washington, D.C. 20002.

ABLA NEWSLETTER. Two times per year. American Business Law Association, c/o Saginaw Valley State University, University Center, Michigan 48720.

ABLE ADVOCATE, THE. Two times per year. American Bar Association, Young Lawyers Division, 750 North Lake Shore Drive, Chicago, Illinois 60611.

ABSTRACTS OF BOOK REVIEWS IN CURRENT LEGAL PERIODICALS. Semimonthly. Brigham Young University, Office of Student Programs, 4th Floor, Provo, Utah 84602.

ABSTRACTS OF LEGAL PERIODICALS; CORPORATE & SECURITIES EDITION. Monthly. Legal Abstracts Publishers, Incorporated, Post Office Box 1363, Brookline, Massachusetts 01246.

ACA UPDATE. Twelve times per year. American Council for the Arts, 1285 Avenue of the Americas, Floor 3, Area M, New York, New York 10019.

Recommended Supplement: *The Standard Directory of Advertising Agencies*

For information on this annual publication (ISBN 087-217-350-X) call National Register Publishing at (800) 521-8110; or fax: (908) 665-2898.

Reference Navigator

Web site: http://www.reedref.com

E-mail: info@internet.reedref.com

Database: LEXIS-NEXIS

CD-ROM: available

Library Reference Number:

_____

Whether you are a student or with an agency, you will find the "Red Books" to be one of your most important resources. Red Books are a constant source of data for new business development, market research, sales lead generation, job hunting, or just about any other need you may have for locating industry information. *The Standard Directory of Advertising Agencies* contains nearly 9,000 agencies and branch offices. Each listing provides complete contact information, including the corporate Internet and e-mail address and fax numbers, names and e-mail addresses of key executives, association memberships, annual billings with a breakdown by media, number of employees, year founded, new accounts acquired since the last edition was published, and a current client roster. Plus, two new sections listing cyberagencies (agencies involved in Internet site consulting, design, and development) and "Who Owns Whom."

The *Standard Directory of Advertisers* provides in-depth information for more than 24,500 companies that have advertising budgets in excess of $200,000 annually. Based on your primary usage, you can select the directory in either a business classification or geographical format. A separate, complete index listing brand names, SIC codes, product categories by state, and personnel is included. Also available with the *Standard Directory* is Red Books *Plus,* a computer service that allows fast, easy access, via your personal computer, for locating specific data found in the Red Books. You can conduct searches using one, several, or all of the 20 available search criteria. It is, according to the editors, the ideal method for gathering data for market research, lead generation, and competitive and industry analysis.

Something to Think About

How many parts are in the *Directory of Business Information* and what does Chapter 2 describe?

C H A P T E R

16 ALMANACS

Description of Publication: *The World Almanac and Book of Facts 1998*

If you would like information on this publication (ISBN 0-88687-820-9) call PRI-MEDIA Reference, Inc. at (201) 529-6900.

 Reference Navigator

Web site: Not available

E-mail: Walmanac@aol.com

Database: OCLC First Search

CD-ROM: available

Library Reference Number:

_____

The World Almanac, which is completely revised each year, was first published in 1868 and has been published every year since 1886, with the goal of making it a "compendium of universal knowledge." According to the publisher, this book is the most comprehensive, authoritative, and up-to-date information source on the market today, boasting nearly 1,000 fact-filled pages. The "General Index" alone is 29 pages of pretty small print—that's *a lot* of information. The subjects of that information can be seen in the table of contents below. The book includes 16 pages of color news photos and 16 pages of color maps and flags.

One "quick thumb" index divides the book into nine categories:

- Special features, news highlights.
- Economy and business.
- Astronomy and calendar.
- Noted personalities.
- Health and nutrition.

- Science and technology, computer.
- U.S. states and cities.
- Nations of the world.
- Sports

Categories of specific business topics within the classifications above include: economics, agriculture, employment, trade and transportation, and consumer information.

There are a great number of facts here, including everything from the world's oldest person to the woman with a lizard attached to her chest. Better keep your mind on your work or you'll become a facts nerd.

Something to Think About

The American Federation of Labor & Congress of Industrial Organizations (AFL–CIO) is listed in the Labor Union Directory as having how many members? Can you name its president?

Public Debt of the U.S.

Source: Bureau of Public Debt, U.S. Dept. of the Treasury

Fiscal year	Debt (billions)	Debt per cap. (dollars)	Interest paid (billions)	% of federal outlays	Fiscal year	Debt (billions)	Debt per cap. (dollars)	Interest paid (billions)	% of federal outlays
1870	$2.4	$61.06	—	—	1979	$826.5	$3,669	$59.8	11.9
1880	2.0	41.60	—	—	1980	907.7	3,985	74.9	12.7
1890	1.1	17.80	—	—	1981	997.9	4,338	95.6	14.1
1900	1.2	16.60	—	—	1982	1,142.0	4,913	117.4	15.7
1910	1.1	12.41	—	—	1983	1,377.2	5,870	128.8	15.9
1920	24.2	228	—	—	1984	1,572.3	6,640	153.8	18.1
1930	16.1	131	—	—	1985	1,823.1	7,598	178.9	18.9
1940	43.0	325	$1.0	10.5	1986	2,125.3	8,774	190.2	19.2
1945	258.7	1,849	3.8	4.1	1987	2,350.3	9,615	195.4	19.5
1950	256.1	1,688	5.7	13.4	1988	2,602.3	10,534	214.1	20.1
1955	272.8	1,651	6.4	9.4	1989	2,857.4	11,545	240.9	21.0
1960	284.1	1,572	9.2	10.0	1990	3,233.3	13,000	264.8	21.1
1965	313.8	1,613	11.3	9.6	1991	3,665.3	14,436	285.5	21.6
1970	370.1	1,814	19.3	9.9	1992	4,064.6	15,846	292.3	21.2
1975	533.2	2,475	32.7	9.8	1993	4,411.5	17,105	292.5	20.8
1976	620.4	2,852	37.1	10.0	1994	4,692.8	18,025	296.3	20.3
1977	698.8	3,170	41.9	10.2	1995	4,974.0	18,930	332.4	22.0
1978	771.5	3,463	48.7	10.6	1996	5,224.8	19,805	344.0	22.0

Note: Through 1976 the fiscal year ended June 30. From 1977 on, the fiscal year ends Sept. 30.

Consumer Price Index

The Consumer Price index (CPI) is a measure of the average change in prices over time of basic consumer goods and services. From Jan. 1978, the Bureau of Labor Statistics began publishing CPI's for 2 population groups: (1) a CPI for all urban consumers (CPI-U), which covers about 80% of the total population; and (2) a CPI for urban wage earners and clerical workers (CPI-W), which covers about 32% of the total population. The CPI-U includes, in addition to wage earners and clerical workers, groups such as professional, managerial, and technical workers, the self-employed, short-term workers, the unemployed, retirees, and others not in the labor force.

The CPI is based on prices of food, clothing, shelter, and fuels; transportation fares; charges for doctors' and dentists' services; drug prices; and prices of the other goods and services bought for day-to-day living. The index currently measures price changes from a designated reference period, 1982-84, which equals 100.0. Use of this reference period began in Jan. 1988.

Consumer Price Indexes, First Half 1997

Source: Bureau of Labor Statistics, U.S. Dept. of Labor

(Data are semiannual averages of monthly figures)

(1982–84=100)	CPI-U (all urban consumers)		CPI-W (urban wage-earners/clerical)	
	1st half 1997	% change 2d half 1996 to 1st half 1997	1st half 1997	% change 2d half 1996 to 1st half 1997
All items	159.9	1.3	157.0	1.2
Food, beverages	157.0	1.2	156.5	1.2
Housing	155.9	1.3	152.6	1.3
Apparel and upkeep	133.3	1.9	132.6	2.0
Transportation	144.7	0.6	144.1	0.3
Medical care	233.4	1.6	232.8	1.6
Entertainment	162.1	1.4	159.5	1.2
Other goods, services	221.8	1.9	218.7	2.1
Services	178.2	1.5	175.3	1.4
Special Indexes				
All items less food	160.5	1.3	157.1	1.2
Commodities less food	133.8	0.8	134.0	0.8
Nondurables	146.1	1.2	145.9	1.2
Energy	111.6	0.0	111.2	–0.1
All items less energy	166.3	1.3	163.4	1.2

Recommended Supplement: *The World Factbook*

For information on this publication (ISBN 0-02-881044-9) call the Central Intelligence Agency at (703) 482-1100; or fax: (703) 613-7871.

Reference Navigator

Web site: http://www.odci.gov/cia   CD-ROM: available

E-mail: Not available   Library Reference Number:

Database: (my guess is they would rather not
have you in it…go to public domain)   _____

The Central Intelligence Agency (CIA) publishes *The World Factbook* annually for the benefit of other government agencies; therefore, the style, format, coverage, and content are designed to meet their specific requirements. The facts about the world are as up-to-date and correct as the U.S. government can make them, which makes this publication particularly useful. All the countries in the world are represented in the book, some with three-page descriptions and some with five or six pages. A small map of each country is shown, with the major cities indicated, plus a scale in kilometers. The description is broken down into the following areas:

Geography	Economy
People	Communications
Government	Defense forces

The descriptions are very brief and exacting. The discussion of the economy is probably the most salient piece for student purposes and is divided into the following areas:

Overview	GDP/fiscal year	Budget
Inflation rate	Unemployment	Exports
External debt	Industrial production	Electricity
Exchange rate	Agriculture	Currency
Economic aid	Illicit drugs	Industries

Want to follow in James Bond's footsteps? The CIA's Career Training Program is one gateway to an overseas career. Qualifications include a bachelor's degree, strong interpersonal skills, the ability to write clearly, and an interest in international affairs.

Something to Do

As an exercise in familiarizing yourself with some of the EU countries' statistics, compare the unemployment and inflation rates in Sweden, Great Britain, Germany, and Italy.

Description of Publication: *Congressional Quarterly Almanac*

For information on this annual publication (ISBN 1-56802-266-2), call Congressional Quarterly, Inc., at (202) 887-6279.

Reference Navigator

Web site: http://www.cq.com   CD-ROM: Not available

E-mail: clientservices@cq.com   Library Reference Number:

Database: Not available   _____

If you want to know what's happening on Capitol Hill, you'd best get familiar with *Congressional Quarterly* (*CQ*) because it reports it all. Anyone interested in politics and business needs to know about this almanac. It's a big book, well over a thousand pages, that draws on reporting and writing done throughout the year by the staffs of the *Congressional Quarterly Weekly Report* and the *Congressional Monitor*. Congressional Quarterly, Inc., is a publishing and information services company and a recognized leader in political journalism. As of this publication date, *CQ* is in the 51st edition, chronicling the course of major legislation and national politics in the first session of the 104th Congress. (*CQ* back issues to 1983 are on the Web.)

The volume includes the following major elements, for example:

• "Inside Congress." The first chapter provides an overview of the year, recounting, for example, the Republicans' takeover of both chambers of Congress. The chapter usually includes statistical information on the session and stories, such as the unique role played by Speaker Newt Gingrich (R, Ga.), about the House and Senate members. Legislation governing Congress as a whole, such as workplace compliance, term limits, and lobbying disclosure, are also included.

• "Legislative Chapters." The next section (nine chapters in this edition) covers the session's legislative action on economics and finance, government and commerce, social policy, defense, and foreign policy.

- "Appropriations." Usually one chapter contains separate stories detailing the substance and legislative history of each of the 13 regular fiscal appropriations bills, as well as an overview of the appropriations process, including the breakdown in negotiations, for example, that twice closed much of the federal government in 1996.
- "Political Report." One chapter covers redistricting, special elections, and governors' races.
- "Appendixes." The volume also includes appendixes on the following topics:

   —"Glossary." A 10-page glossary of terms used in Congress.

   —"Congress and Its Members." A description of the legislative process, membership lists for all committees and subcommittees, and characteristics of Congress.

   —"Vote Studies." Analyses of presidential support, party unity and conservative coalitions patterns, as well as key votes of that particular year.

   —"Texts." Key presidential and other texts.

   —"Public Laws." A complete listing of public laws enacted during the session.

   —"Roll Call Votes." A complete set of roll call vote charts for the House and the Senate during the session.

Another source dealing with comprehensive congressional information is the *Congressional Digest* (ISSN 0010-5899), published by The Congressional Digest Corporation, (202) 333-7332. According to the editors, since 1921 and for three generations, the *Congressional Digest* has continued the tradition set by its founder, Alice Gram Robinson, and her dream of educating fellow citizens by providing an "impartial view of controversial issues in Congress." The masthead proclaims that the *Congressional Digest* is "an independent monthly featuring controversies in Congress, Pro & Con. Not an official organ, not controlled by any party, interest, class or sect." Basically, these folks would like you to know that their perspective on Congress is unbiased, which in Washington is saying a lot. Alice Robinson is a unique personality and provides interesting reading for any young woman (or man) looking for a hero. One of her intentions in founding the *CD* was to inform the woman voter by featuring "opposing views on controversial national questions in facing columns."

Another almanac that could help you navigate the global business and foreign policy community in Washington is *The Washington Almanac of International Trade & Business* (see Chapter 30).

LEGISLATION REDUCES COST OF SBA LOAN PROGRAMS

Lawmakers cleared legislation in late September that reduced the level of federal loan guarantees for small businesses and increased fees on lenders and borrowers. Backers said the bill would reduce the costs to the government of two Small Business Administration (SBA) programs and allow the programs to assist more businesses. President Clinton signed the bill into law Oct. 12 (S 895 — PL 104-36).

House Small Business Committee Chairwoman Jan Meyers, R-Kan., said taxpayers paid $2.74 for each $100 in loans guaranteed by the SBA in 1994. She said that under the bill, the taxpayers' rate would be reduced to $1.06 for each $100 in loan guarantees. The bill was designed to save $255 million over two years in the amount that Congress had to appropriate to cover the loan guarantees. Under credit reform rules enacted in 1990, Congress was required to appropriate a small percentage of the loans guaranteed in a given program was a hedge against defaults.

The main change was to the SBA's popular 7(a) Guaranteed Business Loan Program. The program gave small businesses greater access to commercial bank loans by guaranteeing repayment of a portion of the loan. The SBA guarantee allowed banks to extend the term of a loan for more than the two or three years that was typically offered to small businesses. Under the 7(a) program, a borrower could get a loan term for up to 20 years, though the average term as about 12 years.

Demand for loan guarantees under the program had grown dramatically over the preceding decade, outstripping the funds that were available to support it. In fiscal 1992 and 1993, Congress had provided supplemental appropriations to keep the 7(a) program going. But SBA advocates in Congress were concerned that, with the emphasis on deficit reduciton, funding the program through supplementals had become a thing of the past. Senate sponsor Christopher S. Bond, R-Mo., said the program was due to run out of money Sept. 1.

The bill provided for the SBA to guarantee 80 percent of loans of less than $100,000 and 75 percent on loans that exceeded $100,000. Prior to enactment, the guarantee levels were up to 90 percent for loans of less than $155,000 and up to 85 percent for loans up to $750,000.

The bill also increased the annual fee charged to lenders who sold the guaranteed portion of their loans on the secondary market from 0.4 percent under prior law to 0.5 percent. This fee could not be passed on to the borrower. The bill also established a 0.5 percent fee on the outstanding principal of all 7(a) guaranteed loans that were not sold.

Guarantee fees, imposed when a loan was first granted, were increased to 3 percent on the first $250,000 of the guaranteed amount of the loan, rising to 3.5 percent with the next $250,000. If the guarantee exceeded $500,000, the fee would be 3.9 percent. The fees were paid by the lender but could be passed on to the borrower. Previously, the fee was 2 percent of the guaranteed portion on all loans.

The bill also addressed a second SBA account, the 504 program, which aimed to help small businesses acquire commercial financing for real estate and capital asset acquisition. The measure imposed an annual fee of one-eighth of 1 percent on the outstanding balances of SBA loan guarantees in the 504 program. The implementation of this fee, paid by the borrower, was expected to make the program entirely self-funding.

The bill started in the Senate Committee on Small Business, which approved its version (S 895 — S Rept 104-129) July 13 by a vote of 18–0. Sponsors Bond and Dale Bumpers, D-Ark., won approval by voice vote of an amendment to allow lenders to accept lower guarantee levels in return for lower fees. The Senate passed the bill by voice vote Aug. 11.

In the House, the Small Business Committee gave voice vote approval to its version of the bill (HR 2150 — H Rept 104-239) on Aug. 4. The House passed the measure easily on Sept. 12 by a vote of 405–0. The House then inserted the provisions of HR 2150 into the Senate-passed bill, approved the amended version by voice vote, and sent it to conference. (*Vote 653, p. H-188*)

Meyers said the bill would "significantly simplify the system." She said that the SBA could make an additional $3 billion in new loans without Congress having to appropriate any new funds.

House and Senate conferees agreed on a final bill Sept. 28 (H Rept 104-269). One of the main differences between the two chambers' versions of the bill lay in how the increased annual fees would be calculated. The Senate proposed to calculate fees based on the portion of the loan that was guaranteed by the federal government. The House bill proposed to base the calculation on the total amount of the loan. Conferees accepted the Senate approach. They also included a provision allowing lenders to accept lower guarantee levels.

The Senate adopted the conference report Sept. 28 by voice vote without debate. The House did the same Sept. 29.

Recommended Supplement: *Social Work Almanac*

Reference Navigator

Web site: http://www.naswdc.org

E-mail: info@nasw.org

Database: Not available
(see *U.S. Statistical Abstract*)

CD-ROM: not available

Library Reference Number:

_____

According to the author, Leon Ginsberg, PhD., the second edition of *Social Work Almanac* (ISBN 0-87101-248-0), published by the National Association of Social Workers, (202) 408-8600, makes it easier than ever for human services professionals to find timely social welfare data. Some might ask what social work has to do with business. The answer lies in the social awareness and responsibilities of business. Students can expect that statistics will be required to support their research in this important area, and this book succinctly presents, in one convenient source, the most current statistics related to social work.

Dr. Ginsberg points out that understanding social problems, policies, and programs requires mastery of and knowledge about facts. This is a book, he says, about the major social issues and social programs of the 1990s. It is the second edition of a book that combines national and some international information on population, children, crime and corrections, education, health and mortality, mental health, older adults, and the social work profession itself. It also describes major social welfare and assistance programs, entitlements as well as means-tested benefits, that serve all age groups and address social needs. All people and their societies are in business, whether as consumers or producers.

The book is organized into nine chapters, arranged alphabetically by subject. Not all the information in a chapter is related only to that chapter's subject, because some groups are so important that no one chapter could cover all that needs to be included. For example, although there is no specific chapter on families, which are the central focus of much social work study and practice, every chapter has something to say about families. Most of the material presented comes from data collected, analyzed, and disseminated by researchers and statisticians in the various departments of the U.S. government. The *U.S. Statistical Abstract* (see Chapter 22 of this text) is frequently the source and publishes much of the most current and pertinent data on matters of concern to social workers and corporate strategists involved with the social responsibility of business.

Something to Think About

What do you see as the general assessment of the program called Aid for Families with Dependent Children? Do you see any connection between the thrust of government programs such as these and the American business community?

Description of Publication: *Almanac of Business and Industrial Financial Ratios*

For information on this annual publication call Prentice Hall at (201) 263-7000.

Reference Navigator

Web site: http://www.simonandschuster.com   CD-ROM: not available

E-mail: personal only   Library Reference Number:

Database: not available

Dr. Leo Troy, author of the *Almanac of Business and Industrial Financial Ratios*, is a distinguished professor of economics at Rutgers University and has written the widely praised *Almanac* for more than 20 years.

To the users of financial and operating information—accountants, bankers, business managers, investment and management consultants, lawyers, credit executives, and trade association executives—the *Almanac* gives the answers to such practical and searching questions as: Compared to the industry as a whole and also to corporations of similar size, how well is the company I am now studying performing in its ratio of profit to sales? On net worth? What about costs? What percentage of sales goes to pensions and other benefit plans? How do the company's outlays on compensation of officers, rents, interest, repairs, and advertising compare with the competition? What about internal sources of capital? What share of sales is going to amortization, depreciation, or depletion? And what percentage of net income is held as retained earnings?

Based on the industry's record, the analyst can then ask, are the company's capital allocations in line with competitors? The *Almanac* provides answers to these questions and many others based on corporate activity in the United States as reported in their respective accounting periods and for the most recent year for which authoritative figures derived from tax return data of the Internal Revenue Service are available.

The *Almanac* profiles corporate performance in two analytical tables for each industry. The first table reports the operating and financial information for corporations with and without net income. The second table provides the identical information as the first, but only for those corporations that operated at a profit.

The financial statistics are generated by the U.S. Internal Revenue Service. Computers tabulate the total dollar value of business tax returns line by line. Dr. Troy uses this aggregate data to calculate figures in common size and ratio form (see Chapter 4). The publication appears annually, but there is about a three-year time lag before the IRS data are available. According to Lavin's book, *Business Information*, other weaknesses of the *Almanac* are also a direct consequence of using IRS data. Industry breakdowns are less detailed than those in the RMA *Statement Studies* and from D&B; plus only 180 SIC codes are listed.

Dr. Troy's publication does offer some significant advantages. Data from income statements are more detailed than those found in most other resources. For example, common size analysis for rent, advertising, interest, and other specific expenses are given. Figures are divided into 12 asset-sized categories, plus totals for all companies. In addition to the common size analysis for income and expense items, 10 ratios are calculated. For students doing financial analysis, the availability of these ratios is essential.

Page references to tables for industries with net income are in italic

Agriculture, Forestry, and Fishing
(0400–0600)

Agriculture, forestry, and fishing
Agricultural production   1, 2
Agricultural services, forestry, fishing   3, 4

Mining
(1070–1498)

Metal mining
Copper, lead and zinc, gold and silver ores   5, 6
Other metal mining   7, 8

Coal mining
Coal mining   9, 10

Oil and gas extraction
Crude petroleum, natural gas, and natural gas liquids   11, 12
Oil and gas field services   13, 14

Nonmetallic minerals except fuels
Dimension, crushed, and broken stone, sand and gravel   15, 16
Other nonmetallic minerals, except fuels   17, 18

Construction
(1510–1798)

General building contractors and operative builders
General building contractors   19, 20
Operative builders   21, 22
Heavy construction contractors   23, 24

Special trade contractors
Plumbing, heating, and air conditioning   25, 26
Electrical work   27, 28
Other special trade contractors   29, 30

143

TABLE I
Corporations with and without Net Income

Agriculture, Forestry, and Fishing
0400

Agricultural Production

Money Amounts and Size of Assets in Thousands of Dollars

Item Description for Accounting Period 7/92 through 6/93		Total	Zero Assets	Under 100	100 to 250	251 to 500	501 to 1,000	1,001 to 5,000	5,001 to 10,000	10,001 to 25,000	25,001 to 50,000	50,001 to 100,000	100,001 to 250,000	250,001 and over
Number of Enterprises	1	81725	2466	23113	15653	17126	14091	8431	424	261	91	40	21	9
Revenues ($ in Thousands)														
Net Sales	2	57657688	614304	2326104	3165284	5641046	7651928	12967562	3691471	4816381	3861088	3693241	3889584	5339695
Portfolio Income	3	1454035	6126	53023	100340	152212	256006	369829	99195	127137	32041	59885	87635	110603
Other Revenues	4	3511760	18968	524672	355347	461733	551930	945230	102181	159805	96626	81983	88569	124722
Total Revenues	5	62623483	639398	2903799	3620971	6254991	8459864	14282621	3892847	5103323	3989755	3835109	4065788	5575020
Average Total Revenues	6	766	259	126	231	365	600	1694	9181	19553	43843	95878	193609	619447
Operating Costs/Operating Income (%)														
Cost of Operations	7	57.9	66.2	37.8	32.9	39.9	46.5	49.9	71.4	71.8	79.8	81.2	82.1	63.3
Rent	8	3.9	2.0	13.4	10.3	7.2	6.0	3.8	1.0	1.2	1.2	0.3	0.8	0.9
Taxes Paid	9	2.5	3.5	5.5	3.2	3.4	3.3	2.7	1.8	1.7	1.5	1.3	1.5	1.7
Interest Paid	10	3.3	3.8	3.4	4.7	3.9	4.1	4.4	3.0	2.4	1.8	1.8	2.5	1.6
Depreciation, Depletion, Amortization	11	4.8	8.2	3.6	7.8	6.5	6.2	5.8	3.0	3.5	2.9	3.2	2.8	3.3
Pensions and Other Benefits	12	1.1	0.2	0.6	1.0	1.4	1.0	1.0	0.7	0.8	0.9	0.9	1.6	2.7
Other	13	30.1	20.3	45.9	48.5	43.6	36.8	37.1	21.0	22.8	12.2	12.5	11.3	24.6
Officers Compensation	14	2.9	1.3	14.4	5.1	3.8	3.9	3.4	1.4	1.1	1.2	0.6	0.8	0.5
Operating Margin	15	•	•	•	•	•	•	•	•	•	•	•	•	1.6
Oper. Margin Before Officers Compensation	16	•	•	•	•	•	•	•	•	•	•	•	•	2.1
Selected Average Balance Sheet ($ in Thousands)														
Net Receivables	17	53	•	1	6	18	26	104	757	1751	5351	10566	24721	51950
Inventories	18	80	•	1	8	22	52	183	843	2189	8578	12102	32458	95785
Net Property, Plant and Equipment	19	366	•	18	110	221	436	1141	3499	7225	12385	30743	52823	153081
Total Assets	20	682	•	38	172	358	714	1857	6884	15137	34417	70124	155158	470957
Notes and Loans Payable	21	335	•	33	129	202	315	1038	3572	7394	12115	26285	65615	110171
All Other Liabilities	22	94	•	8	15	23	44	174	1142	2611	10449	19177	41290	117681
Net Worth	23	252	•	-3	28	133	354	645	2170	5133	1853	24663	48253	243105
Selected Financial Ratios (Times to 1)														
Current Ratio	24	1.3	•	0.7	1.2	1.4	1.5	1.1	1.2	1.2	1.7	1.2	1.3	1.7
Quick Ratio	25	0.7	•	0.5	0.9	0.9	0.8	0.6	0.6	0.6	0.7	0.6	0.6	0.6
Net Sales to Working Capital	26	16.1	•	•	35.2	14.5	11.4	30.2	29.3	22.2	6.2	19.2	13.6	7.8
Coverage Ratio	27	1.7	0.7	1.1	1.2	1.3	1.7	1.4	1.8	1.3	2.1	2.1	1.5	5.7
Total Asset Turnover	28	1.0	•	2.7	1.2	0.9	0.8	0.8	1.3	1.2	1.2	1.3	1.2	1.3
Inventory Turnover	29	5.1	•	•	8.3	6.0	4.9	4.2	7.4	6.1	4.0	6.2	4.7	3.9
Receivables Turnover	30	•	•	•	•	•	•	•	•	•	7.9	8.7	7.5	•
Total Liabilities to Net Worth	31	1.7	•	•	5.2	1.7	1.0	1.9	2.2	2.0	1.9	1.9	2.2	0.9

Item Description for Accounting Period 7/92 through 6/93		Total	Zero Assets	Under 100	100 to 250	251 to 500	501 to 1,000	1,001 to 5,000	5,001 to 10,000	10,001 to 25,000	25,001 to 50,000	50,001 to 100,000	100,001 to 250,000	250,001 and over

Selected Financial Factors (in Percentages)

		Total	Zero Assets	Under 100	100 to 250	251 to 500	501 to 1,000	1,001 to 5,000	5,001 to 10,000	10,001 to 25,000	25,001 to 50,000	50,001 to 100,000	100,001 to 250,000	250,001 and over
Debt Ratio	32	63.0	•	•	83.7	63.0	50.4	65.3	68.5	66.1	65.6	64.8	68.9	48.4
Return on Assets	33	5.7	•	10.1	6.7	4.7	5.3	5.2	6.7	3.8	4.6	5.0	4.5	11.5
Return on Equity	34	4.1	•	•	3.7	2.0	3.5	3.2	7.3	0.1	3.9	4.5	3.0	11.7
Return Before Interest on Equity	35	15.4	•	•	•	12.6	10.6	15.0	21.2	11.1	13.4	14.2	14.4	22.2
Profit Margin, Before Income Tax	36	2.2	•	0.4	1.0	1.2	2.8	1.9	2.3	0.7	2.0	2.0	1.3	7.5
Profit Margin, After Income Tax	37	1.5	•	•	0.5	0.8	2.3	1.3	1.8	•	1.1	1.2	0.8	4.8

Trends in Selected Ratios and Factors, 1987–1996

		1987	1988	1989	1990	1991	1992	1993	1994	1995	1996
Cost of Labor (%)	38	4.1	5.4	4.6	4.1	4.3	4.2	4.5	4.4	4.8	4.9
Operating Margin (%)	39	•	•	•	•	•	•	•	•	•	•
Oper. Margin Before Officers Comp. (%)	40	•	•	•	•	•	•	•	•	•	•
Average Net Receivables ($)	41	43	45	47	46	40	48	51	51	47	53
Average Inventories ($)	42	57	56	53	55	67	73	75	80	74	80
Average Net Worth ($)	43	171	178	176	190	193	209	226	234	231	252
Current Ratio (×1)	44	1.0	1.0	1.0	1.1	1.1	1.2	1.3	1.2	1.2	1.3
Quick Ratio (×1)	45	0.5	0.5	0.6	0.6	0.6	0.6	0.7	0.6	0.6	0.7
Coverage Ratio (×1)	46	1.0	1.1	1.0	1.5	1.5	1.5	1.6	1.4	1.3	1.7
Asset Turnover (×1)	47	1.0	1.1	1.1	1.1	1.0	1.0	1.1	1.0	1.0	1.0
Total Liabilities/Net Worth (×1)	48	2.7	2.5	2.5	2.2	2.0	2.0	1.9	1.8	1.8	1.7
Return on Assets (×1)	49	5.69	6.2	5.3	7.5	6.5	6.3	7.1	5.8	4.9	5.7
Return on Equity (%)	50	•	•	•	4.5	4.1	3.6	4.9	2.2	0.9	4.1

Recommended Supplement: Plunkett's Almanacs

Reference Navigator

Web site: http://www.plunkettresearch.com   CD-ROM: not available

E-mail: customersupport@plunkettresearch.com   Library Reference Number

Database: See Web site   _____

According to the editors at Plunkett Research Limited, Plunkett's business and careers reference books (409) 765-8530, or fax (409) 765-8571, are the only complete reference guides to America's fastest-growing industries and the leading players in those industries. At about 700 pages each, these books include compete descriptions of the size, scope, and potential of each industry segment; dozens of tables; indexes by product, services, and geography; plus rankings by company for sales, profits, and research and development. In addition, they provide detailed discussions of key trends directing these burgeoning businesses, and they give an in-depth analysis of careers and occupations within each industry. Combined, their books cover nearly 3,000 fast-growing companies.

Plunkett's delves into the entire scope of each industry, showing you the relationships between technology providers and information managers, manufacturers, financial firms, specialty services, and other players, covering the complete business picture.

They list contact names of leading executives, along with their titles, addresses, phone numbers, e-mail addresses, Web sites, and fax numbers. Their corporate analysis includes complete details on each firm, including corporate culture, financial performance, investments in growth and research, future plans, and tables of products and services—all extensively cross-indexed. Examples of some publications are given below:

- *The Almanac of American Employers: 1998–99* (ISBN 0-9638268-9-1).
- *Plunkett's Health Care Industry Almanac* (ISBN 0-9638268-1-6).
- *Plunkett's InfoTech Industry Almanac* (ISBN 0-9638268-3-1).

These are pretty big books containing complete profiles of the 500 leading firms in each industry. They are your best prospects for marketing, investments, research or job hunting.

17 SELECTED BUSINESS PERIODICALS

Fortune, BusinessWeek, Inc., Hispanic Business, and the other periodicals listed here are not references in the strict sense of the word—a few thousand pages, fine print, black and white, no pictures and requiring a grocery cart for transportation. Because these publications are readily available at most newsstands, a comprehensive portrayal of their table of contents and sample pages are not necessary, but we will point out some strong points and perhaps a weak point or two of these magazines.

Description of Publication: *Fortune*

For information on this biweekly publication (ISSN 0015-8259) call Time Inc. at (800) 621-8000; or fax: (212) 522-7686; European subscriptions: +31 20 487 4232.

 Reference Navigator

Web site: http://fortune.com

E-mail: Fortune@cis.compuserve.com

Database: LEXIS-NEXIS

CD-ROM: 500/1000 lists only

Library Reference Number:

Fortune magazine is probably the best all-around business periodical in the United States, if not the world. According to the Audit Bureau of Circulations, *Fortune* is now the No. 1 business biweekly, which fits neatly with the editors' mission statement: to become "the best magazine in the world which happens to be about business." Toward that end they have worked to increase the utility, the relevance, and the entertainment value of everything they do. The cover stories are colorful and informative. One example is "Killer Strategies That Make Shareholders Rich."

From Nike to Home Depot to Harley-Davidson, the companies that do best for their stockholders thrive by taking risks, breaking the rules—being mavericks. In fact, says the author, a leading strategy guru (Gary Hamel), the ability to "reinvent" the basis of competition within an industry will prove the next competitive advantage.

Fortune's format has been changed to provide significantly more editorial material in each issue. The magazine is now organized in a far simpler way—four sections and a grouping of features—that will make it easier for you to find your way around. There is a beefed-up "Personal Fortune" section in the back of the magazine devoted to helping you make better decisions about how to invest—and spend—your hard-earned money. The "Smart Managing" section will enhance *Fortune's* reputation as one of the best places to discover new management practices. The new "Digital Watch" section stays abreast of the trends and products driving information technology, the most dynamic sector of today's economy. One particularly nice feature at the beginning is "The Index," which shows companies (bold type) and individuals in each issue. Both are indexed to the first page of the article in which each is mentioned. *Fortune*, like a number of other magazines, has a Web site directory to allow you to contact advertisers and a classified section if you happen to be interested in a president's position.

One other publication you should not overlook is the U.S. Chamber of Commerce's monthly publication (ISSN 0028-047X) called *Nation's Business,* (800) 352-1450. This is an excellent resource for anyone interested in keeping up with a smorgasbord of business topics; the table of contents shows the broad coverage of the magazine:

Cover Story: Labor Comes Alive
Managing: Emotions in the Workplace
Transportation: Smart Cars, Smart Roads
Enterprise: Wheels of Change in Bicycle Retailing
Finance: SBA Loans Get Costlier
Technology: From Wireless Phones to Mobile Offices
Small Business Computing: High-Tech Help? It's Your Call
Benefits: Benefit Costs Shift to Reverse
Family Business: A Presence On the Internet
Poll Results: Where I Stand

Nation's Business also offers some excellent services:

- MarketFAX, (800) 597-7363, sells current and past articles from *Nation's Business;* you can choose from a best-seller list, enter the article number, your credit card number and you receive the pages in minutes.

- Top-Rated Business Products, (800) 429-7107, are outstanding selections covering courses, documents, and strategies that save time and money.

Recommended Supplement: *Forbes*

For information concerning this biweekly publication (ISSN 0015-6914) call
Forbes Inc. at (212) 620-2200.

Reference Navigator

Web site: http://www.forbes.com   CD-ROM: not available

E-mail: not available   Library Reference Number:

Database: See Web site

Perhaps one of the first things you notice about *Forbes* is that for a biweekly magazine it's pretty big—sometimes almost 400 pages. Often that size comes from a special advertising section (e.g., "Detroit Making It Better For Business," 33 pages for articles and advertising) or special lists of rankings for which *Forbes* is famous (e.g., "World's Best Small Companies"). In one issue, "World's Best Small Companies" took 61 pages of articles, lists of the best small companies, the 200 best, the best small companies in the world, and CEOs of the best small companies in America. This could all be a little overpowering; one could wonder who except the people on the list really care. However, the Forbes 500 annual directory, compiled annually since 1917, must have a little something for everyone in order to be in demand that long. And the annual report on American Industry, which appears in the first January issue, seems to have a macroeconomic perspective that tells a bigger story.

Something to Think About

Despite the lists, some economics comes with the enjoyable reading. Review "The Forbes Index" as a measure of U.S. economic activity. It is composed of eight equally weighted elements: the cost of services relative to consumer prices, orders for durable goods compared with manufacturers' inventories, total industrial production, new housing starts, personal income, new claims for unemployment compensation, total retail sales, and total consumer installment credit.

Description of Publication: *BusinessWeek*

If you would like to get information on this weekly publication (ISSN 0007-7135) call McGraw-Hill Cos. at (212) 512-2511 or 1 (800) 635-1200.

Reference Navigator

Web site: http://www.businessweek.com

E-mail: bwreader@mgh.com

Database: See Web site

CD-ROM: not available

Library Reference Number:

_____

If you've never heard of *BusinessWeek (BW)*, possibly ... just possibly, you should reconsider going to Harvard B-School. On the other hand this is an outstanding business publication you can become familiar with very quickly. *BusinessWeek* is published weekly except for one week in January. It has a very descriptive table of contents, which briefly annotates the articles. It is also produced in three editions: North American, European, and Asian.

The magazine is broken down into a traditional number of departments, for example:

Cover Story	Science & Technology	Finance
News: Analysis & Commentary	The Workplace	Government
Economic Analysis	The Corporation	Industries
Information Processing	International Business	Features
Personal Business	Sports Business	Marketing

Some departments are used in every issue, some in alternating weeks, depending on the news priorities. The cover story generally is the hot topic of the week. *BusinessWeek* also conducts some special surveys:

- Highest paid executives.
- *BW's* top 1000: America's most valuable companies.
- *BW's* global 1000.
- Quarterly corporate scoreboard.
- Major indicators.
- Selection of the top 500 stock & bond mutual funds.
- The world's best investments.

BusinessWeek also presents frequent live conferences on America Online (AOL) where the reader can ask questions about features from the magazine. Transcripts of all conferences are available for downloading from the *BW* on-line area on AOL soon after each event. *BW* also offers an Internet address directory of some of its advertisers. In addition, on the bottom of the "Technology & You" page, which is featured occasionally, questions and comments are solicited by e-mail, tech&you@businessweek.com, or fax, (202) 383-2125. If you are looking for "Figures of the Week," try figures@businessweek.com. Of particular interest are two sets of statistical references near the back of the magazine:

Business Week Index:

Production Index	Production Indicators	Leading Indicators
Prices	Interest Rates	Foreign Exchange

Investment Figures of the Week:

Commentary	Stocks	Market Analysis	Bonds
Industry Groups	Mutual Funds	Relative Portfolios	The Dollar

In short, *BW* is perhaps one of the best business newsmagazines on the market. Its primary shortcoming is that the articles are not as in-depth as one will find in *Fortune, Harvard Business Review,* and other periodicals of that ilk.

One *BW* specialty worth investigating is its rankings of "The Best B-Schools," which is a good primer for those students seeking careers in business. *Business Week* lists the best B-schools annually, then moves on to *BW*'s methodology for rating the schools (basically, it asks graduates and employers), then as in one case provides some commentaries on PhD pay, networking, and the same old call for abolishing tenure. There is also a personal business guide to speed the way to an MBA—with a little help from your PC.

Something to Do

If you aren't familiar with database formats, check out *Business Week* on ABI (abs), LEXIS-NEXIS (ful-tx), and BPI (ind, abs) to see how the magazine is formatted in each.

Recommended Supplement: *Working Woman: The Magazine for Businesswomen*

Working Woman is published monthly by MacDonald Communications Corporation and can be reached by calling (800) 842-8416.

Reference Navigator

Web site: http://www.womensplace.com   CD-ROM: not available

E-mail: wwedit@womweb.com   Library Reference Number:

Database: See Web site

Working Woman and *Working Mother* (cited below) are published by the same company and offer very similar formats (colorful, 80 to 90 pages, contemporary) right down to the placement of ads (Hallmark on the back page), although the subject content differs for each. *Working Woman* features articles on the success of women, how-to, health, and fashion. The departments focus on self-help such as "How do you map out your small business planning?"; Money, for example, "Four questions to ask before accepting a buyout"; career strategies; and the like. The magazine tries to meet the demands of women in both large and small businesses by providing insights into the needs of women in both categories. The articles are reader-friendly and informative about many aspects of the working woman's life. They are short, about four pages or so, and generally go to the personal side versus the corporate strategy or finance or marketing topics. For example, one feature article portrayed the success of Geraldine Laybourne who built Nickelodeon into the highest-rated basic cable channel in America and now looks to repeat the feat at Disney/ABC Cable Networks. Useful information for research is available in many articles.

    Working Mother is dedicated to incorporating children's issues into the working environment of their mother . . . and helping to ease the pain (e.g., "8 great freeze-ahead family dinners," and "Help your child make friends"). Regular departments include "Just for You" (hair, health and sex), "Children," "Food," and "Buyer's Guide." All in all, the business side is light and the children side heavy. Special issues are sometimes featured, such as surveying corporations for the "100 Best Companies For Working Mothers." Don't look for much research material.

    Another important perspective comes from *Feminist Economics* (ISSN 1354-5701), which is published by the International Association for Feminist Economics, (713) 527-4660 or e-mail to jshackel@bucknell.edu. According to an editorial titled, "Expanding the Methodical Boundaries of Economics," the editors of *Feminist Economics* seek to encourage methods that pay greater attention to women's voices in economic understandings. Given that any scientific findings are only as strong as the data on which they are built, the editors are particularly interested in encouraging research that assesses the quality of traditional forms of economic data. The journal provides an excellent resource for research. The summer 1997 issue included, "Lone Mothers and Paid Work: Rational Economic Man or Gendered Moral Rationalities," by Simon Duncan and Rosalind Edwards.

Description of Publication: *Inc.*

If you need information on this monthly publication (ISSN 0162-8968), call (617) 248-8000.

Reference Navigator

Web site: http://www.inc.com
E-mail: editors@inc.com
Database: full-text back to 1988

CD-ROM: not available
Library Reference Number:

_____

According to the Marketing Research Institute of Pensacola, Florida, 53 percent of employed Americans work for a small business with 250 employees or less. *Inc.* magazine is all about small business and it does one of the best jobs in the nation. It is, as one division of the magazine is called, "hands on" with enough humor and good sense to serve any entrepreneur well.

Inc. has three major departments, which remain mostly the same over the years, as do some of the topics:

- "Hands On"—sales and marketing, managing people, finance, etc.
- Features—anatomy of a start-up, face to face, company profile, etc.
- Columns—FYI, real business, politics, etc.

"Hands On" also includes a unique piece called "The American Dream: Business For Sale." It is a real business for sale, sort of the pick of the month by *Inc.* (even though *Inc.* prints a disclaimer). The article offers a brief overview of the business; price; outlook; price rationale; and pros and cons. The point, one would guess, is to provide some inspiration to those thousands of budding entrepreneurs who ruminate frequently over such opportunities.

Inc. makes a special effort to include the new on-line technology for its readers. For example, in the letters section, the editors solicit comments and do surveys: "Call in your comments on our toll-free line, (800) 238-1756, or send e-mail to editors@inc.com." Articles sometimes include the writer's e-mail address at the bottom of the page.

Inc. has recently come on-line (http://www.inc.com). It offers to be "The full-service electronic consultant for people starting and running their own companies." The service, according to the editors, allows you to build your own Web site on Inc.Online. Plus the Web site provides the current issue of *Inc.* and its archives; tips, interactive worksheets, and list of resources to grow your business; interaction with other entrepreneurs, experts, and *Inc.* editors; and free software, Web tools, and other items to make your job easier.

Inc. publishes two sets of special bonus issues each year:

1. *Inc. Technology* (quarterly); e-mail correspondence to tech@incmag.com or snail-mail it to Inc. Technology, Letters Editor, 38 Commercial Wharf, Boston, MA 02110-3883.
2. *Inc.'s 500 Fastest Growing Privately Held Companies.*

Inc. sponsors a number of annual conferences, such as Growing the Company, Manufacturing Strategies, and CEO Symposium. Call (800) 255-1080 for information.

Inc. also provides a full range of videos, books, and software on small business management; call *Inc.* Business Resources at (800) 468-0800, ext. 5495.

Recommended Supplement: *Entrepreneur*

For information on this monthly publication, call the office of the publisher, Gordon Lee Jones III, at (800) 357-7299, or fax (714) 755-4211.

Reference Navigator

Web site: http://www.entrepreneurmag.com   CD-ROM: not available

E-mail: EntMag@aol.com   Library Reference Number:

Database: See Web site

According to the editors of *Entrepreneur,* America's small-business owners numbered about 23 million and growing.

There is so much information in this magazine (about 230 pages, contemporary format, lots of color, ads, info-boxes, etc.) you really have to buy one to figure out what's going on. For example, there are six to eight features of about three pages each (e.g., "In the struggle between principles and profits, can an entrepreneur have both?" by Janean Chun); 12 columns including topics such as "Travel Smarts," "Entrepreneurial Woman," "Global Vision," and "Books"; and seven departments: Technology, Money, Management, Marketing, Government, FYI, and Opportunity Spotlight.

One can easily see that this is a magazine for entrepreneurs and has dedicated itself to meeting their needs. The magazine is filled with ads trying to sell businesses, and that gets old quickly. If you're looking for substantive articles dealing with substantive research and writing, this may not be the source for you. Nevertheless, the entrepreneurial topics are germane, contemporary, and interesting.

Description of Publication: *Hispanic Business*

For information on this monthly publication (ISSN 0199-0349), call Hispanic Business Inc. at (805) 682-5843; or fax: (805) 687-4546.

Reference Navigator

Web site: www.HispanStar.com

E-mail: info@hbinc.com

Database: see Web site

CD-ROM: not available

Library Reference Number:

_____

The database holdings of *Hispanic Business* (approximately 152 pages) underpin the depth and breadth of its coverage. The annual *Hispanic Business* directory of the 500 largest Hispanic-owned companies, for example, represents the core of the Hispanic middle market in the United States. Students of this market need look no further than this listing to take the pulse of the U.S. economy. The directory includes, rank, address, CEO, type of business, number of employees, year started, and revenues. The article includes half-page profiles of successful Hispanic businesses and a numerical portrait of the largest Hispanic-owned firms, with data by sector, performance, and profitability.

HB magazine features late-breaking developments in law, technological research, education, finance, government, and politics. *HB* has a "Career Opportunities Bulletin" and one of the quickest ways to reach it is on the Web site address above; look for the *National Hispanic Resume Database*.

Ethnic considerations play an obvious role in the magazine, for example, with regard to trade ("NAFTA in the Real World," by Joel Russel), technical services, new business guide, and philanthropy ("The Art of Fundraising: An exhibit featuring the works of Latin American artists benefits a national museum for women," by Patricia Guadalupe). The departments section has at least six categories, with "Career Track" being of particular interest to students.

Since Mexico is a major trading partner with the United States, and NAFTA a recent legislative initiative for future opportunities in Latin America, one publication of special interest is *Bu$iness Mexico*, published by the American Chamber of Commerce of Mexico. The magazine is a quality publication with excellent research opportunities (e.g., Special Edition 1998: "The Strategies Issue: Mexico's top executives look forward to real recovery"). Its Web site is at http://www.amcham.com.mx or e-mail at busmex@mchammex.com.mx. One other publication by the American Chamber called *The American Chamber of Commerce Guide to Mexico* is an outstanding source of business information on Mexico.

See also Chapter 42 for information concerning the *Latin American Weekly Report* and the *Latin American Regional Reports*.

Something to Do

The editors have made a special point of placing Web site information about companies features in their stories at the end of a number of articles. Pick up a copy of *Hispanic Business* and go to one of the Web sites to learn about a Hispanic company of interest to you.

Recommended Supplement: *Black Enterprise*

If you need information on this monthly publication (ISSN 0006-4165), call Graves Publishing Company at (212) 242-8000; or fax: (212) 886-9557.

Reference Navigator

Web site: http://www.blackenterprise.com

E-mail: edmonda@blackenterprise.com

Database: See Web site

CD-ROM: BE's *100*

Library Reference Number:

_____

What is the state of black business this year? Perhaps the quickest way to find out is to pick up a copy of *Black Enterprise* (*BE*). This magazine, in business since 1970, is a slick, organized, well-written publication that focuses on the black community. Every year, a special June edition poses an exhausting challenge for the *Black Enterprise* staff. The "*BE 100s*" is an exclusive list of the nation's largest black-owned businesses and has been published for almost 25 years.

BE's contents are based on business with a black community theme. Each issue includes the usual cover story and feature articles along with about 10 departments covering small business, technology, money, corporate power, education, and more.

One area of the magazine that deserves special attention is the *BE* Board of Economists (BEBE). The eight-member board reviews and considers the economic impact of black-owned companies and the political–economic environment (e.g., viability of a flat tax and prospects for the congressional elections).

Each member of the board is polled on his or her views and the article speaks to their feelings in general.

Regional profiles are also included with specific references to quality of life, employment, professional opportunities, *BE* 100 resident companies, colleges, and entrepreneurialism. Local institutes help with the research; for example, the North Carolina Institute of Minority Economic Development contributed to the North Carolina regional profile. BEBE concludes its message with "The Economic Forecast for Black Americans."

The *BE* 100s are available on disk, a very valuable source of corporate statistics and key executive contacts. To order call (800) 543-6786.

18 INDEXES AND BIBLIOGRAPHIC SOURCES

Description of Publication:
Business Periodicals Index

To obtain information from the H.W. Wilson Company about *BPI* (ISSN 0007-6961) call 1 (800) 367-6770; about *BPI CD-ROM* (ISSN 1076-7053) call (800) 367-6770; about *BPI CD-ROM with abstracts* (ISSN 1057-6533), call (800) 367-6770.

Reference Navigator

Web site: http://www.hwwilson.com

E-mail: info.hwwilson.com

Database: See Web site

CD-ROM: available

Library Reference Number:

_____

The *Business Periodicals Index* is dedicated to business periodicals, 395 of them to be exact. That's not all there are to be sure, but it's a good start. Look up almost any subject matter in business and if it's been written about (since January 1958) you should find the citations and an annotation of the article in the *BPI*. Disk data only go back to June 1982, and abstracts back to June 1990.

These homely blue-covered indexes are pure reference function—no pictures, no graphs, essentially no fun. Nevertheless, they are a very important source, found in almost all libraries. You don't need to have a CD-ROM, or go on-line or through other machinations, although such services are provided by the publisher. The *BPI* is published monthly, except August, with a bound cumulation each quarter and year. It is a cumulative index to English-language periodicals. Selection of periodicals (395 at this date, taken from a list of 522) for indexing is accomplished by subscriber vote represented by the Committee on Wilson Indexes of the American Library Association's Reference and Adult Services Division.

Although no author indexing is available, articles about general subjects, a company, or a person are indexed under the specific name. Bibliographic information may be a little hard to decipher (see the Sample page). Also, the periodicals covered may not be up-to-date. A separate listing of citations for book reviews is at the end. The *BPI* does not have a table of contents.

Perhaps the mother-of-all-indexes is the *Reader's Guide to Periodical Literature*, a cumulative author–subject index to English-language periodicals of general interest. Although not specifically dedicated to business, the periodicals listing are comprehensive. A total list can be seen in the "Periodicals Indexed" section at the beginning of the book.

It's tough to write about indexes without mentioning *The New York Times Index,* published semimonthly with quarterly cumulating and distributed by University Microfilms International, (800) 521-0600. This *Index* has been designed to provide simple access to the contents of *The New York Times*. It can be used by itself for a basic chronological overview of the news, or it can be used as a guide to the location of the full articles in the original newspaper.

The *New York Times Index* contains abstracts of the significant news, editorial matter, and special features published in the newspaper, daily and Sunday. These abstracts (entries) are classified under appropriate subject, geographic, organization, and personal name headings.

Headings and their subdivisions are arranged alphabetically; the entries under them are arranged chronologically. Each entry is followed by a precise reference—date, section, page, and column—to the item it summarizes. All related headings are covered either by cross-references or by duplicate entries. For example:

> European leaders, in their landmark attempt to create a single, unifying currency for the 21st century, officially name it the Euro and agree on a timetable for introducing it by 2002; chronology; photos (M), D 16,1,1:5.
>
> European Union leaders agree to begin formal negotiations with ten Eastern European countries as well as Malta and Cyprus, by the end of 1997 concerning their admission to the union (M), D 17,1,17:1.

The entries include references to an article's length: (S) = article up to 6 column inches in length; (M) = article of 6 to 18 inches in length; (L) article over 18 inches in length.

Something to Think About

The *Business Periodicals Index* is published monthly except which month? What is meant by "quarterly and annual cumulations"? How many journals in business and economics are covered in the *BPI*? Are there other sources that can provide approximately the same information? If so can you list them?

Business Periodicals Index

AUGUST 1995—JULY 1996

@ Cafe (New York, N.Y.)

Marketing

A latte with that log-on? M. Coeyman. il *Restaur Bus* v94 p90 N 1 '95

@Home (Menlo Park, Calif.: Firm)

Cybercitizen Kane is @Home. graph por *Economist* v336 p80 S 16 '95

Service

@Home, Menlo Park, California: Internet access for cable TV customers. L. Rhodes. por *Fortune* v 132 p174 Jl 10 '95

Online content: filling a niche. K. Criner and J. Wilson. Ed *Publ Fourth Estate* v129 p3+ F 3 '96

TCI's @Home teams with Netscape for Internet access. M. Berniker. *Broadcast Cable* v125 p56 O 2 '95 supp Telemedia Week

@Mezzanine (Computer program)

Beefing up document management: Saros to deliver secure info over Internet. S. J. Johnston. *Computerworld* v29 p57+ D 11 '95

@vantage (Online service)

Gartner takes @vantage online. M. Fleming. il *Online* v19 p74–5 S/O '95

1-2-3 (Computer program) *See* Lotus 1-2-3 (Computer program)

1st United Bancorp

Acquisitions and mergers

Order approving the acquisition of a bank holding company, merger of banks, and establishment of branches. J. J. Johnson. *Fed Reserve Bull* v82 p151-2 F '96

2Market (Firm)

Service

Retailing: I-way onramp 2Market. B. Spethmann. il *Brandweek* v 36 p 18+ Jl 10 '95

3-D graphics *See* Computer graphics—Three-dimensional graphics

3-D motion pictures *See* Three-dimensional motion pictures

3-D outdoor advertising *See* Three-dimensional outdoor advertising

3-D video game machines See Three-dimensional video game machines

3Com Corp.

The Internet's golden switch makers [Cisco Systems, 3Com and Bay Networks] tab *Economist* v337 p69-70 D 2 '95

Acquisitions and mergers

3Com is showing a lot of hustle. P. Burrows. il por *Bus Week* p130+ O 2 '95

3Com faces user angst. B. Wallace and L. Didio. il *Computerworld* v29 p6 Ag 7 '95

3Com in 3-D: looking beyond the merger. N. Lippis. *Data Commun* v24 p25-6 S '95

3Com seeks Chipcom for $775M. C. Hardie. *Electron News* v41 p2 Jl 31 '95

Rmon heats up, spark acquisitions [3Com Corp. buys Axon Networks; Bay Networks acquires Armon Networking Ltd.] P. Dryden. *Computerworld* v30 p32 Mr 11 '96

Showtime [3Com has finally made it into the big leagues] J. Epstein. port *Financ World* v164 p29 O 24 '95

Competition

Bonanza time! Cabletron to offer freebies, incentives to entice customers. L. DiDio and B. Wallace. *Computerworld* v29 p1+ Ag 14 '95

Marketing

Server bundle - free switch. B. Wallace and B. Francis. *Computerworld* v30 p1+ F 26 '96

Product development

3Com and Chipcom get down to business. L. DiDio. *Computerworld* v29 p56 Ag 14 '95

3Com unveils virtual LAN master plan. B. Wallace. tab *Computerworld* v29 p16 D 4 '95

Products

3Com hub users say they'd rather fight than switch. B. Wallace. il *Computerworld* v29 p frontcover+ O 23 '95

3Com late with key ATM products. B. Wallace. graph *Computerworld* v30 p4 Ja 2 '96

3Com preps ATM net management package. B. Wallace. il *Computerworld* v29 p6 S 11 '95

3Com switching technology moves along at snail's PACE [Priority Access Control Enabled] B. Wallace. *Computerworld* v29 p6 Ag 14 '95

3Com turbocharges Impact ISDN modem. B. Wallace. *Computerworld* v29 p24 Ag 21 '95

3Com ups switch flexibility: Cellplex 7000 to handle switched, fast Ethernet. B. Wallace. il *Computerworld* v30 p10 Ja 29 '96

3Com's token-ring switch. S. L. Brothick. *Bus Commun Rev* v25 p70 D '95

Chipcom hub users welcome 3Com switching. B. Wallace. *Computerworld* v30 p10 Ap 22 '96

Router software will merge WANs [3Com Corpo., Bay Networks and Cisco Systems] B. Wallace. *Computerworld* v30 p1+ Mr 11 '96

Vendors fortify Internetworking [Cisco Systems, Inc., Hewlett-Packard Co. and 3Com Corp.] B. Wallace. *Computerworld* v30 p20 Mr 4 '96

Recommended Supplement: *Dun & Bradstreet Reference Book of American Business*

For information on this publication, call Dun & Bradstreet Information Services at (908) 665-5000.

Reference Navigator

Web site: http.//www.dnb.com

E-mail: dnbmdd@mail.dnb.com

Database: See Web site

CD-ROM: available

Library Reference Number:

_____

The leading supplier of business credit information since 1841 is the Dun & Bradstreet Corporation. The basic D&B credit document is called a "Business Information Report" and goes for about five pages, focusing on bills past due, debts outstanding, payments made, and the like. Two companies compete for the majority of the credit rating business—D&B and TRW.

The *Reference Book* serves as a printed index to the more than 4 million U.S. companies for which current "Business Information Reports" are available. Companies are arranged geographically by state, and further divided by city, town, or village. Each listing cites the company name, its primary SIC number, telephone number, credit rating, types of reports available, and, for firms less than 10 years old, the founding date. Dun & Bradstreet's *Reference Book of Manufacturers* covers manufacturers only and includes more basic directory information, such as the address, and is arranged by company name. The best features of both publications are combined in a CD-ROM product called Dun's Reference Plus. Unfortunately, it is available only to subscribers of the credit reports.

D&B also provides the *International Business Information Reports,* which contain information and analyses that are essential in evaluating a firm's international operations, profitability, and stability. The reports are prepared by D&B business analysts who are familiar with the local customs and business practices.

Description of Publication: *Wall Street Journal Index*

For information on this annual publication (ISSN 0099-9660), call UMI at (800) 747-9287.

Reference Navigator

Web site: http://www.umipub.com

E-mail: editorial@umipub.com

Database: See Web site

CD-ROM: available

Library Reference Number:

_____

The *Wall Street Journal Index* provides abstracts and comprehensive indexing of all articles in the 3-Star Eastern Edition of *The Wall Street Journal*. It is produced under exclusive agreement with the publisher, Dow Jones & Company. The full text of the 3-Star Eastern Edition and other editions is available on microfilm and CD-ROM (check the Web site to see if they are on-line yet). The index is issued in eight monthly and four quarterly cumulations, as well as a hardbound annual volume.

Indexed material includes news items, columns, feature articles, editorials, letters to the editor, obituaries, certain tabular information, earnings reports, dividend reports, and arts reviews. Items not selected for indexing include most stock tables and any editorial cartoons. For many columns that cover a variety of topics (e.g., Credit Markets, World Markets), only the main topic is indexed.

For ease of access, the index is divided into two parts—corporate news and general news. The first part contains abstracts of all articles indexed with company names, which are arranged alphabetically. The second part contains abstracts of all articles indexed with subject headings, personal names, organization names, product names, and geographic names, all of which are interfiled alphabetically (see the Sample Page).

The subject headings are based on a controlled vocabulary developed by UMI, containing approximately 4,000 general subject terms and authority files containing tens of thousands of personal, corporate, organizational, geographic, and product names. The thesaurus and authority files are continually updated to reflect new subject areas in current events. Most subject headings are in natural word order.

VOLUME II

VOLUME I

D SOUZA, DINESH (BYLINER)

Dinesh D'Souza says that before adopting a course that will determine the future of race relations into the 21st century, Americans must step back from the sound and fury of affirmative action long enough to consider options for dealing with the continuing problem of racial discrimination; illus. (L)S 12 - A, 26:3

DABERKO, DAVID

Edward B. Brandon, chairman and CEO of National City Corp. said he would resign as of Sep 30, 1995. Brandon will be replaced by David A. Daberko, National City's president and COO since 1993. (M)Jl 25 - B 8:1

DACH, LESLIE

Leslie Dach, the former presidential-campaign chief for Michael Dukakis and head of Edelman public relations in Washington DC, has hired Dan Leonard, the communications chief for the GOP's 1994 House campaigns. (S)Ja 13 - A, 1:5

DADA WA (ZHU ZHEQIN)

Hugo Restall profiles Cantonese popular music star Zhu Zheqin. Restall asserts that "Dadawa," as she is known, is largely a figurehead for a marketing effort by Warner Music International and suggests that Asian teenagers have been spending money for Zhu's "packaged spirituality." (M)Je 30 - A, 12:1

DAHL, ROBERT

The Christian Coalition, which is under investigation by the FEC for its tactics in the past two elections, has told Sen Bob Dole (R-KS) that Washington DC lawyer Robert Dahl is its choice for a seat on the agency. Dahl represents Newt Gingrich's former political group, Gopac. (S)O 13 - A, 1:5

DAI XIANGLONG

Dai Xianglong, chief of China's central bank, People's Bank of China, predicted that the 1995 inflation rate would meet the government's 15% target and vowed to maintain an "appropriately tight" money supply. Dai said that controlling inflation would still be the central bank's priority task. (S)O 11 - A, 10:1

DAILY MARKETS

Stock prices were mixed in a sloppy, directionless session on Jan 3, 1995, while bond prices slipped on unsettling price data and the dollar was stronger. The Dow Jones Industrial Average inched up 4.04 to 3838.48; graph. (M)Ja 4 - C, 1:3

A late-session burst of buying sent stock prices higher on Jan 4, 1995 as falling commodities prices indicated a soothing of inflation fears. Bond prices rose and the dollar strengthened. The Dow Jones Industrial Average gained 19.17 to 3857.65. (M)Ja 5 - C, 1:6

Stock prices were mixed on Jan 5 1995 in nervous trading ahead on Jan 6's key release of December employment data. Bond prices moved lower, and the dollar weakened. The Dow Jones Industrial Average fell 6.73 to 3850.92. (M)Ja 6 - C, 1:6

Stock prices finished mixed on Jan 9, 1995 as investors continued to fret about the US's strength and inflationary pressures. Bond prices eased and the dollar weakened. The Dow Jones Industrial Average dropped 6.06 to 3861.35. (M)Ja 10 - C, 1:6

Stock prices ended moderately higher on Jan 10, 1995 in the wake of benign inflation data, backing away from strong midday gains. Bond prices rose on the light inflation news and the dollar was mixed. The Dow Jones Industrial Average was up 5.39 to 3866.74. (M)Ja 11 - C, 1:6

Stock prices finished mixed in a roller-coaster session on Jan 11, 1995 as investors continued to fret about the Mexican financial crisis. Bond prices rose on tame inflation data and the dollar was mixed. The Dow Jones Industrial Average fell 4.71 to 3862.03; graph. (M)Ja 12 - C, 1:3

Stock prices finished mixed in another featureless session on Jan 12, 1995 with stock prices mixed and bond prices lower. The Dow Jones Industrial Average fell 3.03 to 3859.00. (M)Ja 13 - C, 1:6

Stock prices continued to rise and the dollar weakened Jan 16, 1995, while bond markets were closed for the Martin Luther King Jr federal holiday. The Dow Jones Industrial Average rose 23.88 to 3932.34. (M)Ja 17 - C, 1:6

Stock and bond prices finished mixed on Jan 17, 1995, largely shrugging off a batch of reports that showed the economy moving briskly, at least in the industrial sector. The dollar strengthened. The Dow Jones Industrial Average fell 1.68 to 3930.66. (M)Ja 18 - C, 1:3

Recommended Supplement: *Christian Science Monitor Index*

For information on this publication, contact Christian Science Monitor, Inc., New York, at (212) 764-0036.

Reference Navigator

Web site; http://www.csmonitor.com

E-mail: dave@csmonitor.com

Database: See Web site

CD-ROM: not available

Library Reference Number:

_____

The *Christian Science Monitor* is a newspaper with both national and international scope that reports on general topics including business and economics. The *Monitor* provides abstracts and comprehensive indexing of all significant articles in the newspaper. It is produced under exclusive agreement with the publisher. Newspaper editions indexed correspond to those available in microform from UMI. The index is issued in eight monthly and four quarterly cumulations, as well as a hardbound annual volume.

Indexed material includes news items; feature articles; editorials; editorial cartoons; commentaries; sports articles; business and financial news; and reviews of books, art exhibitions, dance movies, music, restaurants, theater, and television programs. Items not selected for indexing include advertising and the daily religious column.

This index is alphabetized according to a word-by-word filing scheme. Subject headings beginning with acronyms or other abbreviations file at the beginning of the alphabet letter. For ease of access, each abstract is assigned an average of three to four subject headings in the index. Personal names, institutional names, product names, and geographical headings are all treated as subject headings and are interfiled alphabetically with topical headings. Material concerning foreign countries is indexed under the country name and under appropriate topical, personal, and institutional subject headings.

Subject headings are based on a controlled-vocabulary thesaurus developed by UMI, containing approximately 4,000 general subject terms and authority files containing tens of thousands of personal, corporate, and product names.

Sample Entry

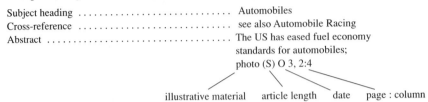

Subject heading .... Automobiles
Cross-reference .... see also Automobile Racing
Abstract .... The US has eased fuel economy
                                          standards for automobiles;
                                          photo (S) O 3, 2:4

      illustrative material   article length   date   page : column

---

Description of Publication: *Books in Print*

For information on this annual publication (ISBN 0-8352 3785-0), call R. R. Bowker at (800) 521-8110, or fax: (908) 665-6688.

Reference Navigator

Web site: http://www.reedref.com   CD-ROM: available

E-mail: info@bowker.com   Library Reference Number:

Database: see Web site

For 49 years, *Books in Print (BIP)* has served the library and book trade communities as the definitive bibliographic resource. A recent edition, covering over 230,354 new book titles, provides coverage of the full range of books currently published or distributed in the United States. This 49th edition of *BIP* contains 1,265,891 active titles published by 49,000 U.S. publishers. Bound in nine volumes, the set includes four volumes arranged by title and four by author. The ninth volume is devoted to publisher information and includes names and addresses of all publishers mentioned in the author and title volumes. (Amazon.com Inc. offers over 2.5 million book titles for sale over the Internet: http://www.amazon.com. We're not talking reference works here, but we just thought you'd like to know.)

BIP doesn't list books that are not published or exclusively distributed in the United States or books that are not available to the trade or general public for single or multiple copy purchase. *BIP* is designed to be easily searchable by both author and title.

Subject Guide to Books in Print, an annual companion volume to *Books in Print,* is produced from the *BIP* database of R. R. Bowker. This database is used to produce a complete, complementary line of bibliographic publications that gives booksellers, librarians, publishers, and all other book, on-line, and microfiche users access to the latest bibliographic and ordering information.

The bibliographic database was begun in 1948 primarily as a listing of titles included in Bowker's *Publishers Trade List Annual* (*PTLA*). The computerization of this database during the late 1960s using the Bibliographic Information Publication System (BIPS) made it possible for Bowker to expand the amount of information included in the bibliographic entries and to increase the number of essential tools of the trade it produced.

During the early 1970s the database was expanded to include information from additional publishers whose titles were not included in *PTLA*. Since then, the database has been compiled from information received on an ongoing basis directly from publishers. Before each publication from the database, publishers review and correct their entries, providing current price, availability, and ordering information, and update their list with recently published and forthcoming titles.

Software Encyclopedia is another Bowker product (see Chapter 21). It is an annual two-volume publication listing software and CD-ROM products for business, personal, and professional use. Bowker also publishes *Ulrich's International Periodicals Directory* (see Chapter 15).

Although there are 1,271,903 entries in *Subject Guide to Books in Print*, users should be aware that certain classes of publications are not represented. These include subscription reference sets, book club editions, books available only to members of a particular organization, subscription-only titles, or those sold only to schools. Books must be available for single-copy purchase to be listed. Fiction, poetry, and drama by a single author are omitted. Collections by more than one author and criticism are included.

B

Gala, Harak, India Open for Business: Guidelines & Opportunities for Companies Worldwide. LC 94-73056 (Illus.). 407p. (Orig.). 1994, pap. 49.95 (0-9645357-0-X, BWI Consult) Balt Wash Intl. A 407 page handbook on HOW TO DO BUSINESS WITH INDIA. A useful guide on JOINT VENTURES, TECHNOLOGY TRANSFERS, EXPORTS, IMPORTS, FINANCING, CONTRACT MANUFACTURING, SOURCING & MORE. "INDIA: OPEN FOR BUSINESS...is specially written for business executives from developed countries. It explains new economic reforms in India & shows how to take advantage of them. This book gives step-by-step instructions, including necessary forms & contact addresses, on several strategic options. "LOUISIANA INTERNATIONAL TRADE BULLETIN, WORLD TRADE CENTER." Books about doing business in India are hard to find. That's what prompted consultant Harak Gala to write this bullish, nuts-&-bolts volume for those considering setting up shop. Thankfully, there are...plenty of charts & appendices. There are also surprising, useful details." TRADE & CULTURE MAGAZINE, "INDIA: OPEN FOR BUSINESS...provides a good breakdown of Indian exports & imports-can serve as a guide to Indian regulations & business practices."

INTERNATIONAL BUSINESS MAGAZINE. Customers include universities, libraries, individuals, small businesses & large corporations. Such as AT&T, ABB, Boeing, Kodak, Texaco, & many more. Contact B W I CONSULTING, 727 Thornwood Drive, Odenton, MD 21113. Tel: (410) 519-3025, FAX (410) 519-3073. *Publisher Provided Annotation.*

Ho, Betty. Hong Kong Contract Law. 2nd ed. Ix, 582p. 1994. text ed. write for info. (0-409-99689-0) MICHIE.

Roebuck, Derek, Cheques, 120 p. (C). 1991. pap. text ed. 22.00 (962-209-288-8, Pub. by Hong Kong U Pr HK) St Mut.

*Roebuck, Derek & Wang Le M, eds. A Digest of Hong Kong contract Law. (Illus). 301p. 1995. 69.95 (7-301-02887-3) Austin & Winfield.

*Shenoy, Georgy T. & Kiat, Toh S. Rights & Obligations of Business in Singapore. 1996. write for info. (0-201-88913-7) Addison-Wesley.

Shum, Clement. Business Associations. 88p (C). 1991. pap. text ed. 22.00 (962-209-308-6, Pub. by Hong Kong U Pr HK) St Mut.

BUSINESS LAW-CHINA

*Bureau of Legislative Affairs of the State Council Staff, compiled by. Laws & Regulations of the People's Republic of China Governing Foreign-Related Matters, 1949-1992, 4 vols., Set. 2684p. (CHI & EHG.). 1994. 445.00 (0-614-11839-5, Pub. by HUWEI Cnslts CH) Am Overseas Bk Co.

Collection of Laws & Regulations of China Concerning Import/Export Commodity Inspection. (CHI). 1994. 145.00

(0-614-11840-9, Pub. by HUWEI Conslts CH) Am Overseas Bk Co.

Large & Middle Enterprises Catalogue of Chinese Printing Industry. -229p. Date not set. 135.00 (0-614-11853-0, Pub. by HUWEI Cnslts CH) Am Overseas Bk Co.

Wang, Guigup. Business Law of China: Cases, Texts, & Commentary. 590p. 1993. boxed 125.00 (0-614-05485-0, SI) MICHIE.

Wang, Gulguo. Business Law of China: Cases, Texts & Commentary. 1994. boxed 125.00 (0-409-99645-9, SI) MICHIE.

BUSINESS LAW-EUROPE

*Buxbaum, Richard M., et al, eds. European Economic & Business Law: Legal & Economic Analyses on Intergration & Harmonization. LC 96-10972. xxii, 374p. (C). 1996. lib. bdg. 168.90 (3-11-014242-2) De Gruyter.

Folsom, Ralph. European Community Business Law: Handbook. 375p. 1994. pap. writer for info. (0-314-03600-8) West Pub.

—European Community Business Law: Sourcebook. 1300p. 1994. pap. write for info. (0-314-03601-6) West Publ.

Folsom, Ralph H. European Union Business Law: Sourcebook, 1995 Edition. 1400p. (C). 1995. pap. text ed. write for info. (0-314-06237-8) West Pub.

Heller, Lober, Bahn & Partners Staff, et al. Hungarian Business Law. 150p. 1990. pap. 56.00 (90-6544-490-4) Kluwer Law Tax Pubs.

*Howells, Geraint G., ed. European Business Law. (European Business Law Library). (Illus). 300 p. 1996. text ed. 69.95 (1-85521-587-X, Pub. by Dartmth Pub UK); pap. text ed. 27.95 (1-85521-600-0, Pub. by Dartmth Pub UK) Ashgate Pub Co.

O'Connor, Bernard, ed. A Business Guide to European Community Legislation. 2nd ed. 1097p. 1995. 145.00 (0-471-95341-5, Pub. by Wiley Chancery Law UK) Wiley.

Scheifele, Bernd & Thaeter. Ralf. Aspects of Business Law in the Czech Republic: Acquisition of Companies, Establishment of Joint Ventures & Formation of Companies. 1995. 70.00 (0-935328-78-5) Intl Law Inst.

Storm, Paul & Ellis, Maarten. eds. Business Law in Europe. 1990. ring bd. 206.00 (90-6544-978-7) Kluwer Law Tax Pubs.

BUSINESS LAW-GREAT BRITAIN

*Bond, Helen J. & Kay, Peter. Business Law. 2nd ed. 378p. 1995. pap. 32.00 (1-85431-437-8, Pub. by Blackstone Pr UK) Gaunt.

Clarke, Michael. Regulating the City: Competition, Scandal & Reform. LC 85-29715. 192 p. 1986. 69.00 (0-335-15381-X, Open Univ Pr); pap. 25.00 (0-335-15382-8, Open Univ Pr) Taylor & Francis.

Gillies, Peter. Business Law. 7th ed. 900p. 1995. pap. 54.00 (1-86287-155-8, Pub. by Federation Pr AU) Gaunt.

Holland, James & Burnett, Stuart. Employment Law: Legal Practice Course Guides. 303p. 1995. pap. 34.00 (1-85431-395-9, Pub. by Blackstone Pr UK) Gaunt.

An asterisk (*) at the beginning of an entry indicates that the title is appearing for the first time.

Recommended Supplement: *Public Affairs Information Service*, Inc.

The Public Affairs Information Service Inc. (PAIS) publishes PAIS International In Print. For information call (800) 288-7247, or fax (212) 643-2848.

Reference Navigator

Web site: http://www.pais.org/   CD-ROM: available

E-mail: inquiries@pais.org   Library Reference Number:

Database: see PAIS International
and PAIS Select   _____

PAIS is a nonprofit association of libraries. It was founded in 1914 and chartered by the regents of the State of New York as a not-for-profit educational corporation index materials in the field of public affairs and public policy. According to the editors, PAIS aims to identify the public affairs information likely to be most useful and interesting to legislators, administrators, the business and financial community, policy researchers and students. The PAIS indexes list publications on all subjects that bear on contemporary public issues and the making and evaluation of public policy, irrespective of source or traditional disciplinary boundaries.

PAIS indexes publications issued anywhere in the world, in any of six languages (French, German, Italian, Portuguese, and Spanish). Another principal resource is the current holdings of the Economic and Public Affairs Division of the New York Public Library, one of the most comprehensive collections of public affairs materials in existence anywhere. PAIS addresses itself to issues of public policy, with emphasis on factual and statistical information. Thus, academic journals in the social sciences are indexed with particular attention to articles that bear on public policy, administration, and legislation. Nevertheless, business topics are extensively covered, with emphasis on economic, management policy making, business-societal interactions, and other broad factors. Visit their home page for current net topics, journal listings, and other valuable information.

19　ENCYCLOPEDIAS

Description of Publication: *Encyclopedia of Ethics*

To obtain information on this book (ISBN 1-55862-153-9) call St. James Press (800) 877-GALE.

Reference Navigator

Web site:　http://www.gale.com

E-mail:　galeord@gale.com

Database:　Dialog

CD-ROM: not available

Library Reference Number:

This encyclopedia is an anthology of 435 signed articles (between 1,000 and 5,000 words each) on topics dealing with, among other things, business ethics; political, social, and legal theory; trends; summaries of leading concepts; and biographical entries. Subjects range alphabetically from abortion to work.

The *Encyclopedia of Ethics,* edited by Laurence and Charlotte Becker, is an extremely handy reference piece on those so-called philosophical subjects that almost always seem to cause controversy. I say "so-called" because few of us would consider ourselves philosophers, yet most would never hesitate to give a person our opinion on abortion, Martin Luther King, happiness, charity, Sartre, child abuse, or war, to name but a few topics. The authors have given careful attention to theories of rational choice and economic analysis; feminist ethics; virtue theory; and moral psychology. The encyclopedia also includes a 13-part, multi-authored, 60,000-word history of ethics from the pre-Socratics through the first nine decades of the 20th century. Each article has a bibliography and the usual cross-references. See-also references are supplemented with two indexes: an analytical index of the text of the articles and an index of authors cited in the bibliographies. The article is signed at the end by its author.

For a more business-like approach to the ethics area, try *Business Ethics: A European Review* (ISSN 0962-8770) by Blackwell Publishers, which is found in the United Kingdom at: http://www.blackwellpublishers.co.uk.

Business Ethics is now entering its sixth year providing incisive and topical articles. It lends itself as a forum for businesspeople and academics to exchange experiences and informed insights on the various moral and ethical challenges and opportunities that increasingly face modern businesses throughout the world.

One bimonthly publication by Sussex Publishers Inc., (212) 260-7210, that also contributes to the investigation of human behavior is *Psychology Today* (ISSN 0033-3107), but some would argue it is not a candidate for this type of business reference text. While it's true to an extent that *Psychology Today* covers many topics outside the world of work, every once in a while it's right on target. In the 1995 March/April edition, for example, it covered the topic of love at work in "Frisky Business," by Mary Loftus.

> Despite the danger of sexual harassment, there's a whole lot of loving going on in the office. The warming of the workplace reflects a complex upheaval in the ways we work. Given endless workweeks, the reclaiming of emotional wholeness, and a new ideal of love as partnership, love at work makes a lot of sense to a lot of people—except the human resources department. Don't look for guidelines just yet in the company handbook.

psychology, discourage preoccupation with issues defined culturally as feminine, or in other ways covertly advance men's interests over women's. Since feminism is essentially a normative stance, and since its meaning is continually contested by feminists themselves, all feminists are constantly engaged in ethical reflection. In this sense, feminist ethics is practiced both inside and outside the academy. Within the academy, its main practitioners are scholars in philosophy, religion and jurisprudence. These scholars represent a variety of philosophical traditions, secular and religious, Anglo-American and continental European; in challenging perceived male bias in those traditions, they draw extensively on feminist scholarship in other disciplines, such as literature, history and psychology.

Scholarly work in feminist ethics often is also responsive to the ethical reflections of nonacademic feminists as these occur, for instance, in much feminist fiction and poetry. In addition, a considerable body of nonfiction, written by nonacademics and directed towards a nonacademic audience, presents itself as feminist ethics. Popular feminist books and journals frequently engage in ethical consideration of moral or public policy issues and sometimes also offer more general discussions of supposedly "masculine" and "feminine" value system. There are even grassroots journals of feminist ethics, such as *Lesbian Ethics,* published in the United States, and *Gossip: A Journal of Lesbian Feminist Ethics,* published in the United Kingdom. *Feminist Ethics,* published in Canada, seeks to combine academic scholarship with accessibility to a general audience. One may note striking parallels between many of the claims made by feminists inside the academy and those on the outside.

Those who currently claim the field of feminist ethics are mainly, through not exclusively, white western women. Nevertheless, a few male philosophers are doing significant work in feminist ethics, and people of color have produced a considerable amount of writing, both fiction and nonfiction, that seems compatible with the moral and theoretical inspiration of feminist ethics. It is predictable that women would be more likely than men to identify themselves as feminists, and both non-westerners and western people of color are less likely than western whites either to be philosophers or, because of feminism's racist history, to be feminists. "Womanist" is a term that many African American authors currently prefer to "feminist"

but they might not object to the description of their work as feminist ethics if feminism could be cleansed of racism and ethnocentrism.

FEMINIST CRITICISMS OF WESTERN ETHICS

Since most feminist ethics is done in a western context, it is western ethics, particularly (though not exclusively) the European Enlightenment tradition, that is the most frequent target of feminist critique. The feminist challenges to this tradition may be grouped conveniently under five main headings.

Lack of concern for women's interest. Many of the major theorists, such as Aristotle (384–322 B.C.) and Rousseau (1712–1778), are accused of having given insufficient consideration to women's interests, a lack of concern expressed theoretically by their prescribing for women allegedly feminine virtues such as obedience, silence, and faithfulness. Some feminists charge that many contemporary ethical discussions continue the tendency to regard women as instrumental to male-dominated institutions, such as the family or the state; in debates on abortion, for instance, the pregnant woman may be portrayed as little more than a container or environment for the fetus, while debates on reproductive technology are alleged to assume frequently that infertility is a problem only for heterosexual married women, i.e., women defined in relationship to men.

Neglect of "women's issues." Issues of special concern to women are said to have been ignored by modern moral philosophers, who have tended to portray the domestic realm as an arena outside the economy and beyond justice, private in the sense of being beyond the scope of legitimate political regulation. Even philosophers like Aristotle or Hegel (1770–1831), who give some ethical importance to the domestic realm, have tended to portray the home as an arena in which the most fully human excellences are incapable of being realized. Feminist philosophers began early to criticized this conceptual bifurcation of social life.

*Please note: Table of Contents from *Encyclopedia of Ethics* is so brief as to be omitted.

Recommended Supplement: *Encyclopedia of Human Behavior*

If you want information on this book (ISBN 0-12-226920-9) call Academic Press, Inc. (a division of Harcourt Brace and Company) at (800) 321-5068.

Reference Navigator

Web site: http://www.apnet.com/   CD-ROM: not available

E-mail: not available   Library Reference Number:

Database: See Web site

_____

This four-volume set is a comprehensive view of human behavior, some of which is depicted specifically in the domain of business (e.g., organizational behavior, social loafing, problem solving, paranoia, motivation, etc.). Some of this material may be deemed too specifically psychological to be particularly useful to the business environment. On the other hand much should be left to the reader's judgment. It is well written in anthology form and clearly formatted.

The *Encyclopedia of Human Behavior* is intended, according to its editor and his advisory board, for use by both students and research professionals. Articles have been chosen to reflect major disciplines in the study of human behavior, common topics of research by professionals in this realm, and areas of public interest and concern. Each article thus serves as a comprehensive overview of a given area, providing both breadth of coverage for students and depth of coverage for research professionals.

The index is located in Volume 4. Each article contains an outline, a glossary, cross-references, and a bibliography. The outline allows a quick scan of the major areas discussed within each article. The bibliography lists recent secondary sources to aid the reader in locating more detailed or technical information.

Description of Publication: *Encyclopedia of Business*

For information concerning this publication (ISBN 0-8103-9187-2), call Gale Research at (800) 347-GALE; or fax: (800) 339-3374.

Reference Navigator

Web site: http://www.gale.com

E-mail: galeord@gale.com

Database: Dialog

CD-ROM: not available

Library Reference Number:

_____

This two-volume set of relatively recent vintage (five years as of this writing) does an excellent job of bringing most of what one considers "business" within the covers of two big books (approximately 1,700 pages total). The books are done in black and white, two columns per page, and almost entirely without pictures or graphs. The writing is clear and easy to read. Each topic is completed with a "Further Reading" section and signed by its author. Average entry length is about 2,500 words. At the back of the second volume are two important features: the "Discipline Index" and the "General Index." If you're in business school, you better memorize where these volumes sit on the shelf, so you can get a solid answer to most of your questions quickly.

According to the editors, the *Encyclopedia of Business's* (*EOB*) combined practical and theoretical approach offers readers a solid explanation of relevant concepts, issues, and terms, covering both current and classical areas of interest and concern. The creators of *EOB* have tried to identify at least four issues that promise to remain very important as we enter the 21st century: entrepreneurship/small business, the globalization of business, quality, and diversity. The editors have delineated three objectives of *EOB*:

1. To create a fundamental and comprehensive reference book on business.

2. To provide current and authoritative information on business terms, ideas, issues, concepts, theories, models, and techniques of importance.

3. To present the information in a clear and concise fashion to the readers.

Something to Think About

EOB defines *discriminant analysis* as a statistical method that is used by researchers to help them understand the relationship between a *dependent variable* and one or more *independent variables*. A dependent varible is the variable that a researcher is trying to explain or predict from the values of the independent variables. Discriminant analysis is similar to regression analysis and analysis of variance (ANOVA). The principle difference between discriminant analysis and the other two methods is with regard to the nature of the dependent variable. What is regression analysis?

Note: The Table of Contents of the *Encyclopedia of Business* is too brief to be included as a sample.

L

LABELING

See: Packaging

LABOR ECONOMICS

According to the MIT *Dictionary of Modern Economics* labor economics is the branch of economics that analyzes "the study of the nature and determinants of pay and employment." Particular emphasis is put on the role played by social institutions and different types of market structures that jointly determine the pattern and mobility or speed of adjustment in the labor market where human labor inputs are bought and sold.

With regard to their speed of adjustment, labor markets are relatively slow in comparison to those markets for nonlabor inputs and commodities. For reasons best attributed to human behavior, worker movement from relatively low-wage areas to high-wage locations is sluggish. Worker retraining aimed at eliminating wage differentials also requires a substantial amount of time, which is generally not the case for other nonlabor inputs and commodities. As a result, the duration of wage differentials has tended to outlast those of other price differentials.

Another prominent distinction is drawn between internal and external labor markets. Internal labor markets refer to the determinants of pay and employment within a firm, while external labor markets refer to the determinants of pay and employment between firms or within and across industries. Many labor economists place substantial theoretical weight on these distinctions when trying to explain how labor markets work. As to the question of which type is more efficient or inefficient in the allocation of labor however, unanimity has been absent.

General Overview

Almost from its inception (and especially during the post-World War II period), the analytical scope of labor economics mushroomed far outside the domain of traditional economics, making it a difficult field to define in strict economic sense. Many labor economics specialists caution that the word "labor" should not be understood as exclusively linked to the discipline of "economics." Instead, they advocate a more interdisciplinary approach that draws critically from insights provided by the disciplines of sociology, political science, psychology, and organizational theory and behavior. As a result, labor economics has concerned itself with a large range of topics, including race and gender discrimination; labor-management relations; demographic economics; personal or social expenditures on education, medical care, and training, referred to as human capital investments; and a multitude of issues surrounding behavior in the workplace, a subject area germane to industrial and human relations schools.

During the last two decades of the twentieth century labor economics has been preoccupied with the problem of understanding and reversing a general economic productivity slowdown in the United States. As a proposed solution, a majority of labor economists and concerned others have recommended. . .

Recommended Supplement: *Encyclopedia of Business Information Resources*

For information about this publication (ISBN 0-8103-6906-0 and ISSN 0071-0210), call Gale Research at (800) 877-GALE.

Reference Navigator

Web site: http://www.gale.com   CD-ROM: not available
E-mail: galeord@gale.com   Library Reference Number:
Database: Dialog   _____

The *Encyclopedia of Business Information Resources (EBIR)* is an excellent reference book. Every business student should become familiar with its ability to portray such information as: title of a publication or database, author or editor, the name and address of the publisher, telephone numbers (regular and toll-free), year or frequency of issuance, and price. Brief descriptive notes are sometimes added to clarify a listing. In addition to printed and electronic sources, *EBIR* also directs you to up-to-date information providing organization names, addresses, and telephone numbers. A supplement issue is published with each edition to keep the reader up-to-date.

According to the authors, *EBIR* has become the first stop in any search for information on business topics. The range of subjects is quite broad because business activity can occur in so many areas of human endeavor. Whether you're interested in such high-tech fields as artificial intelligence, avionics, or urban development, or any one of over 1,200 topics, the search starts here.

To the extent possible, *EBIR* provides citations on the following categories:

General works	Handbooks and manuals
Abstracting and indexing service	On-line databases
Almanacs and yearbooks	Periodicals and newsletters
Bibliographies	Price sources
Biographical sources	Research centers and institutes
Directories	Statistics sources
Encyclopedias and dictionaries	Financial ratios
Trade associations and professional societies	

Perhaps the only drawback is that topics are given in alphabetical order, which is fine, but there is no index so you cannot find specific publications.

Description of Publication: *International Encyclopedia of Business and Management*

For information on this six-volume publication set (ISBN 0-415-07399-5), call Routledge (International Thomson Publishing Company) at (800) 222-7900.

Reference Navigator

Web site: http://www.routledge.com/   CD-ROM: not available

E-mail: info@routledge.com   Library Reference Number:

Database: see Web site   _____

The *International Encyclopedia of Business and Management (IEBM)* is a very contemporary work (1996) that has been written with the goal of meeting the needs of those who are preparing for or working in the rapidly changing organizational environments worldwide. The mission statement of the project authors was "to create a worldwide work of reference covering all aspects of management that is international both in terms of subject matter and its authorship." These authors are from more than 40 countries on five continents and include "a higher than usual proportion of women academics in the field." In addition to covering the main disciplines and subdisciplines that make up modern management, they address wide-ranging topics such as globalization, multinational corporations, transfer-pricing, and so on.

The reference is designed principally for undergraduates studying for degrees in business and management; MBA students and postgraduates; management faculty; and business practitioners.

The project group broke the topics into three primary areas: subject, geography, and biography. The list of subject areas is as comprehensive as possible. The *IEBM* is not only international but also interdisciplinary. A distinctive feature of the *IEBM* is that the team attempted from the outset to inject an international dimension that was largely absent in previous major reference works on management. Also, individual contributions to management thought and practice are considered important.

The encyclopedia contains 517 entries arranged in a single alphabetical sequence through five volumes (see the table of contents). Volume 6 is devoted to a comprehensive index of the key terms, concepts, countries, and names covered in Volumes 1 to 5, allowing users to reap maximum benefit from the encyclopedia. A guide to the index can be found at the beginning of the index. The encyclopedia has been extensively cross-referenced to signpost other entries that are likely to be of interest.

A numbered contents list at the beginning of each entry in the encyclopedia gives the headings of its main sections. The scope and structure of the entry can thus be reviewed and sections of particular interest easily located.

Thematic entries begin with an "Overview" section that serves as a brief introduction to the topic and a useful summary of the entry's contents. Biographical entries begin with a summary of the significant dates and events in the life of the subject and a list of his or her major works. Every entry is followed by a "Further Reading" section.

Another important source to consider regarding international business is the *Exporters' Encyclopedia* (ISSN 8755-013X) published by Dun & Bradstreet Information Services, (610) 882-7000. One can also get immediate help by calling D&B's Export Hotline at (610) 882-7260 or going on the Web to http://www.dbisna.com. The information in the *Exporters' Encyclopedia*, compiled and updated annually, can guide subscribers to broaden their marketing base for greater profits by penetrating international markets. Particular attention must be paid to export markets in Section II comprising the great bulk of the encyclopedia. Each market is divided into country profile, key contacts, trade regulations, documentation, marketing data, transportation, and business travel. These divisions are found in each country market to help you locate specific export information.

Accounting

OVERVIEW

Accounting is a discipline that seeks to provide information about a business entity. Such information is useful to those who are interested in making decisions that may affect the entity or one's relationship with the entity. This entry aims to provide a background to the accounting discipline that will enable the reader to fit the role of accounting into the broader arena of business and economic activity. It serves as an introduction to both managerial and financial accounting areas and related topics such as auditing and sets the stage for other entries which go into greater detail. However, no brief description of accounting can be expected to capture comprehensively the changing faces of the discipline over time or the impact of accounting on all business decisions, current and prospective.

1   INTRODUCTION

The term *accounting* conjures up a variety of images, ranging perhaps from that of a Dickensian clerk painstakingly recording an individual transaction, to that of the annual financial statements of a major multinational corporation, running to many pages of complex data. Both of these notions are valid, even if the clerk now uses the latest computer technology, but how do they fit together?

The term *financial accounting* concerns the whole of the area of the capture of financial data concerning a company's transactions, its organization into a database and the preparation of reports to shareholders, tax authorities and others outside the company, using aggregated data from the database (FINANCIAL ACCOUNTING). The term *managerial accounting* concerns the use of accounting data internally, within a company, to help with management and decision making and to improve profitability.

Techniques developed to meet financial accounting requirements include the preparation of shareholder reports for groups of companies under the same economic control (see CONSOLIDATED ACCOUNTING) and segmental reporting, which concerns the breakdown of aggregated information in annual reports in order to help predict future performance. Inflation accounting addresses the shortcomings of traditional financial accounting measurement methods in a context where monetary values are not fixed (see ASSET VALUATION, DEPRECIATION AND PROVISIONS; INFLATION ACCOUNTING) while the objectives of "creative accounting" are generally to improve reported earnings or to enhance a company's debt/equity ratio (see CREATIVE ACCOUNTING).

Cash flow accounting, an alternative approach to analysing transactions, concerns the preparation of the cash flow statement, which all major companies include in their annual external reporting package (see CASH FLOW ACCOUNTING). The external reports of large companies are subjected to auditing in order to reassure shareholders and other users of their validity (see STATUTORY AUDIT). People who read published accounts have developed special tools for extracting key information (see FINANCIAL STATEMENT ANALYSIS) and the accounts are also used as the basis for corporate taxation (see TAXATION, CORPORATE).

Financial accounting does not comprise a given set of techniques that are undisputed and used uniformly throughout the world. The legal, economic and social context of accounting has an important influence on how it is formulated and, consequently, the measurements and objectives of accounting

Recommended Supplement: *Encyclopedia of Consumer Brands*

If you would like information on this book (ISBN 1-55862-336-1), call St. James Press at (800) 347-GALE.

Reference Navigator

Web site: http://www.gale.com

E-mail: galeord@gale.com

Database: Dialog

CD-ROM: available

Library Reference Number:

_____

Encyclopedia of Consumer Brands provides substantive information on products that have been leaders in their respective brand categories and have had a decided impact on American business or popular culture. Often considered household words, the featured products have become integral parts of the lives of American consumers, and many have gone on to achieve international recognition.

The *Encyclopedia's* three volumes highlight approximately 600 of the most popular brands in America. Coverage in each book emphasizes brands that have been prominent since 1950 and are now on the market, with a few inclusions of instructive debacles such as the Edsel. Younger products that have experienced profound success or have notably influenced their industry are also included. With thousands of new products being introduced to the market each year—and only a handful of them still in existence five years after their launch—much can be learned from the stories behind prominent brands, whose success depends on an elusive combination of careful research, quality development, market savvy, advertising prowess, and precise timing.

Another publication, *Brands and Their Companies* (ISBN 08103-5574-4) a two-volume set by Gale Research and in its 13th edition, provides easy access to more than 282,000 consumer brands and about 51,000 manufacturers and distributors. Brands are presented first in an alphabetic sequence. Company listings follow in a separate section printed on yellow paper, permitting users to locate company information quickly and easily. When available, fax and toll-free numbers have been included.

Description of Publication: *Encyclopedia of Associations*

To obtain information on this book (ISBN 0-8103-6169-8), call Gale Research at (800) 877-GALE.

Reference Navigator

Web site: http://www.gale.com

E-mail: galeord@gale.com

Database: Dialog

CD-ROM: available

Library Reference Number:

_____

If you need to know something about a nonprofit organization this is the place to look. The *Encyclopedia of Associations (EA)* is the only source of detailed information concerning more than 22,000 nonprofit American membership organizations of national scope. (There is also an international edition.) These associations often publish excellent material on their industries; for example, McKinsey Global Institute's *Manufacturing Productivity* is an outstanding source of industrial data worldwide.

In a nation that has encouraged individualism, Americans have always felt the need to belong. Knowing they can achieve more through group efforts than they can individually, Americans have made associations one of the most powerful forces in the United States today. According to Gale Research, a study of 5,500 national associations conducted by the Hudson Institute on behalf of the American Society of Association Executives (ASAE) found:

- Seven out of ten Americans belong to at least one association.

- Associations annually spend $8.5 billion to offer education courses on technical and scientific matters, business practices, and more, to their members and the public. Associations spend more on continuing or specialized education than 49 of the 50 U.S. states.

- Associations spend $14.5 billion on industry standard-setting activities each year, approximately 400 times more than the U.S. government spends on setting and enforcing product and safety standards that affect every American.

Organizations often operate with small, volunteer staffs. Many such groups have requested that all written inquiries be accompanied by stamped, self-addressed envelopes. Replies can then be expedited and costs to the organization kept to a minimum.

The *Encyclopedia of Associations* is composed of three books: Volume 1: Part 1; Volume 1: Part 2; and Volume 1: Part 3. Parts 1 and 2 contain all the citations. Part 3 is the alphabetical index to organization names and keywords.

Entries in *EA* are arranged into 18 subject sections, as outlined on the table of contents page. Within each section, organizations are arranged in alphabetical order according to the assigned principal subject keyword, which appears as a subhead above organization names; therefore, the user need not know the exact name of the organization being sought.

The complete *Encyclopedia of Associations* series (including associations listed in the international and regional, state, and local editions) is available on-line through Dialog as File 114 and through NEXIS as file ENASSC.

The *EA* national edition (EA: National Organizations of the U.S. CD-ROM) is also available as a separate CD. Designed for ease of use, this version features a DOS-based graphical user interface (GUI) that addresses most common research needs and includes convenient search and downloading options. The semiannual CD-ROM version, called *Gale GlobalAccess: Associations*, also utilizes Dialog software.

A second source of association information that exclusively covers business-related associations is the *National Trade & Professional Associations Directory in the U.S.* The NTPA publication highlights meetings and lists approximately 7,000 organizations.

VOLUME 1

PART 1: SECTIONS 1–6

VOLUME 1

PART 2: SECTIONS 7–18

VOLUME 1

PART 3: NAME AND KEYWORD INDEX

SECTION 1
Trade, Business, and Commercial Organizations

ACCOUNTING

★1★ Accreditation Council for Accountancy and Taxation (ACAT)

1010 N. Fairfax St.
Alexandria, VA 22314-1574
Marianne M. Anderson, Dir.
PH: (703)549-2228
FX: (703)549-2984
Founded: 1973. **Staff:** 3. Nonmembership. Participants include accounting and tax practitioners, enrolled agents, certified public accountants, students, and others interested in attaining accreditation in accounting or taxation. Strives to raise professional standards and improve the practices of accountancy and taxation; to identify persons with demonstrated knowledge of the principles and practices of accountancy and taxation, to ensure the continued professional growth of accredited individuals by setting stringent continuing education requirements, to foster increased recognition for the profession in the public, private, and educational sectors. Conducts semiannual accreditation examination in accountancy. Tax credentials obtained through coursework and examination. Designations are: Accredited in Accountancy/Accredited Business Accountant, Accredited Tax Advisor and Accredited Tax Preparer. **Awards:** High Scorer Award. Frequency: semiannual. Type: recognition. Recipient: highest score on accountancy exam ● Type: recognition. **Affiliated With:** National Society of Public Accountants. **Formerly:** (1990) Accreditation Council for Accountancy.
Publications: *Accreditation Council for Accountancy and Taxation—Action Letter,* bimonthly. Advertising: not accepted ● *Accreditation Council for Accountancy and Taxation—Directory,* annual.
Conventions/Meetings: board meeting - 3/year.

★2★ Afilliated Conference of Practicing Accountants International (ACPA)

30 Massachusetts Ave.
North Andover, MA 01845-3413
Julie Vinson, Exec.Dir.
PH: (508)689-9420
FX: (508)689-9404
E-mail acpa@delphi.com
Founded: 1979. **Members:** 72. **Staff:** 3. **Budget:** $344,000. **Regional Groups:** 3. **Local Groups:** 2. Certified public and chartered accounting firms. Encourages the interchange of professional and legislative information among members with the aim of: enhancing service and technical and professional competency; maintaining effective management administration and practice development; increasing public awareness of members' capabilities. Facilitates availability and use of specialists and industry expertise among members in areas such as manufacturing, real estate, legal and medical services, finance, wholesaling, retailing, and municipal government. Makes client referrals; compiles revenue, operating expense, and cost ratio comparisons among firms. **Telecommunication Services:** electronic bulletin board. **Committees:** Quality Control; Regional Management. **Subgroups:** Computer; Employee Benefits; Litigation and Forensic Services; Tax. **Also Known As:** ACPA International.
Publications: *ACPA Directory,* annual. Price: free to members. Circulation: 5,000 ● *ACPA Worldwide Brochure* ● *Perspective.* Newsletter. Includes committee, networks, and membership updates and international news. ● Also makes available press kit.
Conventions/Meetings: annual international conference ● semiannual regional meeting.

★3★ American Accounting Association (AAA)

5717 Bessie Dr.
Sarasota, FL 34244-2399
Craig E. Polhemus, Exec.Dir.
PH: (941)921-7747
FX: (941)923-4093
Founded: 1916. **Members:** 10,000. **Staff:** 12. Teachers and practitioners of accounting. Promotes research and education in accounting. **Awards:** Type: fellowship. Recipient: bestowed to Ph.D. candidates in accounting. **Formerly:** (1953) American Association of University Instructors in Accounting.
Publications: *Accounting Horizons,* quarterly. Price: free to members; $60.00/year for nonmembers (agency discount available) ● *Accounting Review,* quarterly. Journal. Contains scholarly articles on all aspects of accounting; includes annual index. Price: free to members; $90.00/year for nonmembers (agency discount available) ● *Issues in Accounting Education,* semiannual. Price: free to members; $30.00/year for nonmembers (agency discount available) ● Newletter, periodic ● Also publishes special studies.
Conventions/Meetings: annual meeting (exhibits) - always August.

★4★ *American Association of Attorney-Certified Public Accountants (AAA-CPA)*

24196 Alicia Pky., Ste. K
Mission Viejo, CA 92691
Ronald M. DeVore, Exec.Dir.
PH: (714)768-0336
Founded: 1964. **Members:** 1,350. **Budget:** $430,000. **State Groups:** 19. Persons who are licensed both as attorneys and as certified public accountants (CPAs). Promotes high professional and ethical standards; seeks to safeguard and defend the professional and legal rights of attorney-CPAs. Conducts research on dual licensing and dual practice; maintains speakers' bureau, placement service, and a collection of published and unpublished articles on these subjects. Has compiled a list of attorney-CPAs in the United States; conducts biennial economic and practice survey. Maintains liaison with bar associations and accounting groups and offers referral service of potential clients. State groups conduct extensive self-education programs. **Computer Services:** Mailing lists. **Committees:** Continuing Education; Cooperation With Bar and Accounting Groups; Ethics and Opinions; Relations With Government Groups.
Publications: *American Association of Attorney-Certified Public Accountants—Membership List,* periodic. Membership Directory. Available as a computer printout or on pressure-sensitive mailing labels. Price: $135.00 ● *The Attorney-CPA,* 5 year. Newsletter. Contains updates on dual license regulations. Price: $30.00/year. ISSN: 0571-8279. Circulation: 1,800. Advertising: accepted ● *Attorney-CPA Directory,* annual. Membership Directory. Price: $160.00. Circulation: 1,500. Advertising: accepted. **Conventions/Meetings:** semiannual meeting (exhibits) - always June/July and November.

★5★ *American Association of Hispanic CPAS (AAHCPA)*

PO Box 871
Bronx, NY 10465-2455
Robert Rosairio, Dir.
PH: (718)823-6144
FX: (203)259-2872
Hispanic certified public accountants from the private and public sectors, accounting firms, universities, and banks. To maintain and promote professional and moral standards of His-panics in the accounting field. Assists members in practice development and develops business opportunities in securing government contracts for members. Sponsors continuing professional education seminars; bestows scholarships; operates speakers' bureau; provides employment services. **Committees:** Fundraising; Scholarship. **Formerly:** (1982) American Associations of Spanish Speaking CPS's.
Publications: *La Cuenta,* quarterly ● Membership Directory, annual
Conventions/Meetings: annual conference.

★6★ *American Intstitute of Certified Public Accountants (AICPA)*

1211 Avenue of the Americas
New York, NY 10036-8775
Philip B. Chenok, Pres.
PH: (212)596-6200
TF: (800)862-4273
FX: (212)596-6213
TX: 70 3396
Founded: 1887. **Members:** 316,000. **Staff:** 725. Professional society of accountants certified by the states and territories. Responsibilities include establishing auditing and reporting standards; influencing the development of financial accounting standards underlying the presentation of U.S. corporate financial statements; preparing and grading the national Uniform CPA Examination for the state licensing bodies. Conducts research and continuing education programs and surveillance of practice. Maintains over 100 committees including. . .

Recommended Supplement: *Yearbook of International Organizations*

Reference Navigator

Web site: http://www.reedref.com

E-mail: webmaster@www.reedref.com

Database: LEXIS-NEXIS

CD-ROM: available

Library Reference Number:

_____

If you would like to obtain information on this annual publication (ISSN 0084-3814), call Reed Elsevier Inc. at (800) 521-8110; or Union of International Associations (UIA) in Brussels: +32 2 640 18 08; fax: (32 2) 646 05 25.

If you need to find an international organization, this book will get you there. (It was recently integrated with *Who's Who in International Organizations*.) It tells you when the organization was founded; aims; structure; language(s); staff; finance; nongovernmental organizations relations; events; and members. The *Yearbook of International Organizations* attempts to cover all "international organizations," according to a broad range of criteria. It includes many bodies that may be perceived, according to narrower definitions, as not being fully international or as not being of sufficient significance to merit inclusion. You will find that such bodies often are included to enable users to make their own evaluation. For some users, these bodies may be of great interest. (User languages include English, German, French, and Dutch.)

According to the editors at the Union of International Associations, the total number of active organizations appearing in the *Yearbook of International Organizations* in 1994–1995 is 24,197. The breakdown is: 5,191 "conventional" international organizations; 14,719 other organizations; 1,633 recently reported or proposed organizations; 816 religious orders; and 1,838 treaties.

The book is written in three volumes:

Volume 1: Descriptions and Cross-References

(Appearing in alphabetical order of title, with index of abbreviations and other language titles inserted in the same sequence.)

1. Contents of organization descriptions.
2. Types of organization.
3. Legal status of international NGOs.
4. Statistics.
5. Continuity.
6. Editorial policy.

7. Complementary volumes.
8. Use of computers.
9. Union of International Associations.
10. The U.N. and the YIO.
11. Publications index.

Volume 2: Country Directory of Secretariats and Membership

Organizations classified by country of secretariat.

Organizations classified by countries of location of membership.

Statistics: by country and city.

Volume 3: Subject Directory and Index

Organizations classified by subject concerns.

Organizations classified by regional concerns.

Organizations classified by type and statistics: by subject.

Description of Publication: *Encyclopedia of American Industries*

For information on this two-volume publication (ESBN 0-7876-0102-0), call Gale Research at (800) 347-GALE; or fax: (313) 961-6815.

Reference Navigator

Web site: http://www.gale.com   CD-ROM: available

E-mail: galeord@gale.com   Library Reference Number:

Database: Dialog

If you are inclined to believe that an encyclopedia covering American industry is pretty big, you're right. Each of the two volumes is 1,625 pages long with lots of good information. Judging from the references cited at the end of each topic area (called "Industry Information Sources"), it is obvious that the contributors are using up-to-date data.

According to editors, the *Encyclopedia of American Industries (EAI)* is a major new business reference tool that provides detailed comprehensive information on a wide range of industries in every realm of American business. Volume 1 covers 460 manufacturing industries, each in its own essay. Manufacturing industries covered in this volume range from large ones, such as the automotive industry and the pharmaceutical industry, to smaller business sectors, such as the porcelain electrical supplies industry and the waterproof outerwear industry. Volume 2 presents 544 essays covering the vast array of service and other nonmanufacturing industries in America. Industries covered in this volume range from major economic entities, such as the airline industry and the insurance industry, to smaller sectors, such as bookstores and potato farms. Combined, these two volumes provide individual essays on every manufacturing, nonmanufacturing, and service industry in America represented by a four-digit Standard Industrial Classification code. Both volumes of the ***Encyclopedia*** are arranged numerically by SIC code for easy use.

The *Encyclopedia*'s business coverage includes information on historical events of consequence as well as relevant trends and statistics entering the mid-1990s. Sections of coverage in an *EAI* essay may include the following:

Industry Snapshot—provides an overview of the industry in the mid-1990s. Organization and Structure—discusses the configuration and functional aspects of the industry.

Background and Development—relates the industry's genesis and historical development, including major technological advances, scandals, pioneering companies, major products, important legislation, and other factors that shaped the industry.

Current Conditions—provides information on the status of the industry in the mid-1990s, with an eye to industry challenges on the horizon.

Industry Leaders—details specific industry leaders, the companies that reign in such areas as sales, market share, volume of production, and new product development.

Work Force—contains information on size, diversity, and characteristics of the industry's work force.

America and the World—discusses the United States' place in the global marketplace in the industry, as well as trade issues and key international developments and competitors.

Research and Technology—furnishes information on major technological advances, areas of research, and their potential impact on the industry.

Industry Information Sources—provides users with suggested further reading on the industry. These sources, also used to compile the essays, are publicly accessible materials such as magazines, general and academic periodicals, books, annual reports, and government sources, as well as material supplied by industry associations.

The *Encyclopedia of American Industries* also includes hundreds of informative, easy-to-read graphs that detail a wide range of key economic and business information on the diverse industrial landscape of America.

The *EAI* also provides two major indexes to aid the user:

- *General Index*—contains alphabetical references to all companies, associations, key government agencies, and specific legislation cited in the encyclopedia.
- *Industry Index*—contains more than 19,000 alphabetical references to various types of business products and services currently offered in the United States.

Something to Think About

Most burial casket manufacturers employ 100 or fewer people. As of 1991, the top 30 manufacturers employed 17,700 people total and had combined sales of $1.7 billion. Who is the largest manufacturer of burial caskets (SIC 3995) in the United States?

VOLUME ONE:

Manufacturing Industries

Furniture & Fixtures

SIC 2511

Wood Household Furniture

This classification consists of establishments engaged in manufacturing wood furniture commonly used in dwellings, and with the exception of television, radio, phonograph, and sewing machine cabinets; also, millwork production is classified in **SIC 2431: Millwork;** wood kitchen cabinets are classified in **SIC 2434: Wood Kitchen Cabinets.** Cut stone and concrete furniture classified in the major group for stone, clay, glass, and concrete products; laboratory and hospital furniture, except hospital beds, are in the major groups for measuring, analyzing, and controlling instruments; photographic, medical and optical goods; watches and clocks; beauty and barber shop furniture are classified in the major group for miscellaneous manufacturing industries; and those engaged in woodworking to individual order or in the nature of reconditioning and repair are classified in nonmanufacturing industries.

Since the average consumer spends more on furniture within two years of moving into a new house than at any other time, slow growth in housing in the early 1990s undoubtedly depressed household furniture sales. However, housing starts rebounded in 1993 and 1994. Total wood household furniture sales—comprising about 42 percent of household furniture shipments—were $9.3 billion in 1993 out of a total of $22.2 billion for wood, upholstered, and metal household furniture.

An increase in consumer confidence seemed to benefit wood furniture makers such as Bassett Furniture Industries, which earned $27.5 million on sales of $473.4 million in the fiscal year ending November 30, 1992. Chairman and chief executive officer Robert H. Spilman commented in the *Wall Street Journal* that his company had had no backlogs of wood furniture since the stock market crash of 1987. "The opportunity has been much easier in upholstery," Spilman said. Bassett's largest customer was J.C. Penney and most of its efforts concentrated on mid-priced furniture. The company has 44 factories in the United States. The bedroom and dining room furniture segment has been hardest hit, according to Spilman. In 1992, Acton Corp. closed a wood furniture factory employing 200 people in Mebane, North Carolina, citing decreased demand for high-end bedroom and dining room furniture. In the same year, Stanley Furniture Co., a $160 million a year wood furniture company, closed a plant in Waynesboro, Virginia.

Ready-to-assemble (RTA) furniture was the fastest-growing segment of the wood furniture market in the early 1990s, accounting for 13%, or $1.3 billion, of. . .

Recommended Supplement: *Encyclopedia of Global Industries*

For information on this publication (ISBN 0-8103-9767-6) call Gale Research at (800) 877 GALE; or fax: (800) 414-5043.

Reference Navigator

Web site: http://www.gale.com

E-mail: galeord@gale.com

Database: Dialog

CD-ROM: not available

Library Reference Number:

_____

The *Encyclopedia of Global Industries (EGI)* chronicles the history, development, and current status of 115 of the world's most lucrative and high-profile industries. The encyclopedia provides comprehensive, international coverage organized by industry, including:

- Biotechnology
- Computer software
- Information retrieval services
- Pharmaceutical preparations
- Telecommunications
- Commodity trading
- Engineering services
- Motor vehicles and car bodies
- Real estate
- Cable television services

The *Encyclopedia of Global Industries* is the only reference source that provides detailed international coverage organized by industry. This fairly recent publication provides narrative industry outlooks and projections under headings such as "Current Conditions," "Background and Development," "Research and Technology," and "Major Countries in the Industry." It contains more than 500 charts, tables, and graphs that were designed specifically for this publication and includes company and country rankings. It is formatted as follows:

- Alphabetical table of contents.
- Contents organized by industry.
- General index.
- Geographic index.
- Harmonized system/SIC conversion index.
- Industry index.

IV Computer Databases and Vendors

Optional database references:

- *Economic Intelligence Unit (EIU) on the Internet (http://www.eiu.com)*
- *EventLine (http://www.excerptamedica.com/eventline)*
- *WestLaw (http://www.westpub.com)*
- *Industry Insider (http://www.investext.com)*
- *Business Brower AP (http://www.onesource.com/)*
- *Thomson Investors Network (http://www.thomsoninvest.net)*
- *Knowledge Express Data Systems (http://www.KnowledgeExpress.com)*
- *I/PLUS Direct (http://www.investext.com)*
- *Ovid Java Client (http://www.ovid.com)*
- *MCB University Press (EMERALD) (http://www.mcb.co.uk)*

20   DATABASE

Description of Publication

For information on this bimonthly periodical (ISSN 0162-4105) call Online Inc. at (203) 761-1466; or fax: (203) 761-1444.

 Reference Navigator

Web site: http://www.onlineinc.com/database   CD-ROM: not available

E-mail: dbmag@onlineinc.com   Library Reference Number:

Database: not available

Database, which calls itself the magazine of electronic research and resources, is a fun magazine to read. It's well laid out at 115 pages or so and colorful with very informative articles. Two sections of the magazine are particularly useful: (1) "Business and Finance," and (2) "International Business & News."

The "Business and Finance" section offers new information about on-line opportunities from corporations, associations, and government sources. One example is the Coopers & Lybrand Lodging Research Network (http://www.lodgingresearch.com). This on-line information resource for lodging industry research features Coopers & Lybrand's economic forecasts, industry news, market profiles by city, a database of industry-specific real estate acquisitions, financial data of publicly traded lodging companies, new hotel construction data, lodging census and trend data from Smith Travel Research, and a library that includes U.S. economic and demographic statistics. Users can "store, sift, and merge data, as required." If that doesn't spice up the hotel-restaurant management school research assignments nothing will.

The second section, "International Business & News," also has some unique insights into CD-ROM and on-line opportunities. A recent issue announced the availability of two official CIA references, the *World Factbook 1996* and *Handbook of International Economics 1996,* on one CD-ROM from the National Technical

Information Service (NTIS), including search and retrieval software. The *World Factbook 1997* is a basic reference of 267 nations and other entities and includes reference maps (see also Chapter 16). The *Handbook of International Economics 1997* provides basic worldwide statistics from the last five years for comparing the economic performance of major countries and regions, including color maps, figures, and tables. The price of the CD, at this writing, is $40 plus $4 handling; orders can be placed by calling (703) 487-4650) or e-mail at: orders@ntis.fedworld.gov. The Web site is: http://www.ntis.gov

Each *Database* issue features about six articles (contemporary and market oriented, but also useful for research), such as "Mapping a Path to Success: Geographic Information Means Business to Knowledge Manager Cheryl Perkins," by Thomas Pack.

Each issue also includes nine very useful columns for researchers and a "Reviews" section that evaluates services and products. This section is followed by "Editor's Choice." Editor Mary Ellen Bates's August/September 1997 choice was the Wall Street Journal Interactive Edition. She does an excellent job of covering its Briefing Books collection—so pertinent to the goals of *Business Research Sources*, for example:

> Dow Jones's recent foray into Web publishing—the Wall Street Journal Interactive Edition (http://wsj.com)—has been well received, particularly once they added the full Publications Library. Another recent addition to WSJIE (sometimes pronounced whiz-gee) is the Briefing Books service. The Briefing Books are collections of material on publicly traded companies, nicely formatted and (best yet) included in the cost of the subscription.
>
> If you need a quick overview of a company's financial standing, current news and press releases, as well as convenient access to the company's EDGAR filings, the Briefing Book section of WSJIE is a great place to start. Articles in the current day's edition of *The Wall Street Journal* include links from the first mention of a company to that company's Briefing Book. You can also go directly to the Briefing Book search screen: http://wsj.com/edition/resources/documents/bbsearch.htm.

What does a Briefing Book contain? You better buy *Database* and find out! A sister publication to *Database* is called *ONLINE*: *The Leading Magazine For Information Professionals* (ISSN 0146-5422). It is published bimonthly by Online Inc., (800) 248-8466; fax: (203) 761-1444. *ONLINE* starts its 1997 January/February (20th anniversary) issue with this message: "Don't Go Online Without These Essential References For Online & Internet Searching" and then goes on to tout some of its services, such as the ONLINE Deskbook, "ONLINE Magazine's essential desk reference for online and internet searchers." The only desk reference to cover all the major on-line services and the Internet, it helps you identify important online information sources and put them to immediate use. It's loaded with shortcuts, troubleshooting guides, tips, and techniques; and contains the nuts and bolts to get up and running on-line. *ONLINE*'s job is to take you into the intricacies of the Internet, but it also covers databases, such as "ONLINE Magazine's Field Guide to the 100 Most Important Online Databases." It usually boasts of six feature articles, and it also covers recent books and includes a number of interesting columns, such as "ONLINE WORLD Picture Story," by Amy Ferrito.

199

CD-Rom Corner

Walt Crawford

The World on a Platter: CD-ROM Atlases

Some people love atlases for their own sake, exploring maps as a substitute for exploring the world. Good CD-ROM atlases can't duplicate the scope and beauty of the best printed maps—yet I find them fascinating. They can go far beyond printed atlases when it comes to investgating the world, its nations, and its peoples.

This column covers four 1997 world atlas CD-ROMs, including all the atlases that I could find in local stores. (I didn't find Dorling Kindersley's *Cartopedia* in four stores with extended selections and Mindscape's atlases also proved elusive.) These four are 3D Talking Globe from Now What's "Small Blue Planet" series (henceforth "3D Globe"), Compton's Interactive World Atlas 1997 (henceforth "Compton's"), which is bundled with Compton's Complete Street Guide (reviewed separately), ABC 3D Atlas 97 from Creative Wonders (henceforth "ABC"), and Encarta 97 World Atlas from Microsoft (henceforth "Encarta").

THE IDEAL CD-ROM WORLD

My ideal CD-ROM world atlas would include detailed composite satellite views of the earth both by day and by night; accurate geophysical and topographical maps at reasonable levels of detail; accurate political maps with sensible level of detail; and user-controlled options for displays. Large-scale maps would always view the earth as a globe, using flat projections only for smaller areas. Maps would never be pixilated and would always be pleasing, accurate, and meaningful. Legends would be instantly available, and the scale would always be clear.

You should be able to zoom in or out, move around the globe using a hand or pointers, or go directly to a city, nation, continent, or other place from a detailed finding list. The ideal finding list includes all the places you would plausibly look for without absurd or inaccurate details. It makes lookup easy by jumping to the appropriate alphabetic area as you enter a name letter by letter. The ideal atlas includes maps so flexible and detailed that any item in the finding list leads to a visible point on a map.

The ideal CD-ROM world atlas is more than just superb maps. It should also explain the world, its nations, and its people. From any point on a map or by selecting from available lists you should be able to do most or all of the following:

- Get recent population figures and summary descriptive and historical notes on any significant city, and go from there directly to the appropriate country.

- Learn about the geography, history, climate, government, economy, and culture of a country and its people, including detailed statistics; see the flag; hear the anthem; hear samples of local music (fully identified); and see pictures highlighting the country and its people (fully identified and credited).

- Hear native pronunciations of standard phrases, the country's name, and possibly city names.

- Explore the facts and figures of nations and regions through hundreds of relevant statistics, with presentation of those statistics customized to your needs—e.g., ranked tables for selected nations, a region, or the world, statistical maps for a region or the world, and possibly timeline graphs for statistics over time. The source of statistical information should be readily available, as should the dates for changing statistics.

The ideal CD-ROM atlas might even add ways to learn about the world in general—for example, visual essays on aspects of ecology and the environment.

The ideal CD-ROM is stable and attractive, making excellent use of color, scaling to fill high-resolution screens, and offering to export maps, graphs, and textual files with credit attached. It uses screen space efficiently, so that maps, pictures, and essays have plenty of room. It has AutoPlay under Windows

Ratings Summary		
☆☆☆☆	[90–100]	Excellent. Highly recommended.
☆☆☆	[80–89]	Very good. Recommended.
☆☆	[70–79]	Good. Well worth considering.
☆	[60–69]	Fair. Flawed but my meet certain needs.
❏	[1–59]	Poor.

95, installs politely and uses a modest amount of disk space, runs correctly under AutoPlay, and never crashes or hangs the system on exit.

That's a tall order, and none of these products does it all. I'm not sure that you can do all this well within the 660MB limit of current CD-ROMs. Two of these atlases do exceptionally well, however, and between them they meet nearly all the criteria of my ideal atlas—albeit at a total expense of $60 to $100.

I didn't include Mindscape World Atlas 6.0.0 in this review because it's somewhat out of date, but it's useful to

Recommended Supplement: *Gale Directory of Databases*

Reference Navigator

Web site: http://www.gale.com/gale.html   CD-ROM: available

E-mail: 72203.1552@compuserve   Library Reference Number:

Database: Dialog

The July 1997 issue of the *Gale Directory of Databases* (ISBN 0-8103-5754-2) contains contact and descriptive information on more than 11,500 databases, more than 3,700 producers, and more than 2,100 on-line services and vendors/distributors of database products—easily making it the most complete guide to the electronic database industry worldwide. For more information, call (800) 877-GALE.

The *Gale Directory of Databases* is published in two volumes, which are revised and updated every six months:

Volume 1: Online Databases—profiles approximately 5,900 on-line databases made publicly available from the producer or an on-line service.

Volume 2: CD-ROM, Diskette, Magnetic Tape, Handheld, and Batch Access Database Products—profiles more than 5,550 database products offered in "portable" form and through batch processing.

Each volume of the *Gale Directory of Databases* contains three sections of descriptive entries and three indexes:

- "Online Databases" (Volume 1) and "Product Descriptions" (Volume 2) feature complete descriptions of electronic database products, including address/phone number of company; type of material (bibliographic, full-text, etc.); subject coverage; language (usually English); geographic coverage; time span (e.g., 1979 to date); updating; on-line availability; also on-line as part of . . .; alternate electronic formats (e.g., CD-ROM).
- "Database Producers" Includes contact information for database producers and a list of products.
- "Online Services" (Volume 1) and "Vendors/Distributors" (Volume 2) provide contact information for vendors and distributors, conditions of use, and a list of the products they offer.
- "Geographic Index."
- "Subject Index."
- "Master Index."

The *Directory* is available on a subscription basis through GaleNet, a new on-line information resource that features an easy-to-use interface, the powerful search capabilities of the BRS/SEARCH retrieval software, and ease of access through the World Wide Web. For information, call Melissa Kolehmainen at (800) 877-GALE, ext. 1598.

As long as we're on the subject of information technology, it certainly would be wise to include at least one other important source that describes the information highway: *Internet World: The Magazine for Savvy Internet Users* (ISSN 1064-3923). It's available through Meckler-Media Corporation at (800) 573-3062. This magazine, besides being very informative about otherwise esoteric subjects, can also have some pretty racy topics: "Corporate Censors," for example, pointed out that "A Nielsen audit of the *Penthouse* site turned up heavy traffic coming from IBM, Apple, AT&T, Bell, DEC and Hewlett-Packard."

Internet World is a great magazine if only because it reads easy enough to involve most of us in the world of computers, a situation that will become more and more necessary. *Internet World* (130 pages) has a colorful, crisp and sometimes irreverent approach that makes the reader feel at ease with the subject. It has a particular bent for students, such as "Earn a Master's, Virtually," (The Internet gives grad school a new twist—and a new life—as more colleges offer classes through the wire) by Vicky Phillips. Along with the 10 or so feature articles and columns of excellent reference material, the departments offer entertaining and informative essays through "Internet Forum," "Internet News," "The Surfboard," "The Bookshelf," and other sources. The editors also provide a "Home Page Forum" with products and services immediately available through the company's URL. The standard index to advertisers includes an editorial product index that provides a Web site address. The magazine can be reached on the Web at http://www.iworld.com.

You may also wish to get a copy of New Riders' *Internet Yellow Pages 1997* (ISBN 1-56-205-6719). If you are interested in more information go to http://www.mcp.com/Newriders. Be careful when you go to the bookstore though; computer how-to's and directories have to be the longest shelf there.

If you are in business (or just want your own Web site), AT&T Easy World Wide Web offers to give you hassle-free end-to-end solutions, from implementing to managing your Web site. To help you dive right in, it advertises Web site creation tools and access to training. It can also refer you to a team of professional Web developers for help in designing an effective site. Call (800) 7HOSTIN, Dept. 1130, or e-mail: telemark@attmail.com or visit the Web site at: http://www.att.com/easycommerce/.

Look at Lotus's SmartSuite before you retire for the evening. SmartSuite lets you do some real work on the Internet without leaving the familiar business applications you use everyday. With SmartSuite you can jump from one task to the next, from desktop to Internet, without missing a beat. You can find, share, and even publish information to anyone that is available on your internal intranet, if you have one, and on the Internet. You can use whatever browser you want to publish your 1-2-3 models to the Internet or pull information from the Internet into your spreadsheet. Plus, you can easily publish HTML files or create a really cool home page—no special training needed. If you want to work the smart way on the Internet, you may want to check these people out and see what services are available, call (800) TRADE UP, ext. C706, or visit them on the Web at http://www.lotus.com.

21 LEXIS-NEXIS

Description of Database

For information on LEXIS-NEXIS, a division of Reed Elsevier Inc., contact them via e-mail at j.rigg@elsevier.co.uk, or call: (914) 524-9200 or go to an on-line vendor, such as CompuServe or America Online. The address is: http://www.lexis-nexis.com.

For those who remember, and there are many who don't, gathering what is called secondary research data, the stuff somebody else has published and the library is filled with, was usually an arduous task. You had to scour the library; write the government, some corporation, trade association, or otherwise; and often wait several weeks for the reply. "We're sorry, Mr. Jones will be out of the office until next year." Today, of course, that drudgery is over and on-line databases are available by the thousands in every category one can possibly think of, with certainly more to come.

Databases can be classified as either *referral,* which simply point to other databases, or *source,* which generally contain full-text original source data. Subcategories include numeric, bibliographic, full-text, and directory. The advantages of the databases should be obvious: quick access to a large variety of information, lower costs (fewer people needed to stock the bookshelves now), and the little companies get access to the same information the big guys get. Disadvantages are also easy to see—you have to know how to conduct a search. If your dog, for example, has hinted for a quick piece on fleas, you may be courting trouble by searching for "flea." You could end up with a lot of "flea-market" entries. The story goes that one novice researcher working for a famous advertising agency in New York inadvertently punched in a command to call up all stories on one particular topic in their entirety. Once placed, the instructions could not be canceled. The result was a $700 bill for data and telephone lines. Another problem is that if the databases aren't kept up-to-date you may still have to go to the local library anyway. Finally, as you can gather from the story above, searching may prove to be an expensive affair.

At this writing, the LEXIS-NEXIS services, perhaps the world's premier on-line legal, news, and business information services, provide support to customers in more than 60 countries. More than 780,000 active users subscribe to the LEXIS-NEXIS services. There are 6,900 databases between the two services. Just to give you an idea how these guys sell more data than McDonald's does burgers, LEXIS-

NEXIS adds 9.5 million documents *each week* to the more than 1 billion documents on-line. In comparison, the Internet's World Wide Web is estimated to add 300,000 documents each week to a total of between 11 million and 16 million documents currently available on the Web.

The LEXIS-NEXIS service offers three different options of searching for information: FREESTYLE, Boolean, and Easy Search. The FREESTYLE feature is the first plain-English search feature that allows the user to search both legal and nonlegal materials all on one commercial database. Experienced searchers most often select the traditional Boolean search option for precision searching. The Easy Search feature, on the other hand, uses on-line menus and screen prompts to assist novice users in formulating precise search requests and then selects parts of the database to search for the user.

The LEXIS service contains major archives of federal and state case law, continuously updated laws of all 50 states, state and federal regulations, and public records from major U.S. states. The LEXIS service has 41 specialized libraries covering all major fields of practice, including tax, securities, banking, environmental, energy, and international. If, for example, you wanted to do research in accounting, you can, with a single research strategy, have access to federal and state tax information, accounting technical literature and guidelines, financial reports, trade publications, and news. Because the information is on-line, it is updated as changes occur. No more time is wasted wading through a CD-ROM library whose contents are likely to be incomplete and out of date. According to the folks at LEXIS-NEXIS, you'll be surprised how economical on-line researching can be. They offer to help companies control their research costs at economical fixed rates that fit the firm's size and research volume. Rates change and so do services, so if you are trying to work out a program for your own individual research needs, give them a call at (800) 356-6548 and see what they can do for you.

The NEXIS service is a leading news and business information service that contains more than 7,100 sources, of which 3,700 provide their entire publications on-line. These include regional, national, and international newspapers, news wires, magazines, trade journals; and business publications.

The NEXIS service is the exclusive archival source for *The New York Times* in the legal, business, and other professional markets. The NEXIS service also offers several thousand other news sources including the *Washington Post, Los Angeles Times, BusinessWeek, Fortune,* and *The Economist.* It is a one-stop service for both national network and regional television broadcast transcripts, in addition to carrying CNN and National Public Radio news and features. Major news services of China, France, Germany, Japan, Mexico, the United Kingdom, the unified Russian republics, and the United States are vital sources of international business information and news. In addition, the NEXIS service contains more than 2,000 sources of abstracts including *The Wall Street Journal.*

NEXIS also has "Market Library" which focuses on marketing and industry news by specific industry. Topics included are banks, business and finance, computers and communications, energy, entertainment, and environment. There are many other LEXIS-NEXIS features (EdgarPlus, ECLIPSE, FOCUS, etc.) not mentioned here because of the length of descriptions. One service, however, is important to mention because it can be used by nonsubscribers. NEXIS EXPRESS can check citations and find cases or information from the LEXIS legal libraries and the NEXIS business and news libraries. Payment can be made using major credit cards; and documents will be sent via fax, e-mail, overnight or first-class mail. Call: (800) 843-6476 for service.

A second popular database (among many) that you should be familiar with is Dialog. For information on this Knight-Ridder database, go to your on-line vendor (America Online, CompuServe, etc.). The address is http://www.dialog.com.

Dialog is one of the larger, most diversified vendors of on-line services. Dialog Information Retrieval Service offers more than 450 databases, approximately two-thirds of which have direct business applications. Dialog's business information runs the gamut from company directories, financial services, and statistical files, to news wires, periodical indexes, and full-text files of newspapers, journals, and newsletters. With few exceptions, business databases are somewhat expensive to access, regardless of the type of system on which they reside. Government-produced databases, however, offer more reasonably priced alternatives, even when found on commercial systems. Products from government agencies include bibliographic files, numeric databases, and electronic directories. For example, the complete text of the U.S. Commerce Department's *Commerce Business Daily* can be searched on Dialog and several other vendors. On-line systems remain the most heavily used electronic sources for business searching, but they are by no means the only medium at the researcher's disposal. Important business databases can be found with increasing frequency on CD-ROMs (see SIRS in "Commentary") and diskettes for microcomputers.

CompuServe Information Service is one of the largest consumer vendors (according to the *Directory of Business Information*). Over the years it has gradually added more business and financial databases. Current databases include business and financial news (*Reuter Financial Report*), corporate news releases (*Business Wire*), investment statistics (*Compustat, Standard & Poor's*), small business (*Small Business Reports*), and more.

CompuServe Information Service-Knowledge Index was formerly an off-peak-hours database offered by Dialog. It is now cosponsored by Dialog and Compuserve. Knowledge Index is one of Compuserve's gateway services; the files are still kept at the Dialog computer. There is (at this publishing date) a charge of $24 per hour to search the database, and there is an additional charge for downloading information. Knowledge Index includes many databases in addition to the standard Compuserve business databases: *ABI/Inform; Academic Index; Business Software Index; Consumer Reports; Economic Literature Index; GPO Publications Reference File; Harvard Business Review Online; Standard & Poor's Corporate Descriptions; Standard & Poor's Daily News,* and more.

Another business database that is often suggested by librarians is *Edgar Database of Corporation Information* at http://www.sec.gov.

You may have heard of the *ABI/Inform* database because of its value to professionals in all business and management disciplines. It is, according to its editors, a comprehensive source of ideas, concepts, and tested methods in business and management decision making.

ABI/Inform covers business and management periodicals from over 585 journals and provides long, informative summaries of articles. Eighty percent of the journals are published in the United States. Emphasis is placed on cover-to-cover inclusion of some 300 of these 585 journals. All articles are abstracted with the exception of news sections, letters to the editor, book reviews, and similar regular features or columns. The remaining journals are mentioned selectively. *ABI/Inform* is updated monthly with approximately 35,000 citations a year. Call Data Courier Inc. at (502) 583-4111, if you would like more information.

Something to Think About

The LEXIS-NEXIS service offers three different options of searching for information. Do you know what they are? How many countries are serviced by LEXIS-NEXIS? In comparing LEXIS-NEXIS and the Internet's World Wide Web, which do you think adds the most documents each week?

General software sources would not usually have a place in this text; however, so much of the business publications environment is made up of software, there is one reference publication that should not be overlooked. *The Software Encyclopedia* from R.R. Bowker at (908) 665-6770, provides comprehensive and detailed information on microcomputer software. The 11th edition contains 50,000 software titles from 3,000 publishers, including 16,671 unique titles. All software is classified under one or more of the 580 subject headings or applications, which are grouped under 38 major headings. Each title entry contains title, version number, publication date, compatible hardware, operating system requirements, memory required, price, a description of the type of customer support available, package extras (i.e., manuals, etc.) and author if it differs from the publisher, when provided.

The Software Encyclopedia is simply organized. Volume 1 contains the "Title Index," an alphabetical listing by title of all software, and the "Publisher/Title Index," an alphabetical listing of all publishers with full address and telephone, as well as a listing of their titles. Volume 2 contains the "System Compatibility/Applications Index," which provides software organized by system, subject/application heading, and titles.

WebSite Source Book (ISSN 1089-4861) lists the top U.S. businesses, organizations, agencies and institutions that maintain a presence on on the World Wide Web. It is published by Omnigraphics, Inc. (editorial: [954] 525-9422; or sales/customer service: [800] 234 1340). The first edition (1996) contains more than 7,100 individual listings, presented both alphabetically by name and in subject arrangement. Listings provide the name of the sponsoring company or organization and its address and telephone number, together with its World Wide Web address (URL). Most listings also include fax numbers and electronic mail addresses as well as toll-free telephone (if available).

One other Web source not to overlook is *Web Guide Magazine,* which can be found at the newstand or on the net at: http://www.web-guide-mag.com/.

It's All You Need To Know

1,409,246,599

More than 9.5 million documents are added each
week to the more than 1 billion documents available
on LEXIS-NEXIS. Above is the approximate count
of documents currently available on LEXIS-NEXIS.

LEXIS·NEXIS® Xchange™

Including
Business Xchange™ for Business

Government

About LEXIS·NEXIS®

Products & Services

Communications

Customer Service

© Copyright   @ Comment   ⑤ Search the Site

 This site is best viewed using
Microsoft Internet Explorer 4.0.

LEXIS·NEXIS® Channels

HIGHLIGHTS

Just In
What's New
Index
Subscription
Information
Employment
Connect

LEXIS®·NEXIS® and Privacy
Protection
Strong Industry Standards

LEXIS®·NEXIS® Year 2000
Program
Multi-phase program update

LEXIS·NEXIS Around the World
For customers outside the US

LEXIS®·NEXIS® EXPRESS™
Fee-based research for
non-subscribers

LEXIS®·NEXIS® reQUESTer
Now available on the Web

Information Privacy
LEXIS·NEXIS Practices

Content

**Subject
Collections**

**Profound
Sourcebook**

World Reporter

Frost & Sullivan

HOME   CORPORATE   CONTENT   PRODUCTS   SUPPORT   CONTACTS   SITE SEARCH

Subject Collections

Subject Collections details the information by subject area available on the Dialog and DataStar databases. If you require further information on content email us we will be happy to provide additional data.

Data includes the following categories.

- Business and Finance
- Chemicals
- Energy and Environment
- Food and Agriculture
- Intellectual Property
- Government and Regulations
- Medicine
- News and Media
- Pharmaceuticals
- Reference
- Technology
- Social Sciences

Business and Finance
All the information you need to gain a competitive edge with this subject collection. Market research including market share and sales figures, competitive intelligence, corporate finance, business directories, and financials on 14 million U.S. and international companies. Information sources include Dun & Bradstreet, Standard & Poor's, Frost & Sullivan, FIND@/SVP, and SEC filings.
See Company Intelligence Smart Tool sheets
See Products & Markets Smart Tool sheets

Recommended Supplement: *America Online*

AOL is a major consumer on-line vendor (approximately 11.6 million subscribers worldwide) with databases concerning computing, entertainment, education, and references nicely laid out in a colorful screen format. Upgrades to the service are fairly frequent and sometimes substantial. AOL is a relatively young company, but it is adding services steadily, which did cause a problem a while ago, but it has however, overcome these problems. AOL has a growing personal finance unit that includes Morningstar, the comprehensive mutual fund service. It also provides information from the "Nightly Business Report" and the daily TV business broadcast. It is also increasing other business news; for example, *The New York*

Times' current leading stories are available every day. Reuters News Media Inc. provides continuously updated news and financial information from the United States, Europe, and Asia. Additional news comes from special on-line versions of the *Chicago Tribune*, *USA Today*, National Public Radio, and C-Span.

It also carries investor information, such as *Hoover's Handbooks* (see Chapter 2), which profiles the largest and fastest growing public and private companies worldwide. Recent issues of *Worth*, a newsletter, are in the database, and you can easily download interesting material from that source. Stock quotes and portfolio services are also available. Stock movements can be downloaded into spreadsheets for tracing complete portfolio results on a personal computer. America Online can compute your portfolio, and you can buy and sell stock on-line.

One other source that's been around for awhile and had its ups-and-downs is Prodigy (from Knight-Ridder). It provides business and financial databases, financial planning, investments, office services, and real estate information.

Something to Do:

UMI, a Bell & Howell company, is one of the world's largest information archivers and distributors, offering value-added information via microform, paper, CD-ROM, and the Internet to users in more than 160 countries. ProQuest Direct is UMI's (The Answer Company™) premier online information service. They provide powerful, convenient search and retrieval, right from your desktop, to one of the world's largest collections of information, including summaries of articles from over 5000 pulications, with many in full text, full image format. A particularly useful service is their source of 1.4 million citations for doctoral dissertations, over one million of which are available in full text. You should give them a call at (800)521-0600, or email: info@umi.com. Check out their products and services by visiting their UMI info store online at http://www.umi.com, or contact them by phone (800)248-0360 or fax (734)761-1032.

Commentary

The Future of Libraries*

The future library is being built today. In many major cities, such as San Francisco, Portland, Denver and Cleveland, there is a revival of dowtown areas and libraries are part of this dowtown cultural revival. Even though there is concern about taxes, citizens are often willing to pay for cultural centers and the libraries within them. University libraries are also undergoing buildng booms, as they

---

*This section was written by Eleanor Goldstein, who with her husband, Elliot, co-founded SIRS, Inc. (Social Issues Resources Series), in 1973. Goldstein is director of research and development at SIRS; she is also the publisher of Upton Books, a division of SIRS.

strive to prepare for the future, while high school libraries are feeling the pressure to provide electronic opportunities for their students. New technology requires renovation in libraries across the nation, and this is one area that does not face much opposition. No one dares to say that we don't need to provide our citizens with better opportunities for learning.

What Are These New Libraries Like? And What Is the Mission of These New Libraries?

The library is a multifaceted institution. Its mission varies, as do the needs of its patrons. Public libraries are far different from university libraries, which are far different from small college libraries, which are still far different from public school libraries. One question, however, that each of these libraries faces is the role of technology. Enamored as Americans are with the concept of the information superhighway, we can be sure that few, if any libraries, when thinking about the future, will ignore that highway. We are led to believe that if we are not connected, we will be lost in the past. No one wants to be left behind. The *information superhighway* is the path we must all follow—for it is the way to the future.

Public libraries are often masterpieces of architecture. The new library in San Francisco, which opened in April 1996, is an example:

> From its light-filled asymmetrical atrium to the high-tech grid beneath its floors, San Francisco's new library is a stunning piece of architecuture . . . 'This is a library that was made to be friendly from the beginning,' says James Ingo Freed, principal designer of the library.[1]

Public libraries are also community centers, where activities take place morning, noon, and night. The public library in Fort Lauderdale, Florida, for example, was selected as library of the year in 1996, and Director Sam Morrison takes pride in the fact that his library system provides "something for everyone."[2] Film screenings, poetry readings, art shows, concerts, book reviews, and story hours fill the days and nights of the main library and its many branches. Citizens love their libraries. In a 1995 budget survey published in *Library Journal,* 85 percent of the libraries that responded "reported increases in their total budget, with growth averaging 7 percent a year."[3] Furthermore, U.S. News & World Report/CNN found, in a recently conducted poll, that "67 percent of American adults went to a library at least once in the past year—up markedly from the 51 percent who visited in 1978."[4]

---

1. Daniel Sneider, "San Francisco Library Marks Trent Toward Urban Revival," *The Christian Science Monitor,* April 3, 1996.

2. Interview with Eleanor Goldstein.

3. Marilyn Gardner, "Public Libraries Bounce Back—With Help from Their Friends," *The Christian Science Monitor,* October 3, 1995.

4. "The Resilient Library," *U.S. News & World Report,* March 18, 1997, available from http://www.usenews.com/usnews/issue/11outpol.htm.

Paul LeClerc, the New York Public Library president, said, "If you look at what's happening in many places around the country, you see a level of investment in library collections and access that is unparalleled to anything we've seen in this country since the time of Andrew Carnegie."[5] *Newsweek* magazine substantiates this claim, pointing out that we are "in the midst of a coast-to-coast library boom. Cities are racing to rewire and even rethink their libraries, rounding up all the new tools they can afford to get ready for a new millennium."[6] Only 8 percent of Americans think "computers will render libraries obsolete; 91 percent say libraries will still be needed,"[7] according to a recent Gallup poll.

Universities are facing a major challenge regarding their libraries. Since the beginnings of university libraries, their mission has always been to build collections. Now, that is becoming an obsolete idea as universities strive to provide the most accurate, current, and cutting-edge information. University libraries' purpose will change from building collections to providing databases, as location becomes irrelevant. *Issues in Science and Technology* magazine warns that "the library must either become the facilitator of retrieval and dissemination or be relegated to the role of a museum."[8]

The director of the library at Florida Atlantic University, Bill Miller, says, "The role of the library in the future will be more central than ever anticipated. It will be up to the library to supply, organize, pay for, and facilitate the acquisition of information. Libraries will have to license information and instruct people in the use of databases. Good databases are expensive and the cost will not be viable for individual purchase."[9] Miller sees the role of the library in the future as expanding—not declining—as might have been anticipated with the Internet and access to every home. Passwords will be necessary to access many databases, and the cost of acquiring these passwords will likely be borne by libraries.

Small liberal arts colleges, which do not have significant need for specialized research databases, do not play the role of public libraries where activities are constantly taking place or that of university libraries, where expensive databases will be housed. The future of these college libraries will be largely with computerized databases and interlibrary loans. A professor at one of these colleges remarked that the library is rarely busy. It does not compare to a nearby university, which has extended nighttime and weekend hours. Although books will not go away, CD-ROMs will be the most applicable format, since on-line databases will be more costly and less necessary.

"Secondary school libraries are not part of curriculum collaborative efforts of teams of facilitators and students," according to Roger Ashby, librarian at

5. John Markoff, "Data On-Line and on Shelves: Libraries of the Future," *The New York Times,* April 15, 1996.

6. Laura Shapiro, "A Mall for the Mind," *Newsweek,* October 21, 1996, pp. 84–86.

7. "The Resilient Library."

8. William A. Wulf, "Warning: Information Technology Will Transform the University," *Issues in Science and Technology,* Summer 1995, pp. 46–52, reproduced in *SIRS Researchers CD-ROM* (Boca Raton, FL: SIRS, Spring 1997), *Technology 1995,* vol. 4, art. no. 53.

9. Interview with Eleanor Goldstein.

Bloomfield Hills Schools in Michigan. "The world is our resource—students are doing visual digital imaging and interacting with a similar group near Perth, Australia," Ashby says. "Kids in a one-room schoolhouse are connected in the media center area to a Baltimore inner-city school. Traditional and electronic media blend in a wonderful mix, which allows kids 55 miles from town to be attached to the rest of the world."[10]

Hilda Weisberg, librarian at Morristown High School, says "Libraries are becoming more integrated into the education program. As textbook limitations are being left behind and students need to develop flexible research strategies using changing technological formats, they require new skills to help them sift and filter through the information glut that includes propaganda, 'junk mail,' nonrelevant and noncredible sources along with the jewels they are trying to find." She further comments that "all kids need to learn to recognize propaganda when they see it. It's now a basic communication skill. The Internet is the most unbalanced collection available. A good library has fringe groups represented as a minor part—on the Internet the fringe predominates."[11]

According to Dave Loertscher, a librarian in San Jose, California, "School librarians are becoming information coaches and collaborators. They speak library with a technology accent."[12]

So, it appears that libraries are more important than ever. Technology is moving in, where it will predominate at the university level and play a significant role in the public schools. The public library seems to have a future as a great monument to the word, whether it be written or encapsulated on a CD-ROM, or even on-line. The public library is a cherished community asset, vibrant and enduring.

SIRS

For information on SIRS Inc. (*The Knowledge Source*), call (800) 232-SIRS or fax: (561) 994-4704.

Reference Navigator

Web site: http://sirs.com   CD-ROM: available
E-mail: info@sirs.com   Library Reference Number:
Database: available

The original concept for this entry was SIRS's strong representation in libraries throughout the world (over 30,000) and its quality CD-ROM workstations. However, SIRS is no longer simply in the research-printing and CD-ROM business; it

---

10. Interview with Eleanor Goldstein.
11. Ibid.
12. Ibid.

also is on the Internet. However, where American Online is a vendor, and Dialog and NEXIS are business databases, *SIRS excels in CD-ROM workstations for the library and commercial use.* SIRS has a number of databases; only those involving business and economics are listed below:

- *SIRS Renaissance*—the first electronic reference tool providing diverse current perspectives on the arts and humanities. This PC-compatible CD-ROM reference tool provides selected full-text articles from more than 500 newspapers and magazines.

- *SIRS Researcher*—a general reference database with thousands of full-text articles exploring social, scientific, historic, economic, political, and global issues. Carefully selected articles from more than 1,200 domestic and international newspapers, magazines, journals, and government publications can be accessed instantaneously. Articles are from 1988 to present. Some articles are accompanied by graphics, charts, maps, diagrams, and drawings. SIRS flagship database is available in a variety of CD-ROM and on-line versions: DOS, Macintosh, and Windows.

- *SIRS Government Reporter*—an electronic database bringing together a wide range of information published by and about our federal government. The information is presented in six databases: (1) U.S. Government Documents, (2) U.S. Supreme Court Decisions, (3) Justices' Directory, (4) Historic Documents, (5) Congressional Directory, and (6) Federal Agency Directory.

SIRS is built on the premise that many excellent resources never get to the classroom or library, such as magazine, journal and newspaper articles, and government documents. The mission of SIRS is to locate current information; organize it into a meaningful structure, omitting redundancy of information; obtain permission to reprint; and make the information readily accessible via a variety of platforms: print, CD-ROM, and World Wide Web.

Today, SIRS information systems can be found in approximately 30,000 institutions around the world, including all U.S. Air Force bases, Department of Defense schools, Native American schools, universities, colleges, public and private schools (K-12), and libraries.

V STATISTICS, DEMOGRAPHICS, AND CONSUMERISM

Optional statistic and demographic references:

- *U.N. Demographic Yearbook*
- *Business Statistics*
- *The State of Small Business*
- *Statistical Yearbook*
- *Vital Statistics of the United States*
- *Dictionary of Demography*
- *A Bibliographic Guide to Population Geography*
- *Recent Social Trends in the United States 1960–1990*
- *County and City Data Book*
- *Crime in the United States*

22   STATISTICAL ABSTRACT OF THE UNITED STATES

Description of Publication

For information on this publication (ISBN 0-89059-055-9), call the U.S. Government Printing Office at (202) 512-0000.

 Reference Navigator

Web site: http://www.access.gpo.gov/su_docs   CD-ROM: available

E-mail: bybssys@access.digex.net   Library Reference Number:

Database: see Web site

"One of, if not the best single publication from our government."

Economic Developer/Chamber of Commerce

"Single most valuable reference tool."

Librarian

If that hasn't whetted your appetite, you probably lack that proverbial thirst for knowledge. The *Statistical Abstract of the United States*, published since 1878, is the standard summary of statistics on the social, political, and economic organization of the United States. It is designed to serve as a convenient volume for statistical publications and sources. The latter function is supported by the introductory text to each section, the source note appearing below each table, and Appendix I, which comprises the "Guide to Sources of Statistics," the "Guide to State Statistical Abstracts," and the "Guide to Foreign Statistical Abstracts." This volume includes a selection of data from many statistical publications, both government and private.

As can be seen in the table of contents, there are 31 sections in the book. Therefore, it behooves one to look closely at the table of contents to get a feel for an otherwise very thick book (approximately 1,050 pages).

Originally, I thought that not all these categories would interest the average business student. But when I tried to list only categories that business students would be interested in, I found there were none that could be considered outside the interest of business studies (the lone candidate—Section 8: "Elections"—might arguably be construed as peripheral to business interest until you stop to think who writes the laws that control business). The bottom line is: scan all of them.

There is also a handy three-page "Telephone Contacts List" in the front of the book that lists telephone numbers and addresses of federal agencies with major statistical programs. These agencies will provide general information on their statistical programs and publications, as well as specific information on how to order their publications.

Although both the *Statistical Abstract of the United States* and the *Survey of Current Business* address the economic perspective in part, a useful addition to these figures would be the regional Federal Reserve's own publications dealing with the economy. One example is the Federal Reserve Bank of Atlanta's *Economic Review* (ISSN 0732-1813). This is a very thin publication (40 pages) but has some interesting articles. It presents analysis of economic and financial topics relevant to Federal Reserve policy. In a format accessible to the nonspecialist, the publication reflects the work of the Research Department. It is edited, designed, produced, and distributed through the Public Affairs Department. Free subscriptions are available by calling (404) 521-8020 or on the Internet at http://www.frbatlanta.org.

It's hard in this environment not to get involved in some trivia from the *Statistical Abstracts,* soooo . . . to make things interesting (answers below):

1. The median age of the resident population on July 1, 2050, will be?
    Fairly easy, no? Almost all of you got it, I'll bet. How about this one though.

2. The median age of the resident population on July 1, 1850, was?
    Ha! Want to bet your Mustang convertible?

3. The state with the largest number of drivers licenses issued in 1993?
    So . . . if it's that easy, then how many?

4. As of 1990, which state had the largest percentage of the population with a college degree?
    Yeah . . . it is getting boring, just one more.

5. Per capita, in 1993, which was consumed the most—milk, coffee, or beer?

(Answers: 1. 39 years; 2. 18.9 years; 3. California; 20,123,000; 4. Colorado; 5. Beer)

Business Enterprise

In Brief

Patents issued in 1994: 113,600
Percent issued to foreign country residents: 43%
Bankruptcies filed in 1994: 845,257
Business: 7%
Nonbusiness: 93%
Change from 1993 –8%

This section relates to the place and behavior of the business firm and to business initiative in the American economy. It includes data on the number, type, and size of businesses; financial data of domestic and multinational U.S. corporations; business investment, expenditures, and profits; sales and inventories; and business failures. Additional business data may be found in other sections, particularly 27 and 28.

The principal sources of these data are the *Survey of Current Business,* published by the Bureau of Economic Analysis (BEA), the *Federal Reserve Bulletin,* issued by the Board of Governors of the Federal Reserve System, and annual *Statistics of Income* reports on the Internal Revenue Service (IRS), *The Business Failure Record* issued by The Dun & Bradstreet Corporation, Milton, CT, and *Fortune* and *The Fortune Directory,* issued by Time, Inc., New York.

BUSINESS FIRMS

A firm is generally defined as a business organization under a single management and may include one or more establishments (i.e., a single physical location at which business is conducted). The terms *firm, business, company,* and *enterprise* are used interchangeably throughout this section. Examples of series where the industrial distribution is based on data collected from establishments are those on capital stock, those on gross domestic product by industry, and those on employment and earnings (section 13). Examples of company-based series are those on business expenditures for new plant and equipment, those from IRS *Statistics of Income,* and those on corporation profits by industry. A firm doing business in more than one industry is classified by industry according to the major

activity of the firm as a whole. The industrial classification is based on the *Standard Industrial Classification (SIC) Manual* (see text, section 13). The IRS concept of a business firm relates primarily to the legal entity used for tax reporting purposes. The IRS *Statistics of Income* reports present data, based on a sample of tax returns before audit, separately for sole proprietorships, partnerships, and corporations. Data presented are for active enterprises only. A *sole proprietorship* is an unincorporated business owned by one person including large enterprises with many employees and hired managers and part-time operations in which the owner is the only person involved. A *partnership* is an unincorporated business owned by two or more persons, each of whom has a financial interest in the business. The "persons" could be individuals, estates, trusts, or other partnerships, or corporations. A *corporation* is a business that is legally incorporated under state laws. The IRS recognizes many types of businesses as corporations, including joint-stock companies, insurance companies, and unincorporated associations such as business trusts, etc. While many corporations file consolidated tax returns, most corporate tax returns represent individual corporations, some of which are affiliated through common ownership or control with other corporations filing separate returns.

ASSETS AND LIABILITIES

In its annual report, *Statistics of Income, Corporation Income Tax Returns,* the IRS presents balance sheet and income estimates for all active U.S. corporations. The Bureau of the Census issues the *Quarterly Financial Report for Manufacturing, Mining, and Trade Corporations* (QFR), which presents quarterly income account and balance sheet data for manufacturing, mining, and trade industries. This report was prepared by the Federal Trade Commission until responsibilities for QFR were transferred to Census beginning with the fourth quarter 1982 report.

One of the most comprehensive measures of the investment position of the business sector (and the only measure adjusted to current replacement cost) is the BEA capital stock series.

Recommended Supplement: *Survey of Current Business*

If you would like information on this publication (ISSN 0039-6222), call the Bureau of Economic Analysis (BEA), Department of Commerce at (202) 606-9900.

Reference Navigator

Web site: http://www.stat-usa.gov	CD-ROM: available
E-mail: stat-usa@oloc.gov	Library Reference Number:
Database: Stat-USA (call [202] 482-1986)	_____

The *Survey of Current Business* is a monthly journal containing estimates and analyses of U.S. economic activity. Most of BEA's work is presented in the *Survey*, either in full or summary form. It includes the "Business Situation," a review of current economic developments, and regular and special articles pertaining to the national, regional, and international economic accounts and related topics. Among the special articles that appeared in 1995, for example, were "Mid-Decade Strategic Review of BEA's Economic Accounts: Maintaining and Improving Their Performance," and "Regional and State Projections of Economic Activity and Population to the Year 2005." Current estimates of the national income and product accounts appear every month.

The Bureau of Economic Analysis provides basic information on such key issues as economic growth, regional development, and the nation's role in the world economy. The "User's Guide to BEA Information" lists the most recent and most frequently requested BEA products and helps users locate and obtain that information.

BEA's current national, regional, and international estimates usually appear first in news releases, which are available to the general public in a variety of forms: on recorded telephone messages, on-line through the Economic Bulletin Board (EBB), by fax through STAT-USA/FAX, on the Internet through STAT-USA Internet, and in printed *BEA Reports*. The BEA news releases contain reports on gross domestic product, personal income and outlays, regional reports, and international reports.

One other document worth looking into is *The Economic Report of the President* (U.S. Council of Economic Advisors), which is published each February and transmitted to Congress by the president and his advisors. This is unquestionably a partisan publication, so take the message with a rather large grain of salt. (It *is* worth mentioning that our country is over $5 trillion in debt.) The narrative of economic issues is reader-friendly and contains a five-year outlook for the U.S. economy, including projections for the GDP.

During the Reagan administration, so the story goes, President Reagan once asked an aide how much the federal debt amounted to and when told that it approximated $5 trillion said, "Well, Jim, what exactly does that look like?" Jim confessed he didn't know but would return shortly with an example of what it looked like. After a few hours he returned and said, "Mr. President, a stack of $1 million in thousand-dollar bills, would reach four inches high. A stack of $1 trillion in thousand-dollar bills would reach 67 miles high. And since by the year 2000 we will be somewhere over $5 trillion in debt, then I guess the stack will reach 335 miles high and growing." Maybe, the president was heard to have said, we should measure it in ten-thousand-dollar bills.

Something to Think About

Which section, in the *Statistical Abstract of the United States,* presents data on the construction industry and on various indicators of its activity and costs; on housing units and their characteristics and occupants; and on the characteristics and vacancy rates for commercial buildings?

---

23 AMERICAN DEMOGRAPHICS

Description of Publication

American Demographics and Consumer Trends (ISSN 0163-4089), a publication of Cowles Business Media in Stamford, Connecticut, (203) 358-9900, should get the award for the best little information box in the publishing business when it comes to, "How To Reach Us."

Subscriber Service: (800) 828-1133

Offices: 607/273-6343

Fax: 607/273-3196

E-Mail: editors@demographics.com

Website: http://www.demographics.com

Snail Mail: P.O. Box 68, Ithaca, NY 14851

Database: Lexis-Nexis; No CD-ROM (author added)

This is a great little monthly magazine (about 60 pages) that integrates the science of demographics with consumerism. It is colorful, interesting, reader-friendly, informative, very well formatted, and with pertinent messages about society and business. It has the cover story, feature articles, regular departments (e.g., "Demographic Forecasts," "Index of Well-Being," "New Frontiers," etc.), plus "Business Reports." An example of a features article (usually six or seven pages) is *"The Frontiers of Psychographics,"* by Rebecca Piirto Heath ("In an effort to understand consumers, marketers are fueling a resurgence of qualitative research and retooling it for the 21st century").

The advertising in *American Demographics* is particularly useful because it represents the services of many research/analysis and database providers, such as:

American Business Information (800) 624-0076

HSDF, Inc. (502) 899-7768

Tetrad Computer Applications (800) 663-1334

Langer Associates, Inc. (212) 391-0350

Business Location Research (800) 316-2572

Urban Decision Systems (800) 633-9568

Woods & Poole Economics (800) 786-1915

Bernett Research (800) 276-5594

Mediamark Research, Inc. (800) 310-3305

Spatial Insights, Inc. (800) 347-5291

Third Wave Research Group (800) 977-9283

CACI (800) 292-CACI

Hispanic Marketing Communications Research (415) 595-5028

Sometimes when you log on to a Web site it turns out to be a disappointment because it doesn't have much to offer. *American Demographics'* Web site, http:www.demographics.com, has a lot of genuinely useful information. Once you've accessed the site, you can connect to discussion groups, place an order for any of the company's publications (at a discount), or peruse *American Demographics,* marketing tools, and forecast to your heart's content. If you want to search the database, simply complete a brief survey, give yourself a password, and you're in business.

Searching the site's database uses concept-based criteria. Submit your request and moments later, you'll have a screen filled with links to in-depth summaries of all available articles related to your topic. If one article is especially useful, you can request links to similar articles.

If you need additional resources, the *Marketing Tools Directory* and *American Demographics Book Catalog* offer industry contacts, along with books and data sources for marketers. If you wish to go to the source, the Bureau of the Census, Bureau of Labor Statistics, and the Consumer Expenditure Survey are all there 24 hours a day.

FEATURES

DEPARTMENTS

KALEIDOSCOPE

Marketing Street Culture
Bringing Hip-Hop Style to the Mainstream

Many of the hottest trends in teenage music, language, and fashion start in America's inner cities, then quickly spread to suburbs. Targeting urban teens has put some companies on the map with the larger mainstream market. But companies need an education in hip-hop culture to avoid costly mistakes.

The Scene: Martha's Vineyard, Massachusetts, a bastion of the white East Coast establishment. A teenaged boy saunters down the street, his gait and attitude embodying adolescent rebellion. Baggy jeans sag atop over-designed sneakers, gold hoops adorn both ears, and a baseball cap shields his eyes. On his chest, a Tommy Hilfiger shirt sports the designer's distinctive pairing of blue, red, and white rectangles.

Four years ago, this outfit would have been unimaginable to this cool teen; only his clean-cut, country-club peers sported Hilfiger clothes. What linked the previously preppy Hilfiger to jeans so low-slung they seem to defy gravity? To a large extent, the answer lies 200 miles southwest, in the oversized personage of Brooklyn's Biggie Smalls, an admitted ex-drug dealer turned rapper.

Over the past few years, Smalls and other hip-hop stars have become a crucial part of Hilfiger's open attempt to tap into the urban youth market. In exchange for giving artists free wardrobes, Hilfiger found its name mentioned in both the rhyming verses of rap songs and their "shout-out" lyrics, in which rap artists chant out thanks to friends and sponsors for their support.

For Tommy Hilfiger and other brands, the result is de facto product placement. The September 1996 issue of *Rolling Stone* magazine featured the rap group The Fugees, with the men prominently sporting the Tommy Hilfiger logo. In February 1996, Hilfiger even used a pair of rap stars as runway models: horror-core rapper Method Man and muscular bad-boy Treach of Naughty by Nature.

Threatened by Hilfiger in a market he had profited from but never embraced, it hardly seems coincidental that Ralph Lauren recently signed black male super-model Tyson to an exclusive contract. Even the patrician perfumier Esteé Lauder recently jumped on the Hilfiger bandwagon, launching a new cross-promotion series with the clothing company. The name of one of Lauder's new perfumes says it all. "Tommy Girl" plays on both Tommy Hilfiger's name and the seminal New York hip-hop record label Tommy Boy. Hilfiger also launched a clothing line for teenaged girls in fall 1996, projected by the company to gross $100 million in its first year on retail racks.

By Marc Spiegler

Recommended Supplement: *Commercial Atlas & Marketing Guide: Rand McNally*

For information on this annual publication (ISBN 0-528-20507-2), in its 127th edition as of this publishing date, call (800) 284-6565 or (847) 329-8100.

Reference Navigator

Web site: http://www.randmcnally.com   CD-ROM: not available

E-mail: personal only   Library Reference Number:

Database: See Web site   _____

The *Rand McNally Commercial Atlas & Marketing Guide* (*CAMG*) is probably the easiest book in the library to find because it is by far the biggest (open, it's about 2 feet by 4 feet, somewhat hard to get photocopies from when you're in a hurry). So look for a large table with a monster book on it and you'll probably find it. *CAMG* brings together the most current economic and geographic information. With maps, tables, and charts, this atlas combines maximum demographic coverage of the United States with an authoritative interpretation of business data.

The *CAMG* is organized into six sections, each of which is preceded by an introduction summarizing the content of that section. It also provides the definitions of terms and concepts used, and describes some ways to effectively use the data. These sections are: (1) United States and metropolitan area maps; (2) transportation and communications data; (3) economic data; (4) population data; (5) state maps; and (6) index of statistics and places by state.

The U.S. and metropolitan area maps section provides a U.S. city, county, and state map, as well as detailed coverage of 14 major U.S. and Canadian metropolitan areas. The transportation and communications section supplies data on the U.S. transportation (highway, railroad, and airline) and communications (telephone and postal) systems. The economic section describes business activity for states, counties, cities, metropolitan statistic areas, basic trading areas, and the largest corporations in America. Income buying power and retail/wholesale trade are also included, along with censuses of manufacturers, retail trade, and wholesale trade. The largest corporations in American business include:

- The 50 largest advertising agencies.
- The 50 largest commercial banks.
- The 50 largest financial companies.
- The 200 largest industrial companies.
- The 25 largest life insurance companies.
- The 50 largest service companies.

- The 25 largest retailing companies.
- The 25 largest transportation companies.
- The 25 largest utilities.
- Summary table of headquarters cities.

The population section provides 1990 Census figures and current population estimates for states, counties, cities, metropolitan statistical areas, and Ranally metro areas (you can look in the book's "Glossary of Terms" to get definitions for these concepts). In addition, projected population figures for counties and metropolitan statistical areas and their component counties are given.

The state maps section provides detailed, large-scale, color maps of all 50 states and the District of Columbia. The index of statistics and places by state follows the state maps and is arranged alphabetically by state. This index section provides basic business data for counties; lists principal cities and towns; and supplies statistics for virtually all inhabited places in the United States. In fact, according to the editors, over 128,000 places are described in the index of statistics and places by state. Any number of CD-ROMs are now available with geographic and demographic data. They are easy to install and will give the interrogator a tremendous amount of information with a global, region, country, or local perspective. On-line capability is also available through American Online, CompuServe, and others.

Another source of world information that should not be overlooked is the *Hammond New Comparative World Atlas*. It is a new computer-generated edition of the most popular and best-selling education atlas. This state-of-the-art atlas is perfect for students who are studying geography, history, international relations, economics, or any subject that deals with global issues. It is a very economically priced atlas and also features a wide variety of thematic maps and charts—including environment, population, climate, languages, standards of living, structure of the earth, transportation, global alliances—to help students gain a better understanding of the complex relationships between people and their environment. It includes an easy-to-use 2,000-entry master index, quick reference guide, world statistical tables and time zone map. For information, call (800) 526-4953.

While you are looking through atlases, it wouldn't hurt to get a good perspective on the world geographical sources of information either. One place you really need to look and enjoy is the *World Geographical Encyclopedia* (ISBN 0-07-911496-2) published by McGraw-Hill, (212) 512-2000. This encyclopedia was originally published in Italian, and just one of the benefits is the magnificent photographs of people and places throughout the world. Each area of the world is covered by its own volume for a total of six volumes. Another source of geographical information is the *Encyclopedia of World Cultures* (ISBN 0-8161-1808-6) published by G. K. Hall & Company (MacMillan), (800) 223-2348. Despite the *Encyclopedia of World Cultures'* theme, appropriate space is given over to the economy, industrial arts, trade, division of labor, and so on. The encyclopedia comprises 10 volumes, ordered by geographical regions of the world.

24   CENSUS CATALOG AND GUIDE

Description of Publication

For information on this annual publication (ISBN 0-16-048723-4), call the Bureau of the Census at (301) 457-4100; fax: (301) 457-4714; or Superintendent of Documents, Government Printing Office: (202) 512-1800.

 Reference Navigator

Web site: http://www.census.gov/   CD-ROM: available

E-mail: staff addresses on web site   Library Reference Number:

Database: Stat-USA

The *Census Catalog and Guide: 1996,* the 50th edition of the publication, is both a comprehensive catalog and a substantial guide to the programs and services of the Census Bureau. As a catalog, it describes or lists the products (such as reports and machine-readable files) issued from mid-1993 through 1995. Those issued since 1995 appear in the *Monthly Product Annoucement* (see "Recommended Supplement"). Readers interested in Census Bureau products issued from 1988 through 1993 should refer to *Census Catalog and Guide: 1994,* which provides a generally complete record of those years. The *Census Catalog and Guide: 1996* also includes a number of features, such as a chart on product series in the "Product Overview" chapter and an extensive "Sources of Assistance" appendix. Chapter introductions provide key information about the censuses, surveys, and other programs that are the sources of data products described in the chapters. Most products are organized by subject into such chapters as agriculture, business, and foreign trade; but a special section combines references for the 1990 Census of Population and Housing, which is particularly useful for marketing research.

    Business Information (described in Chapter 1 of this text) does an excellent job explaining the census process in the United States. Laven has even written a separate book on the subject, *Understanding the Census: A Guide for Marketers, Planners, Grant Writers and Other Data Users* (ISBN 0-89774-995-2) at Oryx Press, (800) 279-6799, or at Web site: http://www.oryxpress.com. Designed as a textbook, a handbook, and a ready-reference tool, *Understanding the Census* is written in a student-friendly narrative style with research tips, background information, and appendixes that provide valuable support data, answering such important questions as:

- How was the Census planned and conducted?
- What is the purpose of each Census question?
- How are the geographical boundaries determined?
- How are the data organized?

Business Information reports:

> One of the most important categories of business information is statistics on people and their characteristics. The mother lode of demographic data in the United States is the decennial Census of Population and Housing. Only the federal government could attempt to collect systematic information about every man, woman, and child. The results of such an immense undertaking are necessarily complex. Census materials are widely regarded as the most difficult and frustrating of all statistical publications. It is essential, however, for researchers to have a clear understanding of what they contain and how they can be used. No other single body of data is as comprehensive as the decennial Census.

In short, the decennial Census provides information on the number and basic characteristics of both the people and the housing situation in the United States. There are, according to Lavin, two reasons the Census is unique among statistical resources: it is the only complete survey of all people in the nation and it is the only one that provides data at the city block level.

Something to Do

If you are thinking of using Census data to solve a research problem, you must first translate the terms of your demographic questions into the Census format. Think you can do it? Find the appropriate terms for the examples given below:

Question Asked	Census Language
Children per household	Household relationship; Family composition
Female head of household	Family type, Household type *(fill in the right Census terms)*
Size of household	
Currently divorced	
Ever divorced	
Foreign-born	

MANUFACTURING AND MINERAL INDUSTRIES

MA35U. Vending Machines (Coin-Operated): Annual 1994.

MA36A. Switchgear, Switchboard Apparatus, Relays, and Industrial Controls: Annual 1994.

MA36E. Electric Houseware and Fans: Annual 1994.

MA36F. Major Household Appliances: Annual 1994.

MA36H. Motors and Generators: Annual 1994.

MA36K. Wiring Devices and Supplies: 1994.

MA36L. Electric Lighting Fixtures, 1994.

MA36M. Consumer Electronics: Annual 1994.

MA36P. Communication Equipment: Annual 1994.

MA36Q. Semiconductors, Printed Circuit Boards, and Other Electronic Components: 1994.

MA36C. Fluorescent Lamp Ballasts, Summary 1994.

MA37D. Aerospace Orders: Annual 1994.

MA38B. Selected Instruments and Related Products: Annual 1994.

MA38R. Electromedical Equipment and Irradiation Equipment: Annual 1994.

GENERAL AND REFERENCE

The products listed below are either reference sources or they cover both manufacturing and mineral industries and, in some cases, other fields, too.

Introduction to the 1992 Economic Census (EC92-PR-2)

Free introductory booklet. Request from Customer Services.

Manufacturing and Trade: Inventories and Sales

See abstract number 84 in the General and Reference chapter.

New! (900.5) Manufacturing Measures: Census Bureau Data for Manufacturing

Subject content—Explains the programs providing manufacturing statistics, including the surveys conducted once a year or more often and the economic censuses. The report also describes data products that include manufacturing statistics among others, and it describes other demographic and economic programs, foreign trade, for example, that might be of use to manufacturers in marketing, site location, and other activities. The report includes several brief use illustrations and shows how the data can be used via computer and otherwise. It concludes with telephone contact lists.

This report contains only illustrative statistics.
28 pp. 1995. Single copies free from Customer Services.

1992 Economic Census (CD-ROM)

See abstract number 1.4 in the General and Reference chapter.

1992 Industry and Product Classification Manual (SIC Basis) (EC92-R-3)

See abstract number 2.2 in the General and Reference chapter.

(901) Numerical List of Manufactured and Mineral Products (MC92-R-1, 1992 Census of Manufactures and Census of Mineral Industries)

Subject content—Includes a description of the principal products and services published in the 1992 Census of Manufactures and 1992 Census of Mineral Industries. The seven-digit products and services are generally arrayed in ascending numerical/alphabetical sequence code order within their respective five-digiet product classes, the product classes in order within their four-digit industries, and the industries within their two-digit major groups.

This list contains descriptions of the more than 6,300 products collected in the 1992 Census of Manufactures and Census of Mineral Industries. In addition, it includes the approximately 4,500 products for which information is collected monthly, quarterly, or annually in the Bureau's Current Industrial Reports (CIR) program.
GPO Stock No. 003-024-08689-1.
290 pp. 1993. $17.
Also avaliable on CD-ROM (see abstract number 1.4 in the General and Reference chapter) and microfiche from Customer Services.

Recommended Supplement: *Monthly Product Announcement*

To update bibliographic references in the *Census Catalog and Guide,* subscribe to the *Monthly Product Announcement (MPA),* a free publication that lists all Census Bureau products as they come out. *MPA, Census and You* (a monthly newsletter), and other useful Census Bureau reference sources are briefly described below.

MPA lists all new Census Bureau products—primarily publications and data files—and includes ordering information and order forms. Unlike the *Catalog and Guide,* the *MPA* does not describe every data product; it usually presents abstracts of one or two new ones, briefly describes several others, and lists the remainder.

Each *MPA* covers products for a month and may be discarded when the annual *Catalog and Guide* including the period is published. For example, no further reference to the February 1997 MPA (which covers December 1996) or earlier issues is necessary for users of the *Census Catalog and Guide 1997,* since it reports on products released through December 1996.

Students (and all data users) may arrange to receive *MPA* free of charge by contacting Customer Services at (301) 457-4100.

Census and You, a monthly newsletter issued by the Bureau of the Census, highlights new statistical findings and keeps data users informed about important new bureau products, census and survey plans, and other program developments. CENDATA TM is the Census Bureau's on-line data system, which can be reached through CompuServe (800) 848-8199, or Dialog (800) 334-2564. It contains the following menus:

Census Bureau Products	Business Data
U.S. Statistics at a Glance	Construction/Housing
Press Releases	Foreign Trade Data
Census and You (excerpts)	Government Data
Product Information	International Data
Profiles and Ranking	Manufacturing Data
Agriculture Data	Population Data

1990 Census Data

Something to Think About

Was the fundamental purpose of the U.S. Census as stated in Article I of the Constitution to provide an enumeration of the population for the apportionment of representation in Congress or to establish legislation for interstate commerce?

Out of Print

Infatuation with the Information Superhighway, Part 10

By Robert J. Samuelson

My name is Robert, and I am a numbers junkie. I compulsively scour the *Statistical Abstract* for intriguing indicators of our national condition—the fact, for example, that state lotteries collect $25 billion annually. Naturally, I am also a big fan of the Census Bureau, which publishes the abstract and conducts surveys on everything from our incomes to our housing patterns. So it pains me to report that Census is now committing a colossal blunder. It is slowly going out of print. Literally.

The *Statistical Abstract* momentarily seems safe, but scores of other printed reports are simply being eliminated. In 1992 Census issued 1,035 reports; last year the number was 635, and the retreat from print has only begun. Gone are, among others: "Earnings by Occupation and Education"; "Poverty Areas in the United States," and "Language Use in the United States." This is absurd. We go to great trouble to collect this information, and now Census is suppressing it.

The losers are not just statistics addicts. Our public conversations depend heavily on these dry numbers. They shape our concept of who we are, of how society is performing and of what government should or shouldn't do. Political speeches routinely spit out statistics, which can be made to tell stories: some true, some not so true. Keeping the conversations honest requires that the basic data be easily accessible to anyone who wants it.

When I say Census is "suppressing," I don't mean that it's deliberately hiding its surveys. As a reporter, I've asked Census for information hundreds of times; I can't recall an instance when answers, when available, weren't provided quickly. The culture of the place is to release information. By its lights, Census isn't abandoning print so much as it's shifting its data to the Information Superhighway. Statistics are being distributed by CD-ROMs and the Internet. Already, Census brags that its Internet site is receiving 50,000 hits a day. Sounds amazing.

It isn't. Those 50,000 daily hits are a lot less breathtaking than they seem, even if the figure is accurate (and I have my doubts). In May, *Interactive Age*, a trade publication, surveyed Internet sites. It reported that Pathfinder (the site for Time Warner publications, such as *Time* and *People*) had about 686,000 daily hits, *Playboy* had about 675,000 and Hotwired (the site for *Wired* magazine) had

about 429,000. I mention these popular Web sites because they belong to magazines. As yet, none is forsaking the printed page for the glories of the Internet.

There are good reasons for this. One is that the number of daily hits on a Web site exaggerates how many people use it; the same person may hit the same site repeatedly. Another reason is that the Internet hasn't yet evolved into an effective platform for advertising. But the main reason is that, for many purposes, the printed page is still superior to the computer screen. You can flip pages faster than you can search computer files. You can read a magazine standing in a subway or lying in a hammock.

Census's shift from print clearly discriminates against people (including me) who don't surf the Internet or use CD-ROMs. We remain the vast majority. *American Demographics* magazine recently reported a number of surveys that tried to measure U.S. Internet use in 1994. The surveys put usage on the World Wide Web between 2 million and 13.5 million people, which is at most about 5 percent. The average income of Internet households was $67,000, which is the richest fifth of Americans. But it's not just computer clods or the unaffluent who will suffer.

Carl Haub is a demographer at the Population Reference Bureau in Washington. He's a big user of Census statistics and is comfortable cruising in cyberspace. "It's going to be a disaster for the average analyst," he says. Downloading and printing data from the Internet can take hours. Getting a number from a CD-ROM is often a lot harder than getting it from a book. To Haub, Census is transferring a lot of the cost—in time and money—of making statistical information useful to people like him.

Martha Farnsworth Riche, director of the Census Bureau, admits as much. "If someone else can do it, let's shift it to the outside," she says. "We've had a hiring freeze since at least 1992, and those [printed] reports take an enormous amount of time from professionals." They need to concentrate on doing surveys of "an economy and population that are changing dramatically. Our statistics have fallen behind." Only Census can collect much of this data, she says. Let academics and analysts prepare reports.

Up to a point, Riche has my sympathies. The Constitution created the census (Article 1, Section 2), and social and economic surveys are a basic function of modern government. Some congressional proposals to cut the agency's budget sharply are stupid beyond words. But that said, the new approach is misguided. The danger of overrelying on outsiders to organize and analyze basic data is that statistics may fall hostage to special pleaders or incompetents. Printed Census reports provide an easy way to check self-interested or faulty claims.

Print's other great virtue is that it guarantees a historic record. Computer technology is changing so rapidly that data committed to one technology may no longer be easily accessible if that technology vanishes. "The CD-ROMs that we're so excited about today—20 years from now, no one will use them," says Richard Rockwell, director of the Inter-University Consortium for Political and Social Research. "The book is a highly advanced technology for preserving some kinds of information." Exactly.

Let's not become too infatuated too soon with the Information Superhighway. Census should be issuing its data in computer-friendly ways, but not as a substitute for printed reports. A jaunt on the Internet—piloted by my friend Steve—only affirmed my skepticism. Steve typed the Census Web address (http://www.census.gov) and up popped the "home page" designating me as the 567,352d visitor. Unless the count began 10 days earlier (and it didn't), that was a lot fewer than 50,000 daily hits. I informed a Census official. He was mystified. After checking, he said there were other ways of accessing the Web site that didn't raise the count. Hmm. Could be. But it also shows how, on the Information Superhighway, we're still navigating in the dark.

25   CONSUMER REPORTS

Description of Publication

If you would like information on this monthly publication (ISSN 0010-7174), call Consumers Union at (914) 378-2000, or fax: (914) 378-2900.

 Reference Navigator

Web site: http://www.consumerreports.org

E-mail: Subscriber only

Database: LEXIS-NEXIS

CD-ROM: available

Library Reference Number:

_____

Consumer Reports is published by Consumers Union, an independent, nonprofit testing and information organization serving only consumers. It is a comprehensive source for unbiased advice about products and services, personal finance, health and nutrition, and other consumer concerns. Since 1936, its mission has been to test products, inform the public, and protect consumers. Income is derived solely from the sale of *Consumer Reports* and other services and from nonrestrictive, noncommercial contributions, grants, and fees.

    Consumer Reports has been around a long time, but it keeps up with the times. The format is colorful and contemporary; articles are written in a no-nonsense style, and the subject matter is broad (my all-time favorite: "The bald truth about hair replacement," under "Your Health" in the departments section). The "Cover Reports" are written to meet the needs of demanding consumers who in many cases are the paid subscribers (members) themselves. Perhaps a good generalization about these "Cover Reports" is that they are substantive (i.e., around 15 pages) and comprehensive. There are approximately six to eight feature articles in each issue (e.g., "Finding a clean, safe beach"; "Weight control: Do diet pills work?"; "Personal pagers," etc.). As in other magazines the departments include "Letters," "Memo to Members," "Product Updates," "Your Health,"

"Your Money," and more. One particularly useful attribute is the one-year index in the back that lists reports made over the last 12 months.

Consumer Reports is an independent data source of consumer information that can be relied on to be accurate and, for students doing research, loaded with good reference material. The magazine makes the point by stating: "We buy all the products we test off the shelf." They test the products and services, survey their readership to get reliability information, and report on current issues of concern to consumers.

The magazine also provides a host of other services, including:

- New car price service
- Travel letter
- Used car service
- *Zillions* (bimonthly magazine for kids)
- Auto insurance price service
- Television
- Electronic publishing
- Special publications
- Facts by fax
- Health
- Reprints
- Consumer Reports Cars: The Essential Guide (CD-ROM)

A major competitor to *Consumer Reports* is *Consumer Digest*, and they sit right next to each other on the newsstand. *Consumer Digest* (ISSN 0010-7182) is published bimonthly by Consumer Digest Inc., (212) 685-9489; and fax: (212) 685-9528.

Unlike *Consumer Reports, Consumer Digest* does accept advertising. *Consumer Digest* has seven or eight feature-like articles; regular departments (such as, "Consumerscope," "Money Watch," "Health Digest" and "CD Investment Adviser"); and sometimes a special section (e.g., Life Insurance Buying Guide) which is very comprehensive in the how-to and the educated consumer sense. Some of the information is useful for reference material but may be of limited value (e.g., 25 Safest Insurance Companies). Two examples of the articles are:

"1997 Complete Car & Truck Review"—"The fresh model year is bringing a wealth of brand-new and significantly improved vehicles to market. Here's a comprehensive overview of what's coming among 1997 cars, trucks, vans and sport-utility vehicles."

"Testing Today's Hottest Fitness Equipment"—"Sales are booming for the popular new/old riders or upright rowers. But are they better than others?"

GETTING STARTED

NEW CARS

USED CARS

DEPARTMENTS

How to Buy or Lease a Car
You Needn't be a Car Expert or a Financial Whiz to Get a Good Deal on a New or Used Car

Shopping for a car can be a rational process or an emotional odyssey. There are practical considerations like overall performance, safety, and reliability. And there are abstract considerations like aesthetics and image. Whether you buy or lease, new or used, the more your practical side prevails, the better your chances of getting the best transportation at the lowest price.

NEW OR USED?

Industry sources estimate that nearly two out of every three cars sold last year were used cars. It's easy to see why. Compared with a good-quality used car, a new car is a poor investment.

Some large and expensive sedans lose nearly half of their original value in their first three years. Such models make especially good used-car deals, because the previous owner has taken the biggest hit in depreciation. In the years that follow, those same models depreciate much more slowly.

Since a used car costs less, you may also save money by paying cash and avoiding finance costs. And insurance coverage on a used car is cheaper.

But the choice of new versus used goes beyond dollars and cents. Important benefits of buying new include the reliability that the car's newness conveys and the warranty the car comes with. A used car may have been driven abusively by its previous owner, or vital maintenance may have been neglected. Furthermore, a used car will have used up at least part of the factory warranty. Dealers may provide their own warranty on a used car, but it's often not as comprehensive. And if you buy from a private owner, you buy as is.

Shopping carefully can lessen your odds of buying someone else's lemon. See page 17 for a list of simple tests you can perform even if you're not a car expert.

Another pitfall in buying used is that important safety features like dual air bags and antilock brakes were less common a few years ago. That puts an added burden on you to search out a used car that has all the latest safety equipment.

BUY OR LEASE?

That's the next important decision you must make. One out of three new cars will be leased rather than bought this year—no doubt because of the lure of low monthly payments and low down payments featured so prominently in lease advertising.

Lease payments are lower than car-loan payments because you pay mostly for the amount the car depreciates during the time you have it, plus an interest charge. But at lease's end, you no longer have a car. If you keep leasing, your monthly payments never end.

All told, a lease my be the cheapest way to get behind the wheel, but it may not be the cheapest way to stay there. A good, honest lease can be competitive with buying on time. But the potential for sharp tactics makes leasing a tricky proposition.

Leasing may hold a clear advantage if you lease an expensive car for business use. You may then be able to deduct more of the cost than if you buy the car. Leasing may also make sense if you need transportation immediately but lack a down payment to buy a car.

Recommended Supplement: *Journal of Consumer Research*

If you wish information on this quarterly publication (ISSN 0093-5301), call the University of Chicago Press at: (773) 753-3347; or fax: (773) 753-0811.

Reference Navigator

Web Site: http://www.journals.uchicago.edu/jcr/   CD-ROM: not available

E-mail: orders@journals.uchicago.edu   Library Reference Number:

Database: See Web site   _____

The *Journal of Consumer Research,* founded in 1974, is published quarterly (March, June, September, and December) by the University of Chicago Press. It used to be said that the demographics and geographics of marketing were determined by those simple questions of*: who, where, when,* and *what.* And this was accomplished by surveying or counting the obvious. The tricky part came about when one had to speculate about *why* people did things. Psychographics was born. The consumer, consumption, consumer culture, and markets created an interactive set of concepts that are no longer culture or nation bound and have the potential for earth-shaking consequences (e.g., Chlorofluorocarbons in underarm deodorant destroying the ozone layer). This observation could have been better said by many, and often is by those who contribute to the *Journal of Consumer Research.*

The "20-year Summaries and Index" of the *Journal of Consumer Research* is a guide (author and subject) to the first 20 volumes of *JCR*, complete with abstracts and cross-referenced by authors and keywords. Each journal usually has seven or eight articles, such as "Asymmetric Decoy Effects on Lower-Quality versus Higher-Quality Brands: Meta-analytic and Experimental Evidence," by Timothy B. Heath and Subimal Chatterjee.

The only time I have delved into the "decoy effects" of things was to determine if there was enough lead shot in my duck decoys when readying myself for the Eastern Shore of Maryland bird season. If this is true for you, and you can't figure out what the authors mean by *meta-analytic* you may wish to take a marketing course or two before jumping to the *Journal of Consumer Research.*

Something to Think About

Reproduction of *Consumer Reports* in whole or in part is forbidden without prior written permission but is usually permitted for what type of purpose? Do you see any relationship between the goals of *Consumer Reports* and those of the *Journal of Consumer Research*? Why or why not?

VI GOVERNMENTAL AFFAIRS AND NONGOVERNMENTAL ORGANIZATIONS

Optional Government Affairs References

- *National Economic, Social and Environmental Data Bank*
- *Economic Indicators*
- *Technology and the American Economics Transition*
- *The Economic and Budget Outlook*
- *Equal Employment Opportunity File*
- *A Competitive Assessment of Various Industries*
- *Minerals Yearbook*
- *Quarterly Financial Report for Manufacturing, Mining and Trade Corporations*
- *Balance of Payments Statistics*
- *(see state and local government publications by name or state)*

26 MONTHLY CATALOG OF UNITED STATES GOVERNMENT PUBLICATIONS

Description of Publication

For information on this monthly publication (ISSN 0362-6830), call the Superintendent of Documents of the U.S. Government Printing Office at (202) 512-1800; or fax: (202) 512-2250.

 Reference Navigator

Web site: http://www.access.gpo.gov/su_docs   CD-ROM: available

E-mail: bybsys@access.digex.net   Library Reference Number:

Database: See Web site

The *Monthly Catalog of United States Government Publications* (*MOCAT*) is the major tool for finding information about government publications. The catalog marked its 100th year of publication in 1995. In the preface of the January 1895 issue, the superintendent of documents, Francis A. Crandall, expressed the hope that it would be the "initial number in a long series of official Monthly Catalogues."

Over the years many changes have occurred. A significant change took place in 1976, when "Anglo-American cataloging rules" were first used to catalog publications appearing in the *Monthly Catalog*. Availability of the *Monthly Catalog* in electronic formats, first on tape and later in other formats, has enabled the Government Printing Office to make information on federal documents available to a greater number of people. Beginning in 1996, a CD-ROM version of the *MOCAT* was introduced. Most of the features of the traditional paper version were included in the CD-ROM version. An on-line version of the catalog is also now available on the World Wide Web. These new *MOCAT* formats will make it easier for users to retrieve information about federal publications. The paper version of the *MOCAT* will continue to be available with shorter entries and a keyword title index. The problem with the paper version, however, is that you'll be lucky to find one (the microfiche version was discontinued after the December 1995 issue). This is just one example of how books and paper libraries may become things of the past; in the future we will have "media centers."

The bibliographic entries in the *Monthly Catalog* are arranged in Superintendent of Documents classification number order. Each record is also assigned a unique catalog number, which consists of a two-digit prefix representing the catalog year, followed by a sequential number beginning with 1 in the first issue of each year. Within this arrangement, the publications of each government author are further identified by the name and address of the issuing agency.

Catalog entries in *MOCAT* may be accessed by title keyword index (an alphabetical list of truncated titles, arranged by important words selected from publication titles). You should consult the CD-ROM or on-line version of the *MOCAT* for indexing accessed by:

- Keyword
- Author
- Title
- Series/report number
- Subject
- Stock number
- Contract number and classification number

The GPO operates 24 bookstores in major metropolitan centers around the country. Also, nearly 1,400 libraries participate in the Federal Depository Library Program as information links, while 53 are designated as regional depository libraries. These collections, which are tailored to public needs, are open to the public. To find these bookstores and libraries, consult the Superintendent of Documents on the World Wide Web. One thing to keep in mind is that some of these publications qualify as "public domain" (i.e., as a taxpayer they belong to you), so if you want to print them and sell them, you can.

Something to Think About

How about testing your basic knowledge of the *MOCAT*? What does the acronym *MOCAT* stand for? Which agency of the U.S. Government publishes the *MOCAT*? Do you know how to get in touch with the Government Printing Office? In the "Recommended Supplement" below, which two sections of the *Guide to Popular U.S. Government Publications* should most concern business students?

Users now have access to cataloged records of Federal publications in the following formats:

Monthly Catalog of United States Government Publications on CD-ROM (Monthly issues cumulate from beginning of year includes cumulative indexes)

Monthly Catalog of United States Government Publications (paper edition) (This new paper version of the MOCAT has short entries and a title keyword index (the CD-ROM version will include other indexes formerly included in paper version))

Online version of MOCAT available on GPO Access Federal Locator service via World Wide Web. (Users of the online Locator service can identify publications and locate a depository library that includes them in their collection. New records may be accessed daily on the Internet at: http://www.access.gpo.gov/su_docs)

GPO Cataloging Tapes may be purchased from:

Library of Congress
Cataloging Distribution Service
Customer Services Section
Washington, D.C. 20541-5017 U.S.A.

Question, or comments regarding this service? Contact the GPO Access User Support Team Internet e-mail at gpoaccess@gpo.gov; by telephone at 202-512-1530; or by fax at 202-512-1262

AGRICULTURE DEPARTMENT
Washington, DC 20250

96-9779   A 1.36:1847
Accounting for the environment in agriculture. —[1995]
    iv, 27 p. : — (Technical bulletin ; no. 1847) Shipping
    list no.: 96-0225-M. •Item 0016 (MF)
        OCLC 34528527

96-9780   A 1.38/2:996
Agriculture fact book.
    v. ; Shipping list no.: 96-0131-P. Issue: 1996 •Item
    0013-A-01 S/N 001-000-04623-3
        OCLC 31747093

96-9781   A 1.75:718
Soil erosion and conservation in the United States. —[1995]
    iii, 28, [1] p. : — (Agriculture information bulletin ; no.
    718) Shipping list no.: 96-0122-M. •Item 0004 (MF)
        OCLC 34497005

FOREST SERVICE
Agriculture Dept.
Washington, DC 20250

96-9782   A 13.2:W 58/9
White Pass Scenic Byway update. —[1994] 1 v.
        OCLC 34563010

96-9783   A 13.13:g 37/2
Gila National Forest environmental analysis program. —
    [1995] 1 v.
        OCLC 34495112

96-9784   A 13.13:W 66/5
Wilderness visitors—. —[1996?] 1 folded sheet (8 p.) :
        OCLC 34428689

96-9785   A 13.36/2-6:R 9-CNF-R G-019-96
Campgrounds in the Chequamegon National Forest. [1996] 1
    map ; Shipping list no.: 96-0187-P. •Item 0086-C
        OCLC 3451426

96-9786   A 13.40/2:R 31/2
Research natural areas. —[1993?] 1 sheet :
        OCLC 34542024

96-9787   A 13.78:FPL-RP-543
Roof temperatures in simulated attics. —[1995] 14 p. : —
    (Research paper FPL ; RP-543) Shipping list no.: 96-0122-
    M. •Item 0083-B (MF)
        OCLC 34553139

96-9788   A 13.78:NE-699
Dynamics of white pine in New England. —[1995] 8 p. : —
    (Research paper NE ; 699) Shipping list no.: 96-0122-M.
    •Item 0083-B (MF)
        OCLC 34553101

96-9789   A 13.82/2:N 81/2/3.11
Tree shelters. —[1996] 4 p. : — (Northern hardwood notes ;
    3.11) Shipping list no.: 96-0143-P. •Item 0079-E
        OCLC 34578287

96-9790   A 13.88:NE-200
Status of and attitudes toward aquatic macroinvertebrate mon-
    itoring on national forests and districts of the Bureau of
    Land Management. —[1995] 15 p. ;— (General techical
    report NE ; 200) Shipping list no.: 96-0125-M. •Item 0083-
    B-06 (MF)
        OCLC 34553180

96-9791   A 13.88:PNW-GTR-320
Eastside forest ecosystem health assessment. Fire and weather
    disturbances in terrestrial ecosystems of the eastern Cas-
    cades. —[1994] 52 p. : — (General technical report PNW
    ; GRT-320) Shipping list no.: 94-0249-M. •Item 0083-B-06
    (MF)
        OCLC 34606991

96-9792   A 13.88:PNW-GTR-351
FRAGSTATS, spatial pattern analysis program for quantifying
    landscape structure. —[Version 2.0].—[1995] 122 p. : —
    (General technical report PNW ; GTR-351) Shipping list
    no.: 96-0125-M. •Item 0083-B-06 (MF)
        OCLC 34553045

96-9793   A 13.88:RM-GTR-267
Forest health through silviculture. —[1995] 246 p. : — (Gen-
    eral technical report RM ; GTR-267) Shipping list no.: 96-
    0151-M. •Item 0083-B-06 (MF)
        OCLC 34505091

Recommended Supplement: *Guide to Popular U.S. Government Publications*

Reference Navigator

Web site: http://www.lu.com

E-mail: lu.books@lu.com

Database: See Web site

CD-ROM: not available

Library Reference Number:

_____

According to its author, William Bailey, the main purpose of this guide (ISBN 1-56308-031-1), published by Libraries Unlimited, Inc., fax: (303) 220-8843, is to call attention "to the diversity, instruction, and value found in government publications." The *Guide to Popular U.S. Government Publications,* now in its fourth edition, consists of about 2,500 titles.

Arranged alphabetically by title under main topic and subtopic, the entries include information on issuing agency, date of publication, illustrative material, stock number and price, and Superintendent of Documents classification number. While Mr. Bailey is the compiler of the material he gives credit to LeRoy Schwarzkopf for the selection criteria, which Mr. Bailey says has not been altered. In Schwarzkopf's words, the criteria remain "currency or long-term popular interest" with the publications "geared to the general reader, rather than to the professional or technician." In selecting publications, William Bailey read each introduction, noting whether a statement indicated the text was for laypersons; he chose only those that were. He selected congressional committee reports for their full complement of expert and citizen testimony on current issues of importance. Otherwise, he followed one rule, "to select every carefully prepared publication that was absorbing and exhibited wide appeal."

The *Guide*'s table of contents is broken down into a series of parts that cover many aspects of a citizen's life (e.g., birth control, boating, children, climate, etc.). Two sections that directly concern a business student's interest are:

1. Business, Economics, and Industry
   General
   Banking, Finance, Investment
   International Trade
   Small Business

2. Careers and Occupations
   Careers
   Occupations
   Civil Service
   Getting a Job

Mr. Bailey offered one last thought in his introduction:

> About current developments and use of government publications. The best products now going are the *Statistical Abstract,* the *State and Metropolitan Area Data Book,* and the *County and City Data Book* on diskettes and CD-ROMS. These business and educational tools are of exceptional worth. Much of the data contained in the statistical bonanzas are repackaged everyday and sold at a high price. I advise people who need to use authoritative demographic and related data to call and order the products from Customer Services, U.S. Bureau of the Census at (301) 763-4794.

For information on Civil Service careers call the Office of Personnel Mangement, (202) 606-2424.

27 PUBLIC ADMINISTRATION REVIEW

Description of Publication

For information on this bimonthly publication (ISSN 0033-3352), call the American Society for Public Administration (ASPA) at (202) 393-7878; or fax: (202) 638-4952.

 Reference Navigator

Web site: http://www.aspanet.org

E-mail: info@aspanet.org

Database: not available

CD-ROM: not available

Library Reference Number:

_____

If government workers represent 18 percent of the U.S. labor force, why were they victims of about 30 percent of the cases of workplace violence during the years 1987–1992? The 1995 bombing of the federal building in Oklahoma City serves as the most recent and tragic example of public employees being murdered while at work. If you are looking for valuable insight into the public administration arena, the *Public Administration Review* (*PAR*) is an excellent place to start. One is often tempted to simply look at the government as a source of information on regulations and data management. But it is one of the world's largest complexes of organizations both as customer and employer. Despite the general mood of politicians to reduce government size and influence, make no mistake, these organizations will be around for a while, controlling what you do and how you do it.

PAR is published by the American Society for Public Administration. Established in 1939, ASPA is the largest and most prominent professional association in the field of public administration. With a diverse membership composed of more than 12,000 practitioners, teachers, and students, ASPA has emerged as the focal point for intellectual and professional interaction, thereby serving as the principal arena for linking thought and practice within the field of public administration. This is the *only* organization that, in my experience, displays its Code of Ethics on the back of its journal (i.e., "Serve the Public Interest, Respect the Constitution and the Law, Demonstrate Personal Integrity, Promote Ethical Organizations and Strive for Professional Excellence").

PAR continues its 55-year history as the preeminent scholarly journal in the field. It covers a wide range of issues including total quality management, strategic planning, ethics, information technology, administrative systems in other countries, organizational culture. Examples of recent articles are:

"Congressional Budget Reform: The Unanticipated Implications for Federal Policy Making," by Philip G. Joyce, and "Designing Effective Performance-Measurement Systems under the Government Performance and Results Act of 1993," by R. Kravchuck and R. Schack.

Articles (8 to 10 pages) are each preceded by an abstract of approximately 200 words. The journal itself runs approximately 90 to 100 pages with a few ads at the back plus a fairly comprehensive book review section. To get further information, check the Web site at http://www.fedworld.gov.

By the way, if you have your eye on a government job, you may want to apply for the Presidential Management Intern Program (PMI). Graduate students from a variety of academic disciplines completing or expecting to complete a master's or doctoral-level degree from an accredited college or university during the current academic year are eligible. These individuals must also have a clear interest in, and a commitment to, a career in the analysis and management of public policies and programs. PMI winners receive an initial two-year appointment. After successfully completing the two-year program, PMIs may be eligible for conversion to a permanent government position and further promotional opportunities. The Office of Personnel Management facilitates and provides a structured orientation session and graduation ceremony. Additionally, federal agencies also arrange for seminars, briefings, and conferences, as well as on-the-job training and other developmental opportunities. Federal agencies also provide PMIs with rotational assignments. PMI applications can be obtained by calling the Career America Connection at (912) 757-3000.

251

Workplace Violence and Torts
Violence in the American Workplace: Challenges to the Public Employer

Lloyd G. Nigro, Georgia State University
William L. Waugh, Jr., Georgia State University

What do we know about violent crime in the public sector workplace and what can be done to reduce it? Although public employees were only about 18 percent of the U.S. labor force, they were the victims of about 30 percent of the cases of workplace violence during the years 1987–1992. Public concern about occupational violent crime (OVC) is typically a function of media coverage, as shown by the Oklahoma City bombing, but there is great uncertainty about the level of risk that it actually poses for public workers in general and for specific occupational groups. In this article, the authors review the current state of knowledge regarding occupational violent crime in the United States and conclude that the guidance it offers to public employers is limited. It is apparent that a national database on OVC that includes information on social-psychological, organizational, and other variables is needed if current research needs are to be met. In addition to better information, public employers should approach OVC using a strategy that includes prevention methods based on careful assessments of risks, emergency management techniques and systems, appropriate human resources policies, and management training and preparation. Although needed, government regulations may be difficult to implement in the current political environment. Public employers should assume leadership in the effort to prevent OVC and to deal with its consequences.

Among the many problems confronted by public as well as private employers are injuries resulting from occupational violent crime (OVC) or workplace violence.[1] OVC injury is defined as intentional battery, rape, or homicide during the course of employment. The available statistics on OVC in the United States reveal that it is a meaningful risk for many workers and that it may be more widespread and serious in its consequences than these data suggest. To a limited extent, the social-psychological causes of OVC are being explored, but no systematic effort has been made to identify risk factors that may be particularly relevant to the public employer.

There is reason to believe that the public sector is increasingly threatened by anti-government violence involving frustrated clients, terrorist groups with political motives, and individuals who are just plain angry at bureaucrats. The 1995 bombing of the federal building in Oklahoma City serves as the most recent and horrible example of public employees being murdered while at work. Although it is to be hoped that mass murders of government workers will continue to be rare, existing evidence suggests that the more common types of OVC may pose a growing threat to public employees, and the data on homicides reveal that some groups of government employees are at higher risk than the average worker in the United States.[2] The U.S. Department of Justice's Bureau of Justice Statistics reported that of the nation's nearly one million victims of workplace violence in 1994, 30 percent were federal, state, or local government employees (U.S. Department of Justice, 1994). Under these conditions, public policy makers and human resources managers cannot afford to ignore the potential for OVC or to assume that it may be treated as an extraordinary event that does not merit serious investment in its prevention and the mitigation of its consequences.

Recommended Supplement: *Public Personnel Management*

For information on this quarterly publication (ISSN 009-0262), call the International Personnel Management Association at (703) 549-7100, or fax: (703) 684-0948.

Reference Navigator

Web site: http://www.ipma-hr.org

E-Mail: publications@ipma-hr.org

Database: not available

CD-ROM: not available

Library Reference Number:

_____

This association stands as unique in that none of its officers, at the time of this reading, are from universities. The Federal Trade Commission, County of Los Angeles, and City of Pensacola are represented, which along with an impressive list of other agencies ought to inspire confidence in the periodical.

The publication runs approximately 130 pages, which are numbered serially for each quarter. The summer issue for 1997 had nine articles averaging 18 pages or so each and are well annotated. They are an excellent source for research.

For example, "Attributions of Quality Circles' Problem-Solving Failure: Differences Among Management, Supporting Staff, and Quality Circle Members," by Thomas Li-Ping Tang and Edie Aguilar Butler.

Employees with experiences in a quality circle (QC) program were asked to answer a questionnaire that measured the attributions of quality circles' (QCs) problem-solving failure. Seven clearly interpretable factors were identified: Lack of top-management support, lack of QC members' commitment, lack of problem-solving skills, QC members' turnover, the nature of the task, lack of support from staff members, and lack of data and time. The nomological network of the 24-item questionnaire is also examined. Further, management personnel made significantly lower attributional ratings concerning lack of top-management support than supporting staff and QC members.

28 TAX GUIDE FOR SMALL BUSINESS PUBLICATION 334

Description of Publication

For information on *Tax Guide for Small Business Publication 334*, call the Internal Revenue Service at (800) TAX FORM.

 Reference Navigator

Web site: http://www.ustreas.gov

E-mail: not available

Database: See Web site

CD-ROM: private only

Library Reference Number:

_____

URGENT!

Immediate action is required.

We have made several attempts to collect the tax you owe, but we still haven't received your full payment. If you don't respond, we may seize your business, paycheck, bank account, auto or other property. We may also file a Federal Tax Lien. Please pay the amount you owe today or call us at the number below to resolve this issue.

The guys who sent this letter are generally serious and lack a sense of humor when you owe them money. "We" refers to the IRS. So as not to be put in a position to receive such a letter, you may want to do a bit more than just scan *Publication 334*. This publication explains some essential federal tax laws that apply to businesses. It describes the four major forms of business organizations—sole proprietorship, partnership, corporation, and S corporation—and explains the tax responsibilities of each. *Publication 334* is divided into eight parts. The first part contains general information on business organization and accounting practices. Part II discusses the tax aspects of accounting for assets used in a business. Parts III and IV explain how to figure your business income for tax purposes. They describe the kinds of income you must report and the different types of business deductions you can take.

Part V discusses the rules that apply when you sell or exchange business assets or investment property. It includes chapters on capital gains and losses and on involuntary conversions, such as theft and casualty losses.

The chapters in Part VI bring together some specific tax considerations for each of the four major forms of business organizations. Part VII looks at some credits that can reduce your income tax and some of the other taxes you may have to pay in addition to income tax. It also discusses the information returns that may have to be filed. The last part shows how to fill out the main income tax forms businesses use.

Raise your hand if you once thought about starting a "nonprofit" organization but couldn't figure out what nonprofit meant? Keep it up there if you also wondered why you couldn't keep all those profits yourself. That's why you need *Publication 557*. This publication discusses how organizations become recognized as exempt from federal income tax under section 501(a) of the Internal Revenue Code. These include organizations described in section 501(c). The publication also explains how to get an appropriate ruling or determination letter recognizing the exemption, and it gives other information that applies generally to all exempt organizations (see Forms 990, 1023, and 1024).

There is, of course, no end to what you need to know about business procedures and practices when it comes to taxes, but there are at least three publications that come to mind:

1. *Publication 535: Business Expenses*—This publication discusses such business expenses as pay for your employees; fringe benefits; rental expenses; interest; taxes; insurance; employee benefit plans; and certain education expenses for yourself and your employees. It also outlines the choice to capitalize certain business expenses; discusses amortization and depletion; covers some business expenses that may be deductible; and points out some expenses that are not deductible.

2. *Publication 917: Business Use of a Car*—This publication explains the expenses that you may deduct for the business use of your car. The publication also discusses the taxability of the use of a car provided by an employer, and it explains new rules for deducting car expenses.

3. *Publication 587: Business Use of Your Home*—587 can help you decide if you qualify to deduct certain expenses for using part of your home in your business. Deductions for the business use of a home computer are also discussed.

Something To Do

Review the tax publication that would help you plan your tax strategy for using your home as part of your business. What forms would be appropriate for you to use? Review the publication that explains the business use of a car. What forms would be appropriate for you to use?

The art of taxation consists in so plucking the goose
as to obtain the largest amount of feathers with the
least amount of hissing.

Jean Baptiste Colbert
Finance Minister to Louise XIV

So begins the *Tax Guide for College Teachers* (ISBN 0916018-504), published by
Academic Information Services, Inc., fax (only) at (202) 347-0079, which is
designed to keep college teachers informed about the latest tax rules. Perhaps one
of the most important deductions is that for home office. Although a full discussion is given in the home office chapter, it will remain for future IRS rulings and
court cases to interpret the (1994) rules in a variety of situations. As usual, the
current-year edition of the *Tax Guide for College Teachers* includes the new laws,
court cases, and IRS rulings of interest to college teachers. New information is
given on maximizing student aid, deducting the cost of lunch, satisfying Zoe
Baird rules for paying taxes (assuming there are those who still remember Zoe)
on household help, and so on. The editors ask you to remember that saving on
taxes is worth more than a raise in salary. The extra salary gets ravaged by federal and state taxes at the highest bracket your taxes reach. But the money you
save by knowing the tax laws goes into your pocket. The table of contents covers
the following items:

Basic rules	Home office
Expensing	Interest
Medical expenses	Household services
Withholding	Income shifting
State and local taxes	Estate and gift tax
Investing your money	Moving expenses
Audits	Tax deductions for homes
Travel	Expenses of attending school
Retirement	Outside business activity
Tax-free grants	Research expenses
Books, supplies, equipment	Casualty loss
Expenses and depreciation	Divorce/separation
Charitable contributions	Entertainment
Automobile expenses	Foreign income
Tax-sheltered plans	Sample tax return

A duplicate of the table of contents and sample pages will not be supplied
here. All tax information can be obtained by calling the numbers above or use the
Internet.

Recommended Supplement: *The Securities and Exchange Commission Publications*

Reference Navigator

Web site: http://www.sec.gov

E-mail: 102476.2726@compuserve.com

Database: Lexis-Nexis

CD-ROM: not available

Library Reference Number:

_____

The Securities and Exchange Commission (SEC) is not the title of a reference piece. Rather, it is a quasi-government agency. Nevertheless, the SEC, (212) 748-8000) is a very important source of information that needs to be understood by any well-informed business student.

A good description and source of information on the SEC can be seen in the *Directory of Business Information* (see Chapter 15). Publicly held companies and some private ones are required to tell the SEC—and the world—quite a bit about themselves. They must file specific reports disclosing business and financial conditions. This required filing of reports has also created a mini-industry. An estimated 40,000 business and investment entities now report to the SEC. They include public companies, investment funds such as mutual funds, and private companies that issue public debt such as bonds. You can also get a lot of SEC information in derivative reports from major company or industry sources such as *Moody's* and *Standard & Poor's* (see Chapter 3). Company reports required by the SEC include registration statement (operating data); prospectus (new public offering); proxy statement (annual meeting agendas); and Williams Act filings (mergers and acquisitions). Plus

10-K: a company's annual report to the SEC.

10-Q: a quarterly financial report.

8-K: a report on major unscheduled events (bankruptcy, etc.).

13-F: a quarterly report of institutional stock holdings.

13-G: (or 13-D) ownership reports and intentions.

14-D: a tender offer.

There are numerous ways to get SEC company reports; you can visit one of the SEC reference rooms in Washington, New York, or Chicago, or call the Washington information line at (202) 942-8088. The SEC also publishes an annual directory called *Directory of Companies Required to File Annual Reports with the Securities and Exchange Commission*. It is inexpensive and is available from the GPO or can be seen at federal depositories.

29 BUSINESS AMERICA

Description of Publication

For information on this monthly publication, call the International Trade Administration at (202) 205-2000.

Reference Navigation

Web site: http://www.ita.doc.gov

E-mail: tic@ita.doc.gov

Database: stat-usa (800) 782 8872

CD-ROM: available

Library Reference Number:

_____

Business America: The Magazine of International Trade (*BA*), first published by the State Department under another name in October 1880, is the oldest U.S. government magazine. After more than a hundred years of continuous publication, *Business America* still has the same mission: to help American companies sell their products overseas. That mission has been turned over to the U.S. Department of Commerce, International Trade Administration (ITA). The ITA has over 50 commercial districts around the country and in Puerto Rico. Many, but not all, of the offices have trade specialists who are available for counseling: the offices, addresses and telephone numbers plus trade specialist positions are listed at the end of the journal.

BA is a brief publication of approximately 35 pages that focuses on special trade topics (e.g., "Reinvented Government Programs: Paving the Way for Exporters Into the 21st Century") that are designed to inform, instruct, and motivate American businesspersons. The format is simple, but jazzed up considerably (for the government that means two-color separation and big fonts) in the last few years. The magazine leads with "Trade Watch," which gives brief sketches on the most recent trade activities involving the United States (e.g., "U.S. Economy"; "U.S. International Transactions"; "World Bank Sets Up Infrastructure Project Database"; etc.). Examples of some articles—written by ITA trade specialists—are:

"Reinvention Efforts Spread Through the Internet, As the Information Age Meets International Trade."

"American Cosmetics Are Looking Beautiful in Foreign Markets."

"US-China Commission Finds New Ways to Build Bilateral Partnerships."

BA also features a number of useful services that are highlighted in boxes, colors, diagrams, and the like, such as "New Books and Reports"; "Calendar for World Traders"; and "International Trade Exhibitions."

The Department of Commerce also publishes *Commerce Business Daily,* which can be searched on Dialog (see Chapter 21). It lists major federal contract awards and requests for proposals issued by civilian and military agencies. State agency databases also appear on commercial systems. To make researching the best markets easier, the Commerce Department's Commercial Service offers a variety of market research tools and trade lead sources. Call the National Trade Data Bank (NTDB) at (800) Stat-USA. *Business America* is the door to a lot of information; you will benefit by using it. For example:

- The National Trade Data Bank (NTDB) is a "one-stop" source of international trade data collected by federal agencies (CD-ROM available).

- Country Commercial Guides (CCGs) are comprehensive reports focused on single countries that cover topics important to exporters.

- Best Markets Reports (BMRs) describe the best prospects for U.S. sales abroad.

- Industry Sector Analyses (ISAs) are structured market research reports produced on location in leading overseas markets.

- International Market Insights (IMIs) are short profiles of specific foreign market conditions or opportunities prepared at embassies or development banks.

- Customized Market Analysis (CMA) program is market research made to order (prices range from $1,000 to $5,100 depending on the country).

- Trade Opportunities Program (TOP) provides timely sales leads from international firms seeking to buy or represent U.S. products and services.

- Agent/Distributor Service (ADS) is for companies seeking a customized search for qualified agents, distributors, or representatives abroad.

- International Company Profiles (ICPs) portray the reliability of prospective trading partners.

- Commercial Service International Contacts (CSIC) provides contact and product information on more than 46,000 firms abroad interested in U.S. products.

If you are just beginning your search and do not want to limit it to any particular agency within the U.S. government, try the U.S. government international-trade related Internet sites at http://www.business.gov/trade.html. Some other sites of interest are:

U.S. Business Advisor:	http://www.business.gov/trade.html
Stat-USA & NTDB:	http://stat-usa.gov
Economics and Statistics Administration	http://www.esa.gov
U.S. Trade Representative:	http://www.ustr.gov
Export-Import Bank of the U.S.:	http://www.exim.gov

Information on the U.S. Trade Commission may be obtained by calling: (202) 205-2000.

REINVENTED GOVERNMENT PROGRAMS:

PAVING THE WAY FOR EXPORTERS INTO THE 21ST CENTURY

American Cosmetics Look Good in Foreign Markets, and the Future Appears Even Brighter

By George Ruffner and Ronald Soriano, Commercial Service Italy

Not all that glitters is high-tech—especially in terms of U.S. exports. In fact, in 1995, American cosmetics manufacturers exported $1.9 billion worth of products. And the future looks even brighter if the results of the U.S. pavilions at the annual COSMOPROF show are any indication.

THE GREATEST (COSMETICS) SHOW ON EARTH

COSMOPROF is the world's largest and most important cosmetics trade show. Every year, for the past three decades, it has been held in Bologna, Italy, a bustling center of industrial and agricultural activity in Italy's heartland. Each year, the crowds of trade visitors get bigger. This year, COSMOPROF attracted some 1,272 exhibitors and close to 115,000 trade visitors, including more than 16,000 from 126 foreign (other than Italy) countries. They came to see the latest in beauty, skin care, and hair grooming products.

As usual, the United States brought the largest foreign delegation, organized by Commercial Service Italy and the Department of Commerce in Washington (Trade Development). In fact, with 93 firms participating, this American delegation was the largest ever. Seventy-five firms participated directly while 18 were represented in a catalog display organized by the Los Angeles District Office.

In 1989, the Independent Cosmetic Manufacturers and Distributors (ICMAD) enlisted U.S. Department of Commerce support to organize the first-ever U.S. pavilion, which featured 24 exhibitors—a cooperative effort that continues today and yields outstanding results. In 1993, the Beauty and Barber Supply Institute (BBSI) joined ICMAD and Commerce to promote participation to its members. COSMOPROF has become an important showcase for American cosmetics products and services; today, demand to participate in the show by American companies is so great that there are in fact three U.S. pavilions in three different halls at the Bologna Fairgrounds.

The Department of Commerce, through Trade Development's Office of Consumer Goods and CS Italy, continues to recruit for the pavilion with the close collaboration of ICMAD and BBSI. ICMAD and BBSI have looked to Commerce to provide the important institutional framework required to support their memberships' participation and their own recruitment efforts.

A BEAUTIFUL SUCCESS!

The 75 American exhibitors—all small- and medium-size—displayed an impressive array of top quality and innovative cosmetics products, which attracted the attention of some of the world's leading buyers. The results were astounding—a whopping $6.5 million in off-the-floor sales and 108 representation agreements signed with agents and distributors from 47 different nations. Subsequent sales could raise the final figures into the tens of million of dollars, a truly beautiful success!

Why are the U.S. pavilions at COSMOPROF so successful? In part, of course, there is the recognition that the American cosmetics industry is a world leader in a broad range of products from nail polish to natural skin care. Price competitiveness, as well as quality and innovation, underlie the attractiveness of American firms in this sector. The visibility and identification with the United States provided by the Commercial Service banner, and the various services provided to the exhibitors by CS Italy (interpreters, booth logistics, meeting areas), act as magnets for potential buyers and agents. As Nisso Benattar, vice president of Carlstadt, N.J.-based Cobra Henna stated, "if we were in any other pavilion, we would not get the. . .

Recommended Supplement: *WorkAmerica*

For more information on this publication call the National Alliance of Business at (202) 289-2888.

Reference Navigator

Web site: http://www.nab.com   CD-Rom available

E-Mail: info@nab.com   Library Reference Number:

Database: see Web site   _____

The National Alliance of Business (NAB) is a business-led nonprofit organization dedicated to building a competitive American work force by enhancing the skills and knowledge of workers to meet the needs of business. This seemingly governmental goal is one undertaken by what is now called an NGO, or Non-Governmental Organization, dedicated to the social good, in this case, the NAB. The NAB wants to help build an internationally competitive work force dedicated to continuous improvement; it's the old treadmill thing—if you are not working to keep up then you automatically fall behind. Today, the key to American business competitiveness lies in a quality work force—where every citizen should be educated and trained to world-class standards beginning in the classroom and continuing in the workplace.

WorkAmerica, the NAB's monthly newsletter, keeps you informed about the latest initiatives by business leaders to improve work force quality in communities nationwide. It highlights the best practices of community-led efforts in education reform, training, and quality work force programs. Through analysis of data and work force trends, and spotlights on innovative corporate practices, *WorkAmerica* helps organizations define solutions to business work force quality issues. Another source of good reference material is the NAB's *Legislative Update,* which comes out 10 times a year. This newsletter also focuses on work force-related developments in Congress that affect human resources policies and practices. It covers such topics as OSHA, pensions, education standards, job training, immigration, employee participation teams, health benefits, and so on. *Workforce Economics* is another valuable NAB publication devoted to economic analysis of work force development policies and investments.

If you have a predilection to peer into the future, you may wish to get a copy of *Workforce Development Trends,* published by the NAB. It profiles the current and future national work force.

OK, how many of you know when to celebrate National Manufacturing Week? Thought so. In 1998 it was the third week in March. If you want to learn about manufacturing, and you should, join the National Association of Manufacturers (NAM), (202) 637-3000; fax: (202) 637-3402.

The NAM celebrated its 100th anniversary in 1995. It has been the foremost voice in Washington for industry since 1895. Today, it speaks for more than 13,500 member companies and subsidiaries that provide nearly 80 percent of the manufactured products and manufacturing jobs in the United States. The NAM advocates policies that promote economic growth and efficiency in American industry. The Manufacturing Institute is the educational and research affiliate of the NAM; you can call it at (202) 637-3107; or http://www.nam.org on the Internet.

The NAM is a particularly good reference source because it has a catalog of excellent publications, which can be obtained by calling (800) 637-3005. One of the catalogs is *Complying With the ADA: A Small Business Guide to Hiring and Employing the Disabled* (Catalog # 0220-24-02):

Designed especially to serve the practical needs of small business owners and managers who can't afford the high-powered lawyers to interpret the Americans With Disabilities Act's (ADA's) provisions, this simple 210-page handbook shows exactly how to meet the ADA's guidelines on hiring and employing—easily and economically.

Incidentally, if you're civic-minded, you may wish to join The Newcomen Society of the United States. This publicly supported, tax-exempt, education foundation was founded in 1923. The society's name perpetuates the life and work of Thomas Newcomen (1663–1729), the British pioneer whose invention in 1712 of the first practical atmospheric steam engine brought him lasting fame in the field of the mechanical arts. The Newcomen engines paved the way for the Industrial Revolution. The purposes of the Newcomen Society are to:

- Encourage and stimulate original research and writing in the field of business history through a continuing system of **grants and fellowships.**
- Preserve, protect, and promote the American free enterprise system.
- Honor corporate entities that have made significant contributions.
- Publish the histories and achievements of such enterprises.

30 WASHINGTON INFORMATION DIRECTORY

Description of Publication

For information on this annual publication (ISBN 0-87187-908-5), call Congressional Quarterly Inc. at (202) 887-6262; fax (202) 822-6583.

Reference Navigator

Web site: http://books.cq.com

E-mail: pmcclure@cq.com

Database: Oracle

CD-Rom: not available

Library Reference Number:

Anyone who needs to contact a governmental organization or person in Washington should not be without this book. The editors of this directory have organized more than 5,000 information sources into 19 chapters on different subjects. These chapters list names, addresses, and telephone numbers of members of Congress and officials of federal departments and agencies as well as private nonprofit groups in the Washington area. Each entry describes the work and responsibilities of the organization listed. The Washington Information Directory includes a section on the Internet and Related Technologies as well as an enlarged section on Executive Reorganization. It also features e-mail addresses of many agencies, congressional offices, and nonprofit groups; and eight new organization charts.

The *Washington Information Directory* is designed to make your search for information easy and quick. Each of the 18 chapters in the directory (see the table of contents) covers a broad subject area. You will find, for example, chapters on energy, health, science and space, and national security. Within the chapters, information is grouped in narrower subject areas. A detailed table of contents can be found at the beginning of each chapter. This subject arrangement allows you to find in one place the departments and agencies of the federal government, congressional committees, and private, nonprofit organizations in the nation's capital that have the information you need.

The directory divides information sources into three categories: (1) agencies, (2) Congress, and (3) nongovernmental organizations. When you look up a subject, you usually will find entries under all three categories. Each entry includes the name, address, and telephone number of the organization; the name and title of the director or the best person to contact for information; and a brief description of the work performed by the organization.

Students have a tendency to call first and contemplate second. This process generally doesn't work well because hardworking Washingtonian bureaucrats have this thing about being called with ill-conceived questions from what has often been called the sticks, the hinterlands, and other names of affection for the outlanders like us. So when you are writing or calling:

1. Start with a specific question. If necessary, do some homework before you contact a source (don't call the Department of Commerce, for example, and say, "Have you got any information on automobiles?").

2. Call the information telephone number first. Often you can get the answer you need without going further. If not, a quick explanation of your query should put you in touch with the person who can answer your question. Rarely will you need to talk to the top administrator.

3. Call or write your own member of Congress rather than a congressional committee. Your representative has staff people assigned to answer questions from constituents. Contact a committee only if you have a technical question that cannot be answered elsewhere.

4. Address letters to the director of an office or organization. Your letter will be sent to the person who can answer your question.

5. Keep in mind the agency or organization, not the name of the director. Personnel changes in Washington are common. When someone retires or moves, that individual's office and telephone number usually remain the same.

All addresses and telephone numbers in the *Washington Information Directory* are in Washington, D.C., unless otherwise indicated. Each Washington entry includes the name of the agency or organization, the building or street address, the Zip code, and the telephone number. The area code for the District of Columbia telephone numbers (202) is not included.

Another definitive tool to help you navigate the global business and foreign policy community in Washington is *The Washington Almanac of International Trade & Business*. When you need to find the right information about the international landscape in Washington and the individual who knows it, there is no substitute for a comprehensive, proven reference of those to contact. Call Almanac Publishing Inc., (202) 296-2297.

Something to Think About

CAP stands for Capitol in the WID. What do the letters H and S before the room numbers of congressional members and committees indicate? What does the acronym CHOB stand for? Can you find the phone number of the Banking, Housing and Urban Affairs Committee?

2
Economics and Business

CONTENTS:

BUSINESS AND ECONOMIC POLICY

General

AGENCIES:

Census Bureau (Commerce Dept.), Economic Programs, Federal Bldg. 3, Suitland, MD 20233; (301) 457-2112. Thomas Mesenbourg, acting associate director. Fax, (301) 457-3761.

Compiles comprehensive statistics on the level of U.S. economic activity and the characteristics of industrial and business establishments at the national, state, and local levels.

Commerce Dept., Main Commerce Bldg., 14th St. and Constitution Ave. N.W. 20230; 482-2112. Ronald H. Brown, secretary; David J. Barram, deputy secretary, 482-4625. Information, 482-2000. Press, 482-4901. Library, 482-5511. Fax, 482-4576.

Acts as principal adviser to the president on federal policy affecting industry and commerce; promotes national economic growth and development, competitiveness, international trade, and technological development; provides business and government with economic statistics, research, and analysis; encourages minority business; promotes tourism. Library reference service staff answers questions about commerce and business.

Commerce Dept., Business Liaison, Main Commerce Bldg. 20230; 482-3942. Melissa Moss, director. Information, 482-1302. Fax, 482-4054. Business assistance, 482-3176.

Serves as the central office for business assistance. Handles requests for information and services as well as complaints and suggestions from businesses; provides businesses with a forum to comment on federal regulations; initiates meetings on policy issues with industry groups, business organizations, trade and small-business associations, and the corporate community. Business Assistance Office provides information, advice, and guidance on federal policies and programs, selling to government markets, financial assistance programs, and domestic and international business statistics.

Commerce Dept., STAT-USA, Main Commerce Bldg. 20230; 482-0434. Kenneth Rogers, director. Fax, 482-2164.

Develops and maintains macroeconomic models and other analytical tools necessary to analyze a broad range of economic policy issues such as the effects on business of federal legislation, regulations, and programs. Maintains and makes available for public use the Economic Bulletin Board (EBB), the National Trade Data Bank (NTDB), and the National Economic, Social, and Environmental Data Bank.

Comptroller of the Currency (Treasury Dept.), 250 E St. S.W. 20219; 874-4900. Eugene A. Ludwig, comptroller. Information, 874-5000. Fax, 874-4950.

Regulates and examines the operations of national banks; establishes guidelines for bank examinations. Library open to the public.

Council Economic Advisers (Executive Office of the President), Old Executive Office Bldg., Rm. 314 20500; 395-5084. Vacant, chairman; Thomas P. O'Donnell, chief of staff. Fax, 395-6958.

Advisory body of three members and supporting staff of economists. Monitors and analyzes the economy and advises the president on economic developments, trends, and policies and on the economic implications of other policy initiatives. Prepares the annual Economic Report of the President for Congress.

Domestic Policy Council (Executive Office of the President), The White House 20500; 456-2216. Carol H. Rasco, assistant to the president for domestic policy. Fax, 456-2878.

Coordinates the domestic policy-making process to facilitate the implementation of the president's domestic agenda in such areas as business and economics.

Recommended Supplement: Congressional Directory

For information on this biannual publication (ISBN 0-89059-049-8), call the Joint Committee on Printing at: (202) 224 5241.

Reference Navigator

Web site: http://www.access.gpo.gov   CD-ROM: not available

E-mail: not available   Library Reference Number:

Database: see Web site   _____

The *Congressional Directory* is the official Who's Who of Congress. It is published at the beginning of each two-year term of Congress. The book is one of the oldest working handbooks within the government. The first *Congressional Directory* was published in 1821 for the 16th Congress. The format has not changed much over the years, even though it has grown 10 times larger. The Senate is responsible for publishing the *Congressional Directory,* but it is printed by the Government Printing Office (GPO). Call GPO Products at (202) 512-1800.

The book is almost 1,200 pages of detailed facts focusing on Congress. The first part of the *Directory* contains biographies of the vice president, the 100 members of the Senate, the 435 members of the House of Representatives, and officials of the U.S. Territories. (If you want information from the Canadian government, try FaxLink International (613) 994-6500, or Web site: http://www.ic. gc.ca.)

The biographies cover the general background of each representative, party affiliation, education, and family circumstances. Addresses and phone numbers are also listed. An overview of the State delegations, assignments to standing committees of the Senate and House, joint House and Senate committees, and their respective addresses and telephone numbers are given.

There is also a federal section covering the 17 departments from Agriculture to Veterans Administration, who's in charge, their biographies, and the departmental contact. The diplomatic section lists foreign representatives and consular offices in the United States. Don't forget that there are jobs in all those offices!

Something to Think About

Do you know which congressional body publishes the *Congressional Directory?* Do you know who your congressional representatives are? Do you know which committees they sit on, and have you ever asked for their help in your education?

---

31 POLITICAL HANDBOOK OF THE WORLD

Description of Publication

If you wish to obtain information on this book (ISBN 0-933199-10-4), call CSA Publications, State University of New York at (607) 777-2119; fax (607) 777-2117.

 Reference Navigator

Web site: http://www.polsci.binghamton.edu/
   handbook.htm

E-mail: phw@bingvmb.cc.binghamton.edu

Database: not available

CD-ROM: not available

Library Research Number:

_____

This very large (e.g., 1,216 pages) "handbook" seems to belie its title. Nevertheless, it does cover in four to five pages the essential political information of each country in the world. It is broken down into categories of: heads of state and government, cabinet members, leaders and programs of political parties, representation in national legislatures, mass media, and the composition and activities of major intergovernmental organizations. The section on intergovernmental organizations is particularly useful for getting a comprehensive and rapid explanation of their history and obligation.

In an attempt to assess in highly compressed form the past and present politics of the global community, the editors have continued a publishing tradition under way since 1928 when the Council on Foreign Relations issued the first handbook. A major problem facing the compilers of a global compendium turns on the rendering of both geographic and proper names. Despite a number of international conferences on the subject, the problem is becoming more acute, in part because of an increasing tendency toward linguistic "nationalization"; thus, *Burma* is now *Myanmar.* In addition, throughout the Third World (particularly in

Africa) Christian given names are commonly being abandoned as lingering relics of colonialism. The difficulty this makes in finding references is obvious.

In 1989, for the sixth year in a row, no newly independent territory entered the community of nations, and it appeared that the post-WWII march toward independence by the world's dependent peoples was virtually completed. At present it seems that if the post-colonial era has ended, a new period of fractionalization is under way. Thus, the Soviet Union has dissolved into 15 autonomous entities (at least for a while), Yugoslavia into 5, and Czechoslovakia and Ethiopia into 2 each.

The intergovernmental organizations selected for treatment are presented in a separate alphabetical sequence based on their official (in a few cases, customary) names in English. Where an organization is conventionally referred to by initials, these are appended to the official name. A list of member countries of most organizations is printed in the body of the relevant article; for the United Nations and its principal associated agencies, the memberships are given in Appendix C. While the editors admit the political significance of various nongovernmental organizations (particularly multinational corporations), they have limited this section to groups whose memberships are composed of more than two states, whose governing bodies meet with some degree of regularity, and which possess permanent secretariats or other continuing means for implementing collective decisions.

The handbook is broken down into the following sections:

I.   Preface   IV. Appendices (A – E)

II.   Governments   V.   Index

III. Intergovernmental Organizations

To narrow the focus a bit, look at *Politics in America* (ISBN 087187-775-9), published by Congressional Quarterly Inc. (see also Chapters 16 and 30). If you need some assurance about its quality, listen to Roger Mudd of the "Newshour with Jim Lehrer": "I have yet to learn how to leave home without it and doubt that I will. *Politics in America* is always in my suitcase. It is my road map for every congressional district in the country—where to go, what to look for, and who to talk to." The book aims to shed light on the multidimensional challenge of governing America by looking at the 535 individuals of the House and Senate who work as advocates for the districts and states that elect them. The editors examine the motivations of those whose ambitions take them to Congress and the desires of the Americans who sent them there. In writing the profiles, they do not try to decide what members ought to be for or against; their goal is to explain how members express their views and to assess how effective they are. It is, after all, a complex business to make laws for a nation of 260 million people . . . and counting.

Something to Think About

If asked, could you write an overview of the Austrian economy according to the *Political Handbook of the World?* Do you know why Jeane Kirkpatrick, Garrick Utley, and Felix Rohatyn, as well as being on the Board of Advisors of *Foreign Affairs,* are famous?

INTERGOVERNMENTAL ORGANIZATIONS

276

ASIA-PACIFIC ECONOMIC COOPERATION (APEC)

Established

At a meeting of foreign and economic ministers of twelve nations at Canberra, Australia, on November 6–7, 1989; objectives and principles set forth in Seoul Declaration approved during ministerial meeting at Seoul, South Korea, November 12–14, 1991; Declaration of Institutional Arrangements adopted September 10–11, 1992, at Bangkok, Thailand.

Purpose

To provide a forum for discussion on a broad range of economic issues and to promote multilateral cooperation among the market-oriented economies of the region.

Headquarters

Singapore.

Principal Organs

Annual Ministerial Meeting (all members), Senior Officials Meeting (all members), Working Groups, Secretariat.

Executive Director

Shiyiro Imanishi (Japan).

Membership (18)

Australia, Brunei, Canada, Chile, China, Hong Kong, Indonesia, Japan, Republic of Korea, Malaysia, Mexico, New Zealand, Papua New Guinea, Philippines, Singapore, Taiwan ("Chinese Taipei"), Thailand, United States.

Observers: Association of Southeast Asian Nations, Pacific Economic Cooperation Conference, South Pacific Forum.

Official Language

English

Origin and development

In early 1989 (then) Australian Prime Minister Robert Hawke proposed that a permanent body be established to coordinate economic relations among market-oriented nations of the Pacific rim, with particularly emphasis to be given to dialogue between Western Pacific countries and the United States. The proposal was endorsed by the Pacific Economic Cooperation Conference (PECC-a group of business, academic, and government representatives who had been holding informal discussions since 1980) and the first APEC meeting was held at Canberra, Australia on November 6–7. Ministers from twelve nations (Australia, Brunei, Canada, Indonesia, Japan, Republic of Korea, Malaysia, New Zealand, Philippines, Singapore, Thailand, and United States) attended the inaugural session, debate centering on how to proceed in adopting formal APEC arrangements.

Due primarily to concern among some members of the Association of Southeast Asian Nations (ASEAN-see separate article) that they might be "overwhelmed" by the "economic giants" such as Canada, Japan and United States if the organization moved too quickly, the Canberra session decided to keep APEC as a loosely-defined, informal grouping, officially committed only to an annual "dialogue" meeting. As regional economic cooperation gained momentum in other areas of the world, however, pressure grew within APEC for a more structured format. Consequently, the Ministerial Meeting at Seoul, South Korea, in November 1991 adopted a declaration outlining APEC's objectives, established additional organizational structure, and approved the membership of China, Hong Kong, and Taiwan. The "institutionalization" of APEC was completed during a Ministerial Meeting at Bangkok, Thailand, on September 10-11, 1992, with the decision to establish a permanent Secretariat in Singapore as of January 1, 1993. Mexico and Papua New Guinea were admitted in November 1993 while Chile's membership application was approved effective November 1994. The latter was the subject of debate within APEC, some officials suggesting that admission of South American countries could cost the organization its "focus". Consequently, a moratorium on any additional APEC members was declared until at least 1996 (see Activities, below, for subsequent developments).

Structure

APEC's governing body is the annual Ministerial Meeting, whose chairmanship rotates each year among the members. Since 1993 overall guidance has been provided by a summit of the heads of state and/or government of APEC members, who have been meeting annually immediately following the Ministerial Meeting. Responsibility for policy implementation rests with a Senior Officials Meeting (SOM), which convenes as necessary. Reporting to the SOM are ten Working Groups (Trade and Investment Data, Trade promotion, Investment and Technology, Human Resource Development, Regional Energy Cooperation, Marine Resource Conservation, Telecommunications, Transportation, Tourism, Fisheries) . . .

groups (Regional Trade Liberalization and Economic Policy). A small Secretariat is led by an Executive Director appointed for a one-year term by the nation chairing the upcoming Ministerial Meeting. In addition, an Eminent Persons Group was established in 1992 to analyze how trade should be conducted in the region to the year 2000.

Activities

The November 1992 Ministerial Meeting authorized a $2 million annual budget for APEC's new permanent Secretariat and directed it to establish an electronic tariff data base for the region, survey members regarding investment regulations, and study ways to harmonize custom procedures and reduce impediments to "market access" among members. Additional emphasis in the telecommunications, tourism, and environmental sectors was also approved at the November 14-18, 1994, Ministerial Meeting at Seattle, Washington. On the other hand, the APEC ministers postponed action on what were seen as "modest" recommendations from the Eminent Persons Group regarding development of a Pacific free trade area. Ongoing apprehension in some Asian nations (most pointedly Malaysia) was also a background issue at the much-publicized summit of the APEC heads of state convened at the request of US President Bill Clinton immediately after the Ministerial Meeting. Nevertheless, the summit endorsed a broadly worded "economic vision" for its members and agreed to establish "nonbinding" codes for investment and the transfer of technology.

Hoping to impel integrationist sentiment in the region (which controls more than one-half of the world's economy and conducts over $1 trillion in intraregional trade annually), the APEC finance ministers met for the first time on March 18-19, 1994, at Honolulu, Hawaii. Among other things, plans were endorsed to double the capital of the Asian Development Bank, to promote cross-border investment, and to study ways of facilitating the financing of large infrastructure projects. The mood of the meeting was described as "upbeat" although caution was still expressed about tension between the United States and Japan over the Japanese trade surplus and disagreement between Washington and several Asian capitals, particularly Beijing, over US efforts to couple trade and human rights issues.

A potentially historic step was taken at the second APEC summit, held November 15, 1994, at Bogor, Indonesia, with the adoption of a "declaration of common resolve" to pursue "free and open trade and investment" over the next quarter-century. The loosely worded accord called upon the region's developed nations to dismantle their trade barriers by 2010, followed by similar action on the part of the developing nations by 2020. However, many observers cautioned that it would be extremely difficult to translate APEC "resolve" into action, one journalist suggesting there was a "never-never land quality about a pledge 25 years into the future." On the other hand, proponents argued that the Bogor Declaration represented a crucial "psychological breakthrough" on the way to creation of what would the world's largest free trade zone.

Recommended Supplement: *Foreign Affairs*

For information on this bi-monthly publication (ISSN 00157120), call the Council on Foreign Relations at (212) 434-9400; or fax: (212) 861-2759.

Reference Navigator

Web site: http://www.foreignaffairs.org   CD-ROM: not available

E-mail: ForAff@email.cfr.org   Library Research Number:

Database: see Web site

Foreign Affairs has been a mainstream publication for many years, boasting a horde of famous names on its board of advisors (e.g., Garrick Utley, Jeane Kirkpatrick, and Felix Rohatyn). It has three primary sections: Comments, Essays, and Book Reviews. All are annotated to give the reader a quick review of what may be of interest. The articles are written by experts in foreign affairs, well annotated, easily read with little or no academic jargon, presented in large print, and well researched. An example from the May–June 1997 issue is "The Dollar and the Euro." by C. Fred Bergsten.

> With the creation of a single European currency, the dollar will have its first real competitor since it surpassed the pound sterling as the globe's dominant currency. As much as $1 trillion of international investment may shift from dollars to euros. The political impact of the euro will be just as great. Europe could try to export its high unemployment by undervaluing the euro's initial exchange rate. Protectionist battles could break out. The euro's arrival need not cause instability in world markets, but it will probably cause volatility. A smooth transition to a stable dollar and euro system will require a quantum leap in trans-atlantic cooperation.

A second international affairs periodical is *Foreign Policy* (ISSN 0015-7228), published quarterly by the Carnegie Endowment for International Peace, (202) 483-7600. This publication is an excellent reference resource, but somewhat formidable in the length of its articles. A standard length for *Foreign Policy* articles is 4,000 to 6,000 words. The publication's web site is at www.foreignpolicy.com.

One particular interesting note for students is Foreign Policy's Internship Program, which offers challenging staff assistant internships (unpaid) for highly motivated individuals concerned with global policy issues. Interns learn the editorial aspects of publication by assisting in fact-checking, reviewing manuscripts, and proofreading, as well as helping with other editorial office duties. Interns are responsible for seeing two or three edited articles through to publication. Qualified applicants have completed at least their junior year of college with course work or experience in foreign affairs. Candidates must have solid research, writing, and interpersonal skills. The Carnegie Endowment for International Peace is one of Washington's most prestigious foreign policy research organizations.

VII THE ORGANIZATIONAL FUNCTIONS

Optional Company References

- *Finance Facts Yearbooks*
- *Statistics in Marketing (Simmons)*
- *Facts on File Directory of Major Public Corporations*
- *The National Job Bank*
- *The Career Guide*
- *Who Owns Whom*
- *Macmillan Directory of Leading Private Companies*
- *Annual Reports Q File*
- *Million Dollar Directory*
- *Directory of Corporate Affiliations*

32   TRADE JOURNALS

Description of Publication: *Industry Week*

For information regarding this publication (ISSN 0039-0895), call Penton Publishing, Inc., at (800) 326-4146, or fax: (216) 696-6023.

    Reference Navigator

Web site: http://www.industryweek.com

E-mail: 74774.2327@compuserve

Database: See Web site

CD-ROM: not available

Library Reference Number:

_____

This is an excellent resource for young managers interested in the industry perspective. The format is well designed; it leads the reader to punchy articles dealing with industrial themes (growth, technology, logistics management, teaming engineers, etc.). The departments are broken down into short, but informative specialties such as "The Bookshelf," which reviews new books, three in one particular issue, and even offers the telephone numbers of the publishers for more information. Also included are "Global Watch," "Economic Trends," and "InfoCenter." One particularly interesting section is the *Industry Week* LitDigest and the *IW* ResourceFile, which shows pictures of the literature covered, gives a brief description of each of their contents, provides their telephone and fax numbers, and offers free copies. Tough to go wrong there! Here's an example of one:

> "Expanding Or Moving Your Business?" If so, take advantage of the NAM's (National Association of Manufacturers) free plant-site selection service. Through the NAM's exclusive arrangement with Plant Site Locators, Inc., you can save time and money on your plant-site search.

Also, *Industry Week* teams with CNBC to present "Industry Week's Management Today," a weekly half-hour cable TV program exploring the management issues facing today's executives. It airs Saturdays and Sundays at 10:30 a.m. (ET).

Call (800) SMART TV for the cable channel in your area. This type of programming lends itself to class assignments that are original, professionally presented, contemporary, and delivered in a medium the students are comfortable with.

IW also offers two other services. Online: *IndustryWeek* Interactive is an online forum hosted by the CompuServe Information Service. The forum provides access to feature articles, as well as electronic communication and networking opportunities with other online users, featured personalities, executives, and the editors of *IW*. For information on joining *IndustryWeek* Interactive and to receive a free membership kit, call (800) 326-4146 and ask for the *IW* representative. If you already are a CompuServe subscriber, simply type GO INDWEEK. *IW* also produces conferences on topics important to executives and managers. For example, *IW* sponsored (with others) a global leadership forum in October 1996 that included, among other notable speakers, General Colin Powell (USA Ret.). For more information on conferences, call (800) 326-4146 or see the InfoCenter located near the back of the magazine. Training videos and lists of executives are also available.

Finally, *IW* conducts an annual search for America's best plants that highlights manufacturing excellence. In some cases, as Associate Editor George Taninecz writes, "it uncovers industrial dramas as well as potent performance—epics of pragmatic market ascension, triumph over corporate tragedy, and poignant tales of competitiveness combined with community spirit."

This is a very active publication, covering an important aspect of our economy, with informed research and a penchant for communication. The publication is selectively distributed throughout industry to qualified executives with management responsibilities and through subscriptions, but it is not available on newsstands.

From the academic perspective, the journal *Industrial Relations: A Journal of Economy and Society* (ISSN 0019-8676) is published quarterly by Blackwell Publishers, (800) 835-6770. The journal offers themes (e.g., Symposium on Compensation) for some issues, which would include four or five articles, such as "Earnings Mobility and Long-Run Inequality: An Analysis Using Matched CPS Data," by Maury Gittleman and Mary Joyce.

There probably are few students today who do not realize that the service industry sector of the economy is bigger than the manufacturing side. While the *International Journal of Service Industry Management* (ISSN 0956-4233), published by MCB University Press, (800) 633-4931, is not a "trade magazine" per se, it fits in closely with industry topics. Unfortunately, there seem to be very few other service industry journals...most articles of such ilk would fall within the retail categories. Contact can be made on the World Wide Web at http://www.mcb.co.uk. An example of an article from the June 1997 issue is "Market Orientation in UK Multiple Retail Companies: Nature and Pattern," by Hong Liu and Gary Davis.

Also, *Industrial and Corporate Change* (ISBN 0960-6491) has industry as its primary focus. Contact the Institute of Management, Innovation and Organization, Haas School of Business of the University of California at (501) 642-1075. The articles are very comprehensive and excellent for research support. An example of an article from its June 1997 issue is "Technological Regimes, Industrial Demography and the Evolution of Industrial Structures," by D. B. Audretsch.

Something to Think About

In reviewing "Economic Trends" in *IW,* could you compare Global Aggregates (Real GDP/GNP in percentages) between the G-7 countries for 1997 and Latin America?

Industry Searches

Special attention should be paid to searching for industry information because such data often serve as the foundation for any thorough macro- or microeconomic analysis. Aside from the government, trade associations are well-known sources of industry information. (According to Gale's *Encyclopedia of Associations*, see Chapter 19 of this text, there are over 8,000 trade associations specifically relating to business and industry.) However, according to Jan Davis Tudor ("Industry Insider," *Database,* December 1997), the data collected and generated by associations are often published in the form of reports that are difficult to find or restricted to association members. She points out that complete reports have rarely been included in on-line databases and only small sections of the reports are quoted in magazines, newsletters, Web sites, or press releases. And once contact is made it can be difficult (and/or expensive) to persuade personnel to send the data in a timely manner, assuming the information is available in the first place.

This problem is being overcome by a new database, called *Industry Insider,* created by The Investext Group (TIG) and available from TIG's Research Bank—Global Edition, a Windows-based CD-ROM-dedicated workstation, and I/PLUS Direct, an on-line service. TIG, (800) 662-7878, solicited and included the data that are most useful to its clients, such as growth trends, production rates, forecasts, import and export data, sales figures, and other statistics. According to Tudor, the database was likely to contain data from 200 trade associations worldwide by the spring of 1998. TIG is also including data from international organizations, with emphasis on the United Kindgom, Asia Pacific, and Europe. The earliest reports date from 1994 and all reports will continue to be archived.

Tudor states that some of the most valuable industry-related information she finds on the Internet is on trade association home pages. But she also offers the caveat that not all trade associations post their research data on the Internet, and those that do often publish only a segment of a complete report. In fact, the *Industry Insider* product manager studied the content of trade association Web site data versus the data contained on *Industry Insider.* She found that only four percent of association information available on *Industry Insider* was also available on the Internet. Tudor did her own minisurvey of 15 reports she received from *Industry*

Insider to determine if the information was also available on the Internet. She found that *only one* short report was published on an association Web site.

Tudor's verdict: "All in all, I am impressed with *Industry Insider.* Although my searches were occasionally met with 'hit and miss' results, I was often amazed to find incredibly specific data. One example of a good 'find' on *Industry Insider* was a market share analysis of the tomato sauce industry from The Food Institute's 'Food Markets in Review: Tomato Products.' This one-page report provided detailed financial information of specific product lines from large food conglomerates, details that are extremely hard to find from traditional sources. This report, faxed to me within five minutes of finding it, cost a very fair price of $20." (You can contact Ms. Tudor at JT Research, e-mail: jantudor@halcyon.com)

FEATURES

DEPARTMENTS

IW on the woeb: We have bench-marking covered with our virtual communities such as Best Plants, as well as our Special Issues databases.

Industry Focus: Chemicals
The Race Is On

Chemical-industry giants continue to jockey portfolios and capital resources to take profitable, long-term advantage of global market opportunities.

By Tim Stevens

Last year was marked by a continuation of tremendous action in the worldwide chemical industry, as multibillion-dollar companies made blockbuster shifts in holdings and capital investments to improve returns, increase competitiveness, and dampen industry cyclicality.

Monsanto Co. announced a spinoff of its entire $3 billion chemical business to concentrate on life science. The UK's ICI PLC paid $8 billion for Unilever Group's specialty-chemicals business in May. Germany's Bayer AG committed $9 billion to capital expenditures and R&D through the year 2000 in the United States, and German Hoeschst AG has undergone a drastic reorganization to reemerge as nine separate companies, all with global organizations.

"The chemical industry is no longer a predictable mix of products and companies," says Du Pont & Co. CEO John A. Krol. "Now it has become a powerful $1.5 trillion global economic system in the throes of evolutionary change. The dynamic is one of fierce competitiveness coupled with tremendous opportunity all around the world."

THAT'S LIFE (SCIENCE)

Some might suggest that a number of changes—the recent emphasis on life science, for instance—are not so evolutionary. "Life science is seen as a pot of gold, but some chemical companies find it hard to mix that with traditional chemical businesses so they can exploit it," says Michael Ekstadt, vice president and chemical-industry analyst at the consulting firm A.T. Kearney, New York.

For Monsanto, chemicals and life science don't mix—at least they cannot flourish under the same roof. So the company will split this fall into two separate publicly traded companies. One will be a lean diversified, $3 billion chemical operation managed for some growth, but mainly for cash generation. The other will be a $6 billion agricultural, human-health, and food-ingredient operation managed for rapid growth in markets Monsanto predicts will converge as biotechnology allows creation of food products tailored to deliver favorable health benefits.

"It became clear that the two different segments had very different needs, and appealed to different markets and to a completely different group of shareholders," says Monsanto chief economist Nick Flippello in St. Louis. "In the new organization, both companies can operate more optimally."

With perhaps less fanfare, but with equal decisiveness, other chemical companies have shifted emphasis to life science. The blockbuster Hoescht restructuring shows four of the nine new businesses competing in this arena.

"We are now concentrating our resources on the forward-looking markets of health and nutrition, which offer the greatest leverage for growth, employment, profit improvements, and thus shareholder value," says Hoechst Chairman Jüergen Dormann.

One of the companies, Hoechst Marion Roussel Inc., Kansas City-based maker of ethical and consumer pharmaceuticals, posted an operating margin of 14.3% in 1996, one of the highest ever achieved at Hoechst, which has been hovering around 5% as a company since 1993. The goal is for the pharmaceutical business to yield a margin of 20% by 1999, according to Dormann.

Recommended Supplement: *Restaurant Business*

For information on this monthly publication (ISSN 0097-8043), call Bill Communications at: (212) 592-6650.

Reference Navigator

Web site: http://www.restaurantbiz.com

E-Mail: 200-4782@MCIMAIL.COM

Database: See Web site

CD-ROM: not available

Library Reference Number:

_____

This is absolutely not a magazine to be taken lightly. Any reader who can peruse this periodical with its advertising examples of what appears to be delicious and exquisitely prepared foods without a craving for breakfast, lunch, or dinner has incredible self-control.

Considering that there are hundreds of trade magazines covering every industry imaginable (see *Business Marketing* in Chapter 34) choosing a few to represent the industry is difficult. However, perhaps nothing can be closer to the daily life of a human being than eating, therefore, the use of *Restaurant Business (RB)* in this text is selected as only one of many examples of an industry or trade magazine.

Trade magazines usually mean a lot of ads and a few good articles; however, the feature articles in *RB* (one or two) are for the most part substantive and well researched and written. The format is colorful and contemporary. A recent cover article focused on *RB*'s fourth annual CEO compensation ranking highlights (according to a survey by compensation consultants William M. Mercer). The entire article takes 14 pages. It is a good example of *RB* reporting, covering such areas as:

"Tighter Times"	"Exit Packages"
"Overview"	"Women Execs
"Compensation Rankings"	"Bargain CEOs"
"Salary Analysis"	"Odds and Ends"
"The Bonus Situation"	"Youngest and Oldest"

This type of coverage is appropriate for good reference work and reflects the work of a professional editorial staff. The departments include eight columns covering such useful items as: Calendar, Equipment IQ, Index, etc.

Something to Think About

What department in *Restaurant Business* covers information on conferences?
What is the largest restaurant in the world?

---

33   BUSINESS LAW

Description of the Publication: *West's Encyclopedia of American Law*

For information on this annual publication (ISBN 0-314-22770-9), call Gale Research at (800) 877-4253, or fax: (800) 414-5043.

 Reference Navigator

Web site: http://www.wld.com/wealad.htm   CD-ROM: available

E-mail: 72203.1552@compuserve.com   Library Reference Number:

Database: Dialog   _____

I doubt this comment will be news to anybody, but in the past decade or so, Americans in all walks of life have become increasingly affected by the law. Contributing factors include the extensive development and growth of federal and state legislation as well as rules and regulations that have far-reaching impact on everyday life. According to the editors of *West's Encyclopedia of American Law*, there has been a dramatic increase in administrative proceedings and litigation to interpret and enforce such measures. Over the years the public has made repeated demands for an effective and timely system of justice. As a result, Americans need a readily available research source to consult to gain greater knowledge and understanding of the principles, institutions, and people that through the law provide stability and structure to daily life. *West's Encyclopedia of American Law (WEAL)* presents in one reference set a panorama of the American legal system, which while comprehensive in scope is specific in its explanations of legal topics. This unique multi-volume work brings together diverse features and accurate text written in plain English that transcends the traditional format of legal encyclopedias and other secondary sources (translated that means it's more fun to read). *WEAL* provides current information on 5,000 legal topics in 12 volumes.

WEAL (which replaces *The Guide to American Law*) not only encompasses legal principles and concepts, but also contains landmark documents and important acts, accounts of famous trials, historical movements and events, and biographies of prominent individuals. *WEAL* also provides information relating to key federal regulatory agencies and departments; discussions of legal education, philosophies, and the legal profession; and legal maxims and famous quotations, all of which contribute to the highly developed and dynamic tableau of national jurisprudence. Another nice aspect of this publication is its treatment of international law concerning the rights of business, public and private institutions. In short, it's an excellent resource.

For researchers wanting to learn more, at the end of an entry, additional topics discussed in *WEAL* are listed to help readers fully explore a topic of interest. "In Focus" articles accompany many entries, providing additional facts, details, and arguments that help researchers gain a deeper understanding of controversial issues such as the legislative process, abortion, and capital punishment.

If are you looking for a simple yet effective way to integrate technology into your research, consider Marianne Jennings' *Business: Its Legal, Ethical, and Global Environment, 4th edition*, (ISBN 0-538-87094-X). It has the answer—integrated Internet coverage, designed for students to use at their option. This text is the first legal environment book to offer Internet margin notes within every chapter, right next to the relevant topic, and a professionally designed World Wide Web site called Bridging the Gap: http://www.thomson.com/swcp/bef/jennings/jennings.html.

Why just talk about the Federal Trade Commission or the International Court of Justice, when you can visit via the Internet? Why generalize about NAFTA or the Uniform Commercial Code, when you can review the primary texts on-line? The Internet offers sites for government departments, legislatures, and judiciaries; sites for states, treaties, and court opinions; and sites for businesses, organizations, and associations. If you want to surf in some neat waters, call the Academic Resource Center at (800) 423-0563.

*They [corporations] cannot commit
treason, nor be outlawed, nor
excommunicate, for they have no souls.*
SIR EDWARD COKE

CORPORATE VEIL

A legal principle that relieves an officer, director, or stock-holder of a corporation of individual, personal liability for its obligations as long as it engages in business and is not an ALTER EGO of those individuals.

When a corporation is a sham that is used only for the personal benefit of its officers, directors, or stockholders who want immunity from liability for their wrongful acts, a court will PIERCE THE CORPORATE VEIL, disregard the corporate status of the organization, and impose personal liability upon those responsible for wrongdoing carried out in the name of the corporation.

CORPORATION

An artificial entity possessing legally enforceable rights and reciprocal obligations and which is created pursuant to the authority of a state or a nation for the accomplishment of a specific purpose or the undertaking of a particular business.

Although a corporation is comprised of natural persons, it has a distinct and separate legal existence independent of them. It has the capacity to endure perpetually, in spite of changes that might be affected in its membership. In addition, a corporation has many rights and powers that individuals do, including the right to take, hold, and convey PROPERTY, to enter into CONTRACTS, and to sue and be sued. It can also exercise any powers it is given by the law under which it was formed.

Historical Background

The concepts underlying the creation of corporations have early historical roots. The idea of CORPORATE PERSONALITY derives to a certain degree from the CODE OF HAMMURABI and Roman law acknowledged corporate personality when allowed by the state. Corporations that were ultimately embodied in English law were initially formed following the Roman conquest of Britain.

Although corporations were established in the American colonies by English kings and Parliament, state governments took on the authority to grant corporate CHARTERS after the colonies achieved independence. Such charters were, however, restricted for a number of years mainly to public enterprises, such as the building of roads and bridges.

The Industrial Revolution and resulting commercial expansion that took place in the nineteenth century advanced the development of corporations. The corporation was the optimum vehicle for the furtherance of large business enterprises, since it joined centralized direction and control with moderate financial investment by, ideally, an unlimited number of people.

Initially, corporations existed primarily in states that were heavily industrialized or where businesses necessitated extensive financing, such as banking and manufacturing enterprises. The life of a corporation was usually restricted to a term of either twenty, thirty, or fifty years, and most of the incorporators were obliged to reside in the state of incorporation. Corporate powers and the amount of indebtedness was strictly regulated by the government.

Laws governing corporations were eventually liberalized in nonindustrial states to lure new corporations and their revenues. Industrial states responded in a similar manner in order to retain the revenues brought in by corporations which were originally established within their geographical boundaries.

Modern Corporations

The corporation is currently the predominant type of business organization in the United States due primarily to the advantages of limited liability and its indefinite duration. Since the corporation is a distinct and separate entity from those who organize and run it, the corporation alone is liable on the business contracts into which it enters. In addition, a corporation theoretically has perpetual existence and, therefore, can continue regardless of various changes in its members.

A corporation also has centralized management, readily transferable interests, a collection of rules to direct its operation, tax advantages, and the facilitation of financing through the issuance of STOCK which enhance its popularity as a valuable tool to conduct business.

Certain disadvantages, however, exist in the formation of a corporation. Such a business organization is subject to extensive formalities, publicity, and state and Federal governmental regulation, such as SECURITIES REGULATION.

Types of Corporate Organizations

Corporations encompass private corporations, nonprofit corporations, and MUNICIPAL CORPORATIONS.

Private corporations are created with the purpose of engaging in business for profit, whereas nonprofit corporations are ordinarily formed to benefit the public at large. Municipal corporations are organizations, such as cities and towns, organized to aid the state in conducting the processes of government in local communities.

Corporations that would ordinarily be regarded as private are regarded in the law as quasi-public when their business is of a nature directly related to the needs of the public. Since such corporations are devoted to a public use, they generally possess the power of EMINENT DOMAIN and can thereby acquire property under government. . .

Humor for Review

In the interest of relief from sometimes challenging reference pieces in this text, you may wish to review the following questions taken from official court records nationwide. They were compiled by a client of the Salt Lake City law firm of Johnson & Hatch and distributed on the Internet.

Q: The truth of the matter is that you were not an unbiased, objective witness, isn't it? You, too, were shot in the fracas?

A: No, sir. I was shot midway between the fracas and the navel.

Q: Did he pick the dog up by the ears?

A: No.

Q: What was he doing with the dog's ears?

A: Picking them up in the air.

Q: Where was the dog at this time?

A: Attached to the ears.

Q: Doctor, how many autopsies have you performed on dead people?

A: All my autopsies have been on dead people.

Q: Mrs. Smith, you do believe that you are emotionally unstable?

A: I used to be.

Q: How many times have you committed suicide?

A: Four times.

Q: When he went, had you gone and had she, if she wanted to and were able, for the time being excluding all the restrains on her not to go also, would he have brought you, meaning you and she, with him to the station?

A: Mr. Brooks. Objection. That question should be taken out and shot.

Recommended Supplement: *Business Lawyer*

For information on this quarterly publication (ISSN 0007-6899), call the American Bar Association (ABA) at (312) 988-5000.

Reference Navigator

Web site: http://www.abanet.org   CD-ROM: not available

E-mail: Personal only   Library Reference Number:

Database: See Web site   _____

The purpose of this quarterly is to provide members of the legal profession and the public generally with articles and reviews by individual authors and reports and surveys by various committees of the ABA Business Law Section in the fields of law. These areas of business law include (without limitation, according to the editors), constitutional, corporate, banking, commercial, financial institutions, business financing, securities, partnerships, bankruptcy, and environmental law, at the state, federal, and international levels, whether arising in the context of international agreements, legislation, regulation, litigation, or private transactions . . . so, still want to be a lawyer?

These people have been publishing *Business Lawyer* for the last 51 years or so, and, if the author's math is correct, they have added about 10 pages to each article for every decade in business. If you planned on reading one of the articles during lunch, you better take about two hours. An example of an article is "Reorganizations of Investment Companies" by Michael L. Sapir and James A. Bernstein, which runs 62 pages:

> Over the past decade, the tremendous growth and maturation of the mutual fund industry has been accompanied by considerable consolidation and transactional activity. This Article provides a general overview of investment company reorganizations under federal and state laws and reviews the numerous disclosure requirements and legal and regulatory constraints to which a mutual fund reorganization is subject. The Article is designed to guide the practitioner through the regulatory labyrinth from board consideration to preparation of filing to closing the transaction.

34   MARKETING

Description of Publication: *Sales & Marketing Management*

To obtain information on this publication, call Sales & Marketing Management at (800) 821-6897 or (609) 786-9085.

To order *Survey of Buying Power* and *Survey of Media Markets,* call (800) 443-2155; fax: (212) 592-6309.

 Reference Navigator

Web site: http://www.salesandmarketing.com   CD-ROM: available

E-mail: 758.3876@MCIMAIL.COM MCI   Library Reference Number:

Database: See Web site   _____

S&MM is a well-formatted publication with good articles about marketing and management, good editing and useful "how-to" inserts, and *all* business students should be familiar with its contents. Plus, its annual *Survey of Buying Power* is an outstanding statistical review of the marketplace. Buy the magazine and learn how to use the *Survey of Buying Power* (www.sbponline.com)**.** Getting to know the *S&MM* monthly editions is an easy task in any case because one has only to look at the table of contents to get a feel for some of the excellent reference material offered in the monthly edition (see "Table of Contents").

According to the editors, the *Survey of Buying Power* is more than a data listing. "It is a dynamic tool, designed for marketers and researchers to use for a wide range of applications. From advertising and media planning, to territory analysis and test market selection, the *Survey* contains valuable information for every organization." The *Survey* is divided into three sections:

Section A: User's Guide & Highlights

Section B: Summaries & Metro Market Rankings

Section C: Metro, County, & City Data by State

Section A is the user's guide on how to apply Section B and Section C. "Designing a Path to Success" leads off Section A and shows an example of putting the *Survey* to work by presenting (in this instance) a case study on health care with the suggestion that the reader draw appropriate parallels to his or her own industry or market. The article offers some "typical applications for the data in the *Survey of Buying Power* as they relate specifically to the health care market," for example:

- Media planning and buying
- Measuring market potential
- Territory analysis
- Test market selection

This section is also essential for understanding three other important aspects to applying the data:

- How to construct a custom BPI (Buying Power Index).
- How the survey is conducted (using EBI, effective buying income).
- Definition of terms (e.g., BPI, EBI, SIC, PMSA, SAI, etc.).

Sections B and C provide data on state summaries and metro market rankings. The easiest way to explain them is to display them, so, review the samples offered in this chapter under "Sample Page: *Survey of Buying Power*."

S&MM relies on supplements to help communicate its message. Since 1996 the *Survey of Buying Power* and the *Survey of Media Markets* have been combined into a single publication. Savvy marketers make it their business to stay one step ahead of change, and one way they do this is by knowing what lies ahead in terms of a market's growth. To help piece together a reliable picture of the future, the *Survey of Media Markets* includes five-year projections of population, effective buying income, retail sales, and the Buying Power Index for metropolitan areas and their component counties, information that can be used in a number of different ways to help planners uncover areas of emerging opportunity.

Survey of Media Markets has five sections:

Section I: User's Guide & Highlights
Section II: Media Market Profiles
Section III: 5-Year Metro Market Projections
Section IV: Merchandise Line Sales
Section V: Zip Code Areas

S&MM publishes a number of other supplements during the year that try to catch emerging issues and public interests.

Statistical data is always handy, and the *Survey of Buying Power* and *Survey of Media Markets* are excellent assets for those studying the market in the United States. An international source for marketing reference material is *International Marketing Data and Statistics* (ISBN 0-8-6338-568-0), which is a compendium of statistical information on the countries of the Americas, Asia, Africa, and Oceania. Published annually by Euromonitor International Inc., (312) 922-1115, it provides a wealth of detailed and up-to-date statistical information relevant to international market planning. The information is regularly updated and held on an international database of market information comprising 24 subject areas. *International Marketing Data and Statistics* is now in its 20th edition. The data coverage includes a considerable number of 15- and 16-year trends, which permit the analysis of socio-economic trends over a longer time span as a basis for forecasting.

Something to Think About

Which government office designates markets as MSAs or PMSAs? Are you prepared to offer a reasonably comprehensive definition of BPI and EBI? According to the *Survey of Buying Power,* the per capita EBI, which appears in the "Regional and State Summary of Effective Buying Income" table in Section B, is an arithmetic average obtained by dividing total population into total EBI. It is used primarily to measure an area's spending power by eliminating the impact of population size. However, because total population includes residents of all age groups, such a figure assigns income to a sizable portion of the population that _____ (please complete the sentence).

FEATURES

COVER STORY

HIRING

COMPENSATION

MANAGING

PRESENTATIONS

COLUMNS

DEPARTMENTS

BEST PRACTICES

299

Leading Edge

Edited by Andy Cohen
The News Digest for Sales and Marketing Executives

SALES STRIKES OUT ON CAMPUS

A new survey of college students reveals their bad feelings toward the selling profession.

So, it's been a good year. Revenues are up. Profits are soaring. Deals are closing like locks on Fort Knox. And now it's time to prepare for 1998 by adding more salespeople to keep up with the industry's rising demand. Just a couple of young, energetic, recent college graduates who want to learn and grow with your company, right?

Forget it. College students couldn't care less about selling.

A recent survey conducted jointly by the University of Rhode Island and South Bank University in the United Kingdom reports that students—both here and abroad—have very low opinions of the sales profession. The study asked 544 students (about one-third each from the United States, the United Kingdom, and Thailand) to rank, in order of career preference, seven job opportunities in marketing: advertising, direct marketing, market research, product management, retailing, sales, and wholesaling. Advertising ranked first overall, and sales came in fifth, ahead of only retailing and wholesaling. In the United Kingdom and Thailand, sales ranked sixth. While more than 72 percent of the respondents agree with the statement that "the financial rewards from selling are excellent," 40 percent believe that a salesperson's job security is poor.

"College-age people aren't convinced that sales is viable as a career," says Eugene Johnson, professor of marketing at the University of Rhode Island and co-author of the study, "Attitudes of College Students Toward Selling." "They believe there is money to be made in sales, but they often don't want to do the necessary things to make that money."

If these are the attitudes of college students, then how are companies attracting young talent to sales? "They need to be creative with the ways they present the jobs to students," says Stephen Mader, managing director of Christian & Timbers, an executive search firm based in Cleveland. "Students today are interested in running their own businesses, so companies should show that sales can be an autonomous job which can be both lucrative and lead to career advancement."

John Marshall, executive vice president of sales for WTC Electrical Corporation, has experienced the problem of enticing college graduates to the sales profession. This year he had to hire 12 new salespeople for his growing electrical wiring firm in Mesa, Arizona. Looking for recent college graduates that WTC could train and mold into successful salespeople, Marshall placed want ads in college papers and local magazines and newspapers. The response was minimal. "The ad said 'Looking for entry-level salespeople,'" Marshall says. "I think people were turned off by it."

He placed another ad in the same papers looking for marketing people, and suddenly the résumés poured in. When students came for interviews, Marshall made it clear that the position was for sales, but he presented the job in a way they could relate to. "I knew college kids would need money, so I stressed the fact that there was a great opportunity to make a lot of money," he says. "I also showed them the responsibility they would have in a sales position, and they were impressed with that. Growing up, they've heard bad things about sales. You need to make it more glamorous than they think it is."

Metro & County Total

Florida (continued)

S&MM Estimates: 1/1/95

Effective Buying Income

Metro Area County City	Total EBI ($000)	Median Hsld. EBI	% of Hslds. by EBI Group: (A) $10,000 $19,999 (B) $20,000 $34,999 (C) $35,000 $49,999 (D) $50,000 & Over				Buying Power Index
			A	B	C	D	
Gadsden	403,298	22,195	23.4	24.0	15.8	14.5	.0104
Leon	3,503,392	33,491	15.3	21.8	17.5	30.5	.0827
• Tallahassee	2,104,494	28,750	17.5	22.3	15.7	25.9	.0564
SUBURBAN TOTAL	1,802,196	35,135	15.0	22.2	19.3	30.9	.0367
TAMPA-ST. PETERSURG- CLEARWATER	36,418,644	31,409	18.3	26.0	18.8	25.5	.8638
Hernando	1,683,468	28,315	20.9	31.6	18.9	18.1	.0377
Hillsborough	14,473,921	33,985	16.1	23.8	19.3	29.3	.3535
• Tampa	4,431,026	27,541	19.6	24.2	17.2	21.7	.1272
Pasco	4,129,667	25,756	23.9	30.3	17.1	15.5	.0955
Pinellas	16,131,588	32,116	18.0	25.7	18.8	26.7	.3771
• Clearwater	1,934,713	32,272	18.2	24.9	18.5	27.4	.0471
Largo	1,225,322	29,655	20.6	28.7	19.6	21.0	.0284
Pinellas Park	685,297	31,989	18.1	27.4	21.9	23.1	.0189
• St. Petersburg	3,933,772	28,915	20.0	24.8	17.8	23.2	.1047
SUBURBAN TOTAL	26,119,133	32,413	17.7	26.6	19.2	26.6	.5848
WEST PALM BEACH- BOCA RATON	21,289,570	38,187	14.2	22.1	18.9	35.5	.4561
Palm Beach	21,289,570	38,187	14.2	22.1	18.9	35.5	.4561
• Boca Raton	2,114,771	49,098	9.9	17.6	17.5	48.9	.0476
Boynton Beach	996,749	33,868	16.6	25.4	20.4	27.8	.0230
Delray Beach	1,217,488	36,794	15.2	21.9	18.1	34.5	.0391
• West Palm Beach	1,222,485	31,215	16.6	23.9	18.3	25.9	.0386
SUBURBAN TOTAL	17,952,314	38,024	14.3	22.3	19.1	35.2	.3699
OTHER COUNTIES							
Baker	229,140	31,201	16.2	26.0	21.3	22.0	.0054
Bradford	281,301	29,624	18.2	26.1	20.8	19.6	.0065
Calhoun	125,198	22,541	21.8	27.9	14.2	13.2	.0029
Citrus	1,500,791	25,474	23.9	29.2	15.9	17.4	.0348
Colombia	571,190	26,211	20.4	25.9	18.0	18.5	.0160
De Soto	279,226	22,781	26.6	29.8	13.9	12.9	.0070
Dixie	101,721	17,171	27.9	24.1	11.6	7.4	.0026
Franklin	115,998	22,326	22.3	26.7	12.7	15.2	.0027
Gilchrist	142,085	24,793	23.1	28.7	18.1	13.1	.0027
Glades	106,412	26,119	22.1	30.7	14.6	19.0	.0020
Gulf	140,092	25,446	19.7	26.3	18.3	17.0	.0031
Hamilton	97,651	18,465	23.2	26.5	12.5	8.3	.0026
Hardee	202,265	23,472	25.1	28.0	15.2	14.2	.0056
Hendry	304,507	27,904	20.9	26.6	19.1	18.9	.0079
Highlands	1,015,644	24,336	24.0	31.3	15.1	13.9	.0276
Holmes	179,923	21,571	25.1	25.3	15.5	12.5	.0040
Indian River	1,846,873	32,326	17.5	26.1	19.1	26.7	.0402
Jackson	489,967	23,942	21.5	24.0	15.8	17.2	.0134
Jefferson	147,935	27,094	18.2	25.1	17.1	20.4	.0031
Lafayette	75,580	26,896	19.1	25.5	17.2	19.3	.0015
Levy	311,630	21,921	25.1	25.1	15.8	12.7	.0080
Liberty	84,216	27,937	20.2	25.6	18.5	20.8	.0016
Madison	207,482	22,235	22.3	23.6	14.7	16.0	.0047
Monroe	1,712,994	34,043	16.2	25.5	19.1	29.4	.0388
Okeechobee	330,059	23,840	24.0	29.3	15.7	13.5	.0094
Putnam	821,505	24,272	23.0	25.4	15.6	17.6	.0197
Sumter	379,126	21,905	25.6	27.1	15.2	11.7	.0092

Florida (continued)

S&MM Estimates: 1/1/95

Effective Buying Income

Metro Area

County City	Total EBI ($000)	Median Hsld. EBI	A	B	C	D	Buying Power Index
Suwannee	349,046	24,150	22.7	27.5	15.4	16.1	.0090
Taylor	207,127	25,981	20.9	23.9	16.6	20.1	.0049
Union	123,766	26,935	20.3	27.6	22.3	14.2	.0025
Wakuila	199,651	28,191	19.5	26.6	21.1	17.8	.0043
Walton	439,265	27,429	19.4	25.4	17.0	21.1	.0104
Washington	194,558	22,646	25.5	26.8	14.7	13.9	.0045
TOTAL METRO COUNTIES	223,462,940	33,435	16.5	24.5	18.9	28.7	5.2707
TOTAL STATE	236,776,864	32,883	16.8	24.7	18.7	28.0	5.5894

Georgia

S&MM Estimates: 1/1/95

	Population									Retail Sales by Store Group						
				% of Population by Age Group												
METRO AREA Country City	Total Population (Thousands)	% Of U.S.	Median Age Of Pop.	18-24 Years	25-34 Years	35-49 Years	50 & Over	Households (Thousands)	Total Retail Sales ($000)	Food ($000)	Eating & Drinking Places ($000)	General Mdse. ($000)	Furniture/ Furnish Appliance ($000)	Automotive ($000)	Drug ($000)
Albany	**117.4**	**.0448**	**30.9**	**10.4**	**14.4**	**22.1**	**21.9**	**41.2**	**1,011,962**	**172,968**	**100,306**	**170,943**	**60,001**	**222,928**	**40,511**
Dougherty	98.1	.0374	31.0	10.8	14.0	21.4	23.0	35.0	997,412	165,299	100,273	170,937	59,359	221,244	40,493
• Albany	80.2	.0306	30.5	11.0	14.1	21.0	22.6	28.6	981,426	161,253	99,012	170,939	59,199	217,869	36,714
Lee	19.3	.0074	30.3	8.3	16.8	25.6	16.6	6.2	14,550	7,689	33	6	642	1,684	18
SUBURBAN TOTAL	37.2	.0142	31.6	9.0	15.5	24.5	20.3	12.6	30,536	11,735	1,294	4	802	5,059	3,797
ATHENS	**134.6**	**.0514**	**29.2**	**20.1**	**15.7**	**21.0**	**19.9**	**50.2**	**1,232,811**	**190,488**	**121,334**	**209,334**	**55,084**	**248,307**	**48,106**
Clarke	91.0	.0347	27.0	25.7	15.7	18.8	18.6	34.8	1,032,615	152,530	110,383	168,880	46,742	237,681	35,141
• Athens	88.4	.0337	24.5	35.7	14.1	13.6	19.7	33.8	1,032,615	152,531	110,383	168,879	46,744	237,681	35,141
Madison	23.0	.0088	34.2	9.0	15.2	24.2	24.6	8.3	77,383	18,316	5,065		2,267	6,488	3,537
Oconee	20.6	.0079	33.7	7.9	15.1	27.3	20.8	7.1	122,813	19,642	6,007	40,454	6,075	4,183	9,430
SUBURBAN TOTAL	46.2	.0177	37.3	9.6	18.5	35.2	20.4	16.4	200,196	37,957	11,072	40,455	8,340	10,626	12,967
ATLANTA	**3,384.9**	**1.2906**	**32.5**	**9.9**	**18.1**	**25.8**	**19.7**	**1,254.9**	**32,090,797**	**5,194,163**	**3,746,257**	**4,267,840**	**2,028,321**	**7,716,510**	**1,058,768**
Barrow	35.0	.0134	32.1	9.4	17.0	21.7	23.4	12.4	250,317	48,198	22,579	24,428	6,892	86,616	11,639
Bartow	62.5	.0238	32.7	9.7	16.1	23.0	23.3	22.4	427,554	94,153	41,893	51,956	25,278	108,429	11,857
Carroll	77.3	.0294	31.6	12.8	15.1	22.2	22.7	27.4	531,405	142,984	48,042	72,406	19,879	108,010	21,698
Cherokee	111.6	.0425	31.7	8.3	19.7	25.9	17.6	38.5	539,163	102,664	62,032	72,886	21,675	150,637	20,891
Clayton	196.8	.0750	30.9	10.6	18.8	24.9	17.3	70.5	2,274,240	248,204	238,381	394,180	145,638	604,998	64,027
Cobb	515.7	.1967	32.8	9.4	19.1	28.2	17.7	197.3	5,737,963	875,350	622,300	962,285	415,004	1,248,156	184,315

302

Household Expenditures for Health Care

Area	($000)	Rank	Area	($000)	Rank	Area	($000)	Rank
New York	6,261,834	1	Syracuse	529,852	70	Lafayette, La.	226,347	143
Los Angeles - Long Beach	5,914,792	2	Tulsa	528,223	71	Reno	222,184	144
Chicago	5,590,152	3	Tucson	523,634	72	Biloxi - Gulfport - Pascagoula	222,122	145
Philadelphia	3,641,131	4	Worcester - Fitchburg - Leominster	521,526	73	Salinas	220,661	146
Washington	3,514,088	5	Fresno	512,377	74	Hamilton - Middletown	218,512	147
Detroit	3,154,487	6	Akron	489,933	75	Utica - Rome	216,824	148
Boston - Lawrence - Lowell - Brockton	2,891,419	7	Omaha	483,176	76	Hickory - Morganton	216,786	149
Houston	2,581,135	8	Ventura	470,690	77	Eugene - Springfield	214,320	150
Atlanta	2,479,249	9	Knoxville	467,651	78	**Total Top 150**	**130,393,672**	
Dallas	2,176,217	10	Albuquerque	463,425	79	Huntington - Ashland	214,299	151
Minneapolis - St. Paul	2,039,597	11	Harrisburg - Lebanon - Carlisle	459,279	80	Fort Pierce - Port St. Lucie	212,053	152
Nassau - Suffolk	1,903,139	12	Allentown - Bethlehem - Easton	453,551	81	McAllen - Edinburg - Mission	211,761	153
Riverside - San Bernadino	1,883,010	13	Scranton - Wilkes-Barre - Hazleton	451,629	82	Montgomery	211,073	154
St. Louis	1,872,892	14	Tacoma	449,519	83	Evansville - Henderson	208,561	155
Orange County, Cal.	1,822,706	15	Sarasota - Bradenton	434,098	84	Macon	208,102	156
San Diego	1,819,701	16	Toledo	429,607	85	Salem	207,752	157
Phoenix - Mesa	1,794,960	17	Gary	420,872	86	Springfield, Mo.	205,419	158
Pittsburgh	1,789,448	18	Youngstown - Warren	420,063	87	Boulder - Longmont	200,938	159
Baltimore	1,787,882	19	Springfield, Mass.	417,793	88	Anchorage	199,406	160
Seattle - Bellevue - Everett	1,754,095	20	Jersey City	404,151	89	Visalia - Tulare - Porterville	196,048	161
Tampa - St. Petersburg - Clearwater	1,686,830	21	Wilmington - Newark	400,067	90	Erie	192,660	162
Oakland	1,664,680	22	Little Rock - North Little Rock	387,786	91	Charleston, W.Va.	189,141	163
Cleveland - Lorain - Elyria	1,624,672	23	Baton Rouge	379,365	92	Portland, Me.	188,366	164
Newark, N.J.	1,463,633	24	Ann Arbor	376,142	93	Binghamton	188,219	165
Denver	1,438,775	25	Bakersfield	373,575	94	Dutchess County, N.Y.	186,265	166
San Francisco	1,334,208	26	New Bedford - Fall River - Attleboro	362,778	95	New London - Norwich	185,455	167
Miami	1,310,600	27	El Paso	359,793	96	Savannah	184,268	168
Portland - Vancouver	1,268,617	28	Wichita	349,173	97	South Bend	182,539	169
Kansas City	1,248,404	29	Melbourne - Titusville - Palm Bay	348,605	98	Kileen - Temple	179,924	170
Cincinnati	1,155,122	30	Charleston - North Charleston, S.C.	341,407	99	Fayetteville - Springdale - Rogers	176,293	171
San Jose	1,136,156	31	Mobile	339,014	100	Tallahassee	175,508	172
Fort Lauderdale	1,134,014	32	**Total Top 100**	**116,689,303**		Fayetteville, N.C.	174,262	173
Fort Worth - Arlington	1,106,500	33	Columbia, S.C.	336,627	101	Duluth - Superior	173,695	174
Indianapolis	1,105,048	34	Fort Wayne	335,137	102	Columbus, Ga.	172,710	175
Milwaukee - Waukesha	1,081,583	35	Daytona Beach	332,167	103	Roanoke	170,404	176
Sacramento	1,075,809	36	Vallejo - Fairfield - Napa	329,288	104	Santa Cruz - Watsonville	169,560	177
Columbus, Ohio	1,053,569	37	Colorado Springs	324,918	105	Lincoln	168,602	178
Norfolk - Virginia Beach - Newport News	1,042,151	38	Des Moines	321,628	106	Galveston - Texas City	164,996	179
Bergen - Passaic	999,551	39	Stockton - Lodi	318,080	107	San Luis Obispo - Atascadero - Paso Robles	160,850	180
Orlando	991,987	40	Kalamazoo - Battle Creek	317,239	108	Barnstable - Yarmouth	160,713	181
Charlotte - Gastonia - Rock Hill	926,927	41	Flint	317,171	109	Ocala	160,369	182
San Antonio	924,187	42	Santa Rosa	316,231	110	Johnstown	160,068	183
New Orleans	889,066	43	Johnson City - Kingsport - Bristol	316,141	111	Odessa - Midland	159,886	184
Hartford	870,398	44	Lancaster	313,363	112	Bremerton	158,091	185
Buffalo - Niagara Falls	867,992	45	Lansing - East Lansing	312,229	113	Springfield, Ill.	155,553	186
Middlesex - Somerset - Hunterdon	866,392	46	Chattanooga	310,389	114	Fort Collins - Loveland	154,953	187
Greensboro - Winston-Salem - High Point	829,367	47	Lexington	310,164	115	Lubbock	152,146	188
Las Vegas	824,363	48	Lakeland - Winter Haven	304,689	116	Green Bay	151,478	189
Monmouth - Ocean	812,424	49	Madison	303,858	117	Asheville	150,893	190
Nashville	797,163	50	Augusta - Aiken	296,586	118	Provo - Orem	148,278	191
Total Top 50	**90,202,122**		Fort Myers - Cape Coral	290,186	119	Wilmington, N.C.	145,337	192
Rochester, N.Y.	797,001	51	Spokane	287,567	120	Naples	144,899	193
West PalmBeach - Boca Raton	795,153	52	Canton - Massillon	284,435	121	Brownsville - Harlingen - San Benito	142,208	194
Raleigh - Durham - Chapel Hill	750,389	53	Saginaw - Bay City - Midland	282,610	122	Olympia	140,899	195
Salt Lake City - Ogden	744,759	54	Jackson, Miss.	274,509	123	Lynchburg	140,502	196
Austin	723,871	55	Portsmouth - Rochester	269,916	124	Amarillo	140,454	197
Memphis	722,595	56	Manchester - Nashua	269,080	125	Brazoria	150,020	198
Louisville	718,814	57	York	267,568	126	Chico - Paradise	139,052	199
Oklahoma City	706,870	58	Santa Barbara - Santa Maria - Lompoc	263,793	127	Cedar Rapids	135,429	200
Dayton - Springfield	700,836	59	Davenport - Moline - Rock Island	261,887	128	**Total Top 200**	**139,034,030**	
Jacksonville, Fla.	698,037	60	Modesto	257,352	129	Burlington, Vt.	134,531	201
Grand Rapids - Muskegon - Holland	688,952	61	Shreveport - Bossier City	257,040	130	Longview - Marshall	134,328	202
Richmond - Petersburg	686,941	62	Rockford	256,444	131	Gainesville	134,152	203
Albany - Schenectady - Troy	661,170	63	Pensacola	256,245	132	Waco	132,173	204
Bridgeport - Stamford - Norwalk - Danbury	660,530	64	Reading	255,777	133	Yakima	131,807	205
Providence - Warwick - Pawtucket	645,776	65	Beaumont - Port Arthur	252,536	134	Racine	130,543	206
Birmingham	624,723	66	Trenton	251,848	135	Fort Smith	126,469	207
Greenville - Spartanburg - Anderson	612,996	67	Peoria - Pekin	250,783	136	Topeka	126,020	208
New Haven - Waterbury - Meriden	609,782	68	Boise	249,345	137	Mansfield	122,794	209
Honolulu	590,232	69	Atlantic - Cape May	242,666	138	Richland - Kennewick - Pasco	121,757	210
			Newburgh	240,776	139	Sioux Falls	116,882	211
			Appleton - Oshkosh - Neenah	238,882	140	Fargo - Moorhead	116,715	212
			Huntsville	236,531	141	Champaign - Urbana	116,529	213
			Corpus Christi	232,932	142	Medford - Ashland	115,493	214

Recommended Supplement: *Journal of Marketing*

For information on this quarterly publication (ISSN 0022-2429), call the Publications Group of the American Marketing Association at (312) 648-0536, or fax: (312) 993-7540.

Reference Navigator

Web site: http://www.ama.org/pubs/jm   CD-ROM: not available

E-mail: infor@ama.org   Library Reference Number:

Database: See Web site   _____

This journal, like a few others previously listed, is an academic publication that is primarily written for upper-level marketing students and faculty. The articles average around 15 pages each, are usually reviewed by a "blind" process, and are well researched and documented. Guidelines for manuscripts are available on the Web site.

The journal also provides book reviews and a somewhat unique "Marketing Literature Review," based on a selection of articles from a comprehensive business literature database ABI/Inform. Marketing-related abstracts from over 125 journals (both academic and trade) are reviewed by the *Journal of Marketing* staff. An example of an article: "Marketing in Hypermedia Computer-Mediated Environments: Conceptual Foundations," by Donna Hoffman and Thomas Novak.

A number of ads in *JM* remind one of the marketing research companies (e.g., Decision Analyst, Inc.; The Burke Institute; etc.) that are prime sources of marketing information. However, perhaps the best known and most complete guide to marketing research companies is the *International Directory of Marketing Research Companies and Services,* an annual publication published by the American Marketing Association and known as the *Greenbook*. It describes over 1,400 firms that conduct marketing surveys, audits, product testing, and the like. Several national research firms such as Mediamark Research and Simmons Market Research Bureau conduct extensive, ongoing surveys of 20,000 or more households to determine the impact of media on consumer preferences. Expenditure surveys are also recorded in publications such as *Lifestyle Market Analyst* and *Simmons Study of Media and Markets.*

Business Marketing (ISSN 0745-5933), a child of *Advertising Age*, contrary to others of its ilk, does not lend itself easily to being rolled up and stuck in your back pocket. It's not thick—25 pages or so—just long (tall?), with lots of great information. According to a study by *Business Marketing*, "U.S. businesses spent $51.7 billion on marketing and communications to sell their products and services to other businesses in 1995." That's definitely worth a second look. *Business Marketing*, according to its editors at Crain Communications Inc., (312) 649-5309 or fax (312) 649-5462, is all about news, new trends, and issues that affect business-to-business marketing.

While you are at it, look at *Industrial Marketing Management*, published by Elsevier Science Inc., (914) 524-9200. The April 1997 issue marked, according to the editor, the third time the magazine has devoted an entire issue to a single topic, in this case, relationship marketing ("The articles in this special issue focus on improving the mutual benefit of buyer/seller relationships") which is enjoying a great following these days. The special issue is a good reason to read the magazine and also a good way to introduce yourself to the area.

Before a consumer can buy anything, all the necessary business-to-business transactions must occur. But this often hidden activity often goes unappreciated by consumers. In June 1995 *Advertising Age's Business Marketing* commissioned Erdos & Morgan Inc., New York, to conduct an original research project to produce valid and reliable estimates of 1995 business-to-business marketing and communication spending. The results of these efforts have begun to be published in a supplement called "OutFront Marketing Research Study." This is, according to its publishers, "the first statistically valid survey that shows how companies allocate their business-to-business marketing dollars against all marketing tools." They hope "to conduct this 'state of the state' census every other year" with a new special section in the December 1998 edition of *Business Marketing*—good news for the marketing majors. This project by *Business Marketing* is the essence of what it tries to offer to its readers. Perhaps the company's founder, G. D. Crain, Jr., (*Class*, March 1916) provided the best description of their mission when he said: "We don't know a blooming thing about general mediums. But we do know class journals, including trade, technical and professional publications."

Another excellent publication that is a useful reference piece and readily available is *Brandweek* (ISSN 0892-8274). It is published 47 times a year by ASM Communications, Inc., a subsidiary of BPI Communications, Inc., (212) 536-5336 or go to Web site http://www.brandweek.com. According to the editors, it reveals the latest successful marketing and media strategies; new products; deals and mergers; trends; segmentation; new laws and regulations; cross-promotions and co-branding; local, national, and international news; demographics and statistics; agency/client changes; and opportunities for you.

A friend once remarked how adept brand managers were at educating people, since your average consumer could walk into any grocery store in the United States and tell you something about the 2,000 or 3,000 brands located on the shelves. The folks who establish these brands are the brand managers and academics who make it their life study. The goal of the *Journal of Product & Brand Management* (ISSN 1061-0421), according to its editor, is to provide the practitioners of marketing with new ideas that will be applicable to their daily work. Each article recommends how the material contained in the piece can be utilized in business practice. The journal, published six times a year, also provides teachers of marketing with actual business examples of how the theories taught in the classroom work in the real world. One good example is "How to Delight Your

Customers," by Kurt Matzler, Hans H. Hinterhuber, Franz Bailom, and Elmar Sauerwein, University of Innsbruck, Management Institute (vol. 5, no. 2, 1996). Internet services to MCB University Press Limited are: http://www.mcb.co.uk or telephone: (800) 633-4931 and fax: (205) 995-1588.

Look at *Journal of Retailing* (ISSN 0022-4359), a quarterly publication by New York University, Stern School of Business, (212) 285-6100. It has about five articles (e.g., "Household Store Brand Proneness: A Framework," by Richardson et al.) of 25 pages each, but offers executive summaries. *The Journal of Services Marketing* (ISSN 0887-6045), also from MCB University Press Limited, covers one of the fastest growing fields in marketing.

Because *Business Research Sources* is about finding and using information resources, some of the communications companies that provide many of the publications and software needs are listed below:

Crain Communications (26 publications):	(312) 649-5200.
CMP Direct Marketing Services:	(516) 733-6700.
Miller Freeman (76 magazines in 16 markets):	(415) 905-2200.
Group1 (marketing software company):	(800) 368-5806.
Penton Publishing (30 publications):	(800) 326-4146.
Chilton (50 publications):	(610) 964-4493.
American Business Press (147 publications):	(212) 661-6360.

Something To Do

It has been my experience in the classroom that the great majority of students do not, as was said in the Preface, take time to read material other than that assigned in the course. The *Journal of Marketing*, like many academic publications, has some excellent book reviews that could help students keep up with the literature. Take the opportunity to read a brief and well-written book review from the *Journal of Marketing*.

35   ADVERTISING

Description of Publication: *Journal of Advertising Research*

For information on this bimonthly publication (ISSN 0021-8499), call the Advertising Research Foundation at (212) 751-5656; or fax (212) 319-5265.

 Reference Navigator

Web site: http://www.arfsite.org   CD-ROM: not available

E-mail: journal@arfsite.org   Library Reference Number:

Database: See Web site

There can be little question that perhaps one of the most popular periodicals in the advertising industry is *Advertising Age* (see "Recommended Supplement"); however, its primary purpose in life is to service the members of its industry with news, after all, it is called a "newspaper." As such, it is not the first source for advertising research. So we will look at the academic side first and scan the industry tabloid magazines second.

The *Journal of Advertising Research* reports research findings in advertising and marketing, including commentary about and from research conferences (the Advertising Research Foundation has its "Conferences/Workshops" schedule on the inside back cover). The March–April 1997 issue was particularly valuable because it focused on the relationship between advertising and the World Wide Web, which is always a good topic of discussion in any advertising class. The editor offered this comment as part of his editorial: "The Web is changing how consumers participate in the marketing communications process. As interactive media evolve further, other media and the creative advertising placed there will have to change to adapt to the Web-spun consumer." The "Table of Contents" and "Sample Page" below give good testament to this look into the future.

The journal is approximately 100 pages long, easily read, and pointed toward the practicality and applications of advertising research. It is a valuable reference tool for those who wish to have the ideas of both the academicians and the practitioners. One need only to look at the Editorial Advisory Board to understand why—The Wharton School, Leo Burnett Co., BBDO, New York University, and the Newspaper Association of America are just some of the experts whose representation gives direction to the policies of the journal. If those folks can't steer you right on advertising research, no one can.

For another academic perspective, one can go to the *Journal of Advertising* (ISSN 0091-3367) published by the American Academy of Advertising at Clemson University, (864) 656-5285. This source deals primarily with the theoretical and sometimes practical aspects of advertising and communication. If your research needs are overseas, look at the *International Journal of Advertising*. For information on getting a copy, send an e-mail to jnlsamples@BlackwellPublishers.co.uk.

A different, but essential tool for advertising research is the *Standard Rate & Data Service* (*SRDS*), (800) 851-7737. It provides information on database or CD-ROM, or the Web at http://www.srds.com that is indispensable for any advertiser—how much does it cost to place an ad, during what period, and for which medium? Such information is the foundation of any advertising budget and must be designed in such a way as to permit the most cost-effective campaign. *SRDS* provides these advertising rates for thousands of newspapers, television and radio stations, magazines, and other media. Major titles are published monthly and include:

Business Publications Rates & Data

Newspaper Rates & Data

Spot Radio Rates and Data

Network Television and Radio Rates and Data

Each title gives a brief but informed description of the individual publication or broadcast station, detailed ad rates, and production specifications. While general information on rates can be expected to be close to those quoted by the media, the user must always contact the advertising director to establish the most recent rates. Some rates, depending on business, could be gotten at substantial savings.

Something to Think About

Could you measure, if asked, the primary TV, radio, newspaper and magazine media sources in your city? Is it possible to use the *SRDS*? How?

SPECIAL ISSUE: RESEARCH UNTANGLES THE WORLD WIDE WEB

The Once and Future Web: Scenarios for Advertisers

Scott C. McDonald
Time Warner Inc.

The form and nature of content, including advertising content, on the Web has been constrained by the bandwidth limitations of the existing Internet "pipeline"—the telephone system. As competition from alternative pipelines accelerates in the coming years, content will adjust accordingly, evolving eventually into formats more akin to contemporary television. This article reviews the state of current competition to build broadband pipelines and concludes that, in the end, there will be multiple pipelines and continued fierce competition in the Internet access business. It also proposes several likely scenarios for near-term and longer-term future of ad-supported Web sites.

Sitting here, early in 1997, the "new media landscape" looks quite different from what it was five, or even three years ago. By early 1992, many observers had already predicted that severe competition would develop around the delivery of broadband services (e.g., Neuman, 1991) and that a convergence of media would be driven by digitization (e.g., Pool, 1990), but no one anticipated the emergence of the narrowband Internet as the primary vehicle for new media development. Yet the rapid growth in 1994 and 1995 of user-friendly proprietary on-line services like Prodigy, Compuserve, and America Online demonstrated that there was a mass consumer market for computer-based communication over a large-area network. With the development of an open-standards hypertext markup language (HTML) in 1992 and the free distribution of the Mosaic browser in 1994, the World Wide Web took off. Its growth since then has been nothing less than breathtaking, with Web sites and Web users proliferating and with all segments of the advertising, media, and research communities scrambling to understand and benefit from that explosive growth.

In this article, I will consider what the growth of the Web means for advertising and for advertising-based media. I shall do so by invoking a somewhat unusual model for thinking about the subject—the notion of base and superstructure. In this decade following the collapse of the Soviet Union, it may be regarded as foolish to invoke a construct that has its intellectual roots in the Marxist economic theory of state and society, but I'll take that risk because I think that the concept of base and superstructure can illuminate the relationship between new technologies and their social effects. The original Marxian version distinguishes between the "base" of society, held to be the economic components that generate jobs and wealth, and the "superstructure" of ideas, laws, conventions, and ideologies; to the Marxist, the two are thought to be dialectically interrelated, but with developments in the base determining developments in the superstructure. Though in the 1990s that simplified schema has been largely discredited as a guide to predicting the evolution of societal change, there may be some merit in borrowing the distinction between base and superstructure for thinking about new media. In the present context, the "base" for the new media is the fundamental technology: the hardware, software, and communication pipelines which enable computers to talk to each other. By contrast the "superstructure" is the content itself: the words, images, and advertising messages that are relayed over the communication networks at the "base." I invoke this notion of base and superstructure because there is a dynamic (dare we say dialectical?) relationship between developments in the fundamental technologies and the developments in Web-based advertising; and to some extent, developments in new media superstructure (content, advertising, etc.) can only go as fast as developments in the technological base permit. Thus, it is not wise to divorce. . .

Recommended Supplement: *Advertising Age*

For information on this weekly publication (ISSN 0001-8899), call Crain Communications at (800) 283-2724 or (212) 210-0100.

Reference Navigator

Web site: http://www.adage.com   CD-ROM: not available

E-mail: Personal only   Library Reference Number:

Database: LEXIS-NEXIS

_____

Advertising Age is billed as "Crain's International Newspaper of Marketing." When you see *Advertising Age* it's big (11 inches by 14.5 inches), but it sure doesn't look like a *newspaper*. Maybe it just started out that way. The newspaper definition by *Webster* is actually pretty mundane, "a paper that is printed and distributed usu. daily or weekly and that contains news, articles of opinion, features, and advertising."

According to its editors, *Advertising Age* is the largest and most quoted marketing publication in the world, available in local languages in 17 countries, and is the only U.S. marketing publication that is edited for all segments of the marketing industry: marketers, agencies, media, sales promotion, special events, and so on. (*Mediaweek,* see below, is aimed only at media buyers at advertising agencies.)

This is a very "busy" newspaper, with short newsy items that have about as much reference use as a sound bite from Bart Simpson if you're not in the know, plus lots of full page ads, as one might expect with a name like *Advertising Age*. However, if you want to know who's who and what's happening, then this is the place. The newspaper has a classifieds section (about three pages of ads offered by region); editorials, "Interactive," Special Report "World Brands," and more. The publication is written for the industry as news—about the people, companies, products and services, and legislation. It is composed of the journalistic questions who, when, where, what, and how. The analytical "why" is seemingly left for other types of journals. Nevertheless, there are at times some good lists that show industry expenditures in the advertising field and other types of similar statistical data.

If you would like to try some other variations on the advertising industry theme, take a peek at *ADWEEK,* (800) 641-2030 or go on-line to http://www.adweek.com. A close sister to *ADWEEK* is *Mediaweek,* and if you really want that job in advertising, you better be familiar with this weekly publication too (ISSN 0155-176X). Call ASM Communications, Inc. (subsidiary of BPI Communications) at (212) 536-5336.

Reference Navigator

Web site: http://mediaweek.com   CD-ROM: not available

E-mail: bgloede@mediaweek.com   Library Reference Number:

Database: See Web site   _____

According to its editors, *Mediaweek* ("The News Magazine of the Media") uncovers the industry's latest key developments and events in TV, cable, radio, magazines, newspapers, out-of-home, and interactive media. It's the only weekly that brings you timely coverage of deals and mergers, new laws and regulations, demographics, research, accounts, and perhaps a tad more. If you want to be (or are) involved in media, advertising, programming, sales, entertainment, or development, *Mediaweek* could be essential.

Mediaweek evidently has a lot to say because it begins saying it on the cover, which serves as a brief table of contents. This is 60 pages of a smaller size *Ad Age*, and like *Ad Age* is obviously for people in the industry and on the go, since all the articles are short with news as their goal, albeit some articles might suffice as a reference source. Some examples are "FCC's Hundt Vows More Activist Role," by Alicia Mundy ("When the election is over, the FCC chairman plans to launch a campaign of his own: Activism in Media"), and "What's the Trouble with Kids Today?" by Scotty Dupree ("Surprising tumble in ratings has nets scrambling to keep advertisers happy").

The departments include "Calendar" (The First Worldwide Television Summit Conference, Nov 19, etc.); "Media Notes"; "Real Money" (advertising activity in the media marketplace); with some statistical information such as the weekly ranking of the top 50 brands' advertising in network prime time; "Media Person"; and last but not least, "Media Dish Extra."

36   MANAGEMENT

Description of Publication: *Management Review*

For information on this monthly publication (ISSN 0025-1895), call American Management Association (AMA) at (212) 903-8393; or fax: (212) 903-8083.

Reference Navigator

Web site: http://www.amanet.org
E-mail: mgmtreview@amanet.org
Database: LEXIS-NEXIS

CD-ROM: not available
Library Reference Number:

_____

The editors of *Management Review* tout themselves as "America's number one publication on successful business management." They do this each month by offering interviews, practical case studies, and in-depth articles about surviving and prospering in the business world. This 65-page magazine is colorful, informative, and compact. It is reader-friendly with contemporary issues, a few cartoons, cases, summary boxes (called "Briefcase"), conference information, and some classifieds. One particularly useful attribute is the "Case Study" which focuses on a specific company, cites the challenge, and offers the solution.

The AMA provides educational forums worldwide, where members and their colleagues learn practical business skills and explore the best policies of world-class organizations through interaction with each other and expert faculty practitioners. The AMA's publishing programs provide tools individuals can use to extend learning beyond the classroom in a process of lifelong professional growth and development through education. If you are interested in the profession, consider joining the AMA, and enjoy the conferences.

Another source that could prove helpful for the campus set is the Society for Advancement of Management (SAM), which publishes the SAM *Advanced Management Journal* (ISSN 0036-0805) on a quarterly basis. For information on publications, conferences, and the like, SAM has a Web site at http://www.enterprise. tamucc.edu, or call (540) 342-5563. SAM has a very active campus association membership. The Society for Advancement of Management was established in 1912 by the father of scientific management, Frederick W. Taylor, and his associates. It is a quarterly, refereed publication, especially designed for the general manager. "SAM Guidelines for Authors" is available in the journal or at the Web site.

One other publication, a new kid on the block so to speak, is *The Public Relations Strategist: Issues and Trends That Affect Management*. This journal is published by the Public Relations Society of America (PRSA); call (212) 460-0360 or fax (212) 995-0757 for information. You can also visit the PRSA Web site at http://www.prsa.org. Membership dues also provide for subscription to the magazine. Young professional managers would be wise to look into the opportunities provided by this large and prestigious management organization. To paraphrase the publisher, Fraser P. Seitel, in a letter to the readers, their intent in recruiting writers of high caliber is to distinguish *The Strategist* from all the other management and communications journals. "Our mandate and market are broader than most others in this field. We seek to be a thought leader on pertinent management issues and to speak to senior managers and CEOs in language they understand. In other words, we want people actually to *read* our publication, not look at the pictures." An example of an article is "View From Abroad," by Sir Adrian Cadbury, former CEO Cadbury-Schweppes. ("The British treat boards of directors differently than do Americans. The head of a national committee to study the work of boards explains the rationale.")

One unique aspect that is useful and hopefully will be continually developed in this and other journals is a section called "Face Off." Both sides of an issue are developed and argued by experts in the field. Also listed in the table of contents is a column that tells what articles are coming in the next edition. An editorial index on the last page lists articles published during the year in specific categories (e.g., Ethics and Values, Media, etc.).

A quality complement to *Management Review* is *The Academy of Management Journal* (ISSN 0001-4273). The *Journal* publishes articles in fields of interest to members of the Academy of Management; call (914) 923-2607. These "fields of interest" can be seen in the list of divisions and interest groups listed on the inside front cover of the *Journal* (e.g., operations management, information systems, research methods, etc.). This is an academic journal for an academic audience and reading these articles could be more than a shade demanding for the average 20-year-old undergraduate.

In its articles, the *Journal* seeks to publish work that develops, tests, or advances management theory, research, and practice. Articles are expected to have well-articulated and strong theoretical foundations, based on all types of empirical methods—quantitative, qualitative, and combinations. In general, there are enough $25 words in practically any article in this journal to satisfy even the most demanding of intellectual sophisticates. Although the journal is not recommended for the average college student, it is included to reach those laboring away in the graduate programs and to balance those whose primary horizons focus on such publications as *Rental Equipment Register, Product Directory and Buyers' Guide,* and *Field and Stream.* You can reach the *Journal* on the Internet at http://www.aom.pace.edu. An example of an article is "Diversifying Entry: Some Ex Ante Explanations for Post-entry and Growth," by Anurag Sharma and Idalene Kesner.

Finally, take advantage of two excellent databases on management that open the door to hundreds of articles: EMERALD (Electronic Management Research Library) and ANBAR Electronic Intelligence (see Chapter 41).

316

Case Study
Avoid Privacy Collisions on the Information Highway

Technology is revolutionizing office communications, but e-mails are neither casual nor private, and what you say in them can be used against you.

By Teresa Brady

That little sex kitten has been driving me wild. She's moaning and begging for it every minute. Last night I was afraid that someone would hear, and we'd be thrown out of the building. But don't worry—all is arranged. Wednesday she gets the knife.

The supervisor of the employee who wrote the above message intercepted it and alerted authorities hoping to prevent a crime. But after the employee spent the evening explaining himself to the police, he was released just in time to get his female cat to the vet to be spayed. The employee sued his boss for invasion of privacy.

There are two important points about this story, which was false and was circulated on the Internet to illustrate the seriousness of electronic communications uses and abuses. First, it shows the need for companies to establish an electronic communications policy that sets forth the rights and liabilities of employees using the e-mail system for nonbusiness purposes. Second, for companies that have e-mail systems and other types of electronic communications, it presents many real issues that must be addressed, such as:

- Whether the sender of the message has a right to privacy.
- Whether the employer committed any criminal or civil liability by breaching any right to privacy.
- Whether employers can intercept or retain e-mail messages.
- Whether e-mail messages can be used for or against a company and/or employee in later litigation.
- Whether any federal and/or state laws are applicable.

Everyone has heard the expression "talk is cheap." But, how "cheap". . .

317

Recommended Supplement: *Journal of Environmental Management*

For information on this monthly periodical (ISSN 0301-4797), call Academic Press at (+44 181 300 3322).

Reference Navigator

Web site: http://www.hbuk.co.uk/ap/journals/v.htm

CD-ROM: not available

E-mail: personal only

Library Reference Number:

Database: not available

_____

If industry and commerce have a dark side, it lies mostly in the rape and pillage of the environment. Unfortunately, not much is being done about the problem by the schools of business around the world, at least from a curriculum perspective. In my somewhat limited experience, I have never seen a senior-level required course in environmental management. The *Journal of Environmental Management* is a rather lonesome voice in the dark, but a voice nevertheless; ironically, no member on its editorial board, at this reading, comes from the country that pollutes and consumes the most—the United States. Examples of some articles from the August 1997 issue are "Environmental Planning, Biodiversity and the Development Process: The Case of Hong Kong's Chinese White Dolphins," (ev970 130) by J. H. Liu and P. Hills, and "Ethics and Environmental Attitudes With Implications for Economic Valuation," (ev970017) by C. L.Spash.

The journal runs approximately six or seven articles per issue, some as long as 20 pages. There is plenty of quality research material. IDEAL, Academic Press's on-line scientific journal library where guest users can freely search and browse journal abstracts, can be found at http://www.idealibrary.com/.

Another source one can take advantage of is *Business Strategy and the Environment* (ISSN 0964-4733), a monthly publication that also addresses the problem of managing the environment. An example of an article from its February 1997 issue is "A Map of Neverland: The Role of Policy in Strategic Environmental Management," by T. Ketola. It is a brief journal, with six or seven articles of approximately 10 pages in length plus book reviews and a "Greening of Industry Network Noticeboard." You can contact the journal in the United States at http://www.wiley.com.

37   HUMAN RESOURCES

Description of Publication: *Training & Development*

For information on this monthly publication (ISSN 1055-9760), call the American Society for Training and Development Inc. at (703) 683-8100, or fax: (703) 683-9203.

 Reference Navigator

Web site: http://www.astd.org

E-mail: ryann.ellis@astd.noli.com

Database: ASTD Information Center

(See Web site)

CD-ROM: not available

Library Reference Number:

_____

This is a very good little magazine (88 pages). There are lots of feature articles, about 8 or so averaging around five to seven pages each. Here are some examples by title (see the table of contents for a more comprehensive view):

"Making Telecommunications Work"

"Make the Most of Teleconferencing"

"Traveling Through Transitions"

"Global Work Teams"

"Up Is Not the Only Way"

"ROI: Search for Best Practices"

Training & Development offers excellent advice on office management by featuring articles that deal with the dynamics of everyday operations. It also features substantive topics such as workplace violence, quality of work life, and communication skills, for example, "What to Do About Anger in the Workplace," by Helen Frank Bensimon ("Downsizing, job insecurity, and 'toxic' companies are making workers mad. Here's how to defuse angry employees and deal with the increasing incidents of aggression").

The articles are creative and well written and definitely useful as referenced work in research papers. The editors make things easy for you by supplying the name, address, and *telephone number of the author*, plus the address and telephone number to get reprints, at the end of each article. That is a *very* unusual formatting technique and one that could be an excellent tool for students.

The table of contents is annotated, and the magazine is laid out with useful work-related departments (e.g., "Training 101," "Career Power," "Law Review," etc.). In short, ASTD provides many communication opportunities, and students would be well advised to become familiar with its publications.

Something To Do

Call up ASTD and get a copy of its annual "Industry Trends Report."

321

In this article: Communication Skills.

Language, Sex, and Power: Women and Men in the Workplace

by Richard Koonce

OK, confession time: To what extent do you believe, along with author John Gray, that men are from Mars and women are from Venus? Forget about how gender differences play out in the bedroom. Let's talk about how they affect what happens in conference rooms, boardrooms, and executive offices.

Legislators on Capitol Hil may debate whether women in the military should be in combat, but women on the front lines of the military and businesses might say that they already are—considering that charges of sexual harassment make the headlines on a regular basis, from Mitsubishi to the U.S. Army.

Then there is the glass ceiling, which, as countless women will attest, remains firmly in place in workplaces across America. In October 1996, the research firm Catalyst reported that only 10 percent of top jobs at the 500 largest U.S. companies were held by women. And there was only one woman CEO among the ranks of the Fortune 500, Jill Bartad of Mattel.

Do those inequities account for the friction between men and women in the workplace, for the daily communication "disconnects," and for the incidents of harassment? What can men and women do to build bridges of better communication and understanding at work?

Those are just a few topics I wanted to cover with author, socio-linguist, and Georgetown University professor Deborah Tannen when I met with her recently in her Washington, D.C. office.

Tannen, a respected and perhaps the best-known expert on workplace communication, is credited with being the first person to bring to the forefront the differences in communication styles between men and women.

Recommended Supplement: *HRMagazine*

For information on this monthly publication (ISSN 1047-3149), call the Society for Human Resource Management at (703) 548-3440; or fax: (703) 836-0367.

Reference Navigator

Web site: http://www.shrm.org	CD-ROM: not available
E-mail: SHRM@shrm.org	Library Reference Number:
Database: not available	_____

Another great magazine! These human resource types really seem to have it together. The 47-year-old Society for Human Resource Management (SHRM) is a worldwide professional association of human resource professionals, boasting more than 70,000 members and more than 430 chapters in 50 states. The periodical (144 pages) is very reader-friendly with an excellent modern format tailored to meet the needs of the group's members.

The publication has approximately seven feature articles averaging around eight pages each, such as "From School to Work, Partnerships Smooth the Transition," "Elder Care Obligations Challenge the Next Generation," and "Severance Plans Shift Away from Cash." It also has "Technology Solutions," various columns (including legal trends and future focus), and eight departments, such as "Bookshelf," "Member Services," "SHRM Fast-Facts," and a special section for human resource products and services called "The Yellow Pages." This magazine has excellent information.

Two other sources of management information of an academic bent are:

1. *The Human Resource Management Journal,* published for over 30 years by the University of Michigan Business School and John Wiley & Sons, http://www.wiley.com.

2. *The Journal of Human Resources.* For information on this publication (ISSN 0022-166X), call the University of Wisconsin Press at (608) 262-4867; fax: (608) 262-6290; or e-mail THAL@MACC.WIC.ED.

Something to Think About

If you haven't thought too much about personal development, you may wish to get in touch with Dale Carnegie, the classic performance people, at (800) 231-5800 or visit the Web site at http://www.dale-carnegie.com.

---

38   ORGANIZATIONS

Description of Publication: *Organization*

For information on this quarterly publication (ISSN 1350-5084), call Sage Publications Inc. at +44 171 374 0645; fax, +44 171 374 8741.

 Reference Navigator

Web site: http://www.sagepub.co.uk/journal/
details/j0113.htmp

E-mail: info@sagepub.co.uk

Database: not available

CD-ROM: not available

Library Reference Number:

_____

In lectures on the topic of organizational behavior, I do my best to point out that we are all experts in organizational behavior since we are both mindless and mindful parts of organizations. The principal aim of *Organization,* "The Interdisciplinary Journal of Organization, Theory and Society," according to the editors, is to foster dialogue and innovation in studies of organization. The journal addresses a broad spectrum of issues and a wide range of perspectives as the foundation for "neo-disciplinary" organization studies relevant to the 1990s and beyond. In doing so, they say, it promotes an ethos that is theory-driven; international in scope and vision; open, reflective, imaginative, and critical; and interdisciplinary, facilitating exchange among scholars from a wide range of current disciplinary bases and perspectives. *Organization* is a relatively new journal, but it has interesting and well-written topics, and good research material can be found here.

The journal encompasses the full range of key theoretical, methodological, and substantive debates and developments in organizational analysis, identifying and assessing their impacts on organizational practices worldwide. "Alongside more micro-processual analyses, it particularly encourages attention to the links between intellectual developments, changes in organizational forms and practices, and broader social, cultural and institutional transformations" (well, that's what *they* said). In addition to established themes of continued significance to the development of the field, topics and themes addressed by *Organization* include:

Issues of gender, race/ethnicity in organizations.	Organizational identities.
Globalization and its discourses.	Organizational imagery.
Organization and disorganization.	Moralities of organization.
Consumption and organization.	Law and organization.
Organizational space and time.	Organization and postmodernism.

There are approximately six articles per issue, some as short as 10 pages and others as long as 35. There are seven or eight reviews of new books, such as Alan Warde's review of Yiannis Gabriel and Tim Lang's *The Unmanageable Consumer: Contemporary Consumption and its Fragmentations.*

If you are interested in organizations, you have to be interested in quality—quality processes that are the heart of any system or organization.

Quality Progress (ISSN 0033-524X), a monthly publication from the American Society for Quality Control Inc., (414) 272-8575, has a "One Good Idea" section that is used as an example of how quality control management has improved a business. An example feature article topic is "Team Up for Quality Improvement," by John Persico, Jr. ("Process improvement teams approach problems from a different direction"). There are usually 10 feature articles like the one above, plus 15 departments, which include "Book Reviews," and "Statistics Corner."

St. Lucie Press, (800) 272-7737, has some excellent books on quality, such as *The Quality Improvement Handbook* (ISBN 1-884015-59-X). You can also browse on-line at http://www.slpress.com.

Some other trade books you may wish to look at are:

The 90-Day ISO 9000 Manual

The Baldrige Award for Education

Total Quality in Higher Education

The EU Directive Handbook

ISO 9000 Quality Improvement Handbook

Inside ISO 14000

Total Quality in Marketing

One opportunity not to miss is hooking up with the International Institute for Learning and the PBS Business Channel for their special satellite broadcasts on current business issues (e.g., "Internal Benchmarking" and "Juran on Quality"). Call (800) 325-1533 or e-mail info@iil.com.

If organizations must be concerned with quality, then students of quality must know about ISO (International Standards Organization). Anyone involved in ISO procedures knows that a lot of training is involved. A select number of organizations can provide the certificate programs necessary to be ISO qualified. For example, the British Standards Institution (BSI) is one of the foremost standards-setting bodies in the world. It was instrumental in establishing ISO 9000 as the world's primary quality system standard, with BSI as the benchmark registrar. It also led the world in creating environmental management standards and in developing the ISO 14001 environmental standards. With nearly 30,000 registrations globally, BSI is the world's largest certification organization. It is a leading registrar for ISO 9000 Quality Management Systems, BS 7750 Environmental Management Systems, and ISO 14001, and a verifier for the EU Eco Management and Audit Scheme (EMAS).

Founded in 1901 to coordinate the development of national standards in the United Kingdom, BSI was incorporated by Royal Charter in 1929. It is a nonprofit distributing organization that works with manufacturing and service industries, businesses and government to help companies compete globally. BSI establishes standards and provides a wide range of supporting services including information services, product testing and certification, quality and environmental systems certification, and public as well as on-site training. For help in research call +44 181 996-9000 or fax +44 181 996-7400. You can reach BSI on-line at http://www.bsi.org.uk.

For training information in the United States, call International Institute for Learning, Inc., at (800) 325-1533; fax (212) 909-0558; or e-mail info@iil.com.

Butler's recommended reading for college and university presidents

Total Quality in Higher Education, by Ralph G. Lewis and Douglas Smith, provides a framework for implementing total quality principles in the college or university environment. It includes the history and principles of quality management and an assessment of factors in the college and university environment that are leading to serious questions concerning higher education effectiveness and efficiency.

328

Maslow, Monkeys, and Motivation Theory

Dallas Cullen
University of Alberta

Abstract. One of the most enduring influences in motivation theory is Maslow's needs hierarchy. The empiracal basis for the needs hierarchy was Maslow's own studies of dominance in monkeys and humans. In both cases, Maslow concluded that one individual's ability to be dominant over others was due to that individual's acknowledged superiority, and that differences in human or monkey groups occurred because of differences in the exercise of dominance by the individuals in those groups. The incorporation of these ideas into the needs hierarchy explains its intuitive appeal: the hierarchy justifies managerial power, while at the same time absolving managers of accountability for ineffective motivational practices. However, recent primatological research reveals serious flaws in Maslow's understanding of the nature of dominance in monkeys and apes. As a consequence, Maslow's theory is based on research which is no longer considered valid by the discipline in which it was done.

The influence of Abraham Maslow's (1943) hierarchy of needs is ubiquitous in management education and theory. Despite the common belief that Maslow's theory is outdated and ignored (see, for example, Greiner, 1992: 61), current textbooks present the theory in approving terms. It is described as the "most widely recognized theory of motivation" (Hellriegel et al., 1995: 174), the "most well-known need theory" (Moorhead and Griffin, 1995: 83) and a "classic paper" (Luthans, 1995: 150). At the level of theory, Maslow's hierarchy is so pervasive that it has almost become. . .

Recommended Supplement: *Journal of Systems Management*

For information on this bimonthly publication (ISSN 0022-4839), call the Association For Systems Management (ASM) at (800) 203-3657; or fax: (216) 234-2930.

Reference Navigator

Web site: http://www.infinet.com/~jdzg/asm

E-mail: 74431.3442@compuserv.com

Database: See Web site

CD-ROM: not available

Library Reference Number:

_____

The *Journal of Systems Management*, founded in 1948, is the leading academic journal in the information systems field. Each issue of *JSM* covers the tools, technology, and techniques of successful business information systems management through its case studies (not long, but interesting), editorials, and in-depth articles, all written by leading IS and business professionals from all over the world. According to the editors, everyone from business executives to information systems managers, analysts, and educators can benefit from the timely, insightful information in *JSM,* whether you're looking for what's new in information technology or tips on how to use and manage it more effectively.

Libraries, corporations, and individuals from more than 40 countries receive *JSM*; the question is whether you have the ability to read and understand the articles. If you haven't taken MIS yet, you may want to hold off on getting a subscription. The magazine is 65 pages long, black and white, and a little heavy on jargon. For example, if you can read this

> It should be apparent that during the stages of requirements collection and analysis, design of various schema, and validation & testing, the human factors play a larger role in the design of an image-based system compared to the design of database system (taken from: "Is it a lot of Hype?" by D. Challa and R. Redmond).

and understand it, then you're in business. If not, take a course in MIS first. The journal is filled with good information, with seven or eight feature articles, plus columns and departments (which includes "Author Guidelines").

39 FINANCE

Description of Publication: *Financial Management*

For information on this quarterly publication by the Financial Management Association International, call the managing editor, FMA, at the University of South Florida: (813) 974-2084; or fax: (813) 974-3318.

 Reference Navigator

Web site: http://www.fma.org   CD-ROM: not available
E-Mail: fma@bsn01.bsn.usf.edu   Library Reference Number:
Database: not available   _____

Established in 1970, the FMA is a global leader in developing and disseminating knowledge about financial decision making. The mission of the FMA is to broaden opportunities for professional interaction between and among academicians, practitioners, and students; to promote the development and understanding of basic and applied research and of sound financial practices, and to enhance the quality of education in finance. FMA has an excellent Web site and serves as one of the most comprehensive links to financial information available on the Internet.

According to its editor, *Financial Management (FM)* serves both academicians and practitioners who are concerned with the financial management of non-financial businesses, financial institutions, and public and private not-for-profit organizations. *FM's* editorial policy is designed to promote interest and knowledge of issues in management and decision making at the company level. The principal criteria are originality, rigor, currency, practical relevance, and clarity. It is an excellent research source. The Web site also has a listing of career centers that *FM* works with at various universities. An example of an article from *FM* is "Resolution of Financial Distress: Debt Restructuring via Chapter 11, Prepackaged Bankruptcies and Workouts," by Sris Chatterjee, Upinder Dhillon, and Gabriel Ramirez. ("Financially distressed firms select a debt restructuring method based on the degree of their leverage, the severity of their liquidity crisis, the extent of creditor coordination, and magnitude of their financial distress".)

A second publication you should look into (but will not be covered here for space considerations) is *Financial Practice and Education.* The following four journals written with differing perspectives are offered as insight for the aspiring young financier to better recognize his or her calling:

1. The *Journal of Banking and Finance* (ISSN 0378-4266) is a monthly publication, the aim of which is to provide an outlet for the increasing flow of scholarly research concerning financial institutions and the money and capital markets within which they function. The emphasis is primarily on applied and policy-oriented research. The *Journal* is thus intended to improve communications between, and within, the academic and other research communities and those members of financial institutions, both private and public, national and international, who are responsible for operational and policy decisions. You can contact the *Journal* at (212) 633-3730; or fax: (212) 633-3680; or e-mail: usinfo-f@elsevier.com.

2. The following is an abstract from *The Review of Financial Studies* (ISSN 0893-9454), which gives a good example of the subject matter and writing from this periodical:

"The Performance of Japanese Mutual Funds."

Jun Cai,   K.C. Chan and Takeshi Yamada
City University of Hong Kong   Hong Kong University of Science and Technology

We analyze the performance of Japanese open-type stock mutual funds for the 1981–1992 period. The results show that, regardless of the performance measures and benchmarks employed, most of the Japanese mutual funds underperform the benchmarks by between 3.6% and 10.8% per annum. These funds tend to invest more in large stocks with low book-to-market ratios. But this feature does not explain the underperformance. A potential explanation is the dilution effect caused by inflows of funds. In Japan, a new investor of an open-type fund only pays in the after-tax value of the net asset value. We conduct a bootstrap experiment to assess the magnitude of this dilution effect.

If you would like information on this type of financial journal, call Oxford University Press at (919) 677-0977 or (800) 852-7323; fax: (919) 677-1714; or e-mail: jnlorders@oup.co.uk.

3. Another journal to consider is the *Journal of Financial Markets,* which publishes high-quality original research on applied and theoretical issues related to securities trading and pricing. The area of coverage includes the analysis and design of trading mechanisms, optimal order placement strategies, the role of information in securities markets, financial intermediation as it relates to securities investments—for example, the structure of brokerage and mutual fund industries, and analyses of short- and long-run horizon price behavior. The journal strives to maintain a balance between theoretical and empirical work. If that

description interests you, call Editor Bruce Lehmann at (619) 534-0945; or fax: (619) 534-3939, or e-mail: blehmann@ucsd.edu.

4. *The Journal of Finance* (ISSN 0022-1082) is the official publication of the American Finance Association and is published five times a year, in March, June, July, September, and December. *The Journal of Finance* is an esoteric publication that primarily serves the needs of the academic community. Theory and conceptualization are the goals of the publication. The *Journal* is somewhat lengthy and the pages serialized to run in sequence with each issue. Each book is broken down into "Articles," "Shorter Papers," "Book Reviews," and "Miscellanea." Each article is abstracted to quickly introduce the reader to the essential character of the message. Also given are sections for dates, place and program for association meetings; announcements; style instructions; book advertisements; and calls for papers. An example of an article is "Time Variations and Covariations in the Expectation and Volatility of Stock Market Returns," by Robert F. Whitelaw.

Another source of economic information comes from the 12 Federal Reserve Banks across the nation. The Board of Governors of the Federal Reserve System can be reached at (202) 452-3244 in Washington, DC. The Federal Reserve Bank of New York, (212) 720-6134 (http://www.ny.frb.org) is somewhat unique in its operational responsibilities and is worth a special look. The Federal Reserve Bank of Atlanta's *Economic Review* (see also Chapter 22) will be used here as an example. It presents analysis of economic and financial topics relevant to Federal Reserve policy (e.g. "To Call or Not to Call? Optimal Call Policies for Callable U.S. Treasury Bonds," by Robert R. Bliss and Ehud I. Ronn). The publication presents its findings in a format understandable to the nonspecialist. If interested, call (404) 521-8020. Also, the bank invites visits on the Internet, http://www.frbatlanta.org, and provides information on, among other things:

- Economic education
- Conferences / speeches
- Dollar index
- Press releases
- Southeast manufacturing survey
- Information about the bank

For an additional international financial perspective, see *Global Finance* (Chapter 41), and *The Financial Times* (Chapter 42).

334

The Board of Directors and Dual-Class Recapitalizations

Curtis J. Bacon, Marcia Millon Cornett, and Wallace N. Davidson, III

Curtis J. Bacon is an Associate Professor of Finance at Southern Oregon University. Marcia Millon Cornett is a Professor of Finance, and Wallace N. Davidson, III, is Rehn Professor of Finance at Southern Illinois University at Carbondale.

This paper examines stock price reactions to announcements of dual-class recapitalizations as they relate to characteristics of the board of directors. Our results show that certain board characteristics provide insight into directors' incentives. We differentiate characteristics of the board that are associated with management attempts to entrench its position and characteristics that may indicate an attempt to improve performance of the firm in the event of a takeover. We find that high levels of insider and affiliated outsider stock ownership, board tenure, and the presence of staggered board elections affect the stock market's reaction to these plans.

A persistent debate in the finance literature concerns the benefits of shareholder-approved issues of dual classes of common stock. According to one hypothesis, shareholders approve the creation of a second class of stock because it gives management more negotiating power in the event of a takeover attempt. A second class allows management to extract a higher bid, and thus it serves the best interests of the shareholders.[1] This hypothesis views the dual-class recapitalization as optimal recontracting that is intended to create shareholder wealth. Takeover-resisting mechanisms have been shown to give target-firm managers bargaining power. As a result, target-firm shareholders experience a positive wealth effect when companies adopt them (see Jarrell, Brickley, and Netter, 1988).

We note that the resulting gains may accrue disproportionately to various constituent groups unless the firm's charter includes a "fair-price" clause that requires all shares to be purchased at an equal price. In the absence of such a clause, a takeover bidder would be expected to bid first for voting equity, which is disproportionately held by management, and second, to freeze out the holders of limited voting stock to the extent legal. Although they do not examine dual-class recapitalization, Jarrell and Poulsen (1988) find that adoption of supermajority provisions, which also give increased bargaining leverage to large blockholders of stock, leads to a small but statistically significant decrease in shareholder wealth. Fair price amendments, which typically impose a supermajority requirement unless all shareholders are offered the same price, have no such statistically significant effect.

Another view is that creating a second class of stock could allow entrenchment of an inefficient management group.[2] That is, the second class of stock can result in a redistribution of voting rights such that an inefficient management team could obtain or maintain voting control, or dilute the voting control of another group that could replace them. This is known as the management-entrenchment hypothesis. Previous studies find that mechanisms that entrench an inefficient management team are detrimental to shareholder wealth (Jarrell, Brickley, and Netter, 1988), and companies whose voting rights are controlled by a single entity can trade at a discount (Junz and Angel, 1996).

The authors are grateful to Pauletta Avery and Shari Garnett who prepared the manuscript, to the two anonymous referees from *Financial Management* who made insightful comments, and to Sandra Moore for her copy-editing assistance.

[1]See DeAngelo and Rice (1993) and Linn and McConnell (1983) for a discussion of this issue.

[2]See Jensen andRuback (1983) for a review of the evidence on the market for corporate control.

Recommended Supplement: *Money*

For information on this monthly publication (ISSN 0272-9970), call Time, Inc. at (800) 633-9970.

Reference Navigator

Web site: http://moneymag.com   CD-ROM: not available

E-mail: money_letters@moneymail.com   Library Reference Number:

Database: See Web site

_____

This publication is not geared toward corporate finance, like those cited above; rather it's personal finance, which should interest even the nonfinance students, but there is some overlap with the corporate environment to be sure. The bottom line is everyone's interested in what money can do for them to some degree or fashion.

Money is a monthly publication, formatted like most market magazines: colorful and contemporary, written for the average person in informative and how-to style. Its table of contents is sufficient but lightly annotated. It has the usual cover stories, features, and departments; for example: The "Briefing Room"; "Markets," which offers quotes, (2) an analytical section called Marketwatch, and portfolio. It also has a "Mutual Fund Center," plus "Money Subscriber Services." The News Department focuses on Money Daily (Earnings Report), Money Business Report, and the Headlines. Not meant to be particularly analytical, it offers special reports on financial topics of interest, such as the midyear report on mutual funds. It also promotes timely live conferences on CompuServe. In a special section called "Your Company," you could expect to find articles like: "How to find and hire good minority employees" and in Business Briefs: "Now when you default you cannot devalue."

Financial World and *Financial Digest* cover corporate financial news and most categories of investment information. Although these journals are primarily directed at the financial professionals, they do have some overlap with the personal investor. *Forbes*, with its often in-your-face style, focuses mainly on investing, covering recent financial and accounting trends, unique securities, and analysis of corporate strategy (Chapter 17; see also *Barron's* and *Investor's Business Daily*, Chapter 6).

A recent book by Warner Books, *The Money Book of Personal Finance*, should be of interest to anyone and particularly business students whose first priority is to have their personal finances in order, whether dealing with personal investments, real estate, insurance, or any of the other fundamental financial obligations one must undertake. Finally, one other source of personal financial assistance is Quicken Financial Network (http://www.qfn.com), which is a new Web site featuring useful financial services from Intuit.

VIII INTERNATIONAL REFERENCES

Optional International references:

- *World Directory of International Enterprises*
- *Directory of American Firms Operating in Foreign Countries*
- *International Journal of Conflict Management*
- *International Security*
- *Europa World Year Book*
- *Encyclopedia of the Third World*
- *The Prince*
- *Facts About India*
- *Journal of International Economics*
- *The Developing Economies*

40 WORLD CONGRESS: BUSINESS INTELLIGENCE BRIEFINGS: WORLD MARKETS

Description of Publication

For information on this annual publication, call the World Congress, Inc., Home and Law Publishing Group Limited, and DRI/McGraw-Hill Inc., London, at (44) 171 428 3002, or fax: (44) 171 428 3035.

 Reference Navigator

Web site: http:www.wmrc.com.uk

E-mail: wmrc@wmrc.com

Database: not available

CD-ROM: available

Library Reference Number:

This publication is an *excellent reference* and one you should be familiar with. Unfortunately it's probably too expensive for the average person, so get your local or campus library to purchase an annual copy.

According to the chairman and the managing director of the World Congress, Inc., this year-round reference work includes not only the insights and unique perspectives from some of the most well-known and highly respected leaders of business, industry, and finance, but also offers a road map to the most intriguing areas of global direct foreign investment.

Each year this publication is produced in conjunction with the annual meeting of the World Economic Development Congress. Held immediately before the IMF/World Bank Annual Meeting, it involves a select audience of senior government officials, ministers, ambassadors, chief executive officers of both established and entrepreneurial corporations worldwide, institutional investors, multinational financiers, and international bankers from more than 100 nations.

World Markets is published annually so the year is always included with the name—*World Markets 1997.* It is the official business intelligence briefings for the World Economic Development Congress. According to its editors, its principle objective is to provide the growing company with an in-depth analysis of 29 countries around the world.

The countries reviewed are chosen on the basis of their year-to-year growth rate in foreign investment in combination with various factors such as their commitment to reform, policies aimed at economic stability, and so on. In short, these are the countries around the world which the editors believe offer the most exciting business prospects for the upcoming fiscal year.

If you were to review *World Markets 1995* for some historical material, for example, you would find that it was divided into eight regions (this pattern carries through in 1996); each region is prefaced by a regional analysis written by a leading expert on the area. Within each region are a number of country sections, which comprise four principle elements:

- A *state policy trading environment* paper describing the country's laws and policies in relation to foreign investors.
- A *financial infrastructure* paper outlining the country's financial system.
- A *physical infrastructure* paper describing the country's energy, telecommunications and transport systems.
- A *market analysis* depicting the country's leading economic indicators (both historically and projected) together with a directory of useful contact information (which is a *great* idea) within the country concerned.

In the majority of cases, the trading environment and financial infrastructure papers have been written by the appropriate government minister and central bank governor, respectively. One other reminder, the ads (e.g., Infonet) are valuable reading for data services and other sources of information.

Another source of profile and analytical information is the *World Business and Economic Review* (ISSN 1351-4725), distributed in North America by Cassell US. This publication covers all countries and includes a business guide/directory, but is considerably less detailed in its analysis than *World Markets.* This is one of those massive books (over 1,000 pages) that is encyclopedic in its coverage and is published biannually. It is best described as a comprehensive encyclopedia of virtually every nation or principality. The country profiles are extensive.

Something To Do

Could you adequately summarize the Eastern Europe Regional Analysis section, and how would you obtain an Expanded Country Section File for the Czech Republic?

South Asia
Regional Analysis

by M.G. Quibria and Narhari Rao

Dr M.G. Quibria is Head, Centre Services Unit of the Economics and Development Resource Centre of theAsian Development Bank and Managing Editor, Asian Development Review. He has MA and PhD degrees from Princeton University. Before joining the Bank he held teaching and research positions at the Universities of Dhaka and Oxford (Nuffield College) and Boston University.

Dr Narhari Rao is Senior Economist, Economics and Development Resource Centre, Asian Development Bank. He has MA and DPhil degrees from the University of Oxford. Before joining the Bank he was an Adviser, Ministry of Commerce, Government of India.

The opinions expressed in this paper are those of the authors and do not necessarily reflect the views of the Asian Development Bank or of its Executive Directors.

ECONOMIC PROSPECTS—AN OVERVIEW

South Asia consists of diverse economies both in terms of size and, to an extent, in economic characteristics. The aggregate GNP of the region is about $362 billion (at 1992 market prices) and a population of 1.2 billion. While the average per capita income as a whole is low, some estimates suggest that the region has about 250 million consumers in the "middle income group" who provide an expanding and potentially lucrative market for indigenous and imported goods. More importantly despite periodic setbacks in terms of uncertain weather conditions, political instability, natural disasters and often inappropriate economic policies, the region's average income grew rapidly in the 1980s (about 6 percent per annum), and with major economic and institutional reforms currently being undertaken, economic growth is anticipated to accelerate further in this decade.

In the past, most countries in the region adopted an inward-looking strategy of planned development involving a rigid regulatory framework that reserved a disproportionately large role for the public sector in production and distribution and permitted considerable bureaucratic discretion in economic decision making.

The embedded distortions created gross inefficiencies, rewards rent seeking and encouraged corruption. International competition was shut off by prohibitive trade restrictions while domestic competition was blunted by excessive regulations, resulting in a high cost and inefficient industrial structure. This led to slow export growth and a declining share of global trade in the region. Worse still, the system started straining the fiscal balances as governments were forced to make good the losses of inefficient public enterprises, support large bureaucracies and populist subsidisation programmes. Growth slowed down considerably below the potential of the region.

In recent years, most South Asian countries have embarked on major restructuring of their economies. The reforms are broadly aimed at restoring macroeconomic stability; liberalisation of the trade and payments regime; partial convertibility of the exchange rate; getting rid of counterproductive regulation; reducing distortion creating susidies and price controls; greater involvement of the private sector; simplifying the procedures and opening up the major sectors of the economy to foreign investment both direct and portfolio; and initial steps towards privatisation of state-owned entities.

Though reforms have made considerable headway, much still remains to be done. Even with partial reforms, the region has started displaying its underlying dynamism; foreign investors are showing more interest and there are indications that, over the medium term, the region will be more closely integrated with the global economy. It is also noteworthy that the region has an excellent track record in servicing external debt obligations; hence, multi-lateral and bi-lateral agencies have been generous in lending resources for high priority projects and programmes.With liberalisation under way, the region is expected to attract more funds from private sources.

RECENT PERFORMANCE AND PROSPECTS

Under an IMF Standby Programme aimed at restoring macroeconomic stabilisation, India recorded a GDP growth rate of about 4 percent in 1993, which was lower than the historial trend over the 80s. The deceleration in growth was due mainly to industrial recession induced by fiscal compression. However, the inflation rate declined to about 9 percent which represents a significant deceleration over recent rates.

Largely in response to the market determined exchange rate policy and rationalisation of the foreign trade regime, merchandise exports grew by

Recommended Supplement: *International Business Resources on the WWW*

For information on the database go to http://ciber.bus.msu.edu/busres.htm.

This comprehensive database has a great number of reference points from which to begin a search. The downside is that the data have to be constantly updated, and that may not always happen on a regular basis. Nevertheless, this is a very good place to start a search on international business topics. The following categories are listed on the database:

- News/periodicals—domestic (United States).
- News/periodicals—international.
- Journals, research papers, articles.
- Market potential indicators for emerging markets.
- Regional or country-specific information (general).
- Regional or country-specific information (Africa).
- Regional or country-specific information (Asia and Oceania).
- Regional or country-specific information (Europe).
- Regional or country-specific information (Central and South America).
- Regional or country-specific information (North America).
- International trade information.
- International trade leads.
- Mailing lists.
- Statistical data and information resources.
- Company listings, directories, yellow pages.
- Government resources.
- International trade shows, seminars, business events.
- Various utilities and useful information.
- Other indexes of business resources.

If, for example, you decide to pursue "Company Listings, Directories, Yellow Pages" you will get a series of choices. The first is "General: Pronett Business Search Engine." If you choose that category you will get a series of choices, one being "General: The Business Page International." If you choose that category you will be given a series of choices, one being: "World Trade Opportunities." If you choose that category you will be given a series of choices, one being: "Setting up Your Industrial Base in China." If you choose that category you will be given a series of choices, one being: "The Lion Group." If you choose that category you will be given a series of choices, one being: Beijing/Mr. Eric Lim (+86 10 591 0964). Following this type of process, the researcher should be able to come to some very specific and useful research sources quite quickly.

41 INTERNATIONAL PERSPECTIVES OF FUNCTIONAL AREAS

At last count there were at least six journals dealing with international business: (1) *Business & the Contemporary World,* (2) *Columbia Journal of World Business,* (3) *International Business,* (4) *Journal of International Business Studies,* (5) *International Business Review,* and (6) *World Business.* This list does not imply any order of importance; however, for student research I prefer *Business and the Contemporary World* and *Journal of International Business Studies.*

Description of Publication: *Business & the Contemporary World*

For information on this quarterly publication (ISSN 1062-6158), contact John Wiley & Sons at (212) 850-8776; or fax (508) 750-4470.

 Reference Navigator

Web site: http://@www.wiley.com

E-mail: info@jwiley.com

Database: see Web site

CD-ROM: not available

Library Reference Number:

_____

Business & the Contemporary World: An International Journal of Business, Economics, and Social Policy is a research-rich publication. The editor is S. Prakash Sethi, a well-known researcher (spsbb@cunyvm.cuny.edu). The quarterly issues run around 250 pages, include about 14 articles averaging 20 pages or so, and are fairly well written (i.e., students can read them). This journal offers occasional special issues; for example, Volume IX, Number 1 (1997) focuses on topics such as "Managing in a Global Context: Diversity and Cross-Cultural Challenges." An example can be seen on the sample page.

The *Columbia Journal of World Business* (ISSN 0022-5428), established in 1963 and published quarterly by Columbia University, (212) 854-3431, is a simply formatted journal of modest size, about 100 pages, that has relevant and non-esoteric articles that provide a decent comfort level for the average student.

As of January 1997 Columbia's School of Business transferred publication of *Columbia Journal of World Business* to JAI Press, Inc., at (203) 661-7602 or fax (203) 357-8446. The name of the publication is now called *Journal of World Business* and is no longer affiliated with Columbia.

According to the editors, the *Journal of World Business* is committed to providing new business insights by emphasizing the importance of the international perspective. It publishes engaging and authoritative studies and opinions on topics of interest to business managers and leaders, top-ranking government officials, prominent members of the business community, and students too. It is an excellent source for international research projects.

Whether it's global finance, marketing, logistics, or emerging markets, *International Business* (ISSN 1060-4073) has the tools you need to be competitive in the global marketplace, according to the editors. There is a little hyperbole in that claim no doubt, but it is a pretty good magazine. It's Web site is at http://www.internationalbusiness.com.

International Business, (212) 683-2426, covers the usual sort of articles dealing with international business (e.g., "The Lure of Foreign Trade Shows," etc.). One particular attribute, however, is its "IBNet," which offers monthly digest news from the IBNet on-line information service.

The editors offer this service as... The Electronic Silk Road®. Called the most comprehensive on-line source of information for international business dealings, IBNet contains more than 300 pages of highly focused information for the internationally oriented executive. IBNet works closely with such important world government agencies as G7 and the ICC. The home page at: http://www.ibnet.com/newshp.html grants easy access to news and research services:

- The International Bureau of Chambers of Commerce (IBCC).
- The International Chamber of Commerce (ICC) "The World Businss Organization."
- International Business Opportunities (ICC-Net) "The Global Business Exchange."
- Finance and Economics International Financial and Economic Service Providers.
- International organizations for trade promotion and other organizations.
- Research center; newswires and research tools.

For additional information, please e-mail jamonteleone@ibnet.com.

It could easily be said that the impetus behind the massive drive toward success in international trade must come from globally competitive communities. But as every person knows, such things are much more easily said than done.

Partners for Livable Communities and The Manufacturing Institute (the education and research affiliate of the National Association of Manufacturers, see Chapter 29) believe that the 21st century belongs to jurisdictions that put export-driven manufacturing at the core of balanced economic growth to maximize their quality of life. They have taken the initiative to describe what is necessary for creating globally competitive communities.

A Globally Competitive Community
- Imparts work ethic to each generation.
- Educates for basics and school-to-work.
- Supports high-performance manufacturing.
- Makes a serious commitment to exporting.
- Develops logical clusters of industry.
- Extends incentives to smaller firms.
- Avoids adversarial regulatory posture.
- Encourages new uses for "brownfields."
- Upgrades all facets of infrastructure.
- Encourages competitive energy supplies.
- Tempers taxation with investment support.
- Improves quality of life for citizenry.
- Promotes access to debt/equity capital.
- Builds public support for economic growth.

Why learn what manufacturers need for a globally competitive community? Every new manufacturing job creates 2.5 other jobs. For each $1 billion increase in manufactured exports, about 17,000 new jobs are created. The Congressional Research Service says manufacturing stimulates economic activity 1.5 times more than services, 1.3 times more than extractive industries, and 1.15 times more than construction.

The *International Business Review* (ISSN 0969-5931) is an academician's delight and has some well-known academicians on its board. Nevertheless, this is a challenging text for undergraduates and requires in some cases more than a casual familiarity with quantitative methods. Some articles are more esoteric than others. Unless you know what you are after, leave these articles for the graduate students and professors. According to the editors at Elsevier Science, (914) 524-9200 (j.rigg@elsevier.co.uk), the objective of this journal is to provide a forum for academics and professionals to share the latest developments and advances in knowledge and practice of international business. It aims to foster the exchange of ideas on a range of important international subjects and provide stimulus for research and the further development of international perspectives. The international perspective is further enhanced by the geographical spread of contributors.

All articles are refereed and concentrate on empirical studies with practical applications (e.g., "Relationship Marketing: Local Implementation of a Universal Concept"), theoretical and methodological developments in the field of business studies, and reviews of the literature in international business. The journal itself is devoted to international business, especially marketing and management issues. The journal offers an editorial, a number of papers (approximately seven or eight), book reviews, information on calls for papers, notes for contributors, volume contents, author index, and keyword index.

If you're interested in going to Columbia's School of Business, expect stiff competition. According to the September 1997 entering class profile: Applications received: 5,257. Percent accepted: 13. GMAT Middle 80%: 610–720. GPA middle 80%: 3.0–3.8. Male: 63%; female: 37%. Minority: 23%. Northeast: 45%. Humanities and social sciences: 36%. If you need more information try online at http://www.columbia.edu/cu/business or call (212) 854-1961.

SPECIAL ISSUE:

Managing in a Global Context:
Diversity and Cross-Cultural Challenges

IN THIS ISSUE:

Introduction to Managing in a Global Context: Diversity and Cross-Cultural Challenges

Ronald J. Burke

The future ain't what it used to be.
Yogi Bera

Contemporary organizations face extraordinary challenges and opportunties. The globalization of business, continued immigration, and increasing numbers of nontraditional workforce entrants (women, minorities) have increased diversity and cross-cultural challenges. In addition, greater use of work teams in organizations has increased contacts employees have with others outside their functions or products.

This introduction indicates the reasons that the management of diversity has become an important issue in industrialized countries. Diversity is first defined. Then selected research conclusions about workforce diversity are presented. Diversity was found to be a double-edged sword having both positive outcomes, such as increased creativity, and negative outcomes, such as lowered satisfaction and group integration. Then cross-cultural diversity concerns are examined. Some dimensions on which national cultures vary are reviewed showing how these can affect organizational performance. Initiatives that provide new ways of conceptualizing diversity issues and addressing them are offered.

Recommended Supplement: *Journal of International Business Studies*

Reference Navigator

Web site: http://gsb.georgetown.edu   CD-ROM: not available

E-mail: jibs@gunet.georgetown.edu   Library Reference Number:

Database: see Web site   _____

For information on this quarterly publication (ISSN 0047-2506), call the Academy of International Business, (519) 661-4031, or Georgetown University, (202) 944-3755. The *Journal of International Business Studies* (*JIBS*), published since 1970, is the world's leading international business journal, according to its editors. It is refereed, relevant, and read by people in 120 countries. The editors say they strive to publish only the best international business research, papers that are exceptional in one or more of the areas of theory, evidence, methodology, or innovation. The focus is on corporations engaged in international activities and comparative cross-cultural research. The journal is comprehensive; each quarterly issue includes about 200 pages of articles, research notes, dissertation abstracts, book reviews, and listings of business books. An example of an article is "Nationality and Subsidiary Ownership Patterns in Multinational Corporations," by M. Krishna Erramilli.

The April 1994 issue of *JIBS* contained a comprehensive 25-year index. Totaling 90 pages, it was divided into three parts: index by author, index by title, and index by topic. Along with the complementary papers in this issue, the index is an important source of information for current and future international business researchers.

The Academy of International Business is a worldwide organization with more than 2,400 individual members in more than 50 countries. Its objectives are:

- To foster the exchange of information and ideas among professionals in academic, business, and government organizations concerned with international business education.
- To encourage research that advances knowledge pertinent to international business.
- To augment the available body of research and teaching materials.

Worldbusiness is an unfortunate and recent casualty to the competitive publishing industry, but its past issues may still be used as an excellent reference piece. It was a bimonthly publication (ISSN 1081-5724) that had established itself as an excellent resource magazine focusing on events in the global marketplace. It was the flagship publication of KPMG, an international consulting firm.

KPMG Peat Marwick LLP, (800) 970-1999, is the U.S. member firm of KPMG Worldwide. KPMG serves clients through 1,100 offices in 837 cities in 134 countries. Students of international business should take those figures to heart as good job opportunities.

Despite its association with a company, the editors used *Worldbusiness*'s mandate of independence to produce an analytical, critical, and illuminative publication addressing central business stories and issues.

Description of Publication: *International Marketing Review*

If you would like information on this publication (ISSN 0265-1335), call in the United States (800) 633-4931; or fax: (205) 995-1588; or +44 1274 777700 in the United Kingdom.

Reference Navigator

Web site: http://www.mcb.co.uk   CD-ROM: available

E-mail: Rneedham@mcb.co.uk   Library Reference Number:

Database: Emerald (full-text)

_____

Although the basic functions of international marketing are essentially the same as those of the domestic market, anyone who has spent time abroad realizes the significant differences. Managing company distribution channels, pricing strategies, promotion, and product differentiation from the international perspective yields potential disasters just waiting to happen. Those who ignore even the subtleties of marketing internationally do so at their own risk. For example, a survey of 7,000 citizens of six EU countries—the United Kingdom, France, Germany, Italy, the Netherlands, and Spain—was conducted by a London-based research center. The results, published in *Frontiers: Planning for Customer Change in Europe*, showed that in Italy, both rich and poor believe in paying high prices to get the best quality, whereas in Germany, even the rich shop for a bargain. Three-quarters of the Spaniards believe the most expensive wine is the finest, compared to only 5 percent of the French ("The New European Consumer," *Eurobusiness*, July 1989).

Therefore, it pays to read the journals that help define and reduce this risk; the *International Marketing Review* is one. It runs articles such as, "Market Orientation and Business Performance," by Leyland Pitt, et al. ("The article, with the aid of helpful diagrams, focuses on market orientation, the marketing orientation-business performance link, measurement instruments used—samples and responses, hypotheses and research conclusions").

As usual in such academic publications, *IMR*'s format is fairly plain, with little advertising and is approximately 80 pages long. It has been published for 13 years. One useful attribute is "Abstracts and Keywords," which provides brief article descriptions. Two exceptional research services provided through MCB University Press, publishers of *IMR*, are Emerald (Electronic Management Research Library) and Anbar Electronic Intelligence. Emerald is a database of 82 management journals on CD. Articles from 1994 and onward are provided in full. Articles from 1989 to 1993 are provided with abstracts and keywords only. All the full articles are also supplied with two unique features: (1) every article has been classified by what kind of article it is—case study, literature review, theoretical with worked example, and so on, and (2) every article has been graded with a unique quality indicator, which indicates levels of readability, originality, and how clearly implications have been made for further research and for practitioners.

The Anbar Management Intelligence (http://www.anbar.co.uk/anbar.htm) database is updated every month on the WWW, building on an archive going back to 1989. It covers every article from over 420 of the world's best management journals (more than most professors read in a night!). The journals included are determined by the Accreditation Board of leading thinkers (e.g., Philip Kotler ensures the quality of marketing coverage and Andrew Campbell is among those examining strategic management). The full-text article of every abstract featured on the database is available within two working hours by fax.

The *Journal of International Marketing* (ISSN 1069-031X) is a quarterly periodical published by Michigan State University and sponsored by the Center for International Business Education & Research (CIBER) and can be reached at (517) 353-4336. Since we are trying to cover as many references as we can in a small space, one other should be covered—the *European Journal of Marketing* (ISSN 0309-0566). Keep in mind that the European Union is a larger economic zone than the United States with more trade, higher foreign reserves, and very close to a common currency (January 1, 1999). You definitely should get to know the attributes of this monthly publication; call (800) 633-4931 or try http://www. MCB.co.uk.

The primary thrust of *Business Research Sources* is to highlight the reference materials available to students. In doing this, business textbooks are excluded because the list is long, they are not readily available, and they don't usually serve as references. However, *International Business Case Studies* by Braaten et al. (ISBN 0-88415-193-X) from Gulf Publishing Co., (713) 529-4301, is unique and a useful *international* example, which is not always easy to find. The 36 cases are interactive, illustrating the cultural diversity of people, products, and issues and can be taught cross-functionally; all are based on actual business experiences, and there is a geographical balance in the countries selected.

Editor
Angela Rushton

Associate Editor
Ashok Gupta

Strategic and Performance Issues Associated with Mode of Entry Substitution Patterns
A Comparison of Canadian and U.S. Manufacturing Firms

Sam C. Okoroafo
College of Business Administration, The University of Toledo, Toledo, Ohio, USA

INTRODUCTION

When a firm's mode of entry or operation (i.e., exporting, licensing, etc.) into a foreign market becomes irrelevant due to evnironmental, ownership, or strategic factors, which alternative mode of operation should it adopt? In most cases, if the firm has preconceptualized a substitution pattern (a sequential path for adoption of entry modes over time), the decision regarding modal choice is clear. If the *incremental pattern* choice is made, the modal choice[1] is simply the next relevant mode in the chain from exporting to investment. However, if the firm is operating under the *non-incremental pattern,* the modal options are broader, from say exporting to investment (Okoroafo, 1991) and the modal decision choice will proceed on that basis. Preconceptualizing a substitution pattern choice would appear to be a useful precursor to modal decision making and be relevant to international strategic planning. It is akin to understanding various routes (i.e. paths) and their implications (i.e. adjustments, networks, paraphernalia) to travel to a destination (i.e. firms' goals) given uncertainties of weather, road conditions, etc. (environmental uncertainties).

Since Johanson and Vahlne's seminal study (1977), increasing interest has focused on tracking the internationalization paths or mode of entry substitutions patterns (MOESP) of firms (Cavusgil, 1980; Young, 1990). Although the evidence is overwhelming that many firms do not follow the same internationalization path, new research continues to aggregate firms from a country or in an industry into one of two or more mutually exclusive paths. Thus, the path to internationalization continues to be treated as if it would be uniform for all firms from the same country. . .

The author wishes to acknowledge financial support from the Canadian Government Faculty Research Grant Program and the Academic Challenge Fund of the Department of Management at the University of Toledo.

Recommended Supplement: *Management International Review*

If you would like information on this journal (ISSN 0938-8249), call Germany: + 49 611 78 78 129; or fax: + 49 5241 8 06 03 80.

Reference Navigator

WebSite: http://www.gabler-online.de

E-mail: Hofius.tina@Bertelsmann.de

Database: not available

CD-ROM: not available

Library Reference Number:

_____

Management International Review (*MIR*) presents insight and analyses that reflect basic and topical advances in the key areas of international management. It stresses the interaction between theory and practice of management by publishing articles, research notes, reports, and comments that concentrate on the application of existing and potential research for business and other organizations.

MIR is a refereed journal that aims at the advancement and dissemination of international applied research in the fields of management and business. The scope of the *Review* comprises strategic management and business policy, international business, and transnational corporations. The editors state that papers are invited and priority is given to those that, based on rigorous methodology, suggest models capable of solving practical problems. The editor, it should be noted, hopes that besides *MIR*'s academic objectives, the journal will serve some useful purpose for the practical world and also help to bridge the gap between academic and business management.

Another functional source to consider is the *International Labour Review* (ISSN 0020-7780). It is published bimonthly in English, French, and Spanish by ILO Publications (fax: 41 22 798 63 58), based in Geneva, Switzerland. ILO stands for International Labor Organization and is a specialized agency of the United Nations. It seeks to contribute to a wider understanding of labor and social issues by publishing the results of original research and comparative studies of international interest in the form of signed articles, news features and background information to provide a perspective on current and emerging issues, and reviews of recent publications. The journal is an *excellent source* for research reference material and provides comprehensive annotations. An example of an article is "Labour Law Reform in Latin America: Between State Protection and Flexibility," by Arturo S. Bronstein.

> Since the early 1980s, employment relationships in Latin America have undergone significant change under the simultaneous impact of gradual democratization and newly introduced economic liberalism. The latter, in particular, caused disruption to the state's interventionist role, which had traditionally extended into the social sphere.

After a brief historical survey of labour legislation, the author details the impact on employment relationships of the various reforms in national labour law. Most of these emphasized labour market flexibility, though some extended traditional social protection, and others combined both. In conclusion, he suggests some possible economic consequences.

Description of Publication: *European Financial Reporting Series*

If you wish to obtain information on one of these books or the series (ISBN 0-415-06202-0), call International Thomson Business Press at +171 497 1422; or fax, +171 497 1426.

Reference Navigator

Web site: www.itbp.com   CD-ROM: not available

E-mail: info@itpuk.co.uk   Library Reference Number:

Database: not available   _____

This series of 12 books (in the process of being updated to 15) covering the European Union is an excellent reference source for individuals that need information on a specific country's business environment, organization, financial system (institutions and markets), taxation, accounting, auditing, and financial reporting. Illustrative financial statements, differences with U.S. accounting procedures, EC directives, and country legislation are all included. The information is presented in a relatively simple format that is easy to read with up-to-date charts and tables. The books are each hardbound, modest in size, and average 250 pages.

During the last decade many of Europe's largest companies have developed new approaches to financial reporting. A principal aim has been to explain the complexities of the business environments in which they operate to the rapidly expanding international investment community. Earnings and other reported figures are greatly influenced not only by the divergent accounting methods adopted in various European countries but also by the specific application of local tax regulations, company laws, and employment practices, as well as the considerable diversity of financial and commercial environments in which a European company may operate.

With the advent throughout the European Union of a harmonized accounting framework, the scene is now set for European companies to use a common approach to financial reporting. Nevertheless, the EU directives cover only a restricted subset of disclosure and measurement issues, and sometimes at a fairly superficial level. For example, under the Fourth Directive alone, there are more than 30 optional areas of harmonization that provide for alternative ways of implementing the directive. Despite this, the immediate impact of the European Commission's actions in the area of financial reporting will be to enhance considerably the level of corporate accountability throughout the EU. At the same time, the latest evidence suggests International Accounting Standards are assuming increasingly important roles.

As a result, the 1990s have witnessed an accounting revolution in Europe. In the next few years the extent of financial disclosure will take a quantum leap forward in many countries, particularly with regard to the publication of consolidated financial statements and audit opinions. In some countries the institutional and legal infrastructure of accounting is already undergoing rapid change. Harmonization may result in a common understanding of the scope of corporate financial reporting in Europe, but there still remain significant differences between Europe's various business environments. The authors of the first 12 volumes in the *European Financial Reporting Series* have produced the most authoritative studies of the European accounting to date. They chart the evolution of accounting thought through to its current position. In particular, considerable attention has been paid to the fiscal, legal, and financial background, and each book contains a detailed examination of current trends and techniques in accounting practice. If you are studying accounting, these books deserve at minimum a comprehensive research paper.

The books are generally broken down into three main parts:

Part I: The business environment.

      1. The country.

      2. Business organization.

      3. The financial system and taxation.

Part II: Accounting, auditing, and financial reporting.

      5. The accounting background.

      6. Accounting principles.

      7. The profit and loss account.

      8. Assets and liabilities.

      9. Group accounting and related issues.

      10. Further developments in accounting practice.

Part III: Appendices.

      A.   Illustrative financial statements.

      B.   The main differences in financial reporting.

Something to Think About

The *European Financial Reporting Series* aims to meet the needs of what three target audiences?

Another source of useful accounting information that comes from Europe is the *EAG* or the *European Accounting Guide* (ISBN 0-12-0499002), a companion volume to the *Guide to US Generally Accepted Accounting Principles* (the Miller GAAP Guide). This publication is a *very* comprehensive book, spanning some 1,100 pages of accounting information; it not only covers the EU, but also Turkey and other Eastern European states. Each chapter runs from 20 to 40 pages. The International Accounting Standards are included in the appendix.

The harmonization within the European Union of those institutional characteristics that directly affect financial accounting and reporting, namely company law, and tax law is (as pointed out above) moving quickly but still only in its initial stages. Thus, European accounting consists of nationally based sets of rules and practices, subject to a limited degree of harmonization in the case of European Union member states as a whole.

Each country chapter has approximately the same contents, for example:

Republic of Ireland
1. Background
2. Published Financial Statements
3. Valuation and Income Measurements
4. Future Developments
5. Specimen Financial Statements

(Sometimes useful addresses and telephone numbers are included.)

PART I

THE BUSINESS ENVIRONMENT

PART II

ACCOUNTING, AUDITING, AND FINANCIAL REPORTING

PART III

APPENDICES

5 FINANCIAL INVESTMENTS

An investment is an asset which has the primary function of being held to generate wealth in forms such as dividends, interest, royalties, rentals, or capital appreciation. (More precise definitions may be found in the Financial Services Act 1986 or International Accounting Standard 25, *Accounting for Investments*).

Because they generate wealth in a different manner from assets used in the production process, and because the income from some investments is conditioned by falls and rises in interest rates, investments are classified separately in the balance sheet. They may be fixed asset investments or current asset investments. The Act requires separate disclosure of different types of asset. It is far from easy to distinguish fixed asset investments from current asset investments. The final exposure draft from the Accounting Standards Committee in 1990, ED 55, *Accounting for Investments,* proposed the rule that an investment should be classified as a fixed asset only where an intention to hold the investment in the long term can be clearly demonstrated or where there are restrictions on the ability to dipose of the investment.

FIGURE 8.2

Marketable securities: valuation basis, by EC country. Based on the proportion of companies in each country disclosing the valuation basis for marketable securities, as reported by FEE survey. A small number of companies using other methods (e.g. face value) have not been included.

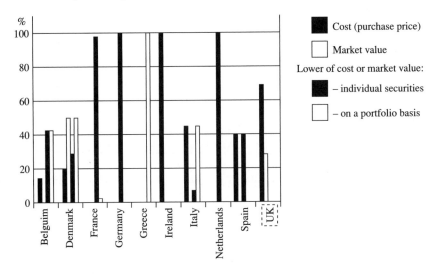

Source: Fédération dex Experts Comptables Européens, *FEE European Survey of Published Accounts, 1991.* London: Routledge, 1991.

Recommended Supplement: *Global Finance*

For information on this monthly publication (ISSN 0896-4181), call Global Finance Media, Inc., at (212) 768-1100; or fax: (212) 768-2020.

Reference Navigator

Web site: under construction

E-mail: jdg@dx.com

Database: not available

CD-ROM: not available

Library Reference Number:

_____

This is one of the those publications that you *have* to have a look at. Fortunately, it's a market magazine; unfortunately, it isn't at too many newsstands. So try at your library or call for a sample copy. *Global Finance* bested *The Economist, Institutional Investor,* and *Euromoney* to win *Financial Digest's* coveted "Most Sophisticated Reportage Award" and earned the prestigious Jesse H. Neal Award for editorial achievement in 1993 and 1995. *Global Finance* writers, the editors tell us, travel the earth to observe where the money is and where it's going. They inform you about regional developments, emerging markets, privatization, bond issuances, private placements, new products, technology, and more. Plus you can get to know more than a few of the players influencing their nation's—and the world's—economies. The magazine is about 160 pages, wonderfully formatted, colorful, and a pleasure to read.

Global Finance is perhaps best at providing independent, accurate, unbiased, clear-sighted coverage of the worldwide financial scene. This is excellent research material with in-depth analysis, focused regional coverage, and monthly *Global Finance* world market indexes that measure international trends.

Global Finance also offers special publications, such as *Best Practices In Risk Management* and *The Global Finance Guide to Direct Investing in Emerging Markets.* At times a special reports section is included at the back and covers topics as unique as they are distant: from hot properties in the Philippines to power plants in India, from investments with the Russian bear to slumbering Brazilian hyperinflation.

The personal side of finance could simply be that one wishes to invest and live internationally. *International Living* (ISSN 0277-2442) is an insider's monthly newsletter on what's happening in international real estate, investments, and travel from Agora Inc., (410) 223-2605, e-mail: 103114.2472@compuserve. com.

In August 1996, *International Living* offered:

> We visit a walled hill city in southern Portugal—viewing it through the eyes of a Canadian Muslim. We look at beautiful Baya California from the height of a kayak. We visit Vicenze—contemplating the site of one of the most transforming moments in the history of architecture. Our intrepid staffers find housing bargains in Venezuela, bicycle bargains in Holland, and budget buys in Japan, of all places.

It's a very informative little publication (I subscribe) and shows you how to invest and live cheaply in all sorts of interesting places from Paris to Belize.

42 INTERNATIONAL NEWSPAPERS AND NEWSLETTERS

Because these and similar newspapers are available on most good newsstands, the table of contents and sample pages will not be included.

Description of Publication: *The European*

If you wish information on this weekly publication, call The European Limited at +44 171 418 7731: fax: + 44 171 713 1855.

 Reference Navigator

Web site: http://www.the-european.com   CD-ROM: not available

E-mail: 74431.1416@compuserve.com   Library Reference Number:

Database: FTProfile   _____

The European is an excellent source of information about Europe and particularly about European business. It covers all of Europe, making sure that Russia and Central Europe get their space. "Europe A La Carte" provides three sections: news and features; sports; and business and economics, which covers 20 pages and is the focus here.

Examples of departments and articles include:

News: "Court blow for Fininvest"; "Euro-plug is pulled back from brink."

Analysis: "The airline giants continue to rule Europe's skies after deregulation."

Comment: "Flexible contracts unlocks the problem of Italian labor gridlock."

Focus: "Contrast of Italy's dynamic new capitalism vs. old secretive model."

Investment: "Telekom sell-off inspires a new investment culture in Germany."

Careers: "CD-ROM courses near France's silicon valley"; "Leuven's cut-
price MBA."

One particularly useful resource is the "Working in Europe" service, a *free*
advertising section that has helped many readers find jobs since it was launched
in 1994. If you want your advertisement to appear in the paper and database write
to: The European Classified Department; 200 Gray's Inn Road; London WC1X
8NE, UK; or telephone: 0171 418 7880.

The European has made a special contribution to the European Union (EU)
by publishing perhaps thousands of articles over the years and disseminating
information about the controversial issues of the EU, the primary source of which
centers on the Maastricht and Amsterdam Treaties. *The European* has published
a booklet called "Maastricht Made Simple" and produced an excellent video by
the same name. It is unusual for a newspaper to take such unique steps in inform-
ing its readership. The paper's efforts have gone a long way toward helping university students understand the issues.

Another newspaper, the *Frankfurter Allgemeine Zeitung*, also has produced
a special publication, but with a different audience and goal. The *Frankfurter Allgemeine Zeitung*, Germany's largest national and business newspaper with a readership of over 1 million, unfortunately does not come out in an English-language
version. But, the editors publish *German Brief (GB)*, a weekly newsletter covering the economics and politics of Germany and published in English. *GB* is published by its Information Services, (203) 656-2701, in the United States, or e-mail
to Germany at: 100336,156@compuserve.com. Politics, companies, industries,
economic situations, and financial issues are among the key topics analyzed in
detail by *German Brief*'s team of editors on a weekly basis. This is an excellent
reference resource. Here are some highlights:

- *Industries: GB* analyzes a full range of industries. Each monthly report
  includes major trends, important production figures, export statistics,
  and more. Performance over the past year is reviewed and the outlook
  for the next year is previewed. *GB* covers all major industries on a regular basis.
- *Company profiles:* Leading German companies, as well as smaller but
  significant exporters, are examined from a financial and strategic point
  of view. *GB* analyzes companies' past performance and outlook for the
  upcoming year.
- *Economic situation: GB* presents key economic data and comprehensive charts, depicting foreign trade, industrial production, unemployment, inflation, and money and interest rates.

Another newsletter with an excellent reputation is *The Kiplinger Washington Letter* (ISSN 0023-1770), which is published weekly (800) 544-0155. Written in a
very pithy, easy-to-read style, it provides current political and economic information. At most you are looking at four pages of material, which may not be sufficient for detailed research work.

Recommended Supplement: *The Journal of Commerce*

For information on this daily newspaper, except Saturdays and Sundays, (ISSN 1088-7407), call The Journal of Commerce, Inc., at Two World Trade Center, New York, at (212) 837-7000.

Reference Navigator

Web site: http://www.joc.com   CD-ROM: available

E-mail: customersvs@joc.com   Library Reference Number:

Database: LEXIS-NEXIS

_____

No matter where I have traveled, with relatively few exceptions, I have always been able to get a copy of the *International Herald Tribune* (http://www.iht.com), which is published as a collaborative effort between the *Washington Post* and the *New York Times*. This is an excellent newspaper, but it is difficult to find in the United States. Many students won't be able to find it easily; so we have used *The Journal of Commerce* instead.

This is a great paper, too. It's been around since 1827 so they must be doing something right. The paper's headquarters is at the Trade Center in New York, where the action is. A sister publication, *Traffic World: The Logistics News Weekly* (ISSN 0041-073X) is also worth looking at.

The Journal of Commerce, Inc., provides comprehensive information on international trade and commerce and on global transportation. According to its editors, *The Journal of Commerce* publishes more usable business news than any other newspaper. You'll find reports on finance, global trade, imports, exports, transportation, foreign investments and markets, logistics, and . . . well you get the idea. Additionally, approximately 200 special supplements are published throughout the year, providing in-depth coverage on topics ranging from geographic regions and insurance, to port authorities, commodities, and other aspects of international trade, transportation, and commerce. For business leads and export advice, "Trade Opportunities" offers 300 buying and selling leads per week. It includes "Export ABCs," "Import ABCs," "Doing Business With . . .," "Country Profiles," and "The Cybertrader," a column that helps you travel easily on the Internet. Plus, the staff is friendly on the phone and happy to help you.

Description of Publication: *The Financial Times*

For information on this daily (except Sundays) publication (USPS 190640), call F.T. Publications Inc. at (800) 628-8088; (212) 745-1340; or fax: (212) 308-2397.

Reference Navigators

Web site: http://www.FT.com

E-mail: Circulation@Financialtimes.com

Database: LEXIS-NEXIS

CD-ROM: See Web site

Library Reference Number

_____

According to an ad in the *Financial Times (FT),* "Over 300,000 influential Russians disappear every Tuesday, Thursday, and Friday." According to *FT*, you'll find them "buried in" (reading) the pink pages of their *Financial Izvestia*. Despite its morbid humor, the ad does point out an important fact, however; the *Financial Times* is a world-class newspaper dealing in business, financial, and economic news from Russia to Australia. It should be one of the first sources a student uses to get up-to-date reference information on the world economic situation. A sample of items from the table of contents includes:

News
- European news
- International news
- Asia-Pacific news
- World Trade news

Markets
- Commodities
- Foreign exchanges
- Wall Street
- Money markets

Features
- Leader page
- Letters
- Observer
- Technology

Surveys
- Polish service industry

Companies and Finance
- International
- International capital markets

The *Financial Times* also has a special supplement called the *Economic Times: Investor's Guide,* which is all you want to know daily about what's hot in making money. That is difficult because trying to read one of these papers front to back will take so long you'll have no time for investing. Another product, the *Financial Regulation Report,* is a monthly newsletter available by subscription covering worldwide regulatory developments. It describes and summarizes new regulations and legislation and comments on the implications for the markets concerned. For information, call +44 171 896 2314.

FT also sponsors conferences on special issues; for example, "The Ninth Annual *FT* Petrochemical Industry Conference: Riding Regional Dynamics." These conferences can provide a great deal of recent research information through speakers and reports. Also keep an eye on the survey agenda for potential research opportunities; contact names and telephone numbers are provided. Special reports (e.g., "Reinsurance: Reports From FT Finance") can be ordered.

FT also has a Business Research Center where, as a client, you can specify the statistics, news, and analysis you want to receive. You can even get a free cost estimate, probably not for doing your research paper though.

Recommended Supplement: *Latin American Newsletters*

For information on these publications, call: +44 171 251 0012, or fax: +44 171 253 8193.

Reference Navigator

Web site: http://www.latinnews.com   CD-ROM: not available

E-mail: 97E@latin.ftech.co.uk   Library Reference Number:

Database: See Web site

The editor of *Latin American Weekly Report* and *Latin American Regional Reports* promises to "deliver to your desk timely and thoroughly researched analysis (economic and political) of news and trends in Latin America." He offers to keep you informed on all the key facts, analysis, and exclusive insight that you need to understand current events in Latin America and "to be ready for the headlines that you'll read tomorrow." That's how, according to the editor, *Latin American* Newsletters has been recognized as the leading information source on Latin America for 30 years.

The *Latin American Weekly Report* provides authoritative information on the economic and political scene, focusing on change, long-term trends, and analyzing the effects for organizations. Each of the *Latin American Regional Reports* focuses on one of five key regions of Latin America: *Mexico & NAFTA Report, Brazil Report, Southern Cone Report, Caribbean & Central America Report,* and *Andean Group Report.* The editor relies on a number of international foreign policy makers and their advisors, world political leaders, top-level journalists, distinguished economists, and businesspeople to share their latest analysis with you.

There are some research possibilities in Latin American newspapers, such as, *Gazeta Mercantil* in Brazil and *The Daily Journal* in Caracas, Venezuelan (562-1122 or fax: 563-1633), which both have English-language editions. You can also find English editions like *The Buenos Aires Herald* from Argentina on the Internet along with a number of others (see the University of Texas, Latin American Center at http://www.lanic.utexas.edu/las.html and also the *Poltical Database of the Americas,* Georgetown University at http://www.georgetown. edu/latamerpolitical/home.html). Looked at from the other perspective, *The Wall Street Journal* has a new Spanish-language edition for Latin America, as does the *Miami Herald* and others.

Latin Trade, *Hispanic Business,* and *Latin American Newsletters* are three excellent resources for students wanting a feel for the Latin American market. However, unless you read Spanish, the opportunities to get analytical information on national economies is difficult. The best source of assistance would come from the commercial attachés at the Latin American embassies in Washington or consulates in some of the major cities around the United States or country desks at the State Department in Washington. Some private (e.g., Bank of Tokyo) and International Development Banks will also have economic and other statistical material (see the *Washington Information Directory* in Chapter 30).

Description of Publication: *The Nikkei Weekly*

If you need information about this newspaper (ISSN 0918-5348), call in the United States (212) 261-6200; subscription department: (800) 367-3405; or fax: (212) 261-6208.

Reference Navigator

Web site: http://www.nikkei.co.jp/enews

E-mail: ecntct@nikkei.co.jp

Database: See Web site

CD-ROM: not available

Library Reference Number:

_____

The Nikkei Weekly is published every Monday, minus one issue in January, by Nihon Keizai Shimbun, Inc. This excellent resource has a number of worthwhile assets other than being the only Japanese English-language newspaper. (*Nikkei Weekly* articles originate in English or are translated from Nikkei's Japanese newspapers.) Usually, a summary is given at the beginning of each separate division (economics, politics, etc.). The front page provides a succinct summary of business activities in the Far East in the first two columns. The paper covers a broad spectrum of topics:

Economy	Politics
Editorial and opinion	Science and technology
Industry	Markets
Topics and people	New products and service
Finance	Asia-Pacific

A new service from *The Nikkei Weekly* is the Nikkei Fax. The first page of the seven-page news brief carries the headlines of 45 of the most newsworthy stories of the day. The remaining six pages are filled with summaries of 25 articles set to run in the morning edition of *The Nihon Keizai Shimbun.* The vital details can be faxed to you every morning (2:30 A.M. Japan time) in English directly from Tokyo. As of this writing, a one-week trial subscription was offered for free; however, it cost $1,500 for six months.

An alternative Japanese newspaper is the *Asahi Shimbun,* which is available through the Web site (http://www.asahi.com) or call + 03 5540 7755.

Recommended Supplement: *Business Standard*

For information on this daily publication, contact the *Business Standard,* at New Delhi at: (91 11) 372 0202: or fax: (91 11) 372 0201.

Reference Navigator

Web site: http://www.business-standard.com   CD-ROM: not available

E-Mail: editor@business-standard.com   Library Reference Number:

Database: See Web site

Two of the major newspapers dealing with business in India are the *Business Standard* and *The Economic Times.* They are both substantial papers, but only the *Business Standard* will be covered in this chapter. The *Business Standard* is published six days a week and is dedicated, according to its editors, to providing high-quality information on India's economy. As part of the daily newspaper, *Business Standard* publishes a set of regular supplements: These are: "Smart Investor" (Mondays), "The Strategist" (Tuesday) and "The Money Manager" (Thursdays). On Fridays, *Business Standard* has been publishing the "Mastering Enterprise" series produced and first published in the *Financial Times* of London.

One very nice attribute of this newspaper is found on the editorial page on Mondays. *BS* previews articles for the week to come by showing six blocks that represent each day, Monday through Saturday. Each day features a different part of the paper; for example, on a Tuesday:

> Two well-known marketing professionals, Shunu Sen and Ravi Kant, tackle the Coca-Cola Company's dilemma as it struggles with a two-bank cola portfolio, in "The Strategist."
>
> In spite of the recent easing up, the RBI continues to discriminate against the NBFCs. An analysis.
>
> Plus: Dr. Ashok. V. Desa talks about Sebi's foibles.

BS is an excellent reference piece for anyone seeking in-depth analysis of the Indian market. *BS* also includes on Mondays a special section called "The Smart Investor" which runs about 24 pages, three-quarters of which are analytical articles and the last quarter stock and bond quotations.

These materials were obtained from the Indian Embassy in Washington, and the staff was very cooperative. They did insist on a fax requesting the material, but that is a small price to pay for learning about some of the more popular Indian newspapers and magazines. Researchers may be well advised to contact the cultural or commercial attachés of countries where they are interested in doing research.

43   INTERNATIONAL AND REGIONAL JOURNALS

Description of Publication: *The Economist*

If you wish to obtain information on this journal (ISSN 0013-0613), call The Economist at (212) 541-5730; or fax: (212) 541-9378.

 Reference Navigator

Web site: http://www.economist.com   CD-ROM: available

E-mail: research@economist.com   Library Reference Number:

Database: LEXIS-NEXIS

                                               _____

The maxim of *The Economist* is to take part in "a severe contest between intelligence, which presses forward, and an unworthy, timid ignorance obstructing our progress." (Another maxim, not quite as vaunted is: "If you laid every economist end to end," as the old saw goes, "they still wouldn't reach a conclusion.") *The Economist* is a business news publication edited for senior management and policy makers in finance, industry, and government in the United States and throughout the world. It is a weekly magazine of approximately 120 pages, small print, and mostly a black-and-white format with few eye-catching pictures. It is an excellent analytical source that should be familiar to all business researchers.

    The articles are clearly written (some a little esoteric), with a couple of major essays that focus on contemporary issues, not necessarily purely political or economic; for example, "Survey: Living With The Car. The free ride is over for the world's biggest consumer product. Now it has to pay its way." This *14-page* article by Iain Carson is a comprehensive perspective on a pervasive technology that is interesting to all people. As can be seen in the table of contents, *The Economist* contains a variety of interesting topics, not the least of which is a classified section for international managers, a section focusing on American news ("American Survey"), and some useful economic indicators at the end.

A subsidiary of *The Economist, The Economist Intelligence Unit* is, according to its owners, the world's most comprehensive provider of country-by-country business information. Published quarterly, its "Country Reports" covers outlook, the political scene, economic policy, the domestic economy, foreign trade and payments, and business news. Plus there's a yearly country profile, giving historical perspective to a country's politics, economy, and industry. For information, call (212) 554-0600.

The Economist Group publishes a monthly periodical (ISSN 1350-1240) called *Business Central Europe,* which, according to the editors, is dedicated to the promotion of successful business markets in Central and Eastern Europe and the expansion of trade within the region and with the rest of the world. The publishers can be reached in Vienna at (43 1) 713 3363; fax: (43 1) 714 0113; or e-mail: 100337.1153@Compuserve.com.

Business Central Europe does a very good job of covering the area it purports to cover, and its articles are substantive and analytical in nature with good supporting statistics that readily lend themselves to research use. Certainly Central Europe is a major area of business and political interest in the forthcoming years. The cover story is usually four or five pages long and focused on current issues, such as "Why Can't Central Europe Grow like Asia?" by Greg Gransden ("Despite its progress in creating market economies and opening up to trade and investment, Central Europe has not yet done enough to ensure high long-term growth") in the June 1996 issue and "Slow Death" ("Poland's National Investment Funds are proving to be a sound way of making privatizing companies more profit-oriented. But there are still 4,000 companies left in state hands. And if the Poles don't sort them out soon, it may be too late") in the April 1997 issue.

The magazine is approximately 75 pages long and covers the region well, particularly with its "Regional Focus"; "Statistics: Facts & Figures"; and "Country Indicators," which are useful for research material. Besides the cover story, the publication lists and does an excellent job of analyzing politics and economics, business, and finance, with such summary items as: "Month in Review," "Profile," "Economic Focus," "Opinion-makers," and the like. One particularly nice attribute is that the editors give an agenda for lead articles coming out over the next 12 months.

If you are looking for a quality monthly covering a heretofore forbidden territory to western business, *Business Central Europe* does it.

Something To Do

Obtain an April 1997 copy of *Business Central Europe* and in the cover story determine what impact the NIF (National Investment Funds) are having on the privatization of Polish companies. "While there are signs that their National Investment Funds are a sound concept for dealing with mass privatization, they only cover 500 companies: there are another 3,700 left in state hands."

The Economist Review

THE FUTURE OF THE EARTH

Adversaries in the Fierce Debate on the Environment Give No Quarter

The Rubbish on our Plates. By Fabien Perucca and Gerard Pouradier. Prion; 240 pages; £8.99. Distributed in America by Trafalgar Square; $14.95

Conspiracy theorists will love this muckraker from two French investigative journalists. People, they allege, are misled about the contents of packaged meals and are unaware that new-fangled food technologies have caused cancer and other terrible illnesses in humans. The only consolation for these consumers, it seems, is that when they die their corpses will be so full of preservatives that they "will take at least twice as long to decompose as they would otherwise."

The authors gloss over the fact that modern farm technologies have enabled food production to keep pace with growth in the world's population, thus avoiding the mass starvation predicted by many pundits. They also gloss over the way such technologies have mostly improved levels of nutrition and health. (Few scientists accept that farm chemicals remain a main cause of cancer.)

Nobody would suggest the food producers have an unblemished record. Mad-cow disease, for example, may yet lead to many deaths among people who ate infected beef. But these two make their case by taking a handful of such legitimate worries and then extrapolating wildly. It all makes for a rip-roaring read which bears little relation to the truth.

The Lost Gospel of the Earth. By Tom Hayden. Sierra Club Books; 269 pages; $22

Much debate on the environment is conducted in the unemotional language of economics. What makes "The Lost Gospel" different is that it discusses an unashamedly touchy-feely subject: the links between religion and nature.

Tom Hayden, a 1960s New Left radical who is now a California state senator, argues that many people have become spiritually disconnected from the earth. He believes that modern societies have become obsessed with economic growth and technological progress. But he also pins the blame for what he calls the "environmental crisis" on various religious teachings. In particular he criticizes versions of Christianity and Judaism that encourage the view that God is separate and distinct from nature.

Mr Hayden wants people to see God, or some sort of spiritual force, within nature. He greatly admires primal religions—such as those practised by American Indians or by his Irish ancestors before the arrival of Christianity—which hold that the natural world is inhabited by spirits. He calls for the world's established religions to rediscover their green roots. Modern Christians, for example, might learn from Hildegard of Beingen, a 12th-century German abbess and mystic who linked God with nature and described Jesus as a "green figure." Centuries ago, Mr Hayden might have risked persecution for encouraging nature worship. These days the worst people will say of him is that he is from California, and hence a little loopy.

Green Backlash. By Andrew Rowell. Routledge; 504 pages; £12.99 and $18.95 paperback

Betrayal of Science and Reason. By Paul and Anne Ehrlich. Island Press; 320 pages; $24.95

Both these tracts could by subtitled "greens hit back." A few years ago, countless environmental doomsayers predicted global disaster would result from a hole in the ozone layer or global warming or the destruction of the tropical rainforest. This stung Greg Easterbrook, Wilfred Beckerman, and Richard North among others into attacking the greens as "doomsayers" overstating the evidence for catastrophe. Now the greens are counter-attacking.

Recommended Supplement: *Asian Perspective*

For information on this biannual publication (ISSN 0258-9184), contact the Institute for Asian Studies at Portland State University at (503) 725-5975 (editor); fax: (503) 725-8444.

Reference Navigator

Web site: not available	CD-ROM: not available
E-mail: mel@ch1.ch.pdx.edu	Library Reference Number:
Database: not available	

Asian Perspective, A Journal of Regional and International Affairs, is an excellent research source, covering Japan, China, Korea, and more with what could be called a fine-tooth comb. The publication includes about seven articles, running from 15 to 50 pages each. Five or six book reviews are also included. The articles are comprehensive, but not esoteric, and include well-developed abstracts. The prime areas of analysis seem to be those in the political and economic areas. For example, the Spring–Summer 1996 issue included "How Trade Liberalization Affects the Political and Economic Performance of Developing Countries: The Application of a Two-Stage Game Model," by Seokwoo Kim.

The major purpose of this study is to investigate how a certain trade policy adopted by a country is related to the performance of its economic and political operations in a changing international environment. More specifically, the study tries to provide an answer to the question of why some developing countries perform much better economically and politically than other developing countries, and how trade politics at both domestic and international levels affects these.

The Editorial Advisory Board has a nice mix of European (Cambridge University), American (Columbia University), and Asian (East-West Center, Japan) scholars that attest to the quality of the coverage and the analytical skills involved.

Description of Publication: *Far Eastern Economic Review*

For information on this weekly journal, call Review Publishing Company in Hong Kong at (852) 2508-4381; or fax: (852) 2503-1530, or in Washington, DC: (202) 862-9286.

Reference Navigator

Web site: http://www.feer.com   CD-ROM: not available
E-mail: subscriptions@feer.com   Library Reference Number:
Database: See Web site   _____

The *Far Eastern Economic Review* is a wholly owned subsidiary of Dow Jones & Company. It has been published since 1946 and in its 50th anniversary year added a yearbook, a television show, and a Web site. The main topics in the table of contents are: "Regular Features," "Regional News," "Arts and Society," "Business," a company index and a classified section. The *Far Eastern Economic Review* is a well-formatted, easily read magazine that covers the Far East in approximately 95 pages. Regional coverage includes one-page articles on China, Thailand, Japan, Taiwan, Hong Kong, Indonesia, and more. The "Business" section is comprehensive, including topics and articles such as:

Banking:	"Philippine National Bank settles debt dispute."
Policies:	"New Zealand seeks jobs from forest-rights sale."
Trade:	"Seoul faces American sanctions on car imports."
Energy:	"Maharashtra agrees to consider Enron compromise."
Industries:	"South Korea's builders survive their own disasters."
Finance:	"Koreans seek tax shelter in long-term bonds."
Projects:	"Bangkok decides on a subway—again."
Media:	"Asia may get more TV choices than it wants."
Currencies:	"Hong Kong dollar resists political pressure."
Economies:	"Japan's economic package is a yawner."
Companies:	"Hopewell's superhighway costs more than expected."

How's that for a business trip around Asia every week? And if that's not enough, one can look at the books special (e.g., "The focus is India, with reviews of four novels, three biographies and books on contemporary politics and Indian art and design"). This magazine covers a lot, particularly about unfamiliar places. If you haven't been doing much reading about the Far East, and you're in business, this is the place to start.

Something to Think About

Can you identify two influential business newspapers in India? They are both cited in this book. The year 1997 is the 50th anniversary of what important date in Indian history? Do you know what tragic incident occurred at a Union Carbide plant in India? Do you know what *crisis management* means?

Finance: Lesson One
Vietnam's Banks Have a Lot to Learn about Commercial Lending

By Faith Keenan in Hanoi

Call it a crash course. Pinned to the walls of a Hanoi classroom are new vocabulary words and phrases, in English: "On the brink of bankruptcy;" "to go bust;" "in the red"—the last in bright red ink.

And a potential cause for all this financial trouble? F-R-A-U-D. The black letters glare starkly from a white board at the Vietnam bank training and research institute in Hanoi. Michael Nordstrand, a Stockholm lawyer, is trying to teach a select group of Vietnam's young but powerful bankers how to recognize fraud, and, better yet, how to avoid it.

But this is not typical pedagogy for the institute, whose three-year course covers such topics as differential calculus but offers little practical knowledge of basics like loan monitoring or risk and credit analysis. "The curriculum was absolutely bureaucratic and useless," says John Theaker, director of a bank-training project jointly funded by the Swedish International Development Cooperation Agency and the International Bank for Reconstruction and Development. "We find people trained as accountants who can't even do project appraisal and cash flows."

And cash flow is key, as many Vietnamese banks are learning the hard way. Some of the country's 52 private "joint-stock" banks (and at least one of its four state-owned banks) have recently missed payments to international creditors. Add to that a towering pile of bad debt at state banks—resulting from years of socialist-inspired lending—and you have a banking sector ill-equipped to finance the transition towards a market economy. Moreover, a draft banking law offers little indication that Vietnamese lenders will become commercially driven any time soon.

The key problem lies within the state banking sector, which accounts for 80 percent of lending. State banks are hostage to a clash of state objectives: The government wants a modern banking sector, but it also requires state institutions to forfeit profitability and flout standard lending principles by extending credit to inefficient state enterprises it somehow hopes will spur economic growth.

The government will bend over backwards to keep its enterprises afloat, partly because they provide about half of state revenues but also because they're politically powerful. Hanoi recently ordered banks to lower lending rates, and exempted certain enterprises from posting collateral for loans. In an unusually frank assessment, a State Bank official quoted in the Vietnam Investment Review recently likened the collateral-free measure to pouring money into torn pockets.

"There is still predominant pressure on the four state banks to lend in ways that they know are not particularly prudent," says Theaker. "It need not be a lack of skills in understanding what to do."

As in China and South Korea, Vietnam's state banks act as arms of government policy, funnelling money to favoured sectors. Capital is increasingly hard to come by, and personal savings are no wellspring: Only 5 percent of Vietnamese have a bank account. The only sure money in Vietnam may be a wager that state-directed lending will inhibit the development of a sound financial system, as it has in other Asian countries.

Loan defaults and allegations of fraud are providing plenty of case studies for one- and two-week intensive training courses offered by the Swedish aid agency. One is Minh Phung, a private textile company based in Ho Chi Minh City that took out deferred letters of credit—a bank's guarantee that it will pay a seller for goods—to import fertilizer. It invested the sales proceeds in property. But the property market collapsed before owner Tran Minh Phung could repay the debts. He and more than a dozen other company officials have been arrested as the State Bank tries to tally the damage.

The fallout reaches farther, however. State-owned Vietcombank failed to repay $5 million owed on letters of credit that it issued, some on behalf of Minh Phung, citing domestic regulatory issues. The explanation left foreign banks aghast at what seemed to be a flouting of international standards governing the instruments.

Recommended Supplement: *China Business Review*

If you would like information on this bimonthly publication (ISSN 0163-7169), call the U.S.-China Business Council at (202) 429-0340; or fax: (202) 833-9027.

Reference Navigator

Web site: http://www.uschina.org

E-Mail: publications@uschina.org

Database: not available

CD-ROM: not available

Library Reference Number:

_____

Until recently, one's ability to do business with the People's Republic of China was very limited. That process is changing, and the demand is for more business information on China. The *China Business Review* is a good start in that direction. The format is fairly basic, some 54 pages of mostly black-and-white columns. The magazine is broken down into three parts: "Focus," "Features," and "Departments." Articles generally target changes in the Chinese economy that sooner or later will provide opportunities for American business investments and exports. Examples of articles are: "Reshaping the Medical Equipment Landscape," by Roberta Lipson and Laurence Pemble ("Reforming China's health care system may make it more efficient, but could make the medical import picture less clear"), and "A Loss of Investor Privileges," by Owen D. Nee, Jr., and Archie Parnell ("The termination of tax and duty preferences on imported capital equipment may make foreign investors rethink their China strategies").

Two areas of particular interest to consider in the "Departments" are:

1. "Council Activities," which keeps the readers up to date on new policy initiatives (e.g., China's most favored nation (MFN) trading status was a key theme at the council's 23rd annual membership meeting, held in Washington.)
2. "China Business," which contains recent press reports of business contracts and negotiations exclusive of those listed in previous issues.

Another useful source is the colorful monthly (65 pages) *Free China Review,* (213) 782-8770, which focuses on Taiwan's cultural environment. Unfortunately, business and economics are not specific themes of the magazine.

Description of Publication: *The Middle East*

For information on this monthly publication (ISSN 0305-0734), call IC Publications Ltd. at +44 171 713 7711, or fax: +44 171 713 7970.

Reference Navigator

Web site: http://www.africasia.icpubs   CD-ROM: not available

E-mail: icpubs@dial.pipex.com   Library Reference Number:

Database: See Web site

(has 7 months' back issues)

_____

In the "Mosaic" section of the magazine, the feature article is "Somewhere Completely Different," meaning Libya, the land of Colonel Gadhafi, considered by the British and American governments to be one of the Middle East's main sponsors of international terrorism. It's being touted here as the playground of well-heeled Western travelers. Any magazine that tries to promote vacationing in a land where most hotels are (according to *The Middle East*) state-owned and Libyans themselves are "a gruff, abrasive people unused to such roles as reception clerks and waiters" has got to be, well, different. (By the way, Americans are banned by law from visiting Libya; fines go as high as $250,000 for trying.) You may want to read this journal just out of curiosity, but some of the articles have research potential, and alternative sources of information are relatively few and far between.

The Middle East is the region's leading current events, business, and cultural affairs monthly since 1974. It is the foremost English-language monthly newsmagazine on the Middle East, covering all major political and economic events with clarity and perception. The cultural section provides a unique insight into the Middle East society. An example of the contents of the magazine are:

Current affairs
Business and finance
- Turkey: "Islamist business forges ahead."
- Jordan: "Jordan is talking politics on-line."
- Regional: "Race for Caspian oil is on."
- Cyprus: "Cyprus consolidates its regional role."
- Gulf: "Slow but steady progress in Gulf stock markets."
- Business briefs
Special report and book reviews
Mosaic

The *Periodica Islamica* is an international contents journal. In its quarterly issues it reproduces tables of contents from a wide variety of serials, periodicals, and other recurring publications worldwide. These primary publications are selected for indexing on the basis of their significance for religious, cultural, socioeconomic, and political affairs of the Muslim world. You can send e-mail to dranees@klcyber.pc.my.

Something to Think About

What is Colonel Gadhafi's home telephone number (please don't mention my name over the phone)?

A list of resources to keep in mind when researching information on the Middle East was compiled by three members of my international business class from Monterrey Institute of Technology: Armando Del Tejo, Rodolfo Garze, and Alejandro Villarreal.

Access Middle East: http://www.accessme.com

ArabNet: http://www.arab.net

Arab World On-Line: http://www.awo.net

Middle East Net: http://www.mideastnet.com

Arab Business Net: http://www.arab-business.net

Institute of Islamic Banking and Insurance: http//www.islamic-banking.com

The International Investor: http://www.tiikwt.com

380

Business & Finance: Turkey
Islamist Business Forges Ahead

John Doxey reports from Istanbul on Turkey's growing Islamist business community, which includes heads of some of the secularist state's biggest companies.

In another sign that separations between Islam and the Establishment are crumbling in Turkey, an Islamist business community is clearly gaining size, status and financial muscle in the secular republic. Signs include the rising number of interest-free financial institutions and the growing number of business people who distinguish themselves as "conscious Muslims," in a country where about 99 percent of the population is Muslim. The business people, often termed "fundamentalists," head some of the country's largest companies, including Ulker Food, Industry & Trading, the region's biggest candy and cookie maker, and Ihlas Holding, a conglomerate involved in the beverage, construction, media and automotive industries.

The trend is best illustrated by the quick growth of Musiad, a nationwide association of business executives and industrialists with a common commitment to Islamic values. Founded in 1990 as an alternative to Tusiad, Turkey's leading industrialists' group, Musiad now boasts more than 2,100 members, 20 domestic branch offices, and eight foreign liaison offices.

Members of Musiad (short for the Independent Industrialists and Businessmen's Association) are mostly young men—just two women belong to the group—who own the kind of mid-size companies that form the backbone of Turkish industry. However, executives from Ihlas, Ulker, the Zaman publishing group and the Kar Group (a conglomerate active in the food, construction and airline industries) also belong to Musiad.

By itself, the rise of a "fundamentalists" business community alarms few secularists, who have generally grown used to signs of religious revivalism, including the rising visibility of Islamic sects (called "tarikat"), Islamic television programming and Islamic-style clothing. But many secularists link Islamist executive to the quick rise of the pro-Islamic Refah Party (RP) in national politics, claiming they—along with supporters in Saudi Arabia, Iran and Germany—are feeding the party's coffers.

Although Refah leaders often state their commitment to democracy and other Western-style institutions, opponents fear the party's religiously conservative leadership seeks to turn this nation of 60 million people—Europe's second-most populous—into an Iranian-style Islamic state. They also fear Algeria-type civil strife between Islamic militants and secular forces should Refah ever take the leading role in a Turkish government.

Secularist circles have occasionally attempted to slow the Islamist business community's rise. The most notable instance followed Refah's stunning by-election victories in march 1994, when RP candidates won mayoral races in Istanbul and Ankara. Several leading pro-secularist businesses tried to organise a boycott of goods produced or sold by companies believed to have supported Refah. By all accounts, however, the effort was a failure.

For their part, Musiad officials and other devout business people deny special ties to any one party. Instead, many say they contribute money to candidates from a variety of conservative parties, including Prime Minister Mesut Yilmaz' Motherland Party and the True Path Party of former Prime Minister Tansu Ciller. "Turkish businessmen are very pragmatic," says Nevzat Yalcintas, a top consultant to Ihlas Holding. "They don't put all their eggs in one basket."

Recommended Supplement: *African Business*

For information on this monthly publication (ISSN 0141-3929), call IC Publications at World Media, (212) 213-8383.

Reference Navigator

Web site: http://www.africasia.com/icpubs   CD-ROM: not available

E-mail: icpubs@dial.pipex.com   Library Reference Number:

Database: See Web site

_____

Perhaps a subscriber can say it best: "Like many other young, up and coming businessmen in Zimbabwe, I am a devoted fan of *African Business,* which in my opinion is the best African magazine around. Perhaps you may not be fully aware that *African Business* is taken very seriously, not only by the business community but also at high levels of government." This is a big compliment for a good but little magazine (42 pages). *African Business* covers all of Africa, offering currency exchange rates, editorials, cover story, technology, finance, "Country file," book reviews, and travel tips. The cover story is usually only three or four pages long, but can be statistically useful for reference purposes, and the magazine itself is often dedicated to industrial articles that promote business research; for example, "African Oil and Minerals," by Jonathan Bearman ("Everybody who is anybody in the oil and minerals industry will be in Johannesburg, attending the annual Sub-Saharan Oil and Minerals conference, which is run in association with *African Business*. Like the conference, our Cover Story this month focuses on the continent's oil and minerals sector. The news is not just good, but very good").

"Countryfile" covers Africa from the regional point of view: Southern Africa, East Africa, and West Africa. The articles are brief—one page—but current and on scene. The magazine makes one feel that Africa is a community of interests, which is a situation that is rarely reflected in the media. There should be more sources like *African Business*. And there are. A second perspective on the African scene is the *Review of African Political Economy* (ROAPE) (ISSN 0305-6244); in the United States call (800) 354-1420, or fax: (617) 354-6875. You can also e-mail to roape@mcrl.poptel.org.uk.

You should also look at *The Mercantile Journal,* "Zimbabwe's Business and Economic Guide to Southern Africa" (+ 263 4 487235). Another source, *African Business Magazine,* in conjunction with *International Book Surveys,* publishes monthly reviews of books on Africa.

Description of Publication: *Business India*

For information on this bimonthly publication, call Business India at Bombay, India: 2024422; or fax: 2875671.

Reference Navigator

Web site: http://www.tajmahal.com

E-mail: not available

Database: WWW Virtual Library: India

CD-ROM: Available for years

1995 / 1996

Library Reference Number:

According to the editors, *Business India* is "India's leading most preferred business magazine." If that's the case, what we are talking about may soon be the world's largest nation of over 1 billion people with a middle class that approaches in number the entire population of the United States. The first thing you may notice about this magazine is that it's big at approximately 286 pages. The CDs promise to cover 7,632 pages for the year 1995. The cover feature is about seven or eight pages long, followed by "Corporate Reports" of three or four pages. The departments have 48 separate categories from advertising to tourism. From a research point of view, the magazine does a very good job of providing statistics on everything from the economy to exports and marketing to retailing in the Indian market. *Business India* is available on the Internet temporarily at www.tajmahal.com while it reconstructs its own website.

Perhaps one of the most difficult things to overcome while reading the articles is the reader's lack of familiarity with the names of people, companies, or cities, which ends up being disorienting. For example,

> Like HFCL, Shyam has also diversified into basic and cellular services. Hexacom India Limited, a joint venture company promoted by Shyam, has licenses to operate cellular phone services in Rajasthan and the North East.

This problem can only be solved by becoming familiar with the area, whether it be the Middle East, Far East, Africa, or elsewhere. A true generalist in world affairs is indeed an educated individual. The days of American, Japanese, and European dominance in the world of trade is coming to a close.

Seeking FDI

The author is the former director-general of NCAER and presently consultant to Business India.

A recent politicians' meeting gives an idea of the kinds of concerns that must be set at rest if India is to improve FDI inflow.

A recent Delhi conference heard the views of thinking and well informed politicians across the political spectrum on multi-nationals coming into India. They give an idea of the kinds of concerns that must be set at rest if India is to improve on its relatively low inflows of foreign direct investment. All of them accepted the need for massive foreign investments in India and in consequence, our need to welcome multinationals. However, each of them qualified his welcome. One view from the BJP was that we should have been more self-sufficient than we are, because, according to him, multinationals, particularly American multinationals, are Trojan horses for the CIA and the U.S. government. A more moderate view from an industrialist from the same party welcomed foreign investment but not in the consumer goods sector. His logic was that MNCs in consumer goods will bring in elitist goods and so further aggravate social tensions.

A CPI intellectual in fact expressed the least suspicions about the motives of multinationals. He preferred the word transnationals to describe them because they had now in many instances transcended the narrow loyalties to the country of their origin. They have gone beyond a single State, and recognise and accept individual country differences. A much travelled and progressive Congress politician pointed out that it was in the nature of corporate citizens to lobby for their interests. MNCs would do so and inevitably find it unavoidable to seek extension of their lobbying to involve themselves in other aspects of the Indian polity. These extra-national influences on India were not in India's interests. Incidentally, every politician present expressed grave concern at the recent judicial activism in areas that the politicians regarded as being in their purview.

A point on which there can be no dispute is the need to raise the rate of domestic saving and investment in India. It is hampered by massive internal and external leakages through tax evasion, illegal activities, over and under invoicing, etc. These must be reduced.

The economists present quoted numbers to show that FDI in India is less than 1 percent of the total investment in the country, while it is 12 percent in China and 30 percent in Singapore; and that a very small fraction of FDI in India has been in consumer goods industries. In the foreseeable future, if India is to maintain its balance of payment deficits at sustainable levels, we would be unable to absorb more than $10 billion a year of foreign investment.

Regarding the fear of a growing role for foreign companies in influencing Indian politics, the example of Malaysia, with over 50 percent of its investment coming from FDI, was given. Prime Minister Mahathir has been very independent and is much wooed by the heads of developed countries for his support. It is the strength of the political leadership, and the transparency of rules and regulations, which can prevent undue extra-national interference in a country's polity. It was pointed out by one politician that multinationals come from different country origins and some countries are known for far greater interference than others. They can be closely watched. Further, the competition between different MNCs will also keep such influences on the Indian polity in check.

It is not clear as to where an industry ceases to be in the core sector and where it becomes a consumer industry. In management literature this is a continuum and there is a point at which it is difficult to distinguish between them. In many countries it is the so-called core industries that are protected from foreign investment. Even India followed this policy for many years. It is observed that in southeast Asia and China, it is the consumer goods industries in which there has been much foreign investment, that generated quick and large levels of employment. They also benefit millions of consumers by giving them larger choice, improved quality, low production costs and therefore reasonable prices. Employment generation has come about by industry in China and southeast Asia because of large and foreign investments in cloth, garments, leather, shoes, food processing, toys and other consumer goods. India has not had such large investments either domestic or foreign in these fields. The scientists pointed to the considerable technological inputs which go into the design and manufacture of consumer goods. The attempt to distinguish technology by whether it is producing potato chips or computer chips was seen as being too simplistic. It does not understand the meaning and role of technology. If Kentucky Fried Chicken teaches us to supply cooked food of the same standard in outlets all over the country, and to serve it in the same hygienic environment, that is also technology, and one that we badly need in India. A definition of *swadeshi* was suggested by P.V. Indresan. "A *swadeshi* firm is the one which invests in Indian talent to promote indigenous. . .

Recommended Supplement: *Latin Trade*

For information on this monthly publication (ISSN 1087-0857), call Freedom Magazines International, Inc., (954) 358-8373.

Reference Navigator

Web site: http://www.latintrade.com

E-mail: Lattrade@aol.com

Database: See Web site

CD-ROM: not Available

Library Reference Number:

_____

Did you know that a while ago the Zapatistas became the first cyber revolutionaries, launching attacks in the southern Mexican state of Chiapas and announcing their actions to the world via the Internet? According to the article below, one can receive the latest Zapatista communiqués, electronic copies of their newspaper *La Jornada,* and communicate with rebel leaders through e-mail. Would Lenin have loved it or what! The dark side, of course, is that innocent people are being victimized by these conflicts. As my father used to say, progress is through evolution not revolution.

This little tidbit of Latin American revolutionary information came from Jeb Blunt's article titled: "www.armed/struggle.latam.ouch" in *Latin Trade* (January 1997). *Latin Trade* is an excellent magazine (See also: *Latin Finance*). It's 80 pages, easily read, and displays a colorful format that has excellent reference material. It usually has one feature article (e.g., "Cover Story: The Bravo Business Awards," "*LT* honors regional business/government leaders for vision, dynamism and insight"). Along with the usual departments—"Trade Calendar," "Marketing,"—it also has three special sections: (1) "Investment Report," (2) "Industry Report," and (3) "Technology Report." An example of an article is "Connection," by Cristina Adams. ("LT launches a new technology section. The section will provide expanded coverage every month of the latest trends in the use of technology in Latin America").

Also take a look at Florida International University's, (305) 348-2000, *Latin American Media Directory*, which lists Spanish and Portuguese newspapers, TV channels, and radio stations, along with Web sites and e-mail. It is available in CD-ROM.

44   WORLD ECONOMIC OUTLOOK

Description of Publication

If you would like information on this book (ISSN 0251-6365), call the International Monetary Fund (IMF) in the United States: (202) 623-7430; Fax: (202) 623-7201.

Reference Navigator

Web site: http://www.IMF.org

E-mail: publications@imf.org

Database: not available

CD-ROM: not available

Library Reference Number:

The *World Economic Outlook* is a meaty little book of 200 or so pages with colorful presentations and published twice a year in English, French, Spanish, and Arabic. It presents IMF staff economists' analyses of global economic developments during the near and medium term. Chapters give an overview of the world economy; consider issues affecting industrial countries, developing countries, and economies in transition; and address topics of current interest. For example, in the October 1997 edition, Chapter 3 covered "The EMU and the World Economy." The projections and analyses contained in the *World Economic Outlook* are an integral element of the IMF's ongoing surveillance of economic developments and policies in its member countries and of the global economic system. The IMF has published the *World Economic Outlook* annually from 1980 through 1983 and biannually since 1984. The *Publications Catalog* is available as a database and can be searched by title, author, subject, series, language, or keyword.

    The survey of economic policies and prospects is the product of an interdepartmental review of world economic developments that draws primarily on information the IMF staff gathers through its consultations with member countries. The country projections are prepared by the IMF's area departments on the basis of internationally consistent assumptions about world activity, exchange rates, and conditions in international financial and commodity markets. For approximately 50 of the largest economies—accounting for 90 percent of the world output—the projections are updated for each *World Economic Outlook* exercise. For smaller countries, the projections are based on those prepared at the time of the IMF's regular Article IV consultations with member countries or in connection with the use of IMF resources. The table of contents is very comprehensive and though the book has only five chapters, it is filled with data presented in special appendixes. For example, the "Statistical Appendix" for member countries includes:

Output	External financing
Inflation	External debt / debt service
Financial policies	Flow of funds
Foreign trade	Medium baseline scenario
	Current account transaction

The "Statistical Appendix" is almost half the book, and the figures are presented in easily read tables of bold print and color (see the sample page). The "Statistical Appendix" presents historical data, as well as projections. It comprises four sections: assumptions, data and conventions, classification of countries, and statistical tables. The assumptions underlying the estimates and projections for 1997–98 and the medium-term scenario for 1999–2002 are summarized in the first section. Three Annexes included in the May 1995 edition covered some dramatic and news worthy topics:

Annex I: "Factors Behind the Financial Crisis in Mexico."

Annex II: "Adjustment in Sub-Saharan Africa."

Annex III: "Structural Fiscal Balances in Smaller Countries."

Also in the May 1995 issue, Chapter 5, "Saving in a Growing World Economy," covers such topics as: trends in saving patterns, important questions about saving, key factors affecting saving, future supply of saving, limits on borrowing the savings of others, global real interest rates as an indicator of saving adequacy, world economic performance under different saving scenarios, conclusions, and policy considerations.

Don't overlook the opportunity to check out the IMF's sister organization, the World Bank, otherwise known as the IBRD or the International Bank for Reconstruction and Development. The World Bank has some great stuff. You can get the catalog by calling World Bank Information Shop at (202) 473-2941 or e-mail books@worldbank.org.

Whenever the word *world* starts getting thrown around, you have to be careful. Everyone *knows* that the NFL Super Bowl winners are the greatest football team in the *world,* even though only American teams play in the league. Nevertheless, *The World Bank Economic Review* is a real class act and *is* top in its field.

The World Bank Economic Review (ISSN 0258-6770) is an excellently researched book, capably written by the World Bank economic staff, (202) 477-1234 or fax (202) 477-6391, and for the most part easy to read. Although the emphasis is on economics, other subjects are covered as well. For example, the January 1996 edition did a thorough study of fertility in sub-Saharan Africa based on a symposium of the same name. It is a sophisticated journal to be sure, but one with important information on a user-friendly basis.

The World Bank Economic Review is a professional journal for the dissemination of World Bank-sponsored research that informs policy analyses and choices. It is directed to an international readership of economists and social scientists in government, business, and international agencies, as well as in universities and development research institutions. The *Review* emphasizes policy relevance and operational aspects of economics, rather than primarily theoretical and methodological issues. It is intended for readers familiar with economic theory and analysis, but not necessarily proficient in advanced mathematical or econometric techniques. Articles illustrate how professional research can shed light on policy choices. I wouldn't recommend this journal, however, if your report or research paper is due tomorrow. If you are in a hurry you can go on-line at http://www.worldbank.org.

You should also know about the Export-Import Bank in Washington, DC (with five regional offices); call (800) 565-EXIM or try the Web site at http://www.exim.gov.

Something to Think About

If you had to respond to a comprehensive exam question (using the *World Economic Outlook*) that required a short essay on capital formation and employment comparing the United States and the European Union, could you do it?

Whenever a publisher makes a statement like, "Introducing the ultimate international economic research tool," you really have to sit up and listen. Business McGraw-Hill and DRI have announced the release of *Encyclopedia of World Economics on CD-ROM*. According to the editors, it's the most current and comprehensive database available on all the significant economies of the world, including the new post-Communist nations.

The *Encyclopedia* provides you with instant access to complete financial, economic, labor, and currency information for more than 80 nations, "90 percent of the world economy," they say (note the disparity from the 50 nations cited above; that's why your professor always wants more than one source on a topic). Does that mean other figures could be off too? You bet! That's why research is research. Coverage includes up to 150 tables of economic facts and 20 years of data for each country. Moreover, the *Encyclopedia* standardizes data from different countries so that individual variables can be compared from country to country. You can get more information about the *Encyclopedia* by requesting a free 3.5-inch diskette; call (800) 722-4726.

Another reference of particularly useful information comes from a book recently published by Walter de Gruyter, Inc., called *European Economic and Business Law: Legal and Economic Analyses on Integration and Harmonization* (ISBN 3-11-014242-2) and edited by R. Buxbaum, G. Hertig, A. Hirsch, and K. Hopt. The main purpose of the book is to discuss the probable evolution of European economic and business law. Some of the topics addressed are accounting, corporate law, and securities regulation. Fundamentally, according to the book's editors, "there is one general assessment regarding future European business law developments: it is not inevitable, it will not happen without a struggle, but it is now conceivable that a single European business law will establish itself." Visit the World Wide Web site at http://www.deGruyter.de (see Chapter 41).

392

I
Global Economic Prospects and Policies

With world output expected to expand by some 4¼ percent in both 1997 and 1998, the strongest pace in a decade, the global economy is enjoying the fourth episode of relatively rapid growth since the early 1970s (Figure 1). The expansion is underpinned by continued solid growth with low inflation in the United States and the United Kingdom; a strengthening recovery in Canada; and broadening of recovery across continental western Europe, notwithstanding persistent weakness in domestic demand in some of the largest countries; robust growth trends in most of the developing world, particularly in China and much of the rest of Asia even though some countries are likely to experience a setback associated with recent turmoil in financial markets in Southeast Asia; and evidence of an end to the decline in output, and perhaps a beginning of growth, in Russia and in the transition countries as a group. It is worth recalling, however, that each of the three previous episodes of relatively rapid growth was followed by widespread slowdown and even recession in many countries. Taking account of this earlier experience, is there a danger that the present expansion may soon run out of steam and give way to a new global downturn?

Although a moderation of world growth is indeed likely to occur at some point, there are reasons to believe that the current expansion can be sustained, possibly into the next decade. First, there are relatively few signs of the tensions and imbalances that have usually presaged significant downturns in the business cycle: global inflation remains subdued and commitments to safeguard progress toward price stability are perhaps stronger than at any other time in the postwar era; fiscal imbalances are being reduced with increasing determination in many countries, which is helping to contain inflation expectations and real interest rates; and exchange rates among the major currencies, taking account of relative cyclical conditions, are generally within ranges that appear to be consistent with medium-term fundamental. Second, cyclical divergences have remained sizable among the advanced economies, and there are still considerable margins of slack to be taken up in Japan and continental Europe. Stronger growth during the period ahead in these countries should help support global demand and activity as growth slows to a more sustainable pace in these countries that have already reached a mature stage in their expansions, especially the United States. . .

FIGURE 1   WORLD OUTPUT AND INFLATION[1]
(Annual percentage change)
The expansion of world output is expected to continue above trend, while inflation should remain contained.

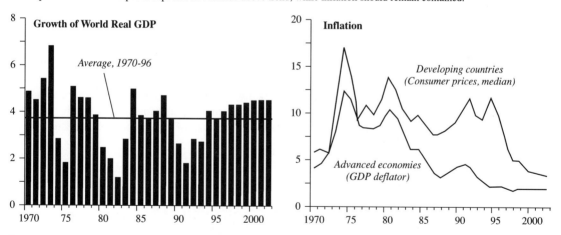

[1]Shaded areas indicate IMF staff projections. Aggregates are computed on the basis of purchasing-power-parity weights unless otherwise indicated.

Recommended Supplement: *Global Competitiveness Report 1997*

If you wish to order this annual publication (ISBN 1-85564-630-7), call World Link Publications Ltd. at + 44 171 779 8324; or fax + 44 171 779 8727.

Reference Navigator

Web site: http://www.worldlink.co.uk   CD-ROM: not available

E-mail: worldlink@pobox.com   Library Reference Number:

Database: See Web site   _____

This is an amazing, *big* book (approximately 800 pages) that compares nations on the basis of their competitiveness in almost any category you can think of; for example, "Willingness to Delegate" (Sweden's best; Russia's the worst). Since it first developed and launched the *World Competitiveness Report* in 1980, the World Economic Forum has been in the forefront of the analysis of country competitiveness. As the *New York Times* noted, the *Global Competitiveness Report* "blends the idea of competitiveness to fit modern growth theory." According to its editors, the *Global Competitiveness Report 1997* is the most authoritative annual audit on competitiveness. It provides critical information to help corporate and public policy decision makers. Its exclusive methodology combines hard quantitative data recorded by international and national organizations with a worldwide executive opinion survey to assess 53 countries on hundreds of competitiveness factors. By combining quantitative and qualitative data, the *Global Competitiveness Report* gives you valuable guidance on both current conditions and future opportunities in the countries analyzed. The *Global Competitiveness Report* is the only analysis that rigorously confines itself to those criteria that have a demonstrated impact on the ability of an economy to sustain growth.

The data tables are constructed on the basis of eight factors of competitiveness:

1. Domestic economic strength   5. Infrastructure
2. Internationalization   6. Management
3. Government   7. Science and technology
4. Finance   8. People

The World Economic Forum, according to its leadership, is the foremost international membership organization integrating leaders from business, government, and academia into a partnership committed to improving the state of the world. "Entrepreneurship in the global public interest" is the motto of the foundation. The World Economic Forum has 1,000 corporate members from among the world's most successful global companies. The not-for-profit foundation, founded in 1971, is independent, impartial, and tied to no political, partisan, or regional interests, and is under the legal supervision of the Swiss federal authorities.

45 U.S. INDUSTRY AND TRADE OUTLOOK 1998

Description of Publication

If you wish to obtain information on this publication (ISSN 0-07-032931-1), call the U.S. and Foreign Commercial Service District Office in your area or the Trade Information Center (TIC) at (800) 872-8723; Department of Commerce: (202) 482-2000.

 Reference Navigator

Web site: http://www.ita.doc.gov/tradestats

E-mail: ita@doc.gov

Database: See Web site

CD-ROM: not available

Library Reference Number:

_____

Last published five years ago under the title *U.S. Industrial Outlook,* this completely revised and updated guide has been renamed *U.S. Industry and Trade Outlook 1998* to reflect its broader scope and in-depth coverage. It is written by a unique partnership among the U.S. Department of Commerce/International Trade Administration, DRI/McGraw-Hill, and Standard & Poor's. It is an outstanding research reference that all business faculty and students should investigate. The *Outlook* covers over 350 manufacturing and service business sectors in 50 chapters—giving readers in-depth overviews of each industry, key factors affecting domestic growth and global trends, and forecasts for the next one to five years. The book is eminently readable with clear charts and tables that provide a quick look at major economic trends, trade patterns, productivity, and other important data. The author of each section is included at the end of the piece along with his or her telephone number and the date the section was written. This person is your contact in Washington and should not be overlooked as a major resource for assisting in research.

Some of its most salient features include:

- Up-to-date information on hundreds of industries, divided into 50 groups.
- New, previously uncovered industries such as electricity production.
- Expanded coverage in both manufacturing and nonmanufacturing sectors.
- New graphical snapshots of economic and trade trends.
- 650 easy-to-read tables and charts.
- New coverage of global industry trends
- Hundreds of industry reviews, analyses, and forecasts.

Until the *U.S. Industry and Trade Outlook 1998,* the Department of Commerce, International Trade Administration (ITA) had published three reports under the Clinton administration. The first, *Competing to Win in a Global Economy,* analyzed the components of U.S. competitiveness vis-à-vis our most important trading partners. The second, *The National Export Strategy,* reported on the accomplishments of 19 federal agencies working together to promote American exports and their plans for the coming year. And a third report, *The U.S. Global Trade Outlook, 1995–2000: Toward the 21st Century,* provided an additional assessment of America's place in the global economy by highlighting growth and trade trends in key countries. Although these publications have been superseded, they are still fairly recent and probably could be found on the shelves of most libraries or through the Department of Commerce ITA.

To help U.S. firms compete in the global marketplace, the U.S. Foreign Commercial Service has a network of district and branch offices in more than 70 U.S. cities. Most offices maintain business libraries containing the Commerce Department's latest reports. District office trade specialists provide the business community with export counseling and a variety of export programs and services, including the "Export Qualifier Program," a computerized program to help firms determine their readiness to export and enhance their exporting ability.

The Trade Information Center is a comprehensive resource for information on all federal government export assistance programs. The center is operated by the U.S. Department of Commerce for the 19 federal agencies comprising the Trade Promotion Coordinating Committee. These agencies are responsible for managing the U.S. government's export promotion programs and activities.

International trade specialists can be reached weekdays on the center's toll-free telephone line. These professionals advise exporters on how to locate and use government programs and guide them through the export process. They are ready to supply general market information and basic export counseling. The TIC is an access point for information on all Federal export assistance programs including those that provide:

Export counseling.

International market research and trade leads.

Overseas and domestic trade events and activities.

Federal environmental export promotion programs and assistance.

Export financing.

Export license advice.

Country Commercial Guides (CCGs) are available through the National Trade Data Bank (NTDB), the government's complete source of international business information, at (202) 482-1986. The NTDB is published monthly on CD-ROM and is also accessible via Internet on the following locations: FTP: ftp.stat.usagov, (2) Gopher: gopher.stat.usagov, and (3) Mosaic: www.stat.usagov.

Country Commercial Guides provide the facts you need to succeed in more than 100 foreign markets. They are prepared overseas by the agencies of the U.S. Trade Promotion Coordinating Committee. Each *CCG* presents a comprehensive view of a selected country's commercial environment, with up-to-date information on topics of crucial interest to you or your company.

The U.S. Export Assistance Centers (USEACs) are customer-focused federal export assistance offices. USEACs streamline export marketing and trade finance by integrating in a single location the counselors and services of the U.S. and Foreign Commercial Service of the Department of Commerce, the Export-Import Bank, the Small Business Administration, and, in Long Beach, the U.S. Agency for International Development. The four pilot USEACs are located in Baltimore, Chicago, Long Beach, and Miami.

Consideration should also be given to the United Nations' *International Trade Statistics Yearbook,* Volume II, where researchers and analysts can learn which countries export and which import their firms' products and the dollar quantities. Furthermore, according to Ball and McCulloch of *International Business,* annual dollar values are given for the past five years, enabling analysts to establish trends for projecting future values. The *Yearbook* uses the United Nations Standard International Trade Classification system based on 1,312 subgroups identified by five-digit codes.

For those who want to know if American competitors are already exporting products, analysts can use two U.S. Department of Commerce foreign trade sources—the *FT925* and the *U.S. Exports of Merchandise,* both of which come on a CD-ROM from the Department of Commerce and replace the old publication *FT447*. The information on the CD-ROM is very helpful because it gives both units and dollar value, permitting the analyst to calculate the average price of the unit exported. It also lists more countries importing and exporting to the United States than the *FT447* did and how much of the amount exported to each destination passes through each U.S. Customs district. Look in the government documents section of libraries and in Department of Commerce district offices for these research sources.

To help in their search for research on markets, students can obtain from the nearest Department of Commerce field office numerous studies prepared by U.S. embassies. *Annual Worldwide Industry Reviews* and *International Market Research Reports* indicate major markets for many products. The *Country Market Surveys* indicate products for which there may be a good market in a particular country. Other countries publish similar data. For example, the data office of the European Community, Eurostat (see Chapters 46 and 47), publishes an annual, *External Trade*.

An on-line database that could prove to be useful is the *Internet Tradeline,* (212) 425-2130; fax: (212) 425-2549. The Web site address is http://www. trade90.com/. *Tradeline* helps traders to find manufacturers and wholesalers, shippers and insurance companies, lawyers and business consultants, banks and factors. It gives, according to its owners, "easy access to the product catalogs, pro forma offers, price list, and shipping terms you need to evaluate international commerce deals."

The World Trade Center Association offers a number of excellent opportunities for gaining information on international trade at the local level. Call this franchise organization, in business since 1970, at (212) 432-2640; or visit the Web site: http://www.wtca.org, If you aren't satisfied with the local approach, go to the World Trade Organization at http://www.wto.org.

The Canadian government also has valuable information on trade, industry, and statistics. Contact it through FaxLink International at (613) 944-6500 or Web sites for Foreign Affairs (http://www.dfait-maeci.gc.ca), IndustryCanada (http://www.ic.gc.ca), and Statistics Canada (http://www.statcan.ca).

Most students, undergraduate or graduate, interested in international business have probably heard of Thunderbird: The American Graduate School of International Management, one of the top institutions of its kind. According to Thunderbird, it is the recognized leader in global business education. Since 1946, Thunderbirds (as they call themselves) have provided management talent for more than 9,000 companies in the United States and around the world. Thunderbird graduates, a powerful group of more than 28,000 global citizens, can, according to the Admissions Department:

- Utilize their business skills beyond their home countries.
- Manage a culturally diverse team.
- Speak the language of their clients and associates.
- Be flexible in changing global markets.

Thunderbird, an American Assembly of Collegiate Schools of Business accredited school, offers:

The Master of International Management degree, requiring courses in international management, international business environment, and any of 10 foreign languages.

The Executive Master of International Management degree, a two-year program for working professionals.

The Post MBA degree, a continuation, at the master's level, of courses focusing on the global market.

If you are interested in getting information from Thunderbird call the Office of Admissions at (800) 457-6940 or go on the Web to http://www.t-bird.edu.

If you've been waiting for an opportunity to work as a U.S. diplomat, you may want to obtain information on the exam and registration materials. Send a letter requesting the Application for the Foreign Service Officer (FSO) Examination to Foreign Service Written Examination, U.S. Department of State, P.O. Box 12226, Arlington, VA 22219. You can take the FSO exam at one of 185 U.S. sites. It consists of three parts: a knowledge test, an English expression test, and a biographic questionnaire. You must then also pass an oral examination, a medical exam, the fitness standards, and a background investigation before being put on the eligible-for-hire register. About 125 new FSOs will be appointed from the group taking the exam each November. To prepare for the exam, use the "Study Guide for the Foreign Service Officer Written Examination and Assessment Procedure," published by the Educational Testing Service, (609) 771-7243 or http://www.ETS.org.

36
Motor Vehicles

Industry Definition The motor vehicle industry includes new, on-road, volume-produced completed vehicles for carrying cargo or passengers (SIC 3711) and truck and bus bodies and cabs for sale separately or for assembly on purchased chassis (SIC 3713). The automotive parts and accessories industry is covered in Chapter 37.

OVERVIEW

The global automobile industry is decreasing the number of standalone companies, unique platforms, unique engines, and unique parts in an effort to reduce investment costs and increase economies of scale. As a result, the major automakers are combining research and development efforts to create platforms and parts that can be used throughout the world. Volkswagen, for example, is working toward reducing the number of unique platforms it produces worldwide from 16 to 4. Yet the total number of vehicles Volkswagen offers will probably increase as the average number of vehicles a given platform supports increases.

Another trend is also related to cost control as well as to timeliness: Manufacturers are using supercomputers and paperless design tools to reduce the time it takes to go from vehicle concept to production. A reduced development time means key decisions affecting product marketability can be postponed until later in the process. It also means that engineers and designers can evaluate several iterations of a given part or even an entire vehicle as computer simulations rather than use the costly and time-consuming method of building and testing actual prototypes. Although this new technology requires significant investments, the payoffs should be fairly immediate.

GLOBAL INDUSTRY TRENDS

Many of the barriers that have separated the world's automotive markets are slowly falling away. As a result, the light-vehicle market (cars plus light trucks) worldwide has become much more integrated with production. Likewise, over time vehicle trends in the world's mature markets (the United States, Western Europe, and Japan) are likely to appear in the developing markets.

The changing face of the world market means that automakers can move production to less-costly locations. In response, the U.S. Big Three automakers (General Motors, Ford, and Chrysler) have been adding production in Mexico, for example. Honda and BMW, however, are moving production to the United States to avoid relatively high domestic labor costs. Another global trend is that production has moved closer to a vehicle's primary market, in part to minimize the effect of currency fluctuations. In keeping with that trend, Mercedes-Benz is building its M-Class sport/utility vehicle exclusively in Alabama, which will make Alabama the worldwide location of M-Class production.

WORLD COMMONALITY

Changes in today's world industry are in ways reminiscent of Henry Ford's idea of mass-producing vehicles in the interest of reaching economies of scale. Today, the industry is moving the concept of economies of scale from the country level to the world level by reducing the number of unique platforms (a vehicle's underpinnings) and components (e.g., engines and transmissions). The idea is to design a single platform or component that can be made and used on several vehicles worldwide. An example of such a vehicle is the Ford Contour (sold and made in both the United States and Mexico), a very similar version of which is the Mondeo, which is sold and produced in Europe.

This global approach has a number of advantages: First, product development costs are reduced (one design in place of many). Second, development costs can be spread over a larger number of vehicles, reducing the development cost per vehicle and thereby allowing lower prices or increased profit margins.

401

Recommended Supplement: *World Trade*

For information on this monthly publication, call World Trade at (714) 798-3500 or fax: (714) 798-3501.

Reference Navigator

Web site: http://www.worldtrademag.com   CD-Rom: not available

E-mail: wtedit@aol.com   Library Reference Number:

Database: See Web site

_____

World Trade is a smart-looking publication of approximately 215 pages that was created "for the Executive with Global Vision." The editors do a credible job in trying to capture the essential trade news.

Feature articles are not done in-depth, being only three or four pages long and not statistically driven. However, some topics are done in serial, which is both good news and bad news. The good news is the topic is well covered; the bad news is (at least from the reader's point of view) you better not miss an issue or you don't get the whole picture. For example, one article, "The 10 Steps of Global Trade," is broken down into a number of issues (e.g., October: step 6, the initial face-to-face with overseas business prospects). This is a good technique for keeping the reader coming back, but makes it a little inconvenient carrying around five or six issues while trying to research an article.

Having said that, the articles are easily read and on top of current issues, for example: "Ford's World Drive," by James L. Srodes. ("Ford Motor Co. wants to be the top carmaker in the world. We talk with Ford chairman and CEO Alex Trotman about the global strategy behind it all") and "A Matter of Survival," by David Wallace ("As Ford and other major automakers look to the future of the global economy and try to produce cars that will satisfy consumers across the world, their push for standardization has touched off a consolidation among its suppliers. How will this affect the $500 billion a year U.S. supply chain, where companies are moving quickly to get in line with Detroit's strategy?").

Although not particularly analytical, *World Trade* is worth reading for its excellent coverage of international trade news and business trade concepts.

Arthur Andersen & Company is a major player in international business consulting. In an advertisement in *World Trade* the company offers to demonstrate its knowledge base and send a free brochure. (It could be a good learning experience for students.) The ad asks: "What's really holding your company back?"

> You'll find out when you discover your real business problems—the ones hidden in your underlying business practices. And that's where our proprietary knowledge base of Global Best Practices can help. In our trained hands, it lets us compare your operating practices to the best in the business world—within your own industry, and

across the board. It's designed to be the most thought-provoking resource of its kind. Driven by an advanced application of CD-ROM technology. Updated throughout our global network. And unsurpassed in its depth and scope. To see a demonstration of our knowledge base or receive a free brochure, call 1- 800-445-5556.

Another publication that deals directly with trade is Joseph Zodl's *Export-Import* (ISBN 1-55870-388-8); call F&W Publications, Inc., at (800) 289-0963. Zodl wrote this book with the intention of giving you many of the answers you need to enter into international trade and pointing out other knowledgeable sources for other answers. The book is geared to the small- to medium-sized company wanting to get involved in exporting or importing products right away with a minimum of complications.

Zodl is a veteran exporter and importer who makes getting started in the export-import business easy, or at least easy to understand. He shows how you can guide your company into international trade and minimize complications. You'll get current information on trade laws. In addition you can see many examples of trade documents such as sight drafts and letters of transmittal. Coverage of many practical aspects of international trading are cited in the book, for example (by chapter):

1. Why You Should Be Exporting or Importing.
2. Risks and Rewards of International Trade.
3. Finding Markets for Products Abroad.
4. Finding Sources for Products Abroad.
5. Where to Go for Help.
6. Terms of Sale.
7. The Pro Forma Invoice.
8. Ins and Outs of Getting Paid.
9. Documentation.
10. Transportation Rates.
11. Alternative Concepts for Export-Import.
12. Planning Ahead for Import.
13. Meeting Customs Laws and Regulations.
14. Glossary, Resources, and Index.

Something To Do

Can you draft a letter of credit? If not, it could be worth your while to visit a local bank to see if it has examples, and if it could spend some time explaining how it uses the letters of credit.

---

46 EUROSTAT YEARBOOK '96

Description of Publication

To obtain information on this book (ISBN 92-826-8940-9), call the Statistical Office of the European Communities at (800) 274-4888; or fax: (301) 459-0056.

 Reference Navigator

Web site: http://europa.eu.int/eurostat.html   CD-ROM: not available

E-mail: eurodata@haver.com   Library Reference Number:

Database: See Web site   _____

This is a good solid publication, published by Eurostat (Statistical Office of the European Communities), whose focus is entirely statistical. The advantage of this reference is the 10-year trends it provides. It has been an annual publication since 1995. As far as possible the data are in a time series covering 10-year periods; for example, 1984–1994. This enables the reader to compare the present situation of member states (European Union) and other countries. This book is high in quality statistics and low in colorful, interpreted presentations.

   The aim of *Eurostat Yearbook* is to offer statistics from the point of view of the user rather than the producer—certainly a nice touch. The layout of pages, tables, and graphs is in a standard format that makes it easier for the user to become quickly familiar with the way data are presented. Be careful, however; not all statistics used for this publication lend themselves to such treatment. For example, some statistics are produced with a higher priority given to reflecting the present situation rather than to comparing them with data published 10 years ago. Germany is included in three different ways. Many tables and graphs include Germany as constituted before the reunification of October 3, 1990. Every table contains suggested further reading. The publications recommended are available through national sales and subscription agencies (use Eurostat Information Office, fax: + 352 4301 32594).

Eurostat Yearbook is for and about the Europeans. It compares significant features of each country of the European Union and of other European countries, those in the European Free Trade Association, (Austria, Finland, Iceland, Liechtenstein, Norway, Sweden, and Switzerland) United States, Canada, and Japan. For ease of comparison, all statistics in this publication are either compiled in the same way or harmonized by Eurostat or accepted as offering sensible comparisons. But even when statistics are compiled in the same way, one has to be careful to allow for people's varied backgrounds—cultural, economic, and climatic.

The book has five chapters of statistics followed by an annex including text on main events of the European Union, a glossary, geographical nomenclature, and classifications of economic activities and commodities. The five chapters are:

1. "The People"—includes figures on life and death, family life, international migration, non-national citizens, age, sex, population increase, education, people in and outside the labor market, earnings and working hours, social protection, consumption and spending, housing, culture and leisure, and crime.

2. "The Land and Environment"—includes figures on population density and use of land, air quality and emissions, fertilizers and pesticides, and . waste and recycling.

3. "National Income and Expenditure"—includes figures on economic growth, contribution to output by industry, consumption and spending, factor incomes, government receipts and spending, consumer prices and interest rates, balance of payments, trade in services, trade in goods, and key figures on the labor market.

4. "Trade and Industry"—includes figures on agriculture, forestry, fishing, industry, manufacturing, energy, water, services, transport, and tourism.

5. "The European Union"—includes figures on institutions and budgets, the ECU, internal economy, the European market, and external trade.

Yves Franchet, Director-General and ultimately responsible for the work, offers a final caveat:

> Statistics are never the absolute truth. But when all is said and done . . . they are undoubtedly the key to unlocking many of the important questions facing today's Europeans.

A strong supplement to *Eurostat Yearbook* is *Enterprises in Europe* (ISBN 92-826-7692-7); call UNIPUB: (800) 274-4888; or fax: (301) 459-0056.

In 1988 Directorate-General XXIII and Eurostat launched a project to improve the collection and compilation of statistics on small and medium-size enterprises (SMEs) as part of a program aimed at assisting them. Two years later this project led to creation of the *European Statistical System on SMEs,* a database containing information on the enterprises by size.

This database has grown considerably over the years. It now covers all economic sectors, except agriculture, in 23 countries (the member states of the European Economic Area, Switzerland, the United States, Canada, Japan, and Australia). It also contains nine size classes based on the number of employees. Its contents are regularly disseminated in commission publications, *Enterprises in Europe, Third Report,* being the latest.

This edition is in two volumes and consists of a descriptive analysis illustrated with graphics and tables of figures, which are supplemented by notes on the methodology. As well as the usual statistics on enterprises, employment, and production, it contains, for the first time figures on the demography of enterprises, which, because of its close link with job creation, is a particularly important issue in periods of economic recession.

An example of its organization is:

Chapter 3—Enterprises in Germany
1. National Perspective
    1.1 General Overview
    1.2 Industry
    1.3 Construction
    1.4 Distribution
    1.5 The rest of services
2. Germany in the EU

Finally, if you're interested in the situation in Europe, particularly the European Monetary Union (EMU), you should pick up a copy of *Business Week's* April 27, 1998 issue which includes, "Special Issue: The Euro."

Here Comes the Euro
Revolution is at hand, and it will go well beyond adopting a new currency. Monetary union will sweep away Europe's national companies, generous pension plans, and rigid work rules. In their place will arise a $6.4 trillion economy—the second-largest in the world—that is more competitive and ripe with new opportunities. But there will be transition pains, and the question is: Can politicians sweat the fallout?

People in the Labour Market

The Community labour force survey applies the internationally-accepted definition of unemployment. According to this, unemployed people are those out of work who are available to start work within two weeks and are actively seeking a job. Only such harmonised unemployment estimates are comparable between EU countries. The concept of registered unemployment (people registered at employment offices), widely recognised in member States, differs widely between them and cannot be used for comparison.

Unemployment rate of men aged 50 to 64

	1983	1984	1985	1986	1987	1988	1989	1990	1991	1992	1993
Eur12	*	*	*	*	6.7	6.1	5.6	5.2	5.3	6.2	7.6
B	6.0	5.5	5.0	5.3	5.4	5.6	4.0	3.5	2.5	2.7	3.9
DK	6.4	4.7	2.7	4.3	5.4	5.1	5.9	6.3	7.2	7.3	8.5
D	4.3	4.1	5.1	5.4	6.1	5.7	5.2	5.1	5.0	6.0	7.7
GR	3.2	3.1	2.7	2.4	2.6	2.3	1.9	1.8	1.8	2.4	3.2
E	*	*	*	12.6	10.8	9.8	9.2	8.4	8.3	9.1	12.0
F	5.1	5.4	6.1	7.0	7.0	6.8	6.4	5.7	5.7	6.9	7.0
IRL	8.8	10.7	11.6	10.6	12.4	12.0	11.6	10.3	10.4	9.4	9.8
I	1.7	1.9	1.7	2.2	2.4	1.9	2.3	1.8	1.8	2.3	2.7
L	*	*	*	*	*	*	*	*	*	*	*
NL	6.4	*	5.8	*	5.4	5.1	4.9	3.6	4.7	2.6	3.8
P	*	*	*	3.1	3.2	2.4	2.0	2.0	1.6	2.5	3.9
UK	9.2	8.5	9.2	9.7	10.3	9.4	7.9	7.5	8.6	10.4	11.9

Reading Labour force survey, 1993. Eurostat.

Unemployment rate of women aged 50 to 64

	1983	1984	1985	1986	1987	1988	1989	1990	1991	1992	1993
EUR12	*	*	*	*	6.8	6.8	6.8	6.1	6.4	7.4	8.1
B	9.1	9.1	7.8	8.6	8.8	8.4	7.0	6.1	4.6	5.1	5.9
DK	6.6	6.2	7.0	7.0	5.4	6.3	8.2	7.9	8.8	8.9	9.8
D	4.8	5.9	6.6	7.6	7.8	8.4	9.3	7.2	7.7	10.2	11.7
GR	2.9	2.3	2.7	2.2	2.3	2.2	2.6	2.5	3.5	3.7	3.4
E	*	*	*	6.7	8.4	8.0	8.4	8.9	8.8	9.6	11.4
F	6.4	7.2	7.4	7.2	8.2	8.3	8.2	7.9	8.0	8.9	8.2
IRL	9.4	12.4	11.7	13.4	13.0	13.2	12.1	11.4	11.1	10.2	9.5
I	3.3	2.7	2.5	3.7	3.6	3.7	3.3	3.6	3.0	3.9	3.8
L	*	*	*	*	*	*	*	*	*	*	*
NL	6.5	*	5.8	*	8.0	9.0	7.7	7.1	7.5	5.5	5.4
P	*	*	*	2.9	2.6	2.0	1.9	2.0	2.2	1.2*	2.8
UK	4.6	5.5	6.3	6.2	6.8	6.2	5.7	4.7	5.2	4.7	5.4

Reading Labour force survey, 1993. Eurostat.

Recommended Supplement: *The World's Women 1995: Trends and Statistics*

The second edition of *The World's Women: Trends and Statistics* is co-sponsored by 11 United Nations partners, an indication of the importance of data on women for United Nations system initiatives (http://www.un.org). In addition to being an official document for the Fourth World Conference on Women, this edition is an independent United Nations publication. Its six chapters cover and update areas previously analyzed on education, population, and public life. It also expands the sections on health, childbearing, and work. These topics—along with such new topics as media, violence against women, poverty, the environment, refugees and displaced persons, and 50 years of women in the United Nations and peacekeeping—reflect the main areas of activity of the co-sponsoring programs and departments and organizations of the United Nations system.

This is a substantive report specifically tailored to its target audiences of people in the media and policy making, governments and nongovernmental organizations, and academic and research institutions. It has been, according to its editors, a major collaborative effort of many individual consultants and other organizations and units of the United Nations to bring together their expertise in policy, programming, data, and analysis.

The table of contents includes:

Overview

1. "Population Households and Families"
    *   Example: Numbers of women—numbers of men.
2. "Population Growth, Distribution, and Environment"
    *   Example: Where women and men live.
3. "Health"
    *   Example: The health of girls and boys.
4. "Education and Training"
    *   Example: The influence of education on childbearing.
5. "Work"
    *   Example: Women's and men's work and time use.
6. "Power and Influence"
    *   Example: Top positions in politics and business.

Did you know U.S. companies owned by minority women, one of the fastest growing categories in small business, surged in number to 1.1 million in 1996? A new report (using estimates from the Census Bureau), focusing mainly on businesses owned by Asians, blacks, and Latinas, was released by the National Foundation for Women Business Owners, the research affiliate of a Washington group that advances the interests of women in business.

A relatively new publication, *The European Journal of Women's Studies* (ISSN 1350-5068), is now available. It is a multidisciplinary, academic, feminist journal that has as its main focus the nature of the complex relationship between women and the diverse regions and meanings of Europe. The journal can be contacted at +44 171 330 1266.

You may also wish to consult the *Statistical Handbook on Woman in America* (ISBN 1-57356-005-7) from American Demographics Bookstore, http://www.demographics.com. It has the latest statistics on employment, earnings, and educational status.

47   EUROPE IN FIGURES

Description of Publication

To obtain information on this book (ISBN 92-827-0075-5), call UNIPUB: (800) 274-4888; or fax (301) 459-0056. In Europe call Eurostat at (352) 4301 4567; or fax: 352 43 64 04.

    Reference Navigator

Web site: http://www.europa.eu.int

E-mail: Eurodata@haver.com

Database: See Web site

CD-ROM: available

Library Reference Number:

This excellent book, the goal of which is to educate people about Europe, lends itself to a comfortable interaction between reader and material. It is well documented with statistics; interpreted data; colorful presentations of charts, graphs, photos, vignettes, and maps; glossary; and further reading. Its quality by far exceeds its price.

Progress in European integration and initiatives taken at the Maastricht Summit has called for a greater understanding of the Community's history and background. In keeping with this need for greater understanding and the availability of more objective information on its economic and social conditions, Eurostat (Statistical Office of the European Communities) created this publication. One of Eurostat's tasks was to provide Europeans and other interested persons with information on developments in European Community policies based on uniform definitions and data-collection methods to enable them to make informed choices and decisions. Eurostat's harmonized EU statistics fulfill that objective.

The book is color coded to refer to Eurostat's various statistical themes:

General statistics.

Population and social conditions.

Economy and finance.

Energy and industry.

Agriculture, forestry, and fisheries.
Services and transport.
Miscellaneous.

External trade/balance of payments.
Environment.

Also, for general information concerning the European Union Commission, go on-line at http://www.cec.lu/welcome.html.

Something to Think About

What is the translation of the following currency acronyms?

DM   =   _____

LIT   =   _____

USD   =   _____

FF   =   _____

Unemployment

In 1990, 12 million persons in the European Community were unemployed (annual average). Unemployment is one of the most worrying aspects of the labour market, affecting 8.4 percent of the active population and women more than men. Youth and long-term unemployment remain high.

Unemployment Rates (%)

	EUR 12	USA	JAP
1970	6.3	4.8	1.1
1975	4.1	8.3	1.9
1981	7.7	7.6	2.2
1983	9.9	9.6	2.6
1986	10.7	7.0	2.8
1987	10.3	6.2	2.8
1988	9.7	5.5	2.3
1989	8.9	5.3	2.3
1990	8.4	5.5	2.1

Unemployment in the EC, 1990

| | Number out of work × 1000 | | | Unemployment rate (%) | | | | | | | |
| | | | | Total | | | Aged under 25 | | | Aged 25 and over | |
	Total	Men	Women	Total	Men	Women	Total	Men	Women	Total	Men
EUR12	11986	5623	6363	8.4	6.5	11.1	16.1	14.0	18.4	6.7	5.1
B	318	125	193	8.1	5.2	12.8	16.0	12.2	20.3	7.0	4.3
DK	230	112	118	8.0	7.2	8.8	10.9	10.6	11.3	7.3	6.4
D	1482	675	806	5.1	3.9	7.0	4.5	4.1	5.0	5.3	3.9
GR	297	115	182	7.5	4.6	12.4	24.8	16.9	33.9	4.7	3.0
E	2407	1146	1261	16.1	11.9	24.1	31.9	26.0	39.1	12.2	9.0
F	2157	906	1251	9.0	6.7	11.9	18.6	15.4	22.0	7.5	5.5
IRL	202	130	73	15.6	15.0	16.8	21.6	23.3	19.5	13.8	13.0
I	2319	968	1352	9.9	6.5	15.7	29.2	23.7	35.6	5.9	3.6
L	3	1	1	1.7	1.2	2.5	3.9	2.9	5.0	1.3	1.0
NL	535	234	301	8.1	5.8	11.9	11.8	10.3	13.3	7.2	4.9
P	223	90	132	4.6	3.2	6.3	10.0	7.5	13.1	3.2	2.2
UK	1314	1122	692	6.4	6.9	5.7	9.3	10.5	7.9	5.6	6.0

Recommended Supplement:
OECD Economic Surveys

If you wish to order this publication (ISBN 92-64-14587-7), call OECD Publications and Information Center at (202) 785-6323; or fax: (202) 785-0350; or in Europe: (33-1) 45 24 8200; or fax: (33-1) 49 10 4276.

Reference Navigator

Web site: http://www.OECDwash.org   CD-ROM: available

E-mail: personal only   Library Reference Number:

Database: not available

Each book is a survey about an Organization for Economic Cooperation and Development (OECD) member, which includes Austria, Belgium, Canada, Denmark, France, Germany, Greece, Iceland, Ireland, Italy, Luxembourg, the Netherlands, Norway, Portugal, Spain, Sweden, Switzerland, Turkey, United Kingdom, United States, Japan, Finland, Australia, New Zealand, and Mexico. OECD was created in 1961 to promote policies of economic growth for its members. OECD Europe (in Paris) can be reached at http://www.oecd.org. The books are unique in that they provide very recent coverage of their members' economies in considerable detail. They are easy to read, but lack any significant effort to present the material in any but the most basic fashion. Nevertheless, the books provide a comprehensive overview of each members' economy.

Each book includes:

Introduction

Chapter 1: Structural Change and Recent Economic Developments.

Chapter 2: Economic Policy and Policy-Making.

Chapter 3: Some regional aspects.

Chapter 4: The Developments of Markets: Corporate Governance, Competition, and Enterprise Behavior.

Chapter 5: Labor Market Mobility and Flexibility.

Chapter 6: Living Standards and Social Protection.

Chapter 7: Conclusions

Notes and Bibliography

Another source that provides ranking information and could supplement the OECD surveys is the *European Business Rankings* (*EBR*) published by Gale Research (ISBN 1-73477-007). The Library and Information Service of the Manchester Business School receives around 800 periodicals and newspapers from around the world, together with an extensive range of directories, statistical series and market reports. These sources are constantly scanned for the inclusion of suitable ranking tables and selected for the *EBR*.

48   YEARBOOK OF THE UNITED NATIONS

Description of Publication

For information on this annual publication (ISSN 0082-8521), contact the UN Publications Sales Section, Room DC 2-853, United Nations, New York, NY 10017.

 Reference Navigator

Web site: http://www.un.org
E-mail: publications@un.org
Database: available on micro-fiche

CD-ROM: not available
Library Reference Number:
_____

Another *big* book that covers the activities of the United Nations on an annual basis is *Yearbook of the United Nations,* which continues the tradition of providing the most comprehensive and up-to-date coverage of the activities of the UN. It is an indispensable reference tool for the research community, diplomats, government officials, and the general public seeking readily available information on the UN system and its related organizations.

The *Yearbook* is subject-oriented and divided into seven parts covering political and security questions, regional questions and peacekeeping, human rights, economic and social questions, legal questions, administrative and budgetary questions, and intergovernmental organizations related to the UN. Chapters and topical headings present summaries of pertinent UN activities, including those of intergovernmental and expert bodies, major reports, Secretariat activities, and in select cases, the views of states in written communications. References are listed either at the end of short chapters or after subchapters, linked to the text by numerical indicators. Subject headings in the report include:

Activities of the United Nations bodies. All resolutions, decisions, and other major activities of the principal organs and, on a selective basis, those of subsidiary bodies are either reproduced or summarized in the respective articles.

Major reports. Most reports of the Secretary-General along with selected reports from other UN sources, such as seminars and working groups, are summarized briefly.

Secretariat activities. The operational activities of the UN for development and humanitarian assistance are described under the relevant topics. For major activities financed outside the UN regular budget, selected information is given on contributions and expenditures.

Views of states. Written communications sent to the UN by member states and circulated as documents of the principal organs have been summarized in selected cases, under relevant topics. Substantive actions by the Security Council have been analyzed and brief reviews of the Security Council's deliberations given, particularly in cases where an issue was taken up but no resolution was adopted.

Related organizations. The *Yearbook* also briefly describes the activities of the specialized agencies and other related organizations of the UN system.

Part Four of the *Yearbook* covers "Economic and Social Questions," which is probably the section most interesting to business analysts and students. Only four sections dealing primarily with the economic perspective versus the social perspective will be covered here:

1. "Development Policy and International Economic Cooperation" (e.g., Science and technology for Development, 849).
2. "Operational Activities for Development" (e.g., Program Planning and Management, 894).
3. "Humanitarian and Special Economic Assistance" (e.g., African Economic Recovery and Development, 931).
4. "International Trade, Finance, and Transport" (e.g., International Investment and Transnational Corporations, 974).

PART ONE

Political and Security Questions

418

PART FOUR:

ECONOMIC AND SOCIAL QUESTIONS

CHAPTER IV
International Trade, Finance, and Transport

In keeping with the recent trend, international trade again exceeded world output in 1994, rising in volume by close to 9 percent, mainly due to expansion of trade manufactures. The prices of many non-oil commodities rose sharply during the year, partly because of an upsurge in demand but also because of speculative trading and a declining dollar. The United States and Western Europe received a strong impetus from exports, especially to the developing countries in East and South-East Asia and Latin America. Although Africa showed a slight improvement in terms of trade, long-term development performance remained depressed by commodity dependence, poor infrastructure, over-indebtedness, low levels of domestic investment, and caution by foreign investors, as well as by political instability and conflicts.

Preparations for the ninth session of the United Nations Conference on Trade and Development (UNCTAD IX), to be held in 1996, began with the approval in March 1995 by the UNCTAD Trade and Development Board (TDB) of a development-oriented provisional agenda. Following an offer from South Africa, received during TDB's September session, the General Assembly in December decided to convene UNCTAD IX in Midrand, Gauteng Province. The Conference was to have the unifying theme: "Promoting growth and sustainable development in a globalizing and liberalizing world economy."

Following consideration of international trade and development issues in December, the Assembly invited UNCTAD to follow developments in the international trading system, particularly their implications for developing countries, and to identify new trading opportunities arising from the implementation of the 1994 Uruguay Round agreements.

Questions of trade, environment, and sustainable development were discussed by the Commission on Sustainable Development and by UNCTAD's Ad Hoc Working Group on Trade, Environment, and Development, which completed its work in 1995. The Assembly invited UNCTAD and the UN Environment Programme to continue their joint programme on trade and environment issues.

The Third UN Conference to Review All Aspects of the Set of Multilaterally Agreed Equitable Principles and Rules for the Control of Restrictive Business Practices took place in November. The Conference requested the UNCTAD secretariat to revise periodically the commentary to the model law on restrictive business practices and to disseminate widely the model law and its commentary. In the area of commodities, the International Natural Rubber Agreement, 1995, was adopted in February and opened for signature in April.

The debt of low-income and some middle-income countries continued to cause concern during 1995. The Assembly in December called on the international community to implement the commitments of the major UN conferences and summits on development, organized since the beginning of the 1990s, addressing the question of external debt.

The newly named Commission on International Investment and Transnational Corporations met in April to discuss trends in foreign direct investment (FDI) and related issues. It recognized the role of investment for development, especially for Africa, and supported international activities to increase FDI flows.

With regard to transport, the Economic and Social Council, having reviewed the work of the Committee of Experts on the Transport of Dangerous Goods, requested the Committee to elaborate proposals for globally harmonized criteria for the classification of flammable, explosive and reactive materials.

PREPARATIONS FOR UNCTAD IX

As requested by TDB in 1994, (1) the Officer-in-Charge of UNCTAD carried out informal, open-ended consultations on the provisional agenda for the ninth session of UNCTAD, to be held in 1996. At the second part of its 41st session (Geneva, 20–31 March 1995), (2) TDB approved the provisional agenda and agreed annotations for UNCTAD IX, requested the Officer-in-Charge to complete the provisional agenda with the customary procedural and administrative items and annexed to its report a background note on the agenda, prepared by the secretariat. On 31 March, TDB noted the Final Communiqué of the Eighteenth Meeting of the Chairmen and Coordinators of the Group of 77 (developing countries) Chapters (Geneva, 14-15 March) (3) and annexed it to its report.

Recommended Supplement: *UN Chronicle*

For information on this quarterly publication (USPS 647-380), contact the United Nations Department of Public Information at (800) 253-9646; fax: (212) 963-3489.

Reference Navigator	
Web site: http://www.un.org	CD-ROM: not available
E-mail: UN_Chronicle@un.org	Library Reference Number:
Database: See Web site	_____

The *UN Chronicle* provides a contemporary overview in 50 pages of some of the main activities taking place at the United Nations; it is in a way the human side of diplomacy. Where the *Yearbook of the United Nations* is a comprehensive set of records dealing with UN activities, the *UN Chronicle* is a set of articles and essays from the folks of the UN community who have the responsibility for making those activities happen. For example, in the No. 2 1997 issue, the Secretary-General (Mr. Kofi Annan) writes an essay, "Our world needs an instrument of global action as never before in history." Another example is "The Chronicle Interview":

"The United Nations has to play a role in promoting dialog between the various sets of countries, in debating policies in order that a consensus on development and the future of the world economy can emerge," according to Professor Nurul Islam, Chairman of the UN Committee for Development Planning.

Examples of other departments include:

- "First Person": Ambassador Shahryar Khan looks back on his tenure as the Secretary-General's Special Representative in Rwanda.
- "Conference Room Papers": Reports on the Status of Women, Narcotic Drugs, etc.
- "Peacewatch": Some questions and answers on United Nations peacekeeping.
- "Regional Perspectives": The global environment outlook, continent by continent.

If there is a drawback, it is that the publication is dedicated to issues that are not necessarily those of business and economics; nevertheless, the publication is a good one and accomplishes its international objectives.

Another international publication that does have economic considerations as its goal is *The OECD Observer* (http://www.oecd.org) published bimonthly in English and French by the Organization for Economic Cooperation and Development, (202) 785-6323. This magazine is approximately 50 pages long, with an appealing and colorful format, that addresses the economic, social, agricultural, technological, and global issues of the world. The articles are relatively brief, only three or four pages; nevertheless they do contain good analytical material for research. For example, the August/September 1997 issue included: "Globalisation: The World Economy in 2020," by Olivier Bouin and David O'Connor, and "Towards Efficiency in Brazilian Agriculture," by Garry Smith.

49   INTERNATIONAL CHAMBER OF COMMERCE PUBLICATIONS

Description of Organization

 Reference Navigator

Web site: http://www. iccwbo.org

E-Mail: icc@iccwbo.org

Fax: +33 1 49 53 2942

CD-Rom: not available

Library Reference Number:

_____

The International Chamber of Commerce (ICC) is the world business organization that works to promote greater freedom of world trade, to harmonize and facilitate business and trade practices, and to represent the business community at international and intergovernmental levels. Whether settling contractual disputes, protecting business from commercial fraud and counterfeiting, or fostering joint ventures in shipping, the ICC provides concrete and practical help to the world trading community in the solution of everyday problems. Regularly scheduled ICC conferences and symposia and training are important features of these services. ICC seminars in Europe, Africa, Asia, and North and South America deal with, for example, the practical and technical aspects of commercial arbitration, international contracts, and banking. ICC-sponsored training programs for developing-country professionals are regularly organized, often with third parties.

The ICC was founded in 1919 by a handful of farsighted business leaders. Today it includes thousands of member companies and associations from over 130 countries. National committees in all major capitals coordinate with their membership to address the concerns of the business community and to put across to their governments the business views formulated by the ICC.

Some ICC Services

The ICC International Court of Arbitration (Paris).

The ICC International Centre for Expertise (Paris).

The ICC International Bureau of Chambers of Commerce—IBMM (Paris).

The ICC Institute of International Business Law & Practice (Paris).

The ICC Center for Maritime Co-operation (London).

ICC Commercial Crime Services (London), grouping:

> The ICC Counterfeiting Intelligence Bureau.
>
> The ICC Commercial Crime Bureau.
>
> The ICC International Maritime Bureau.

ICC Publishing, the publishing subsidiary of the International Chamber of Commerce, produces and sells the works of ICC commissions and experts. It also offers guides and corporate handbooks on topics ranging from banking practice, international commercial arbitration, and joint ventures in eastern and central Europe, to advertising, environment, and telecommunications. Some 100 titles (in English and French)—designed for anyone interested in international trade—are now available from ICC Publishing. Certain titles also exist in other languages.

One popular ICC publication is Guide to Incoterms. This popular companion guide explains the respective obligations of the buyer and the seller when using one of the Incoterms (e.g., FOB, CIF, Ex-Works, etc.) in a commercial transaction and shows how a given term is applied in a sales contract. For information, call (212) 206-1150; fax (212) 633-6025.

There are two possible ways of becoming a member of the International Chamber of Commerce: either through (1) affiliation with an ICC national committee or group or (2) direct membership where no national committee or group exists.

What ICC Has Done for Business

Arbitration

The ICC created the world's first global commercial arbitration system. For more than three-quarters of a century, the ICC International Court of Arbitration has guaranteed companies an impartial and reliable means of settling commercial disputes.

Documentary Credits

The ICC established the rules on documentary credits that banks throughout the world apply daily in letter of credit operations.

Incoterms

Every day, standard trade terms like FOB and CIF are used in countless international business transactions. The ICC standardized these and other Incoterms and provides guidelines on how to use them.

ATA Carnets

The ICC issues its own passports for merchandise. ATA Carnets allow billions of dollars' worth of goods to cross borders temporarily for exhibition at trade fairs or as commercial samples.

Trade

More than 120 chief executives of top global companies publicly backed the successful ICC campaign for a far-reaching trade liberalization pact under the Uruguay Round. The negotiations also led to the creation of the World Trade Organization.

Customs

Customs modernization is now on the WTO's working agenda following ICC insistence that governments tackle border delays as one of the major remaining barriers to international trade.

Environment

The ICC's Business Charter for Sustainable Development, backed by more than 2,000 companies, helps companies to introduce innovative measures to protect the environment.

Standards

ICC experts played a key role in devising the voluntary international standard on environmental management (ISO 14001) now being implemented by companies throughout the world.

Self-regulation

The ICC pioneered business self-regulation with its widely used marketing codes. In 1977 it drew up the first business code of conduct against corruption in international transactions.

Crime Prevention

ICC Commercial Crime Services has saved companies that are exposed to shipping or financial frauds from huge and potentially crippling losses.

E: English **F:** French **D:** German **S:** Spanish **A:** Arabic **I:** Italian **EF:** bilingual English-French **ED:** bilingual English-German **EDF:** trilingual English-German-French **R:** Russian.

BANKING AND FINANCE

Uniform Rules for Collections
This publication assists banks in their collection operations by codifying the main rules to be applied. An indispensable aid in everyday banking operations.
E-F-ED   no 322

Uniform Rules for Contract Guarantees
This booklet presents Rules designed to regulate contract guarantees, as well as an introduction explaining their use. The Rules invest these guarantees with a moral content and strive to achieve a fair balance between the legitimate interests of the parties involved.
E-F-D   no 325

Uniform Customs and Practice for Documentary Credits (1983 Revision)
The constant evolution in transport and communications technology, added to the creation of new documents and new methods connected with the liberalization of commerce, made a revision of the UCP necessary. Implanted since October 1983.
E-F-S-A-ED   no 400

Model Forms for Contract Guarantees
E-F   no 406

Documentary Credits 1974 Rules and 1983 Rules Compared and Explained
This comparative study by B.S. Wheble gives a clear comment and provides the necessary information for every party concerned with documentary credits.
E-F   ISBN 92-842-1019-5
no 411

ICC Best-seller

Guide to Documentary Credit Operations
Some guidance may prove helpful to those who have not had much practice with documentary credits. This Guide will assist the reader regarding the problems and the needs of the commercial parties: the colorfully and clearly illustrated flow charts will help the reader to understand the practicalities and the priorities involved in such a commercial transaction.
E-F   ISBN 92-842-1021-6   no 415

Standard Documentary Credit Forms
Standard Documentary Credit Forms is designed for bankers, attorneys, importers/exporters and everyone involved with documentary credit transactions around the world.
The publication includes :
• comprehensive, easy-to-use standard credit forms,
• enhanced guidance manual with simple, step-by-step instructions to assist bank personnel when using the forms.
E   ISBN 92-842-1026-7   no 416

Standard Forms and Guidance Notes for Credit Applicants
A standardized credit application form to be completed by the applicant has been included in the book with guidelines.
E   ISBN 92-842-1027-5   no 416 A

Projects Planned by ICC Publications

Publication Title	Number
Banking	
• Documentary Credits Insight	nos 9–12
• ICC World Payment Systems Handbook	566
• Queries & Answers on UCP 500	565
• Managing Interest Rate Risks	572
• Guide to Financial Derivatives	562
• ICC Database / CD-ROM on Documentary Credits	
E-100	
• ICC Uniform International Authentication and Certification Practices	
Environment	
• ICC Guide to ISO 14001	573
Business Ethics	
• Corporate Case Studies on Combating Extortion and Bribery in International Business Transactions	
IMB	
• Report of Piracy and Phantom Ships	
• Report on Documentary Fraud	
• Guide to Product Counterfeiting	574
International Trade and Contracts	
• Educational Software on Incoterms, in cooperation with Lille Chamber of Commerce	470
• Export-Import Basics	543
• Transfer of Ownership, a co-publication with Kluwer	546
• Legal Guide to Trade with China	
• ICC International Sales Contract and General Conditions	556
• ICC Model Contract on Franchising	557
ICC Institute	
• ADR in Europe	490/2
Insurance	
• Guide to ICC Uniform Rules for Contract Bonds and Model Forms	536
Intellectual Property	
• Licensing Guides	545
• Enforcement of Intellectual Property Rights	
Law and Arbitration	
• ICC Awards (Vol III) (1991-1995), a co-publication with Kluwer	553
• Collection of Procedural Decisions in ICC Arbitration, a co-publication with Kluwer	567
• International Arbitration Rules for Airline Passenger Liability Claims	
Books to be distributed by ICC Publishing	
• World Trade Almanac (World Trade Press)	
• The Portable Encyclopedia for Doing Business with the U.S. (World Trade Press)	

Recommended Supplement: *The Henry Holt International Desk Reference*

If you would like information on this publication (ISBN 0-8050-1852-2), call Henry Holt and Company, Inc., at (212) 886-9200; or fax (212) 645-2610.

Reference Navigator

Web site: http://www.hholt.com

E-mail: maria_ferrer@hholt.com

Database: not available

CD-ROM: not available

Library Reference Number:

_____

The demand for accurate information about the major trading nations of the world has dictated that professionals in every field, and particularly in business, have at their fingertips a resource work that provides up-to-date, accurate information that is highly organized and easy to use. *The Henry Holt International Desk Reference: (A Guide to Essential Information Resources of the World's Major Trading Nations)* is structured in reference form to provide the essential information one needs. It is organized by geographical region and by country. Covering the Americas, Asia and the Pacific Rim, Europe and Russia, and the Middle East and Africa, each country is divided into 28 sections directing the user to information on such topics as:

Agriculture	Banking	Business development
Consultants	Imports/exports	Laws
Politics	Sales agents	Social agents / tourism

The entries are highly annotated, providing descriptions of services, background information, addresses, telephone numbers, and more. In addition, there are detailed sections on how to use and get the most from the book, as well as a cross-referenced appendix making finding information easy.

The Henry Holt International Desk Reference is organized in four sections, each consisting of a region of the world. The chapters within each section are dedicated to individual countries in that part of the world. Within each country the specific subject headings are arranged alphabetically. If you are looking for cultural information about Singapore, for example, you can look in Section II, "Asia and the Pacific Rim," turn to the chapter on Singapore and look under the "Culture" heading:

Ministry of Information and the Arts
15th Floor, MCD Building
512 Thomson Road
Singapore 1129
Telephone: 350-6102 / Fax: 350-6118

50 WORLD DEVELOPMENT REPORT

Description of Publication

For information on this annual publication (ISBN 0-19-520889-7), call Oxford University Press Inc. at (800) 334-4249.

 Reference Navigator

Web site: http://www.worldbank.org

E-mail: lsms@worldbank

Database: See Web site

CD-ROM: available

Library Reference Number:

The *World Development Report 1996* is the 19th in a continuing annual series of reports from the World Bank that examines the interplay of major issues in the world, such as the environment, developmental strategies, and poverty. Each report furnishes an overview of the goals and means of development. *World Development Report 1993*, for example, examined the issues of human health, health policy, and economic development, while the *World Development Report 1994* covered infrastructure. A similar publication by the UN is published under the name *Human Development Report* (annual) and can be reviewed at http://www.undp.org.

The format of the *WDR 1993* is a good example of how the series addresses world issues. The theme is how business and government must interact in order to accomplish the goals of development. This report on health examines in depth a single sector in which the impact of public finance and public policy is of particular importance. The *Report* advocates a three-pronged approach to government policies for improving health in developing countries. First, governments need to foster an economic environment that enables households to improve their own health. It suggests that growth policies (including, where necessary, economic adjustment policies) that ensure income gains for the poor are essential. Second, it also calls for expanded investment in schooling, particularly for young women; while government spending on health should be redirected to more cost-effective programs that do more to help the poor. Third, governments need to promote diversity and competition in financing and of health services.

World Development Report formerly included the "World Development Indicators" (WDI), a statistical appendix that offered selected social and economic statistics on 127 countries. Now, the *WDI 1997* is a freestanding publication, enlarged to include more than 80 data tables and 600 indicators for single-year observations. It is also available as a Windows™-based CD-ROM that contains most of the underlying time-series data for these statistics, as well as many others. This colorful and powerful CD-ROM package offers more than 500 indicators and over 1,000 tables, with definitions, sources of information, and all the text from the book. You may map and graph data sets and can easily download the information into other software programs.

The World Bank Atlas 1997 is also available. Another new product is *Global Development Finance 1997*, the new name for World Bank's annual authoritative review of external debt and financial flows in developing countries—the *World Debt Tables*—renamed to reflect the changing tide in global capital flows. The content is as rich and varied as before, making it an indispensable reference guide for economists, bankers, country risk analysts, financial consultants, and others involved in investment lending and capital flows around the world.

The UN Center for Economic and Social Information in Geneva publishes *Development Forum Business Edition*, a biweekly newspaper that gives details of all major business opportunities opened by World Bank loans. The newspaper publishes requirements for each project and instructions on how to bid for the business. World Bank publications deal with many areas, countries, and subjects, and the bank issues a periodic "Publications Update." You can get it from the World Bank Information Shop, Washington, DC; call: (202) 473-2941.

Among World Bank reports and publications that can also be helpful to businesspersons and students are its *Annual Report, Statement of Loans* (quarterly), *Guidelines Relating to Procurement under World Bank Loans and IDA Credits, Uses of Consultants by the World Bank and Its Borrowers*, and *World Bank Atlas of Per Capita Product and Population*. Also available are reports of the World Bank's various "General Survey Missions" regarding certain countries and areas.

430

TEXT TABLES

3
Opportunities for Growth

As growth slows, governments turn their attention to reviving it—and to addressing the problems that slower growth creates. Developing countries have taken many steps to improve their economic performance and to adjust to the changing international economic environment. But as they look ahead to the rest of this decade and beyond, they recognize that there is room for further improvement. Better policies are especially needed because the international environment is fraught with uncertainty. Commodity prices and depressed, real interest rates are still above historical levels, and the debt service burden imposes serious constraints on many countries' long-term prospects for growth.

As the economies of the world become increasingly interdependent, future prospects for the world economy depend upon the policies that both the industrial and developing countries adopt. This chapter describes two possible paths for the world economy during the next 10 years and the policies that might bring them about. Both High and Low cases presuppose the same moderate improvements in the economic policies of developing countries. However, if the pace of reform were to quicken, or if more countries were to implement corrective policies, the average growth rates for developing countries would exceed our estimates in each case. As the recent success of countries as diverse as Turkey and China illustrates, it is the developing countries' own policies that determine how much they can take advantage of, or offset, changes in the world economy.

Developing countries cannot assume a stable or favorable external environment. It is, therefore, important to outline the kinds of policy which would improve their ability to adapt to unpredictable circumstances and to use capital flows most productively to sustain growth over the medium term.

POLICIES FOR GROWTH IN DEVELOPING COUNTRIES

A useful way to approach this issue is to consider the distinction between stabilization policies and structural adjustment policies. Stabilization policies include the monetary, fiscal, exchange rate, and income policies that governments use to maintain macroeconomic balance. Structural adjustment policies concern those things which influence production, trade, and distribution decisions: changes in incentives, government institutions, and the rules governing property rights, liability, and information. Obviously, the two sets of policies overlap and can complement each other. An exchange rate adjustment not only stabilizes the current account but also will increase the share of exports in domestic output. Similarly, restructuring a public enterprise may improve its efficiency and also reduce the public sector deficit.

Sometimes the two policies work against each other. A rapid reduction in distortionary trade taxes can, if there are no new revenue-raising measures, increase the budget deficit in the short run. Unless macroeconomic policy is consistent with longer-term structural aims, governments run the risk of having to reverse or abandon policy reforms for the wrong reasons. The Philippines is a case in point (see Box 2.3 in Chapter 2).

While the exact mix of appropriate policies varies from country to country, the overall aim is to restore and maintain economic stability while simultaneously improving the incentive and institutional structure to encourage domestic savings and the efficient allocation of resources. Whether the initial problems are caused by unsustainable. . .

432

Recommended Supplement: *World Resources*

For information on this biannual publication (ISSN 0887-0403), call the World Resources Institute at (202) 638-6300; fax (202) 638-0036.

Reference Navigator

Web site: http://www.wri.org/wri/   CD-ROM: available

E-mail: personal only   Library Reference Number:

Database: See Web site   _____

The *World Resources* series, according to its editors, is intended to meet the critical need for accessible, accurate information on some of the most pressing issues of our time. Wise management of natural resources and protection of the global environment, for example, are essential to achieve sustainable economic development and hence to alleviate poverty, improve the human condition, and preserve the biological systems on which all life depends. Publication of *World Resources* at this date is in its ninth year of the series, reflecting a collaborative effort of the United Nations Environmental Program, the United Nations Development Program, and the World Resources Institute (WRI) to produce and disseminate the most objective and up-to-date report of conditions and trends in the world's natural resources and in the global environment.

This volume, like the *World Development Report*, has a special focus each year. In 1992, for example, the focus was on sustainable development, in support of the upcoming 1992 United Nations Conference on Environment and Development. The 1998–1999 *World Resources* report, contains 450 variables for 200 countries.

The *World Resources* report is divided into specific parts. Part I usually includes three or four chapters on the special topic of that year (e.g., sustainable development), an overview chapter, and some case studies; Part II continues the tradition of examining a particular region of the world in more detail (such as an overview of the severe environmental and resource problems faced by Central Europe); Part III reports on basic conditions and trends, key issues, major problems and efforts to solve them, and recent developments in each of the major resource categories, from population to climate. Where data exist, the chapters give a 20-year perspective on trends in the physical environment. Supporting data from the World Resources Data Base, are found in Part IV of the report.

Something to Think About

Assuming you have a specific region in the world that best holds your interest, try to obtain a copy of the specific *World Resources* report (Part II) that covers your area of interest and review it. Can you integrate the environmental and resource problems faced by Central Europe written about in Part II above with articles from the periodical *Business Central Europe* (see Chapter 43)?

A   SAMPLE SYLLABUS

For a Course on Business Research Reference Techniques

Any University

Course: XXX Business Reference Research Techniques
Syllabus   **(Semester:**   **)**

I. Course Overview:

The purpose of this course is to help prepare senior students for employment in the industry of their choice. The student is assigned the responsibility for selecting an industry he or she is interested in and studying the parameters of that industry (e.g., productivity, unions, exports, technology, profits, legislation, etc.). Once the students have developed a foundation of knowledge in their industry, they must choose a company within that industry that they would like to study and possibly work for. A *company profile* is created that shows the history, personalities, product lines, marketing strategies, and so on, that best portray the activities of the company. Once the profile is created the student must select a product or service from this company and analyze it. Finally, the student must review the political, economic, social or technological issues (or a combination of issues) that pose an opportunity or threat to the company's profitability or even survival. Students should construct a matrix composed of industry, company, and product down the side, and political, economic, social, or technological issues across the top; then identify the appropriate box or boxes that are issue related. Having researched and analyzed these four important areas of the student's interest, he or she should be confident of competitively looking for a job in the student's chosen field.

II. Course Objectives: The objectives of this course are to:

A. *Encourage independent research* on the student's part that is pertinent to his or her career. The independent research is to be carried out in the library and through companies, associations, unions, government agencies, brokers, and other sources of vital information.

B. *Develop teamwork* by having students assist each other in obtaining information regarding their stated interests and goals. The corporate environment requires teamwork; preparation for this should be developed through students helping each other meet the requirements of the course (sharing reference discoveries, telephone numbers, and contact people).

C. *Learn research techniques and obtain pertinent information* that will be of use to the students in their careers. The goal of becoming specialists within an industry is enhanced by students collecting and maintaining information that can be the beginning of their professional literature and reference collections. These objectives will be met by individual research efforts, personal presentations, and report writing. The professor will be seeking to enhance the quality of the performance of the students by requiring that comprehensive reference searches have been conducted in all of the report areas. It's a lot of work, but as said by Viktor Frankl. . . "What is to give light must endure burning."

III. Required Texts:

1. F. Patrick Butler, *Business Research Sources: A Reference Navigator,* McGraw Hill-Companies.
2. Michael R. Lavin, *Business Information: How to Find It, How to Use It,* Oryx Press.

In addition, many textbooks used during the students' academic career are good initial sources to research their assignments. **Most students do NOT have a sufficient command of the resources in the library** and therefore will be expected to significantly improve their familiarity with the reference material available. The librarians are prepared for this course and will initiate a research "reference hunt" on one of the first library visits to introduce the student to the search techniques. The easiest solution to the problem of finding the right reference sources is to ask the librarian. This is *not* the way to learn how to research information. The reference librarians are to be used only as a last resort.

IV. Course Outline:

The course will meet on specific days and times in the library or the classroom assigned or revised as the professor sees fit. The library session is independent research time on the student's part; however, the professor and aide *will be present to assist and check on the progress of the student's activities.*

V. Course Requirements:

A. Industry report:
   - 6 to 8 pages; typewritten/double-spaced.
   - Submitted/presented — (date).
   - Report criteria — student directed.
B. Company report:
   - Six to eight pages; typewritten/double-spaced.
   - Submitted/presented — (date).
   - Report criteria — student directed.
C. Product/service report:
   - Six to eight pages; typewritten/double-spaced.
   - Submitted/presented — (date).
   - Report criteria — student directed.
D. Issue paper:
   - Six to eight pages; typewritten/double-spaced.
   - Submitted/presented — (date).

VI. Grading Policies:

Industry report:	20 percent.
Company report:	20 percent.
Product report:	20 percent.
Issue paper:	20 percent.
Presentation:	20 percent.

Preparations are an example of quality of effort. ***Missed classes*** (3) either in the classroom ***or the library*** without the permission of the instructor; or missed or lack of preparation for presentations (1) ***will cost 20 percent of the student's final grade.***

The format of the reports will be developed *by the students* with only steering assistance of the professor. The students *must* take the initiative to develop the best criteria possible and use this criteria to both write their reports and present their material.

Schedule of Activities

Jan. 9		Class Orientation
	11	Class Orientation, Presentation Assignments, etc.
	16	Reference Training at Library (Database Lecture)
	18	Reference Training at Library (Scavenger Hunt)
	23	*Industry Report: Criteria Development*
	25	Library Research
	30	Library Research
Feb. 1		Library Research
	6	**Industry Reports due: Presenters are:**
	8	*Company report: Criteria Development*
	13	Financial Analysis Lecture
	15	Financial Analysis Lecture continued
	20	Library Research
	22	Library Research
	27	Library Research
	29	Spring Break
March 5		Spring Break
	7	**Company Reports due: Presenters are:**
	12	*Product/Service Report: Criteria Development*
	14	Guest Lecturer
	19	Library Research
	21	Library Research
	26	Library Research
	28	Guest Lecture
April	**2**	**Product / Service report Due: Presenters are:**
	4	*Issue Report: Criteria Development*
	9	Video: TBA
	11	Library Research
	16	Library Research
	18	Library Research
	23	**Issue Reports due: Presenters are:**
	25	Course review day

No final exam scheduled.

Any suggestions or comments for the improvement of this course are actively solicited by the professor.

Chapter 1

Business Information
Reprinted from Business Information: How to Find It, How to Use it by Michael R. Lavin © 1987, 1992 by the Oryx Press. Used with permission from The Oryx Press, 4041 N. Central Ave., Suite 700, Phoenix, AZ, 85012. 800-279-6799. http://www.oryxpress.com

Chapter 2

Hoover's Handbooks
Copyright © 1998, Hoover's Inc., 800–486–8666, Reprinted with Permission.

Chapter 5

GAAP Guide
Excerpts from MILLER'S COMPREHENSIVE GAAP GUIDE by Martin A. Miller and Jan Williams, copyright © 1993 by Harcourt Brace & company, reprinted by permission of the publisher.

Chapter 6

Almanac of Business and Industrial Financial Ratios
From ALMANAC OF BUSINESS AND INDUSTRIAL FINANCIAL RATIOS by Leo Troy. Copyright © 1997. Reprinted with permission of Prentice Hall.

Barrons
1997 Dow Jones & Company, Inc. All Rights Reserved.

The Wall Street Journal
1997 Dow Jones & Company, Inc. All Rights Reserved.

Chapter 8

Harvard Business Review
Reprinted by permission of Harvard Business Review. Copyright 1997 by President and Fellows of Harvard College; all rights reserved.

Chapter 10

MIT'S Technology Review
Reprinted with permission from *MIT'S Technology Review Magazine*, copyright 1997.

Chapter 12

Peterson's Guide
From *Peterson's Four-Year Colleges 1998* © 1997 by Peterson's. With Permission. Available at local bookstores, directly from Peterson's by calling 1–800–338–3282, or via its web site at www.petersons.com

Chapter 13

American Heritage
Reprinted By Permission of AMERICAN HERITAGE Magazine, a division of Forbes, Inc. © Forbes, Inc., September, 1997

Chapter 16

World Almanac and Book of Facts 1998
Copyright © 1997 by PRIMEDIA Reference Inc.

Chapter 17

Fortune
FORTUNE, © 1997 Time Inc. All rights reserved.

Inc. Magazine
Reprinted with permission, INC. Magazine, September 1997.

Chapter 18

Books in Print
Copyright © 1997 by Reed Elsevier Inc.

PAIS International in Print
Copyright 1997 PAIS – Public Affairs Information Service, Inc.

Chapter 19

Chapter 23

Chapter 24

Chapter 25

Chapter 32

Chapter 35

Journal of Advertising Research
Reproduced by permission of Advertising Research Foundation.

Chapter 36

Management Review
MANAGEMENT REVIEW SEPTEMBER 1997 © 1997. American Management Association, New York. All Rights Reserved.

Chapter 38

Organization
Reprinted by permission of Sage Publications Ltd. Copyright Sage Publications 1997.

Chapter 41

Business in the Contemporary World
Copyright © 1997. Reprinted by permission of John Wiley & Sons, Inc.

Notes

Notes

Notes

Notes